Small Governments, Big Ambitions

This book, along with any associated content or subsequent updates, can be accessed at https://hdl.handle.net/10986/45031.

AI Disclosure Statement:

World Bank mAI powered by Claude Sonnet 4.6 was used to support literature review, summarization of background evidence, and editing of draft text. All analytical judgments, policy interpretations, and conclusions were developed, reviewed, and verified by the authors.

Scan to see all titles in this series.

East Asia and Pacific Development Studies

Small Governments, Big Ambitions

Fiscal Policy in East Asia and Pacific

Ergys Islamaj
Aaditya Mattoo
Agustin Samano
Matthew Wai-Poi

WORLD BANK GROUP

1 2 3 4 29 28 27 26

ISBN (paper): 978-1-4648-2318-3
ISBN (electronic): 978-1-4648-2350-3
DOI: 10.1596/978-1-4648-2318-3

Artificial Intelligence: If AI tools were used in the development of this work, page ii of this work will have further information.

Cover art: © Xinling yi fang / Shutterstock.com. Used with permission; further permission required for reuse.

Cover design: Bill Pragluski, Critical Stages, LLC.

Library of Congress Control Number: 2026915405

The manufacturer's authorized representative in the European Union for product safety is Mare Nostrum Group B.V., Doelen 72, 4831 GR Breda, The Netherlands. Email: gpsr@mare-nostrum.co.uk.

EAST ASIA AND PACIFIC DEVELOPMENT STUDIES

The EAST ASIA AND PACIFIC DEVELOPMENT STUDIES explore economic issues in one of the most vibrant regions at a time of rapid technological change. Topics range from improving productivity and jobs to advancing services reform, and from enhancing education and health care to facilitating the green transition. Each volume blends analysis, examples, and policy lessons of interest to scholars, policy makers, and practitioners.

TITLES IN THE SERIES

Small Governments, Big Ambitions: Fiscal Policy in East Asia and Pacific (2026)

Firm Foundations of Growth: Productivity and Technology in East Asia and Pacific (2025)

Future Jobs: Robots, Artificial Intelligence, and Digital Platforms in East Asia and Pacific (2025)

Green Technologies: Decarbonizing Development in East Asia and Pacific (2025)

A Healthy Future: Primary Health Care and the Chronic Disease Epidemic in East Asia and Pacific (2025)

Services Unbound: Digital Technologies and Policy Reform in East Asia and Pacific (2024)

Fixing the Foundation: Teachers and Basic Education in East Asia and Pacific (2023) (World Bank East Asia and Pacific Regional Report)

All books in this series are available for free in the World Bank's Open Knowledge Repository at https://hdl.handle.net/10986/42047.

Contents

Boxes

Figures

Maps

Tables

Foreword

For much of the last 40 years, the East Asia and Pacific region has been a paragon of economic development. In the span of a single generation, hundreds of millions of people were lifted out of extreme poverty and much of the region was propelled to middle-income status. These achievements were supported by a fiscal policy that involved taxing little and spending within countries' means, mostly on infrastructure, primary education, and basic health. The region's lean approach delivered both growth and macroeconomic stability.

That approach, however, is no longer enough. The forces of globalization that powered the region's dynamism are now faltering. The skills demanded by technology-intensive economies are not being developed fast enough. Populations are aging faster than the institutions designed to support them. The climate shocks that once seemed distant are now an accelerating reality. And regional growth has slowed and become less inclusive. In short, the fiscal approach that served the region well during earlier stages of development now needs an upgrade.

The region requires a new fiscal compact, one that moves from enabling growth to enhancing it. This shift depends on governments that are proactive and more efficient. It calls for governments that are adept at complementing private initiatives and markets to build human capital, upgrading infrastructure to accelerate skill- and technology-intensive growth, and strengthening social protection to create safety nets for all citizens. It requires pairing public spending with institutional and sectoral reforms that raise the efficiency of taxation and spending, improve service delivery, and crowd in private investment.

Governments in East Asia and Pacific today collect roughly 20 percent of gross domestic product in revenue—just half the average share in high-income economies. Closing even a fraction of that gap does not require politically difficult increases in income taxes or value added tax rates. It simply requires better use of the tools already available: broadening the indirect tax base by reducing poorly targeted exemptions, pairing those measures with well-targeted transfers that protect the most vulnerable, and modernizing tax systems. Such reforms can strengthen both the efficiency and equity of the fiscal system while helping finance the investments the region needs.

Digital technologies and improvements in fiscal institutions have raised the return to public spending and lowered the cost of tax collection. Advances in data systems, digital public infrastructure, and tax administration mean that governments can identify beneficiaries, deliver services, and collect revenues with a precision that was unattainable a generation ago—even though some new technologies can make it easier to avoid taxes. The frontier of what sound fiscal policy can achieve has shifted.

This book sets out a practical agenda for governments in East Asia and Pacific to advance to the next fiscal frontier. By taking stock of the region's fiscal strengths, vulnerabilities, and reform options, it aims to inform public debate and support the difficult choices governments must now make. The region's challenges are considerable, but so are the region's ambitions—and its capacity to meet them.

Indermit Gill
Chief Economist and Senior Vice President for Development Economics
World Bank Group

Carlos Felipe Jaramillo
Vice President, East Asia and Pacific
World Bank Group

Acknowledgments

This book is a collective endeavor of the Development Economics Office of the Chief Economist, Asia; the Development Economics Research Group; and the East Asia and Pacific (EAP) Poverty and Equity Global Practice of the World Bank.

Izzati Afiqah Binti Ab Raz, Carlos Alberto Brutomeso Panozzo, and Yan Wang provided excellent research and data analysis support. Robert J. Palacios made significant contributions to the pension analysis, and Scott J. Sommers contributed the data analysis for chapter 2 and a background paper on fiscal rules.

Indermit S. Gill, Carlos Felipe Jaramillo, and Lalita M. Moorty provided valuable guidance and helpful comments. We are especially grateful for valuable feedback from Omar Arias, Alessandro Barattieri, Yu Cao, Daisuke Fukuzawa, Duong Le, and Jonathan Timmis. Generous inputs and comments were provided by Jaffar Al Rikabi, Diego Ambasz, Diego Angel-Urdinola, Mehwish Ashraf, Benu Bidani, Fernando Andres Blanco Cossio, Ibrahim Saeed Chowdhury, Amina Coulibaly, Sebastian Eckardt, John Nana Darko Francois, Marco Hernandez, Lars Christian Moller, Panayiotis Nicolaides, Franziska Lieselotte Ohnsorge, Ririn Salwa Purnamasari, Habib Nasser Rab, Laura Rodrigues Takeuchi, Bambang Suharnoko Sjahrir, Liliana D. Sousa, Kersten Kevin Stamm, and Gonzalo J. Varela.

We are also grateful for stimulating discussions and comments from members of the EAP Economic Policy Team and EAP staff who participated in the review meetings. The authors benefited from generous feedback from Arsenio Balisacan, Byunghoon Nam, Allen Ng, Yohei Okawa, Eunmi Park, Andrea Salvador, and other participants at the ASEAN+3 Macroeconomic Research Office (AMRO)–World Bank EAP Roundtable in Singapore on November 3, 2025, and at the 20th East Asia Economic Association International Convention in Manila, the Philippines, on November 8–9, 2025.

We thank Maria Laura Gonzalez Canosa for leading the communications strategy and Narya Ou and Cecile Wodon for their administrative support. Honora Mara copy edited the manuscript, and Gwenda Larsen and Ann O'Malley proofread the book. Stephen Pazdan was the production editor. Cindy A. Fisher and Patricia Katayama provided advice and guidance on the publication process.

About the Authors

Ergys Islamaj is a senior economist in the Middle East, North Africa, Afghanistan, and Pakistan Chief Economist Office at the World Bank. During the production of this report, he was a senior economist in the East Asia and Pacific Chief Economist Office. In that role Ergys also led flagship analytical work, including the biannual East Asia and Pacific Economic Update. Before joining the World Bank, he was an assistant professor of economics at Vassar College, where he taught courses on international finance, macroeconomic theory, and international trade. His research interests span fiscal policy, international spillovers, the Chinese economy, informal labor markets, and household consumption behavior. His research has been published in academic journals, and his policy work has been cited in *Bloomberg*, the *Financial Times*, and the *Wall Street Journal*. He holds a PhD in economics from Georgetown University.

Aaditya Mattoo is director of the Development Research Group of the World Bank. He specializes in development, trade, and international cooperation and provides policy advice to governments. Previously, he was chief economist of the East Asia and Pacific Region; codirector of the 2020 World Development Report on global value chains; and research manager, Trade and International Integration. Before Aaditya joined the World Bank, he was an economic counselor at the World Trade Organization and taught economics at the University of Sussex and Churchill College, Cambridge University. He has published on development, trade, trade in services, and international trade agreements in academic and other journals; his work has been cited in the *Economist*, the *Financial Times*, the *New York Times*, *Time Magazine*, and the *Wall Street Journal*. He holds a PhD in economics from the University of Cambridge and an MPhil in economics from the University of Oxford.

Agustin Samano is an economist in the Macroeconomics and Growth team of the World Bank's Development Research Group. He is based at the World Bank's East Asia and Pacific Chief Economist Research Center in Kuala Lumpur, Malaysia. His research focuses on international macroeconomics and international finance, with a particular emphasis on fiscal policy, sovereign debt, and monetary-fiscal interactions in emerging market and developing economies. His research has been published in the *Journal of International Economics*. Agustin received his PhD in economics from the University of Minnesota in 2021.

Matthew Wai-Poi is a lead economist with the Poverty and Equity Global Practice of the World Bank, working in East Asia and Pacific on measuring and understanding drivers of poverty and inequality in the region along with the design and implementation of policies to address them. He has led various reports on inequality, poverty, the middle class, displacement, social protection and targeting, and female economic empowerment. He was previously global lead for the Distributional Impacts of Fiscal Policies project, and he worked on poverty and inequality issues in the Middle East, including on gender and displacement. Matthew was based in Jakarta with the World Bank for eight years and has a PhD in economics from Columbia University and degrees in business and law.

Overview

Introduction

Over the last three decades, most economies in East Asia and Pacific (EAP) have followed a growth-enabling approach to fiscal policy, taxing little and spending within their means. They have directed limited revenues to public investment, especially in infrastructure. Although this strategy supported growth and macroeconomic stability, propelling much of the region to middle-income status, it led to underinvestment in education, health, social protection, and climate adaptation. Consequently, growth has slowed, becoming less resilient and less inclusive, and putting the region's high-income aspirations at risk.

To achieve its development ambitions, the region must forge a new growth-enhancing fiscal compact. The state will need to play a stronger role in enhancing human capital and upgrading infrastructure to support the shift to more skill- and technology-intensive growth. It must also protect people and the economy from shocks in a region that is rapidly aging and increasingly exposed to extreme climate events. In each case, public spending must be paired with institutional and sectoral reforms that crowd in private investment, raise efficiency, and improve service delivery.

An enhanced role for the state is feasible. Improvements in fiscal institutions and technologies can raise the return to every dollar spent and lower the cost of every dollar collected. Stronger public investment management—transparent procurement, standardized project appraisal, and independent evaluation—can increase efficiency and improve project selection. Reforms in tax administration—simplified payment procedures and risk-based audits—can cut compliance costs and broaden the revenue base. Advances in data and digital technologies can help identify taxpayers more accurately, verify liabilities, and collect revenues owed. These advances can also improve service delivery in health and education, and better target income support to those most in need.

The current fiscal approach has served EAP well. Delivering on the region's higher-income ambitions will require a more efficient and proactive fiscal approach.

Economic developments and the role of fiscal policy in EAP

The EAP region stands out for its robust and stable economic performance compared to other country groups (refer to figure O.1). Between 1999 and 2019, East Asian economies grew at an average annual rate of 5.6 percent—substantially faster than the 4.0 percent recorded across emerging market and developing economies (EMDEs) and more than double the 2.6 percent pace of advanced economies.[1] The region combined rapid growth with relatively low volatility. The standard deviation of annual growth in EAP during this period averaged 2.4 percent, roughly half the level observed across the broader EMDE group (4.0 percent) and below that of advanced economies (2.9 percent). Within the region, the Pacific Island countries are an exception, growing at a lower average annual rate of 3.3 percent and with substantially higher volatility.[2]

East Asian economies have seen two decades of higher and more stable growth than in the past and compared to other emerging, developing, and advanced economies.

FIGURE O.1 GDP growth and GDP growth volatility, 1976–96 and 1999–2019

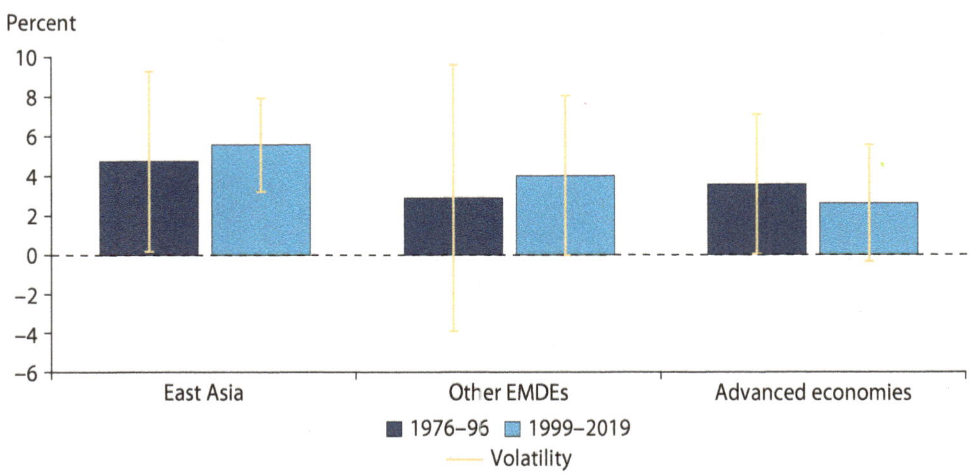

Source: Original figure for this publication based on Penn World Table (Feenstra et al. 2015).
Note: Bar height shows average annual growth rate; lines show average standard deviation over the period. East Asia includes Cambodia, China, Indonesia, Lao PDR, Malaysia, Mongolia, Myanmar, the Philippines, Thailand, Timor-Leste, and Viet Nam. EMDEs = emerging market and developing economies.

Despite that strong performance, growth in EAP has slowed and is increasingly sustained by capital accumulation rather than by improvements in productivity. The contribution of total factor productivity to growth declined from about 0.8 percentage point during 2001–15 to close to zero during 2016–23 (refer to figure O.2). Improvements in human capital accounted for an even smaller share of growth. These trends suggest that the region has become less successful at improving efficiency, fostering innovation, and strengthening human capital—all key drivers of productivity growth and critical to successfully transitioning to high-income status.

Poverty in the region has fallen markedly over the past two decades (refer to figure O.3). The share of the population living in extreme poverty declined from 37 percent in 2001–05 to just 6 percent in 2021–24, reflecting rapid growth and expanding job opportunities. However, about 61 percent of the population across the region, and as much as 76 percent excluding China, has yet to attain middle-class living standards. This situation underscores the fragility of recent progress, the continued prevalence of economic insecurity, and the need to sustain inclusive growth.

Growth in East Asia has slowed and is being driven by capital accumulation rather than by improvements in productivity.

FIGURE O.2 Drivers of growth in East Asian economies, 1971–2023

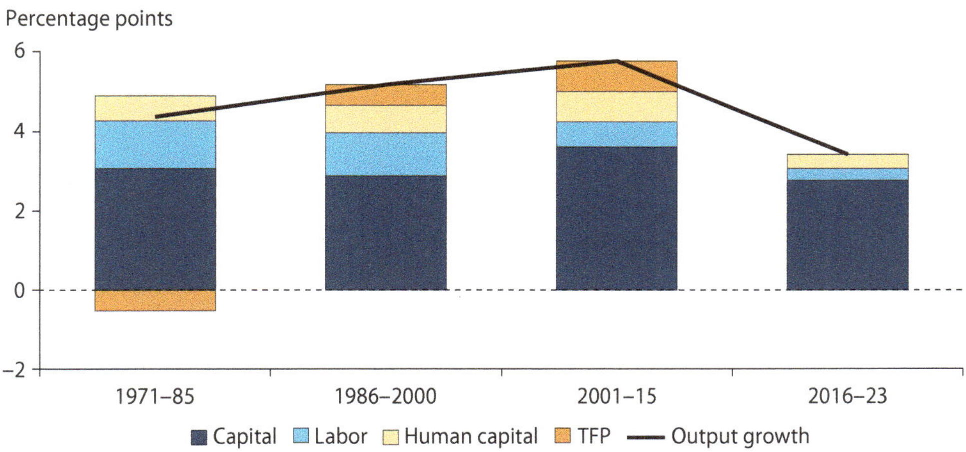

Sources: Original figure for this publication based on Asian Productivity Organization (APO) 2025; Penn World Table (Feenstra et al. 2015).

Note: The figure shows simple averages. East Asia includes China, Indonesia, Malaysia, the Philippines, Thailand, and Viet Nam. TFP = total factor productivity.

Poverty has declined markedly in the region, but 76 percent of the population excluding China has not yet achieved middle-class status.

FIGURE O.3 Poverty in EAP, excluding China, 2001–24

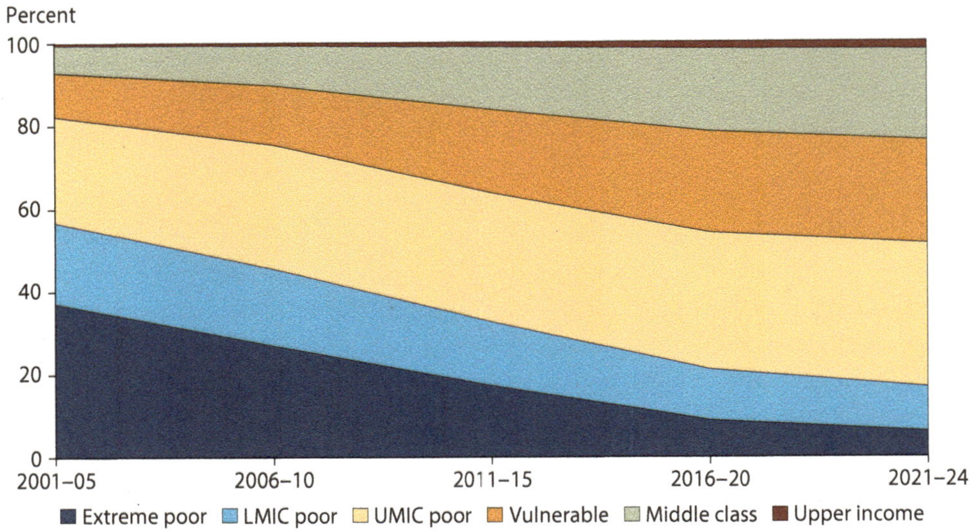

Source: Original figure for this publication based on Krah et al. 2026.
Note: LMIC poor individuals live on less than $4.20 per day; UMIC poor, on between $4.20 and $8.30 per day; vulnerable, on between $8.30 and $15.00 per day; middle class, on between $15.00 and $56.00 per day; and upper income, on above $56.00 per day. The $15.00 threshold follows Chaudhuri (2003) to identify the income or consumption level associated with a 10 percent probability of falling into poverty at the $8.30 (2021 purchasing power parity) line across 20 EAP economies. The median estimate ($15.20) was rounded to $15.00. The upper-income threshold, $56.00 per day, is twice the Prosperity Gap line of $28.00 per day, which reflects incomes typical of countries nearing high-income status; doubling that line better excludes the upper tail while maintaining focus on the middle of the distribution. EAP = East Asia and Pacific; LMIC = lower-middle-income country; UMIC = upper-middle-income country.

As economies in the region have grown richer, inequality has generally declined (refer to figure O.4). Nonetheless, inequality remains an important challenge in EAP. Gini coefficients in some economies remain close to or above 0.40, commonly used as a threshold for high inequality (World Bank 2024b). By the 2020s, the regional Gini index remained above the average for EMDEs. Moreover, evidence from advanced economies suggests that the COVID-19 shock may have reversed part of the earlier progress, disproportionately affecting lower-income households through job losses, school disruptions, and uneven recoveries. These trends highlight the continued role of the state in expanding economic opportunity and reducing inequality.

The EAP region also faces the challenges of a warming world and an aging population (refer to map O.1), both of which will likely slow growth and increase

Inequality has declined but remains high in some EAP economies.

FIGURE 0.4 Income per capita and Gini index, selected EAP economies

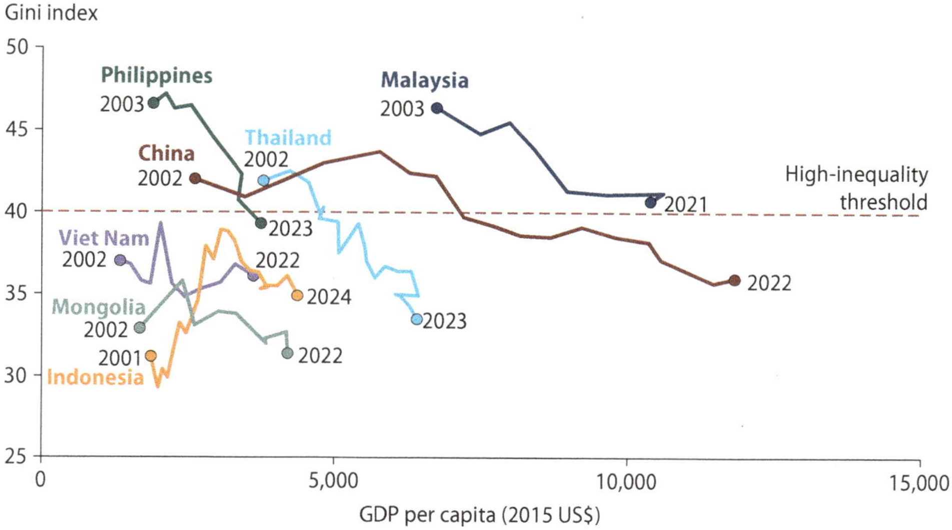

Source: Original figure for this publication based on World Bank Poverty and Inequality Platform, 2026, with major processing by Our World in Data, OurWorldinData.org/economic-inequality.
Note: Malaysia and the Philippines use income as welfare, whereas other countries use consumption.

fiscal pressures. More than half of the annual losses from natural disasters worldwide occur in EAP. Without major adaptation efforts, coastal, river, and chronic flooding alone could lead to gross domestic product (GDP) losses of 5–20 percent by 2100 in China, Indonesia, the Philippines, and Viet Nam. In the region, natural disasters already cost Pacific Island countries over 2 percent of GDP every year, and sea level rise could threaten the existence of entire low-lying atoll island nations (Kiribati, the Marshall Islands, and Tuvalu).

The population of the EAP region is also aging faster and at lower levels of income than in the currently richer and older countries of Europe and Central Asia and of the Organisation for Economic Co-operation and Development (OECD). The transition from aging to aged societies (that is, growth of the age 65 and over cohort from 7 percent to 14 percent of the total population) has taken only 20–25 years for most EAP economies, in contrast to 50–100 years or more in Europe and Central Asia and OECD countries. EAP economies are also becoming aged societies at far lower income levels than their OECD counterparts, with purchasing power parity per capita GDP at peak working age between 10 percent and 40 percent of the level in the United States at the same point in demographic transition.

EAP economies are highly exposed to climate change, and their populations are aging rapidly.

MAP O.1 Climate risk and population aging, EAP and the rest of the world

a. Climate Risk Index ranking, 1999–2019

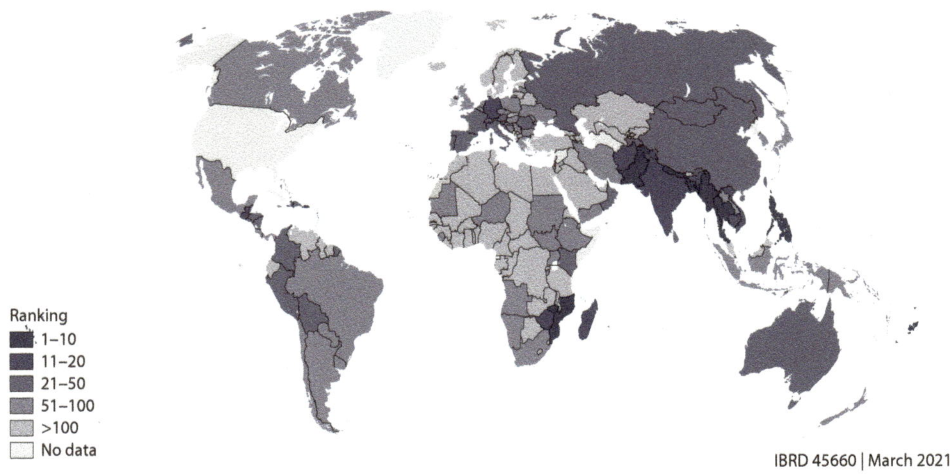

b. Projected share of population age 60+ in 2050

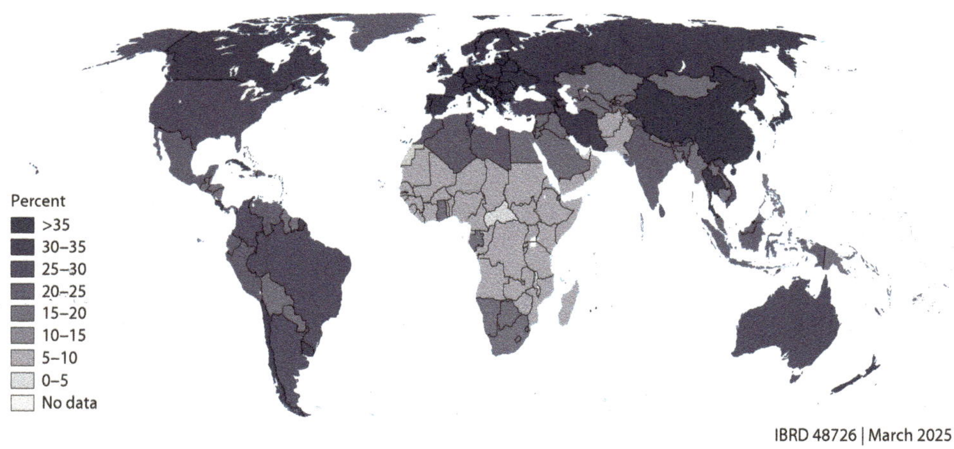

Sources: Original map for this publication based on Eckstein et al. 2021; UN DESA 2022.
Note: EAP = East Asia and Pacific.

Ensuring higher, stable, and inclusive growth amid these challenges will require critical fiscal policy choices (refer to figure O.5). Well-designed government spending can support skill development and resilient infrastructure, helping to crowd in private investment. At the same time, financing these priorities requires effective tax systems that do not unduly distort firms' and households' investment and employment decisions. Sustainable public finances help preserve market confidence and maintain the fiscal space needed to deploy countercyclical measures when shocks occur. Finally, well-targeted transfers, social protection, and sustained investment in human capital can support the transition of vulnerable households into the middle class. Designing such a fiscal compact requires institutional reforms and the adoption of new technologies to raise the effectiveness of public spending and reduce the costs of raising revenue.

Fiscal policy plays a crucial role in shaping outcomes related to growth, stability, poverty, and inequality.

FIGURE O.5 Fiscal policy for long-term growth and productive jobs: A conceptual framework

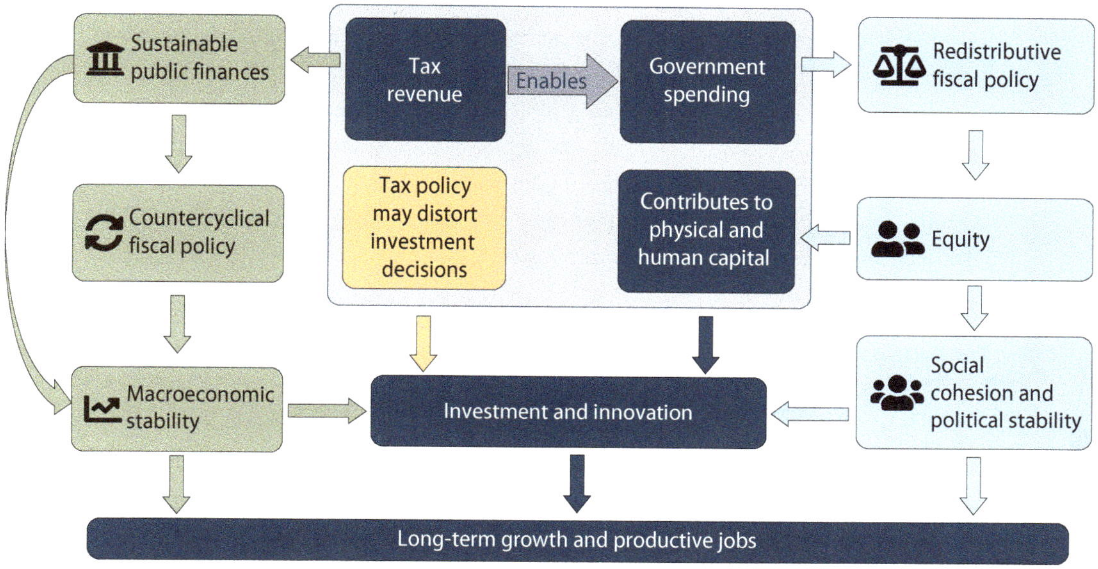

Source: Original figure for this publication.

Fiscal policy: A growth-enabling approach

Fiscal policy has supported the region's historic economic growth. Many EAP governments pursued what this report calls a "growth-enabling" approach: low tax burdens to attract private capital, infrastructure investment to reduce the cost of doing business, and fiscal restraint to keep macroeconomic conditions stable.

Figure O.6 illustrates the anatomy of that model. Three features stand out. First, East Asian governments are low tax collectors. Government revenue as a share of GDP averages 20.4 percent—below the middle-income country average of 25.0 percent and well below the high-income country average of 37.0 percent. Second, overall spending is low. Primary government expenditure averages 14.1 percent of GDP, roughly two-thirds of the middle-income country average and less than half of the high-income country average. Third, public investment is high. At 6.5 percent of GDP, East Asia's average exceeds levels recorded in low-income countries (4.3 percent), middle-income countries (4.4 percent), and even high-income countries (4.6 percent). Governments in the region spend less overall as a share of GDP but allocate a larger share to investment compared to other countries.

This enabling approach describes a broad tendency in the large middle-income economies (Indonesia, Malaysia, the Philippines, and Thailand) that have the potential to increase revenues. Smaller economies (Cambodia, the Lao People's Democratic Republic, and Myanmar) face more binding institutional and administrative constraints. Resource-dependent economies (Mongolia, Papua New Guinea, and Timor-Leste) have relied on resource revenues and not built robust domestic tax systems. Pacific Island countries have relatively high revenues and spending as a share of GDP, but the fiscal scale reflects structural factors rather than policy choices. Their small and less diverse economies, geographic isolation, recurrent shocks, and high fixed costs of service delivery lead to larger fiscal aggregates relative to GDP (World Bank 2017b, 2023e). Despite the large budgets as a share of GDP, Pacific Island countries' even higher spending needs leave them with limited fiscal buffers and significant infrastructure gaps.

Most East Asian governments collect and spend less overall as a share of GDP, but they allocate a larger share to investment compared to other countries. Pacific Island countries tend to exhibit significantly higher revenue, spending, and public investment ratios.

FIGURE O.6 Government revenue, spending, and public investment

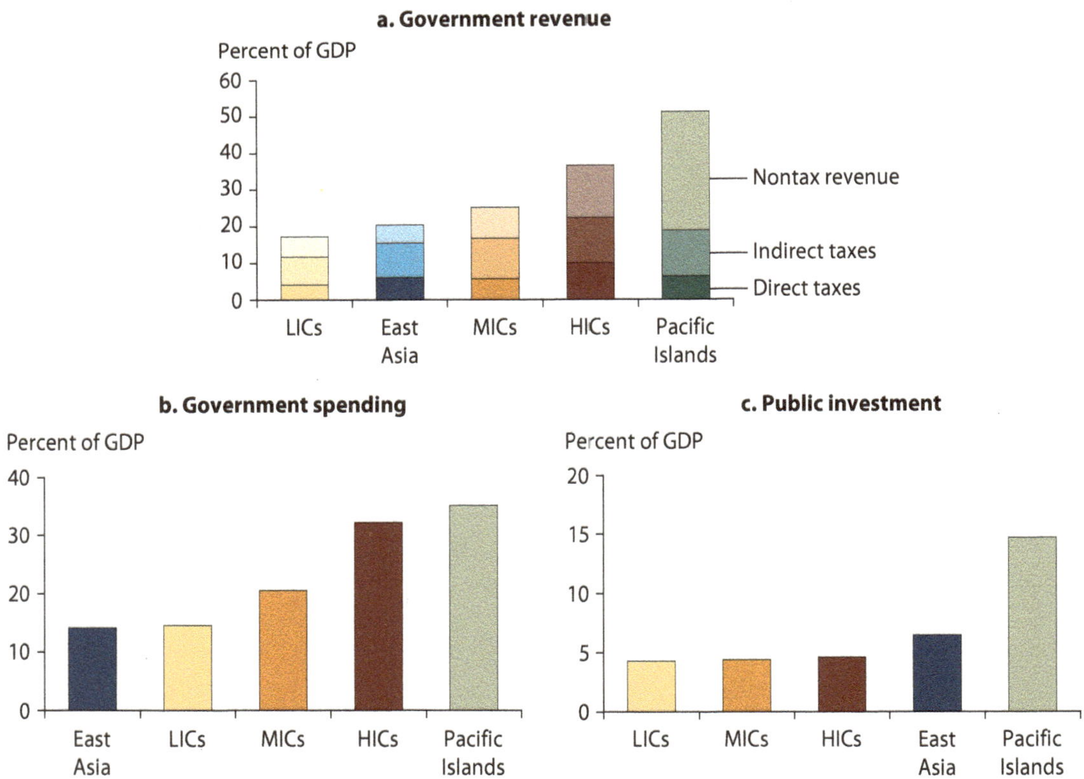

(continued)

FIGURE O.6 Government revenue, spending, and public investment *(continued)*

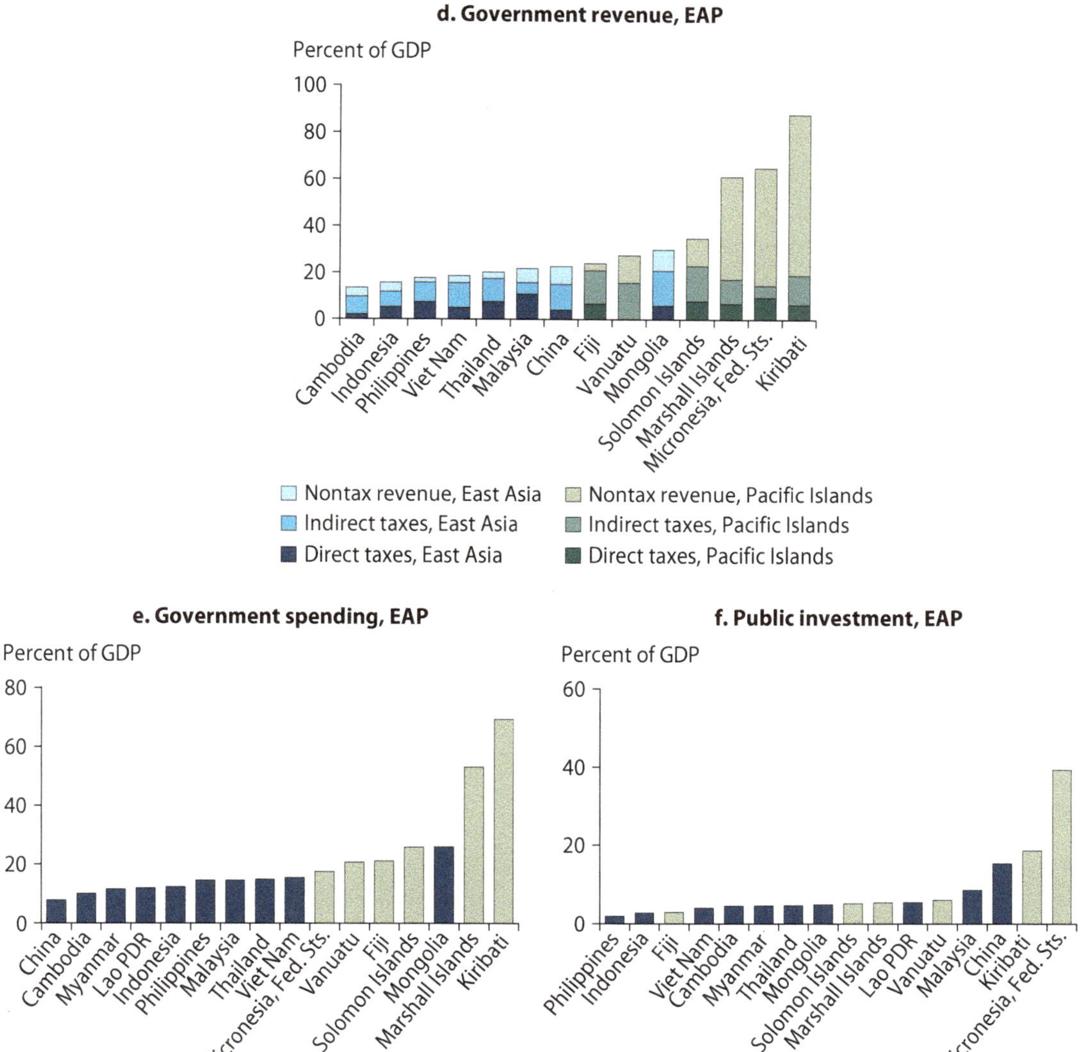

Sources: Original figure for this publication based on Government Finance Statistics, International Monetary Fund (IMF), https://data360.worldbank.org/en/int/dataset/IMF_GFSMAB; Investment and Capital Stock Dataset (ICSD), IMF, https://data.imf.org/Datasets/ICSD; World Economic Outlook (WEO) Database, IMF, https://www.imf.org/en/publications/sprolls/world-economic-outlook-databases; World Revenue Longitudinal Database, IMF, https://www.imf.org/en/topics/fiscal-policies/world-revenue-longitudinal-database.

Note: Revenue and spending show unweighted averages for 2000–22. Public investment shows unweighted averages for 2000–19. In panels a, b, and c, East Asia includes Cambodia, China, Indonesia, Malaysia, Mongolia, the Philippines, Thailand, and Viet Nam. Pacific Islands include Fiji, Kiribati, Marshall Islands, Federated States of Micronesia, Solomon Islands, and Vanuatu. Direct taxes include taxes on corporate and personal income; indirect taxes include taxes on goods and services, and trade; and nontax revenue includes revenue from social contributions and grants, and other revenue from property income, sales of goods and services, fines, penalties and forfeits, non-life insurance, and standardized guarantee schemes as well as current transfers. Government spending refers to total government spending excluding interest payment (WEO) and public investment (ICSD). Total government spending includes expenditure on government consumption, social benefits, grants, subsidies, and other transfers. EAP = East Asia and Pacific; HICs = high-income countries; LICs = low-income countries; MICs = middle-income countries.

Although EAP governments generally spend less as a share of GDP relative to economies at comparable income levels in other regions, the footprint of the state in the region's economies extends well beyond the fiscal budget. State-owned enterprises (SOEs)—and, in some economies, local government financing vehicles and other quasi-fiscal entities—represent a substantial share of economic activity. Viet Nam has among the highest SOE revenues relative to GDP in the world, equivalent to approximately 38 percent of GDP (de Nicola et al. 2025; World Bank 2023a). In Indonesia, approximately 150 SOEs—but primarily the 22 largest—contribute an estimated 15–40 percent of GDP (World Bank 2023a). In China, SOEs' share of industrial assets declined from nearly 69 percent in 1998 to about 42 percent in the early 2010s, but they still account for roughly 30 percent of GDP (World Bank 2014). Off-budget entities, including local government financing vehicles and extrabudgetary funds, add a further layer of state presence, estimated at 8–10 percent of China's GDP in some years (Bai et al. 2016). Although an important aspect of the fiscal picture, this broader presence of the state falls outside the analytical scope of this report.

Tax revenues

East Asian economies have long used relatively low corporate tax rates and generous incentives to attract private investment and foster export-oriented growth. Statutory corporate income tax rates fell from an average of about 40 percent in the 1980s to roughly 20–25 percent by the early 2020s. Over time, however, the rest of the world has also reduced its corporate income tax rates, contributing to a global race to the bottom (refer to figure O.7). Tariffs tell a similar story: most East Asian economies have lower tariffs, on average, than middle-income countries do. Pacific Island countries maintain higher rates, and Cambodia and Myanmar exceed the middle-income country average for tariffs.

Economies in the region not only have low statutory rates but also provide extensive tax incentives to attract investment. Tax holidays, preferential regimes, and special economic zones are prevalent across the region. In several economies, including Indonesia, Lao PDR, Malaysia, and Thailand, corporate tax holidays can extend beyond 10 years. Pacific Island countries offer similarly generous arrangements: Fiji, for example, provides a 13-year tax holiday under its Tax Free Zone scheme, and in some cases tax holidays can reach up to 30 years (World Bank 2015).

Interestingly, the region has relatively high revenues from corporate taxes as a share of GDP despite having comparatively low statutory rates. Since 2000, corporate income tax revenue has averaged approximately 4.3 percent of GDP, about one-third higher than in both middle-income and high-income country groups, reflecting a relatively broad and formal corporate tax base, supported in part by the strong

Historically, EAP has had relatively low corporate tax and tariff rates.

FIGURE O.7 Statutory CIT and effective tariff rates, EAP and comparators

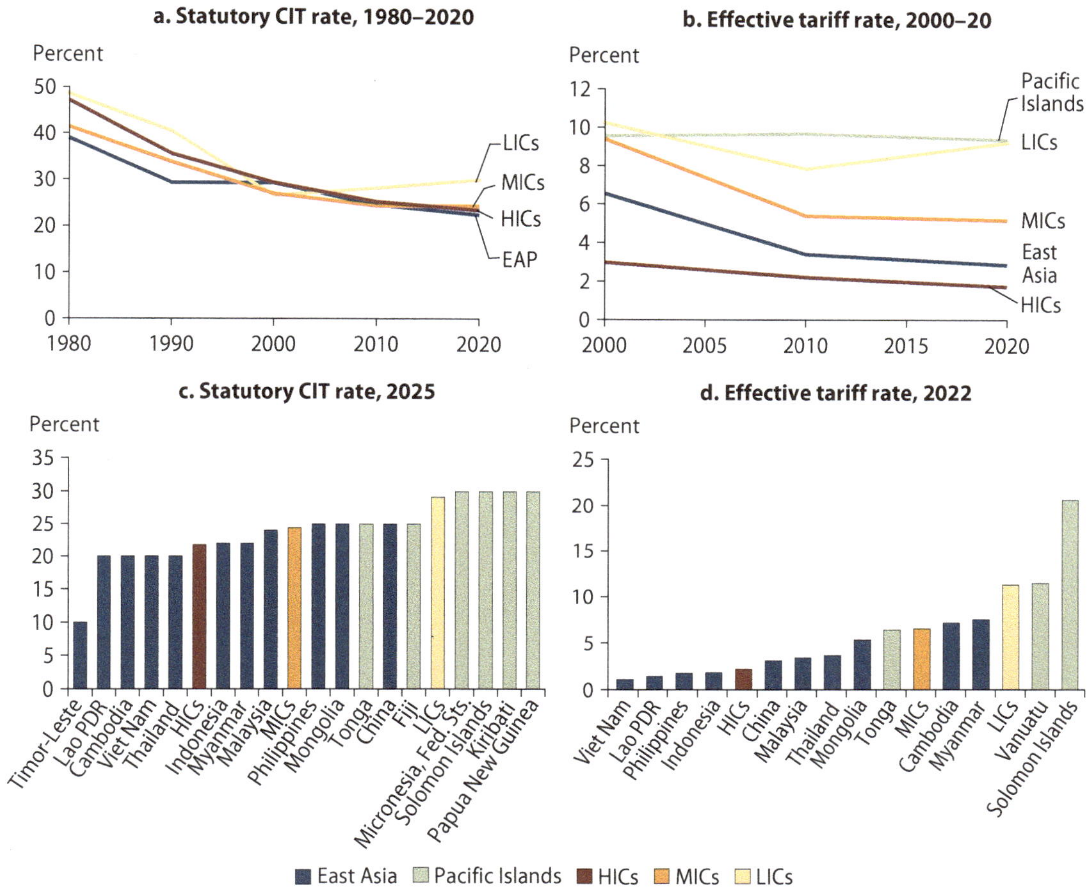

Sources: Original figure for this publication based on Enache 2025; World Development Indicators, World Bank, https://datatopics.worldbank.org/world-development-indicators/.

Note: In panels a and c, CIT rate refers to the standard top statutory corporate income tax rate. In panels b and d, tariff rate refers to the average of effectively applied rates weighted by the product import shares corresponding to each partner country. In panel a, available averages for Cambodia and Viet Nam start at 1990, and for Lao PDR at 2020. In panel b, East Asia includes Cambodia, Indonesia, Lao PDR, Malaysia, Myanmar, the Philippines, Thailand, Timor-Leste, and Viet Nam; Pacific Islands include Fiji, Papua New Guinea, Solomon Islands, Tonga, and Vanuatu. CIT = corporate income tax; EAP = East Asia and Pacific; HICs = high-income countries; LICs = low-income countries; MICs = middle-income countries.

presence of multinational firms. By contrast, other tax instruments generate relatively modest revenues. For example, personal income tax revenue as a share of GDP remains lower than in other middle-income countries, reflecting exemptions, high informality, and low enforcement. Revenue from goods and services taxes also remains low, reflecting a combination of structural constraints and policy design features, including high levels of informality, extensive exemptions, and relatively low statutory rates, which together narrow the tax base and constrain the region's capacity to mobilize stable and broad-based revenue.

Human capital

Because of low tax revenues, government spending in the region remains lower than in most other country groups. Between 2000 and 2022, government spending averaged just 19.8 percent of GDP, about two-thirds of the average for middle-income countries and roughly half that for high-income countries. As discussed earlier, EAP governments have prioritized public investment, particularly in infrastructure. That stance, however, has contributed to underinvestment in human capital (refer to figure O.8).

The current fiscal approach in EAP has come at the cost of human capital investments.

FIGURE O.8 Government spending on human capital: Selected EAP economies and comparators, 2000–22

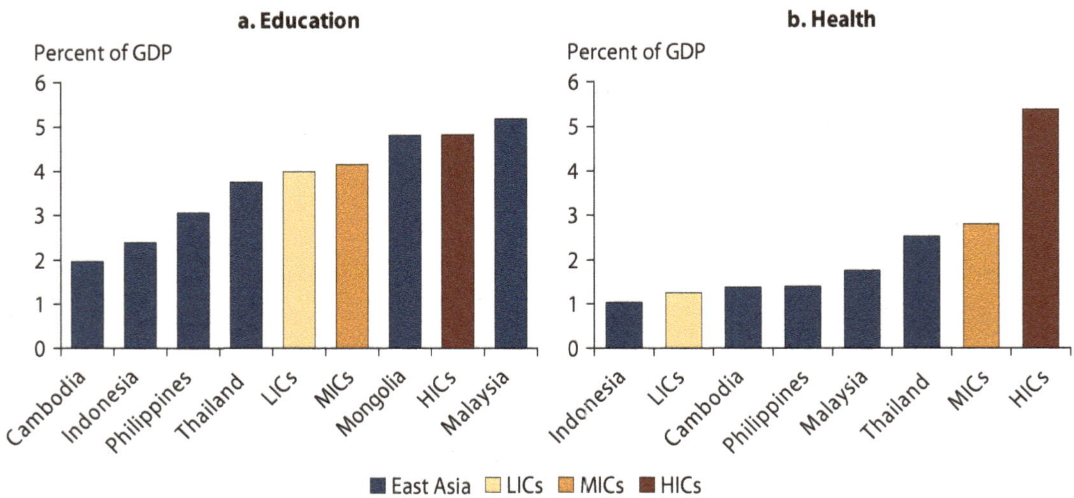

Sources: Original figure for this publication based on Government Finance Statistics, International Monetary Fund, https://data360.worldbank.org/en/int/dataset/IMF_GFSMAB; World Development Indicators, World Bank, https://datatopics.worldbank.org/world-development-indicators/.

Note: EAP = East Asia and Pacific; HICs = high-income countries; LICs = low-income countries; MICs = middle-income countries.

The underinvestment has led to gaps in outcome-based measures of human capital development. For example, the World Bank's Human Capital Index shows that China, Malaysia, Mongolia, Thailand, and Viet Nam score relatively high compared with other middle-income countries but lower than high-income ones—a status to which they aspire. Other economies in the region, especially those in the Pacific Islands, have even lower learning and health outcomes (refer to figure O.9).

The low quality of basic education, which results in weak foundational skills, constrains the contribution of education to human capital in EAP economies. In 14 of the region's 22 middle-income economies, more than half of 10-year-olds cannot read or understand age-appropriate reading material—that is, they experience learning poverty (Afkar et al. 2023). Even in Malaysia and the Philippines, only 24 percent and 16 percent of 15-year-olds, respectively, leave high school with basic literacy and numeracy skills (OECD 2023).

Moreover, EAP economies face a two-dimensional health challenge that prevents people from preserving their human capital despite living longer (Debebe et al. 2026). First, although most economies in the region have achieved significant progress in maternal and child health and nutrition outcomes, levels of child and maternal mortality remain unacceptably high in Cambodia, Lao PDR, Timor-Leste, and most Pacific Island countries. Second, all EAP economies face an increasing burden of noncommunicable diseases (NCDs), such as hypertension, diabetes, and cardiovascular disease, among the adult population. The likelihood of premature death (at ages 30–70) due to NCDs exceeds 30 percent in some EAP economies. The NCD burden affects economies like Mongolia and some Pacific Island countries (such as Fiji and Tonga) more severely than others like China and Thailand. Poor-quality health care—including poor management of NCD conditions and high rates of preventable hospitalization—accounts for one-third of avoidable mortality in EAP (Bales et al. 2022; Kruk et al. 2018). The surge in NCDs leads not only to lower quality of life but also to lower productivity in the prime of life and higher health care costs.

Macroeconomic stability

Fiscal policy is one of the most powerful tools governments have to promote macroeconomic stability. It operates primarily through countercyclical policy—expanding the fiscal stance during downturns to support demand and tightening it during expansions to rebuild buffers. EAP reveals a contrasting picture of fiscal policy: a core of relatively disciplined middle-income economies with some fiscal

On the Human Capital Index, many EAP economies rank below the middle-income country average.

FIGURE O.9 Human Capital Index, 2020

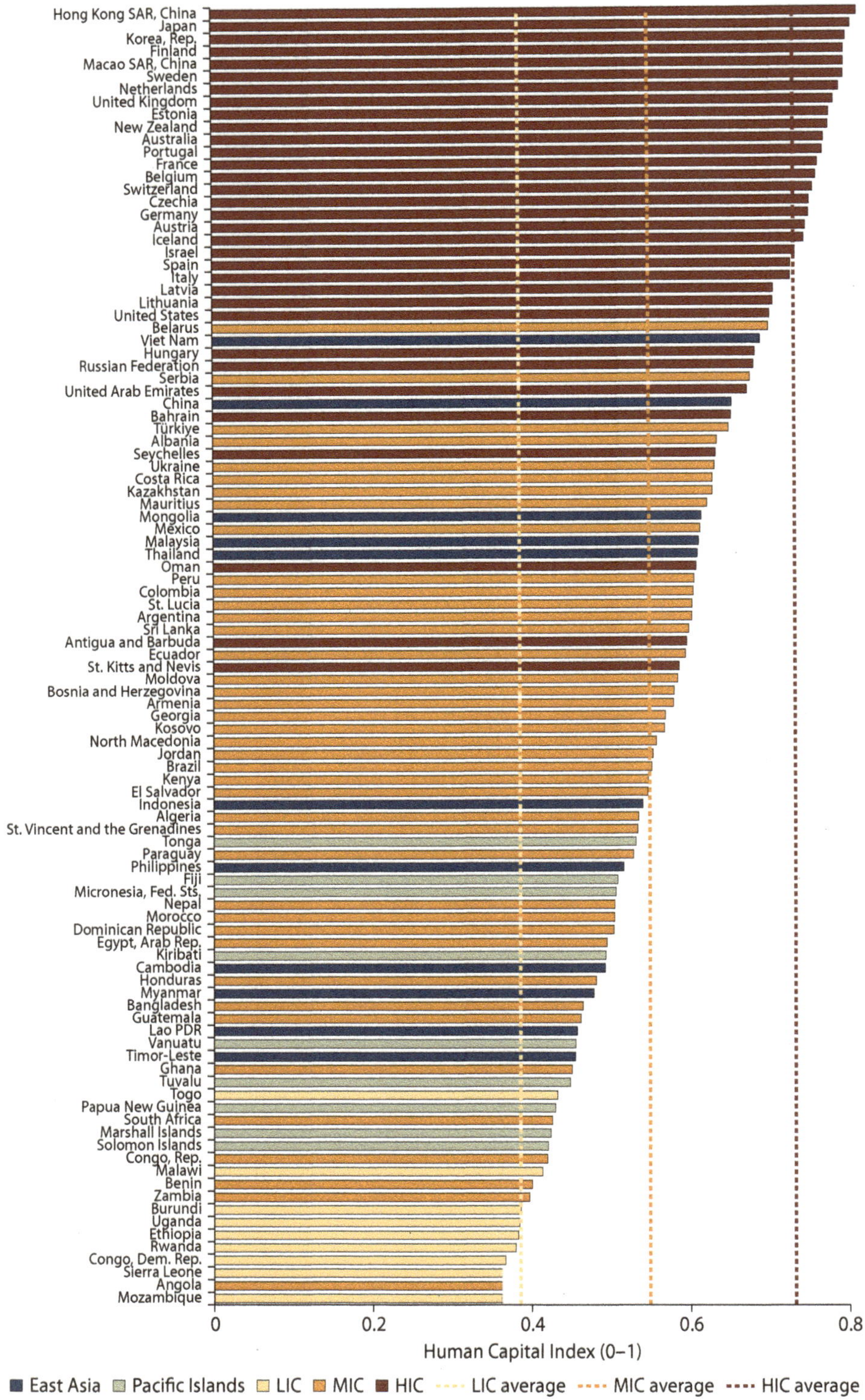

Sources: Original figure for this publication based on Human Capital Index, World Bank, https://humancapital.worldbank.org/en/indicator/WB_HCP_HCI; World Development Indicators, World Bank, https://datatopics.worldbank.org/world-development-indicators/.
Note: The index measures, on a scale of 0–1, how productive a child born today will be as a future worker relative to the benchmark of full health and complete education. EAP = East Asia and Pacific; HIC = high-income country; LIC = low-income country; MIC = middle-income country.

space to conduct countercyclical or broadly acyclical policy, and a periphery of smaller, more vulnerable states with limited fiscal space, where fiscal policy remains highly procyclical, as in Lao PDR and most Pacific Island countries.

The core economies in the region have preserved the fiscal space needed to respond effectively to adverse shocks by containing expenditure and maintaining relatively low deficits and debt levels during economic upswings. This fiscal discipline has also contributed to greater credibility and more favorable financing conditions during economic downturns. Consistent with this pattern, primary balances in East Asia tend to improve during economic expansions and deteriorate during downturns, as governments allow deficits to widen to support countercyclical fiscal policy.

Consequently, government spending in the region is significantly less procyclical than in other EMDEs (refer to figure O.10, panel a). On average, the correlation between the cyclical components of government spending and GDP in East Asia is approximately –0.10, compared with a strongly procyclical correlation of 0.30 in other EMDEs. Moreover, about 89 percent of East Asian economies display either acyclical or countercyclical spending behavior—closely mirroring advanced economies (91 percent) and substantially exceeding the share observed in other EMDEs (41 percent).

In contrast, most Pacific Island countries exhibit highly procyclical government spending. These economies face significantly higher macroeconomic volatility because of their small size, limited economic diversification, and high exposure to external and climate shocks. At the same time, narrow and volatile tax bases, limited access to international capital markets, and frequent natural disasters constrain governments' ability to borrow or accumulate fiscal buffers. Consequently, fiscal policy has limited capacity to smooth economic fluctuations and is often procyclical.

Social benefits and other transfers play a role in the countercyclicality of fiscal policy (refer to figure O.10, panel b). On average, social benefits and public debt in East Asia increase during economic downturns, and decline during economic upswings. This countercyclical pattern contrasts sharply with that observed in other EMDEs, where social benefits typically expand during booms and contract during downturns, and public debt exhibits only limited cyclical responsiveness (refer to figure O.11).

Despite having relatively small governments, East Asian economies have less procyclical spending than other EMDEs, largely reflecting timely provision of social benefits and transfers.

FIGURE O.10 Cyclicality of spending, by size of government and expenditure subcomponent, EAP and comparators, 2000–22

a. Government size and cyclicality

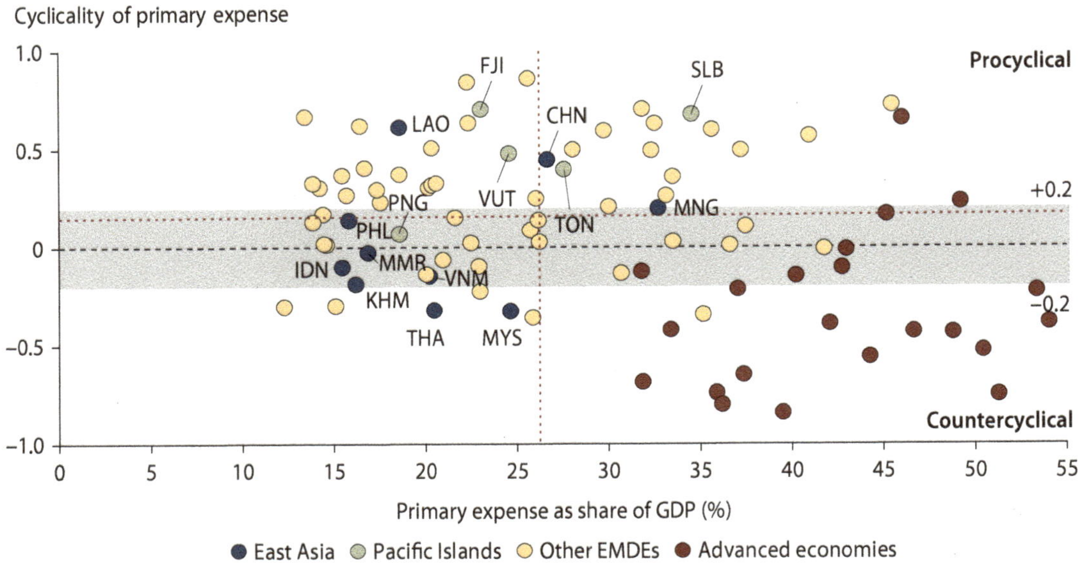

b. Cyclicality, by expenditure subcomponent

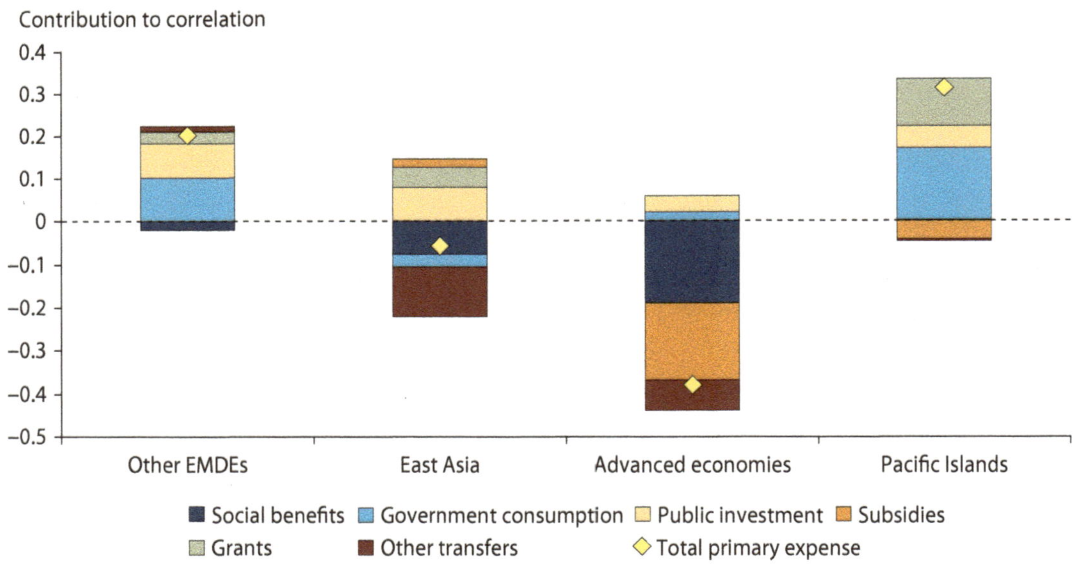

Sources: Original figure for this publication based on Government Finance Statistics, International Monetary Fund, https://data360.worldbank.org/en/int/dataset/IMF_GFSMAB; World Economic Outlook Database, International Monetary Fund, https://www.imf.org/en/publications/sprolls/world-economic-outlook-databases.

Note: In panel a, dashed red lines denote unweighted averages for EMDEs. Cyclicality of government expenditure is calculated as the correlation between the cyclical component of real government expenditure and real GDP. The cyclical component has been estimated using the Hodrick-Prescott filter. Following Fuentes and Soto (2022), fiscal policy is classified as procyclical if the observed correlation is above 0.2, countercyclical if it is below −0.2, and acyclical otherwise (gray-shaded region in panel a). Sample (excluding East Asia and Pacific, and China) includes 66 developing and transition economies, and 22 industrial economies. For a list of country codes, refer to https://www.iso.org/obp/ui/#search. EMDEs = emerging market and developing economies.

By containing spending and public debt issuance in good times, many East Asian economies have preserved fiscal space to respond effectively to shocks.

FIGURE O.11 Social benefits and public debt during the economic cycle, East Asia and comparators

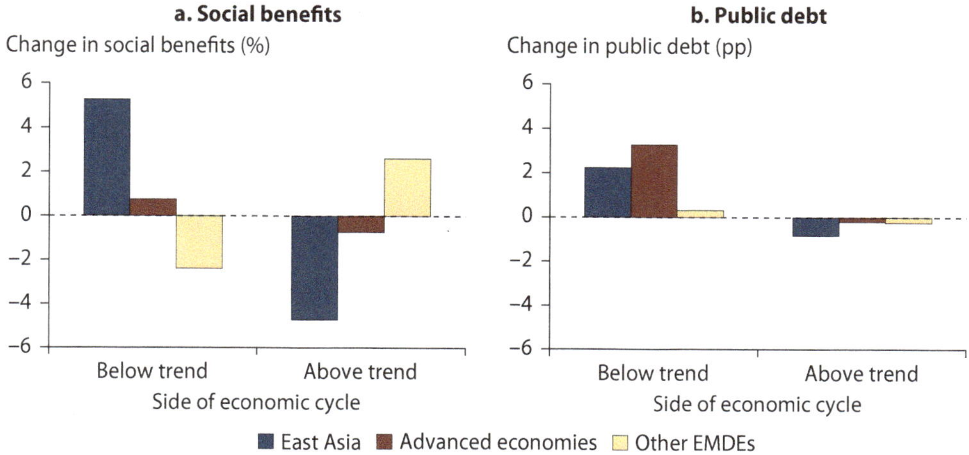

Source: Original figure for this publication based on Government Finance Statistics, International Monetary Fund, https://data360.worldbank.org/en/int/dataset/IMF_GFSMAB.
Note: Below trend and above trend correspond to periods when real GDP is below or above the trend estimated using the Hodrick-Prescott filter. EMDEs = emerging market and developing economies; pp = percentage point.

Countercyclical spending is a necessary but insufficient condition for effective fiscal stabilization. It is difficult to assess whether state spending, which represents a small share of GDP in several EAP economies, had an economically significant impact on dampening fluctuations. The empirical literature suggests that fiscal multipliers for EMDEs are positive but state-dependent: they are larger during recessions than expansions, when fiscal space is ample, and when interventions are well targeted (Huidrom et al. 2020; Ilzetzki et al. 2013; World Bank 2021a). Since the Asian financial crisis, the region has built stronger fiscal frameworks and maintained moderate fiscal deficits, preserving the space to respond forcefully when shocks arrived (World Bank 2023c). Thailand's cash transfer program during COVID-19—representing about 2.5 percent of GDP—was well-targeted to affected households, effectively mitigating their income losses and sustaining consumption (World Bank 2022a). Nonetheless, the size of the fiscal envelope ultimately constrains the macroeconomic cushion governments provide.

Despite the region's general fiscal restraint, the COVID-19 shock sharply accelerated a public debt trajectory that began rising after the global financial crisis of 2007–08 (refer to figure O.12). In the years between that crisis and the

Although interest rates are expected to remain below growth rates, rising debt levels could push up borrowing costs and dampen growth.

FIGURE O.12 Public debt, growth, and interest rates, East Asia

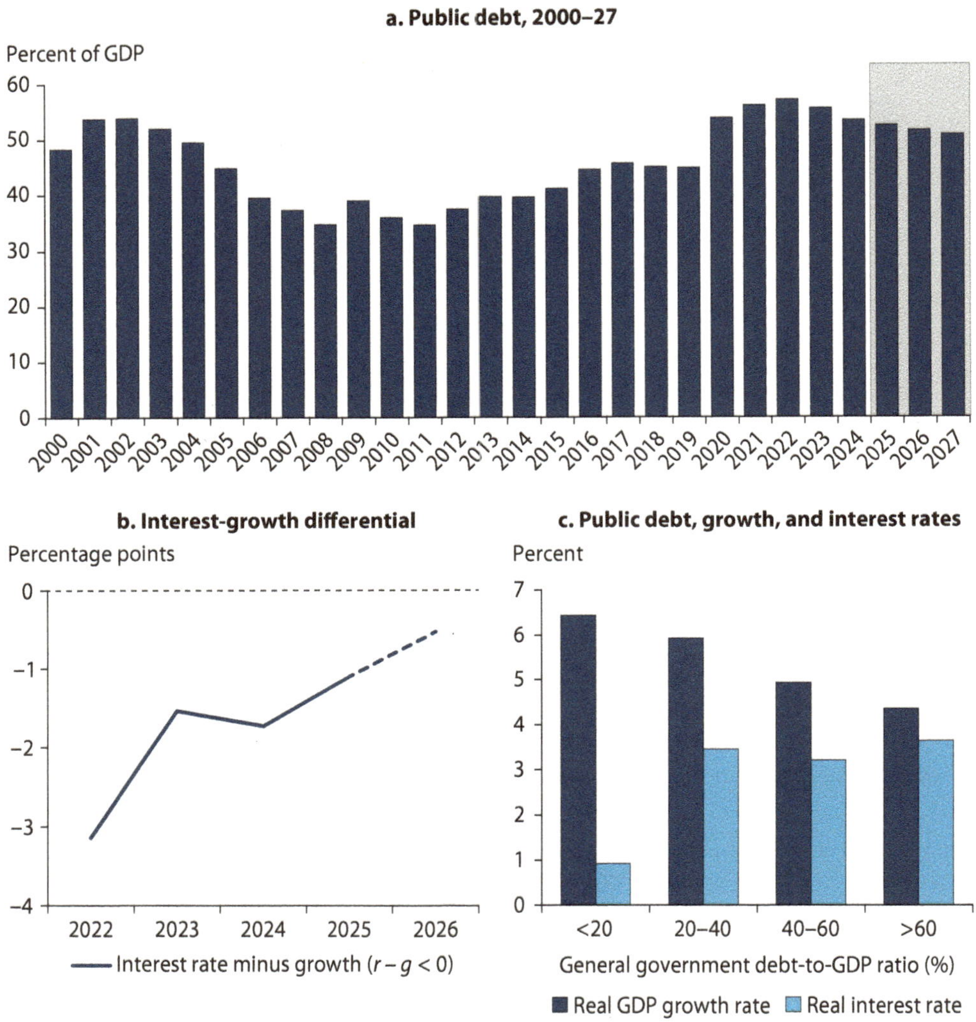

Sources: Original figure for this publication based on International Finance Statistics, International Monetary Fund, https://data360.worldbank.org/en/int/dataset/IMF_IFS; World Development Indicators, World Bank, https://datatopics.worldbank.org/world-development-indicators/; World Economic Outlook Database, International Monetary Fund, https://www.imf.org/en/publications/sprolls/world-economic-outlook-databases.

Note: In panel a, bars show unweighted average. Gray shaded area refers to projections of public debt from the World Economic Outlook. In panel b, interest-growth differential refers to real interest rates (r) minus GDP growth rate (g). Unweighted average for East Asian economies excluding China. Values for 2026 are estimates. Panel c plots the average real GDP growth and real long-term interest rates for different levels of the public debt-to-GDP ratio; the sample includes 50 developing economies (10 of them EAP) with at least 10 observations on $r - g$ and public debt over GDP over the period 2000–19.

COVID-19 pandemic, expanding deficits remained broadly sustainable: low interest rates and strong growth produced favorable interest-growth differentials that kept debt dynamics manageable. Looking ahead, however, higher global interest rates and a more subdued growth outlook could significantly heighten debt vulnerabilities. In several economies—including Indonesia, Lao PDR, Mongolia, and Papua New Guinea—interest payments already consume an increasing share of revenues, constraining fiscal space. As fiscal risks accumulate, the region's ability to undertake countercyclical policy in future downturns may become increasingly limited, underscoring the need to rebuild fiscal buffers.

The impact of population aging on fiscal balances, which are likely to be strained on both the expenditure and revenue sides, presents a further source of concern. On the expenditure side, pressures on public finances will come from rising pension costs and health and long-term care spending. Economies in the region have underdeveloped systems for old-age financial protection, with relatively low coverage of formal pension systems and very modest social pension and social assistance adequacy for older people. Furthermore, existing pension schemes tend to be defined benefit schemes, so that the coverage of contributory pension schemes in many EAP economies remains low (refer to figure O.13). A key driver of both current and projected spending is civil service pension schemes, which in several countries are much more generous than private sector schemes, resulting in significant and rising unfunded liabilities. Economies such as China and Viet Nam have started to reform civil service pensions, but long transition periods mean the fiscal burden will continue for some time. This situation is of particular concern in a low-revenue region like EAP. On the revenue side, the declining size of the working-age population will shrink the contribution base for financing pension, unemployment, and health insurance systems in several major EAP economies, necessitating either ever-increasing and distortionary labor taxes or significant reforms in how governments finance entitlement programs.

Rebuilding fiscal space requires institutional mechanisms that strengthen fiscal discipline, anchor expectations, and ensure access to financing during downturns. Medium-term fiscal frameworks, fiscal rules, and liquidity buffers form a mutually reinforcing system that restores countercyclical capacity (refer to figure O.14). Rules without medium-term fiscal frameworks lack an operational anchor; medium-term fiscal frameworks without buffers limit the ability to respond when shocks materialize; and buffers without rules risk premature depletion.

Coverage of contributory pension schemes in many EAP economies remains low; generous civil service pension schemes have created large unfunded liabilities.

FIGURE O.13 Existing pension schemes and liabilities, EAP

a. Coverage of contributory pension schemes

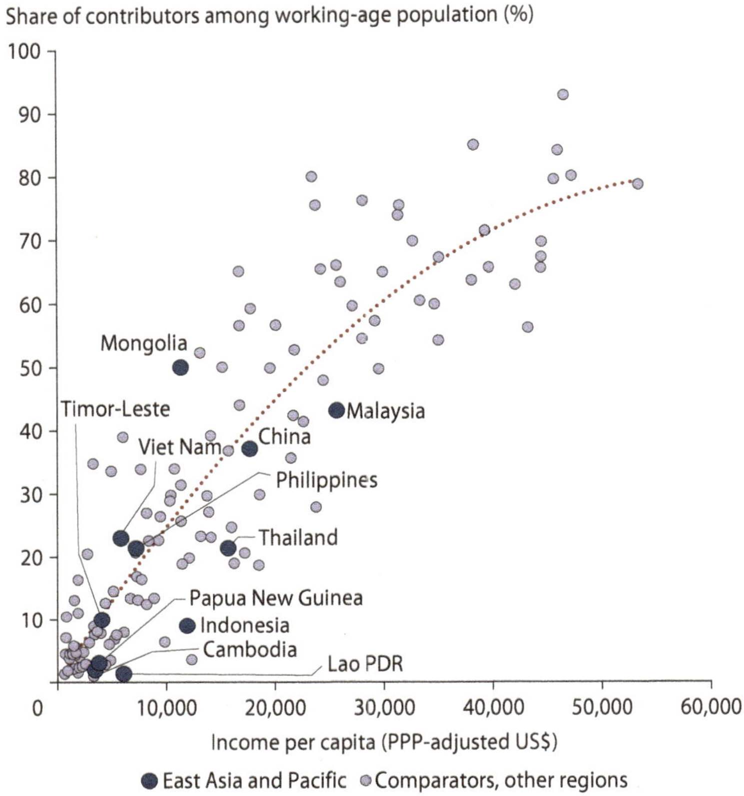

b. Unfunded civil service pension liabilities

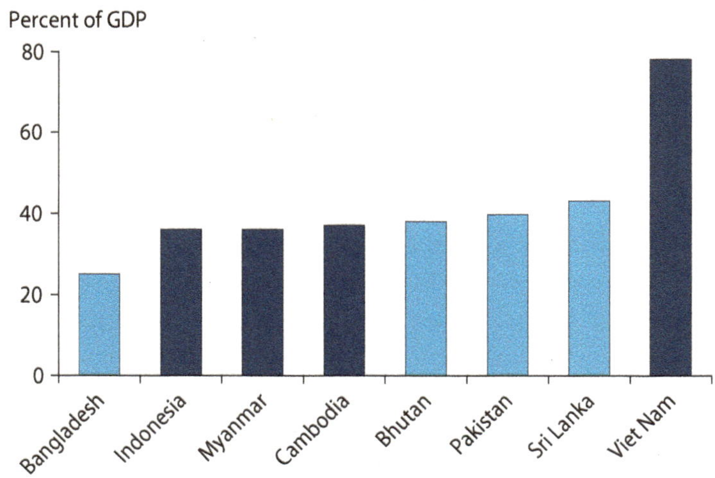

Sources: Original figure for this publication based on World Bank 2025 (panel a); World Social Protection Data Dashboards, International Labor Organization, https://www.social-protection.org/gimi/WSPDB.action?id=32&lang=EN (panel b).

Note: In panel b, bars denote unfunded civil service pension liabilities as a share of GDP in the latest year. EAP = East Asia and Pacific; PPP = purchasing power parity.

Medium-term fiscal frameworks, fiscal rules, and liquidity buffers rebuild fiscal space by aligning revenues and spending, strengthening discipline, and ensuring liquidity during downturns.

FIGURE O.14 Framework for rebuilding fiscal space: Planning, commitment, and resilience

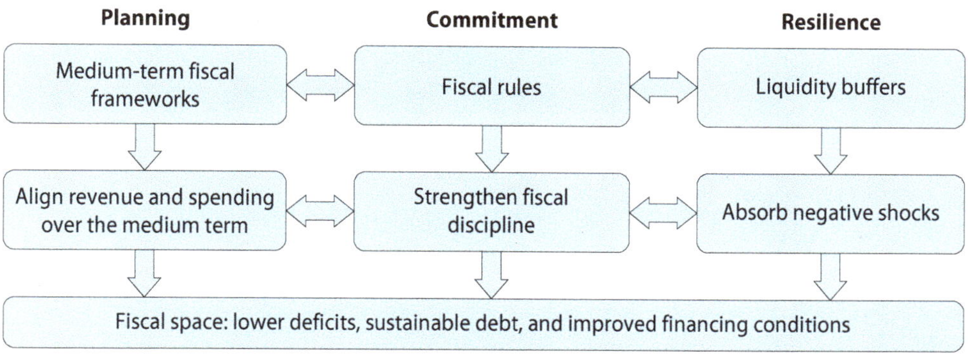

Source: Original figure for this publication.

Poverty and inequality

An examination of the drivers of poverty reduction in EAP highlights the dominant role of economic growth. Broad-based expansion of income and employment opportunities has had far more influence in reducing poverty than has declining inequality or redistributive policies (refer to figure O.15). Although fiscal policy has played a supportive role, it has generally been secondary to growth as a driver of poverty reduction. That said, public spending in EAP has had somewhat stronger poverty-reducing effects than in other middle-income countries, reflecting well-targeted social transfers, conditional cash programs, and provision of basic services. In most EAP economies, however, these effects remain modest; notable exceptions include Mongolia, where social protection programs have significantly helped poverty reduction, albeit on a near-universal basis and at considerable fiscal cost (refer to figure O.16). This pattern suggests that, although growth has been the primary engine of poverty alleviation, potential exists for fiscal policy to complement growth by more systematically supporting vulnerable households and accelerating the transition from poverty into the middle class.

Direct transfers can play a critical role in alleviating poverty by providing immediate support to vulnerable households. Indirect taxes impose a significant burden on lower-income households, which pay such taxes through their consumption. In Fiji and the Philippines, for example, the negative impact of indirect taxation on household income offsets much of the poverty-reducing effect of direct transfers.

Economic growth helped reduce poverty in EAP much more than redistribution.

FIGURE O.15 Drivers of poverty reduction, selected EAP economies

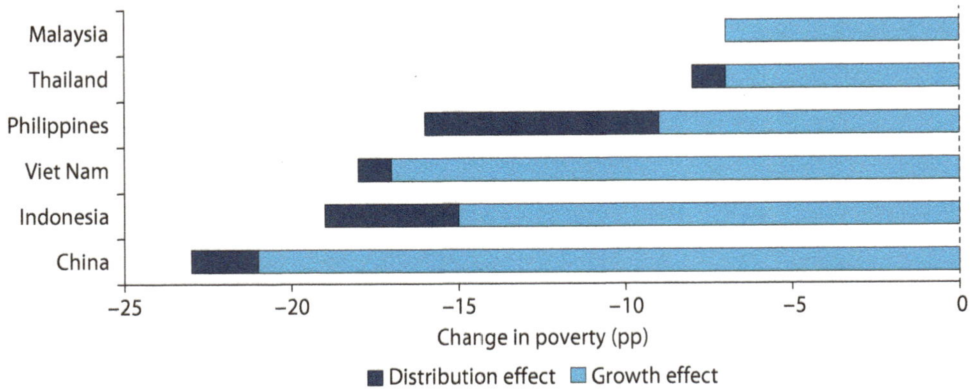

Source: Original figure for this publication based on a growth-redistribution decomposition method from Datt and Ravallion 1992.

Note: Bars show percentage-point change in poverty and the contribution of growth and distribution effects to total poverty reduction at the upper-middle-income poverty line ($6.85/day). Periods for each country were selected on the basis of availability of two comparable surveys over the last decade: China, 2013–19; Indonesia, 2011–19; Malaysia, 2011–19; the Philippines, 2012–18; Thailand, 2011–19; and Viet Nam, 2012–18. A decomposition of poverty changes into growth and inequality components examines whether changes in poverty were driven by growth in mean consumption (income) per capita or by a more inclusive distribution of consumption (income). EAP = East Asia and Pacific; pp = percentage point.

Although fiscal policy has reduced poverty rates in EAP more than in the average low- and middle-income countries, the impacts are small.

FIGURE O.16 Change in poverty rate, by type of government spending program, EAP and comparators

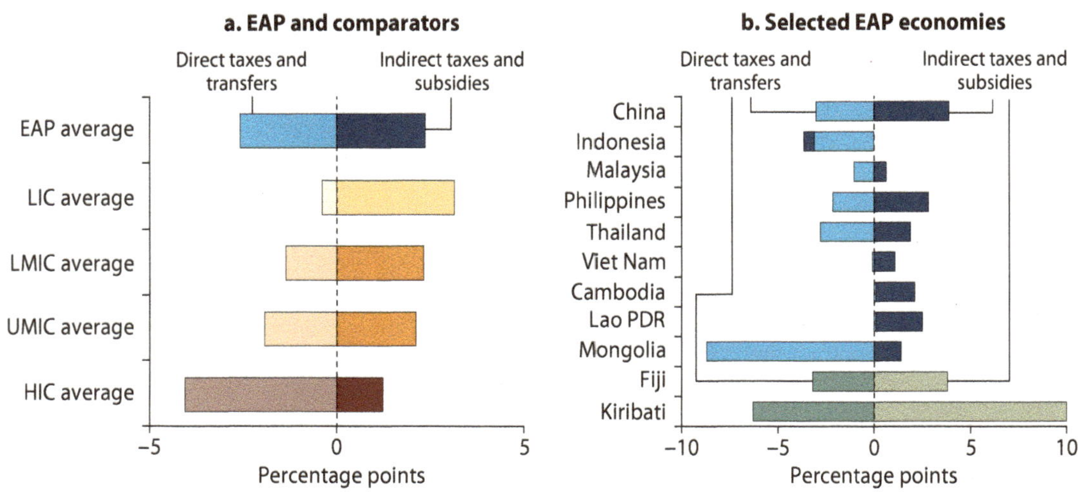

Sources: Original figure for this publication based on Wai-Poi et al. 2025.

Note: Latest available year from 2010–19; refer to table 5 in Wai-Poi et al. (2025) for specific country years and sources. China poverty result is from 2014. EAP = East Asia and Pacific; HIC = high-income country; LIC = low-income country; LMIC = lower-middle-income country; UMIC = upper-middle-income country.

Meanwhile, indirect tax exemptions, intended to protect the poor, largely accrue to wealthier households with higher consumption, and provide little relief to lower-income households that already conduct tax-free transactions in the informal sector (Wai-Poi et al. 2025). By contrast, Indonesia illustrates how substantial increases in transfer programs, and improvements in targeting and delivery mechanisms, can achieve stronger poverty-reduction outcomes. Crucially, Indonesia financed the expansion of transfer and health spending not by imposing higher taxes but by reallocating resources away from expensive and regressive energy subsidies (World Bank 2020).

Finally, an assessment of the distributional impact of fiscal policy in EAP reveals the pivotal role of government spending on health and education in reducing inequality. Investments in human capital, measured as the costs of service delivery, provide larger equity gains than taxes, transfers, and subsidies (refer to figure O.17). Strengthening government spending on health and education not only promotes equity but also supports human capital development, productivity growth, and long-term inclusive development.

In EAP, as in other country groupings, health and education spending is the main driver of inequality reduction.

FIGURE O.17 Change in Gini index, by type of government spending program, EAP and comparators

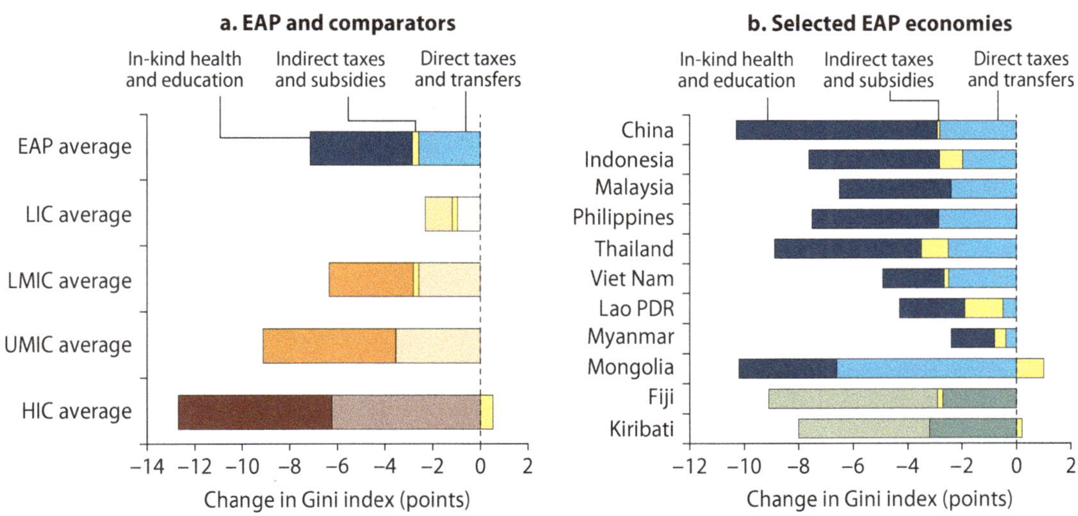

Source: Original figure for this publication based on Wai-Poi et al. 2025.

Note: Latest available year from 2010–19; refer to table 5 in Wai-Poi et al. (2025) for specific country years and sources. China inequality result is from 2019. EAP = East Asia and Pacific; HIC = high-income country; LIC = low-income country; LMIC = lower-middle-income country; UMIC = upper-middle-income country.

Policy implications

In summary, fiscal policy in EAP has been characterized by relatively low tax rates, modest government spending, and comparatively high levels of public investment in infrastructure. This "growth-enabling" approach has supported private investment and economic growth, but it has also meant limited spending on health, education, and social protection. The strategy has also left the region ill-equipped to deal with climate shocks and the fiscal consequences of rapidly aging populations.

Against this backdrop, the report outlines a set of specific policy actions that would constitute a new "growth-enhancing" fiscal compact to support higher, inclusive, and resilient growth in EAP. The compact would have the following three pillars:

Prioritizing spending on health, education, infrastructure upgrading, social protection, and climate adaptation. More state spending in each of these areas would go toward ensuring the provision of more and better public goods (especially in health, infrastructure, and adaptation), generating stronger positive externalities (in health and education), and remedying persistent inequality of access (in health and education, and through social protection). In each case, state spending would need to be complemented by institutional and sectoral reforms that increase the efficiency of spending, encourage private investment, and improve service delivery.

Improving the efficiency and effectiveness of domestic revenue mobilization. Recognizing the constraints on direct taxation in a world where capital and skills are mobile and employment is often informal, revenue mobilization would need to rely more on uniform indirect taxes, as well as on property, health, and carbon taxes. Well-designed reforms can simultaneously reduce tax-related distortions, increase revenue, and improve health and climate outcomes.

Linking tax and spending reforms to increase efficiency, credibility, and political feasibility. The new compact would recognize the need to determine the scale of spending and taxation jointly, with the marginal benefit of spending ideally equal to the marginal cost of taxation. Explicitly connecting new or higher taxes to clear and well-targeted spending priorities can strengthen political support. Anchoring these reforms in a medium-term fiscal framework, combined with fiscal rules and liquidity buffers, would increase credibility and thus public support.

Prioritizing spending on health, education, infrastructure upgrading, social protection, and climate adaptation

To deliver on the region's development ambitions, public expenditure would need to serve three interconnected objectives: improving the quantity and quality of core public goods, particularly in health, infrastructure, and climate adaptation; harnessing stronger positive externalities in health and education; and correcting entrenched inequalities of access through social protection and human capital investment.

Human and physical capital investments

Higher spending on human capital—combined with reforms of education and health—would support growth and reduce inequality. Narrowing the region's human capital spending gaps could yield substantial economic and social returns. For example, raising education spending in EAP economies to the average levels of Japan and the Republic of Korea could boost annual GDP per capita growth by an estimated 0.97 percentage point on average (refer to figure O.18). Economies with the largest gaps stand to gain the most.

Upgrading infrastructure is essential to build resilience and sustain growth. Infrastructure gaps in transportation and digital networks raise logistics costs and inhibit productivity growth (de Nicola et al. 2025). In Indonesia, infrastructure deficiencies contribute to logistics costs of approximately 15 percent of firms' total expenditure (World Bank 2021b). Mobile connectivity has expanded rapidly across the region, but disparities in broadband quality and connection speeds remain

Narrowing the education spending gap in EAP economies could increase annual growth, on average, by 0.97 percentage point.

FIGURE O.18 Additional growth from aligning education spending with average of aspirational countries, selected EAP economies

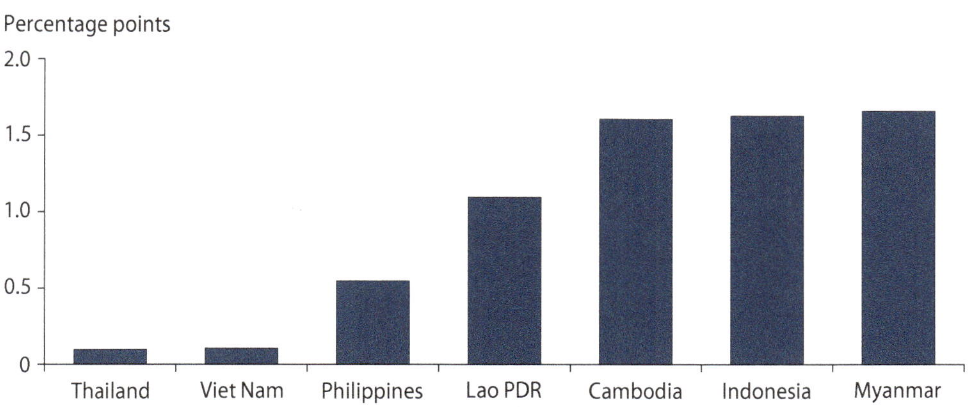

Source: Original figure for this publication based on Acosta-Ormaechea and Morozumi 2013.
Note: The bars represent additional annual growth (pp) if the average government spending on education between 2010 and 2019 equaled the average spending on education by Japan and the Republic of Korea in the same period. The figure does not include Malaysia and Mongolia because they both have higher average education spending within the period than the aspirational average. EAP = East Asia and Pacific.

pronounced both within and across countries (World Bank 2023b). The returns to closing these gaps are high. Benefit-cost ratios for investments in energy and transportation exceed 1 in almost all EAP economies—meaning that additional investment passes a basic social rate of return threshold in virtually every economy in the region (refer to figure O.19). Of course, public investment would be needed in economies that have higher social than private returns to investment, even after implementing the relevant regulatory reforms.

Climate adaptation investments

Climate adaptation investments can deliver a triple dividend (refer to figure O.20, panel a; World Bank 2023c). First, adaptation measures reduce the physical and economic losses associated with climate shocks. For example, upgraded and climate-informed infrastructure reduces direct exposure to floods, storms, heat waves, droughts, and sea level rise. Second, such measures also generate induced economic benefits by lowering uncertainty and encouraging investment.

The social benefits of further investments in energy and transportation exceed their costs in almost all EAP economies.

FIGURE O.19 Benefit-cost ratios for investments in energy and transportation, selected EAP economies

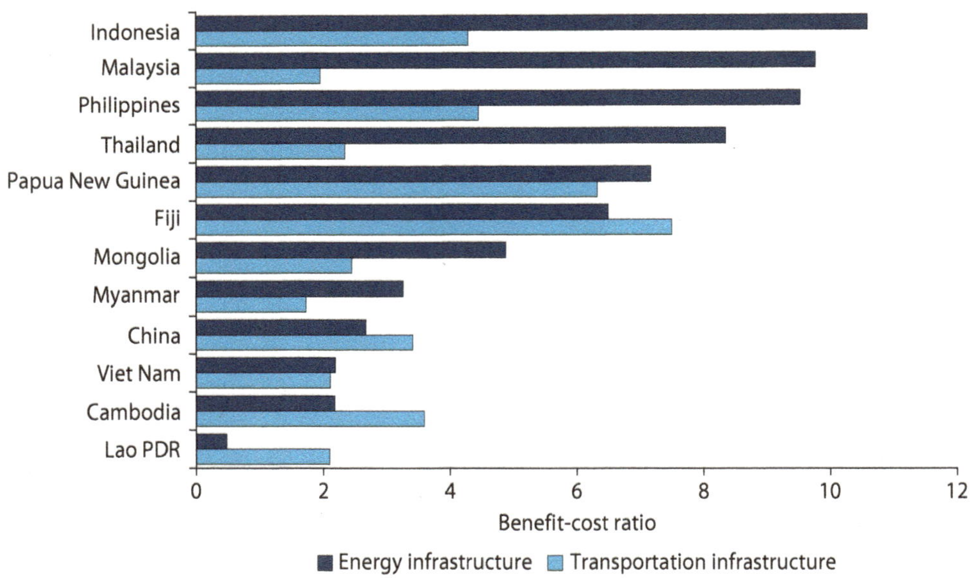

Source: Original figure for this publication based on Straub et al. 2026.
Note: Benefit-cost ratio, termed infrastructure efficiency ratio in Straub et al. (2026), denotes the social rates of return to investment divided by the country-specific borrowing costs and country-sector-specific depreciation. An efficiency ratio above 1 indicates that additional investment is warranted, because it passes a basic benefit-cost threshold.

Third, many adaptation interventions yield social and environmental co-benefits, such as improved access to services, stronger livelihoods, and better ecosystem management. Although the positive externalities and public good aspect of some adaptation initiatives constitute a compelling case for public investment, such investment must strengthen rather than weaken incentives for private action.

Investing in adaptation will deliver a triple dividend; in the Philippines, all sectors will benefit from adaptation investments.

FIGURE O.20 Triple dividends of climate adaptation and the example of sectoral benefits in the Philippines

a. Triple dividends of adaptation

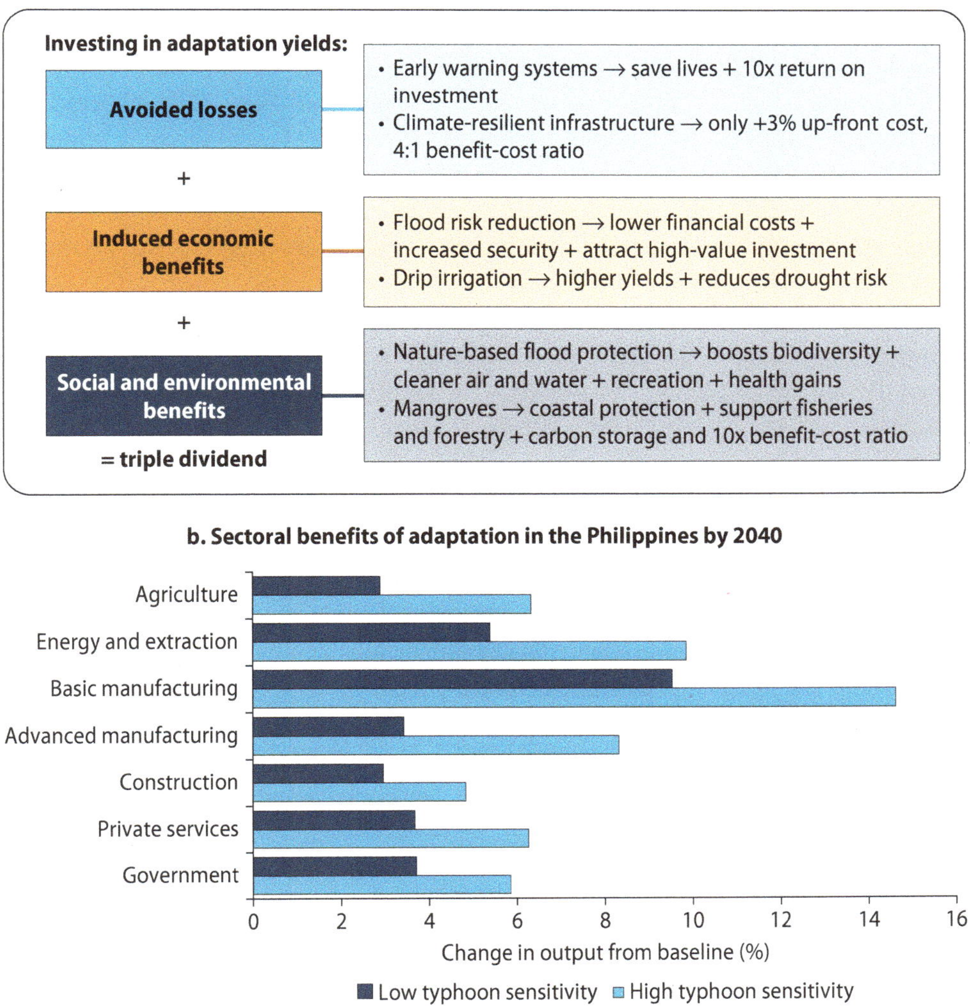

Sources: Panel a: World Bank 2023c, figure O21. Panel b: Original figure for this publication based on World Bank 2022c.

At the sector and macro levels, adaptation investments have clear benefits. For example, in Samoa, investing an additional 2 percent of GDP in adaptation for the next five years would save about 4.5 percent of 2021 GDP in output losses. In the Philippines, all sectors would benefit from climate adaptation measures: investments of less than 1 percent of GDP would avoid losses of 3–5 percent of GDP in many sectors by 2040 (refer to figure O.20, panel b).

Reforming pension systems

Pension systems play an increasingly important role as populations age, providing income support to the elderly while affecting labor markets, national savings, and fiscal outcomes. As demographic pressures rise and coverage gaps widen, pension spending is expected to increase, particularly in systems with large unfunded liabilities (World Bank 2025). In this context, raising the retirement age boosts labor supply and can contain pension costs. Complementary reforms to align benefits and contributions and improve system design can further support sustainability. Many EAP economies, such as China, need to shift from partially funded defined benefits schemes, especially for civil servants, to fully funded defined contributions schemes. The shift can entail a transitional deficit—that is, old pension liabilities are paid off at the same time as contributions are being accumulated in individual accounts—but can eventually lead to an increase in national savings and the more productive use of fiscal resources, with positive implications for economic growth.

Although policy makers need to remain alert to the risk that public investment will crowd out private investment in these areas, there are strong reasons why public investment can crowd in private investment. Investments in basic human capital create the conditions for further investments in higher education. Such investments also reduce inequality by equipping a larger share of the population with skills that act as springboards for upward mobility. Infrastructure investment raises productivity and can strengthen resilience to shocks, both of which spur private investment. Climate adaptation similarly protects existing assets and livelihoods, leading to more stable economic activity over time, and encourages investment by reducing risk. Social protection systems provide income support to vulnerable groups, preserving and encouraging investment in productive assets. Well-designed reforms—such as increasing the retirement age—can help contain fiscal pressures and liberate resources for productive investment. These complementarities underscore that effective spending does not necessarily involve choosing between growth, equity, and resilience, but could often advance all three simultaneously.

Reallocating spending away from subsidies

Complementary reforms can strengthen the effectiveness of public spending by improving both its composition and its efficiency. Reallocating spending away from broad-based subsidies—which tend to be regressive and poorly targeted—can free up resources for higher-impact investments. Well-targeted transfers more effectively reduce poverty and inequality than untargeted subsidies do (refer to figure O.21). At the same time, consolidating fragmented social programs and improving targeting through integrated beneficiary registries and digital delivery mechanisms can reduce leakages and ensure that support reaches those who need it most. The combination of targeted subsidies and uniform indirect taxes (discussed in the later sections under domestic resource mobilization) can efficiently achieve equity goals while ensuring fiscal sustainability.

Targeted transfers have proven more cost-effective than untargeted subsidies at reducing poverty and inequality.

FIGURE O.21 Transfers and subsidy cost-effectiveness, selected EAP economies

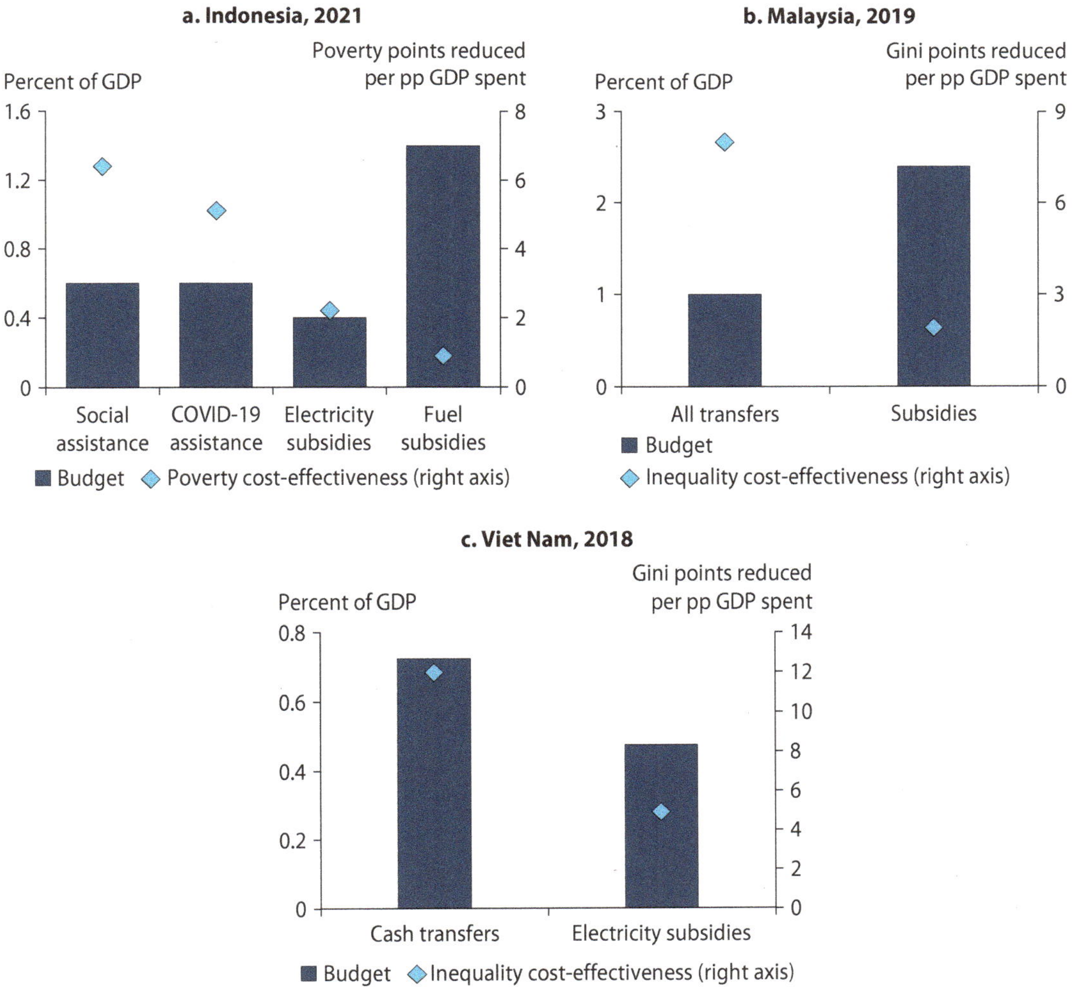

Sources: Original figure for this publication based on World Bank 2022b, 2022c, 2023c, 2023d.
Note: Instrument varies by country depending on the specific study subject. EAP = East Asia and Pacific; pp = percentage point.

Returns to increased public spending and sectoral reforms: The examples of health and education

Some economies achieve strong outcomes relative to their level of public spending, whereas others spend more but achieve comparatively weak results. Policy choices and the regulatory environment largely explain the difference, confirming the importance of sectoral reforms in enhancing the returns to public investment.

The high-efficiency cases are instructive. Viet Nam ranks consistently among the high performers as measured by Programme for International Student Assessment (PISA) scores, reflecting not higher spending but a strong emphasis on teacher quality, accountability, and parental involvement (Afkar et al. 2023). Teacher quality in turn comes from improved teacher selection, training, and incentives. Korea built world-class human capital by sequentially concentrating education budgets at the primary level before moving resources upward—spending more at each level only when the previous level was functioning (World Bank 2018b). Thailand's Universal Health Coverage expansion between 1998 and 2008 paired budget increases with provider payment reform and centralized pharmaceutical procurement, generating both coverage expansion and efficiency gains (Tangcharoensathien et al. 2011). As populations age and urbanize, China and Thailand are showing the way in addressing the epidemic of chronic diseases including diabetes, hypertension, and heart disease—all of which affect workers in their prime, erode productivity, and escalate health care costs—by focusing on prevention, screening, early diagnosis, and care management (Debebe et al. 2026).

The cautionary cases are equally telling. Despite large per-student spending increases, Thailand's Programme for International Student Assessment scores have stagnated (Afkar et al. 2023; World Bank 2023f). This stagnation results from allocative inefficiency, with too much spending on an oversized network of small primary schools and too little at preprimary and secondary levels, which offer higher returns. Timor-Leste spends per student at broadly comparable rates to Indonesia, the Philippines, and Viet Nam, yet literacy rates and child survival indicators lag significantly, pointing to structural inefficiencies in teacher deployment and budget allocation rather than insufficient resources (World Bank 2023g).

Improving the efficiency and effectiveness of domestic revenue mobilization

Funding human capital and resilient infrastructure demands effective tax systems—ones that draw on uniform indirect taxes and levies on property, health-related goods, and carbon emissions without unduly distorting investment and employment decisions.

Rationalizing value added tax exemptions and zero-rated items

Tax reforms in EAP should prioritize broadening the tax base by rationalizing exemptions and reducing preferential treatments. Countries in the region could, on average, raise an additional 2 percent of GDP through more effective collection of goods and services taxes (including excises). The largest opportunities are concentrated in Malaysia, the Philippines, and Viet Nam, where goods and services tax revenues currently fall substantially below potential levels (refer to figure O.22).

Value added tax (VAT) is often viewed as regressive, but recent evidence suggests that it can be more progressive than commonly assumed in economies with high informality (refer to figure O.23). In Indonesia and the Philippines, informal consumption—largely outside the VAT net—accounts for a much larger share of total consumption among lower-income households than among higher-income

GST revenue in most East Asian economies falls short of estimated capacity, pointing to significant untapped revenue potential of about 2 percent of GDP.

FIGURE O.22 GST revenue and capacity, selected East Asian economies, 2000–20

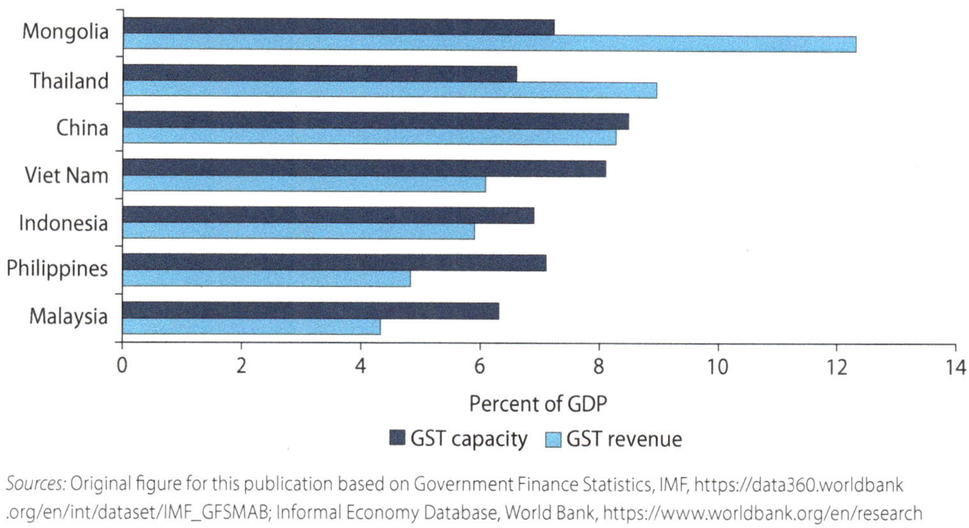

Sources: Original figure for this publication based on Government Finance Statistics, IMF, https://data360.worldbank.org/en/int/dataset/IMF_GFSMAB; Informal Economy Database, World Bank, https://www.worldbank.org/en/research/brief/informal-economy-database; International Country Risk Guide data set, PRS Group, https://www.prsgroup.com/explore-our-products/icrg/; World Development Indicators, World Bank, https://datatopics.worldbank.org/world-development-indicators/; World Economic Outlook (WEO) Database, IMF, https://www.imf.org/en/publications/sprolls/world-economic-outlook-databases; World Revenue Longitudinal Database, IMF, https://www.imf.org/en/topics/fiscal-policies/world-revenue-longitudinal-database.

Note: GST revenue refers to collected GST revenue; GST capacity refers to predicted GST revenue that could be collected. GST capacity is obtained from the ordinary least squares estimation of the following equation: $GST/GDP_{it} = \alpha + \beta_1 \, GDPPC_{it} + \beta_2 \, AGR_{it} + \beta_3 \, Corruption_{it} + \beta_4 \, Population_{it} + \beta_5 \, Trade_{it} + \beta_6 \, Informal\ output_{it} + \beta_7 \, Consumption_{it}$ + regional dummies + time dummies + ε. *GDPPC* refers to GDP per capita, *AGR* to share of agriculture in GDP, *Corruption* to an index of corruption, *Population* to total population, *Trade* to exports plus imports as a share of GDP, *Informal output* to share of informal output in the economy, *Consumption* to consumption as share of GDP, ε to statistical error, and *i* and *t* to country *i* and time *t*, respectively. Refer to chapter 1 for further details. GST = goods and services tax; IMF = International Monetary Fund.

VAT is not as regressive as expected: informal consumption of standard-rated items makes VAT mildly progressive, and informal consumption of exempt items limits their utility while sacrificing considerable revenue.

FIGURE O.23 Consumption patterns, by income decile, Indonesia and the Philippines

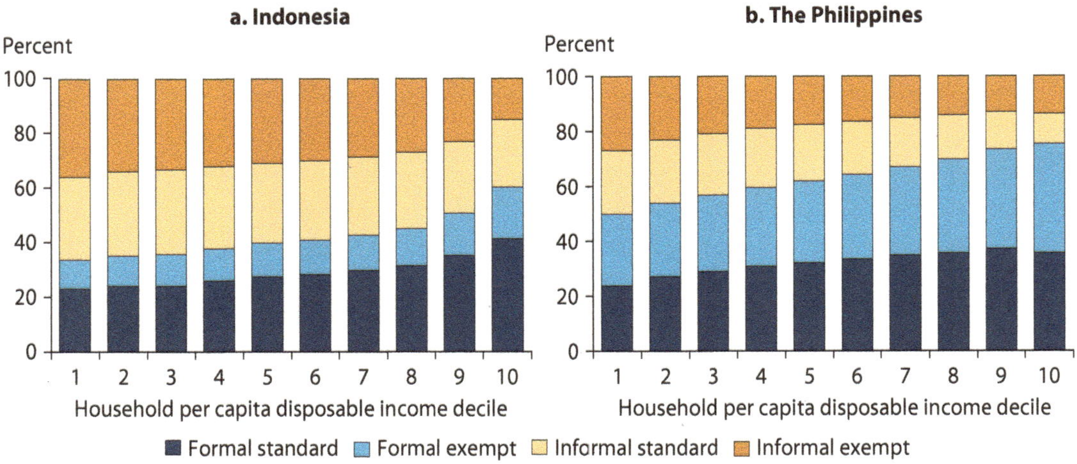

Sources: Original figure for this publication based on National Socioeconomic Household Survey, Rand, https://www.rand.org/health/surveys/bps/susenas.html (Indonesia); Family Income and Expenditure Survey, Philippine Statistics Authority, https://psa.gov.ph/statistics/income-expenditure/fies (Philippines).

Note: Informal purchases can be from a vendor below the threshold for VAT registration who does not need to charge and remit final VAT or from a vendor above the threshold who is noncompliant. Informality estimates for Indonesia and the Philippines are imputed using countries with similar VAT efficiency gaps in Bachas et al. (2024). VAT = value added tax.

groups. The high informal consumption of standard-rated items among poorer households implies that broadening the VAT base can raise revenue while maintaining progressivity (Bachas et al. 2024). As coverage expands and more consumers are brought into the tax net, this implicit progressivity may diminish. Nonetheless, deliberate VAT exemptions offer an ineffective and inefficient way of mitigating indirect tax impacts on the poor. The high informal consumption of exempt items means the poor do not benefit from the exemption; at the same time, considerable revenues from richer households are forgone (Wai-Poi et al. 2025). Over time, a sustainable and equitable revenue system can combine indirect taxes with stronger direct taxation, including personal income and property taxes.

As an alternative to VAT exemptions, economies could maintain a broad tax base while compensating vulnerable households through targeted transfers, as noted earlier, or rebates. In practice, such instruments can achieve similar or better distributional outcomes than exemptions, which tend to be poorly targeted and distort the tax base (Wai-Poi et al. 2025). Countries such as Brazil have introduced personalized VAT rates with point-of-sale or periodic rebates; however, simple

Singapore labels its transfer a "VAT voucher" and communicates the net VAT burden across the income distribution.

FIGURE O.24 Effective VAT rate, by income decile, after accounting for the enhanced VAT voucher, Singapore

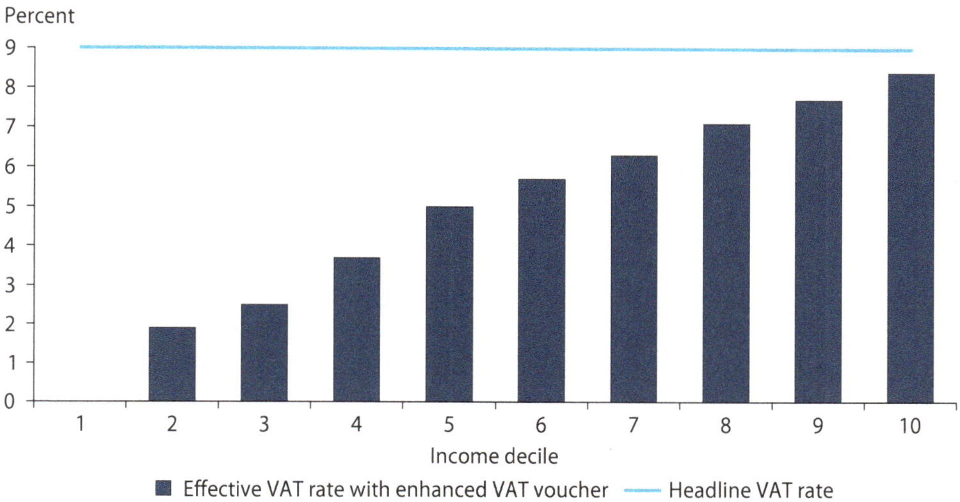

Source: Government of Singapore, GST Voucher: Overview, https://www.govbenefits.gov.sg/about-us/gst-voucher/overview/.
Note: VAT = value added tax.

mechanisms—such as VAT rebate vouchers calibrated to household income—can replicate the intended benefits of exemptions without requiring complex tracking of individual consumption (Bachas et al. 2024; Cebreiro-Gómez et al. 2022). This approach preserves revenue efficiency while strengthening equity, and has been implemented in practice, for example through Singapore's VAT voucher system (refer to figure O.24).[3]

Strengthening the personal income tax base

Personal income tax (PIT) can be a key instrument for both raising revenue and achieving equity objectives. PIT is a progressive tax with most of the revenues coming from the richest or second-richest income decile (Wai-Poi et al. 2025). Only in OECD countries, however, do progressive direct taxes like PIT and corporate income taxes provide the bulk of tax revenues (OECD 2024). In low- and middle-income countries, high informal employment and low incomes may limit the scope of these taxes in the near term (IMF 2023a). At the same time, exemptions and evasions result in low effective tax rates for the richest households, reflecting weaknesses in both administrative capacity and the political will to tax the rich (Chancel et al. 2022; Junquera-Varela et al. 2017). Strengthening the PIT base through various policy changes can increase short-term revenues. Reducing or removing exemptions and deductions could increase the taxable income of rich households, and all sources of household income can be made subject to PIT, including capital income and capital gains. At the same time, aligning top marginal PIT rates with corporate income tax rates could prevent avoidance. Increasing PIT revenues significantly will take time: improving compliance and collection will require investments in tax administration capacity; an increased use of technology and data can make it easier to identify payers and verify their liability (IMF 2011; OECD 2010). In the longer term, greater formal employment and higher incomes could help bring more households into the PIT base.

Increasing property tax revenues

The property tax is one of the most underused revenue instruments in EAP, despite being the most efficient and progressive form of property taxation. Property is visible, immobile, and largely owned by higher-income households. Those attributes make property taxes simultaneously more efficient, less distortionary to labor and investment decisions, and more progressive than most other instruments available to EAP governments.

Across the region, however, recurrent taxes on immovable property generate well below 0.5 percent of GDP in most countries, compared to an OECD average of about 1.9 percent of GDP (OECD 2024). Indonesia collects just 0.1 percent of GDP, Thailand 0.2 percent, Viet Nam a mere 0.05 percent, and Malaysia effectively nothing from recurrent property taxes (OECD and ADB 2022). In the Philippines, property taxes contribute about 9 percent of local tax revenues; however, even there, collection rates represent only about 50 percent of assessed liabilities, and the tax base relies on outdated valuations, leading to property tax collections accounting for only 0.47 percent of GDP in 2020 (World Bank 2024a).

The reasons for underperformance, apart from political resistance of the rich and powerful, are consistent across countries. Land registers are incomplete; assessed values are not linked to market prices and go years or decades without revaluation. Administrative capacity—particularly at the local government level where property taxes are typically assigned—is limited. The fiscal opportunity is significant. Closing even a fraction of the gap with structural peers would meaningfully expand fiscal space, particularly for subnational governments responsible for service delivery.

Pricing negative externalities through carbon and health taxes

Carbon pricing—through carbon taxes or emissions trading systems—can mobilize substantial and stable revenues while addressing environmental externalities. Establishing a predictable and gradually increasing carbon price trajectory, however, is critical to guide private investment and avoid policy uncertainty. In EAP, economies such as Singapore have implemented a carbon tax with a preannounced path of increases, enhancing credibility and enabling firms to adjust investment decisions over time (World Bank 2024c). China has developed the world's largest emissions trading system, demonstrating the feasibility of scaling up carbon pricing instruments in large emerging economies. Evidence shows that well-designed carbon pricing can generate significant fiscal revenues while supporting decarbonization objectives.

Health taxes—particularly on tobacco, alcohol, and sugar-sweetened beverages—can raise revenue while addressing negative health externalities. These taxes are relatively easy to administer, have low efficiency costs, and are good for health (Chaloupka et al. 2012; World Health Organization 2015). Several EAP economies provide examples: the Philippines significantly increased excise taxes on tobacco and alcohol, generating revenues exceeding 1 percent of GDP while helping finance universal health coverage, and Thailand has long used earmarked excise taxes to fund health promotion initiatives (World Bank 2018a, 2023f). Together, carbon and health taxes illustrate how fiscal policy can expand revenue mobilization while remedying negative externalities, particularly when supported by transparent communication, predictable policy frameworks, and effective administration.

Linking tax and spending reforms to increase efficiency, credibility, and political feasibility

Efforts to increase public spending and revenues must be paired with institutional and sectoral reforms and technology adoption. Institutional and sectoral reforms can crowd in private investment, raise efficiency, and improve service delivery. Linking new or higher taxes to clear spending priorities and anchoring reforms in a medium-term fiscal framework would strengthen both political support and credibility.

Improving spending efficiency and fiscal capacity through reforms and technology adoption

Government spending and taxation are in principle jointly determined. The economically optimal fiscal scale is reached when the marginal benefit of the last dollar spent equals the marginal cost of raising it through taxation (Barro 1990). The optimal scale of government is not fixed over time; rather, it can expand as the effectiveness of public spending improves and the cost of revenue mobilization falls. Institutional reform and technological improvements shape both benefits and costs.

Strengthening public investment management can substantially raise the effectiveness of spending. Transparent procurement systems, standardized project appraisal, and independent evaluation help reduce leakages and improve project selection. In developing EAP, leakages in public investment have been estimated at 50–60 percent of funds invested in some economies, implying that institutional failure cuts the effective return to a dollar of spending roughly in half before it reaches its intended purpose (Riera-Crichton et al. 2014; World Bank 2018a).

Taxation reforms such as simplified payment procedures and risk-based audits can lower compliance costs and strengthen enforcement. Bribery demands, arbitrary audits, and opaque enforcement increase compliance costs and discourage participation in the formal economy (Junquera-Varela et al. 2017). Firms in Lao PDR and Viet Nam spend 540 and 362 hours per year, respectively, meeting tax obligations, compared to 67 hours in Singapore (World Bank 2017a; World Bank Group and PwC 2017). This situation highlights substantial scope to improve tax administration and reduce compliance costs in the region.

Institutional reforms following the Asian financial crisis strengthened fiscal institutions across much of EAP, but the reform momentum has slowed. In the decade after the crisis, Country Policy and Institutional Assessment scores on budget management and revenue mobilization improved for most EAP economies eligible for assistance from the International Development Association.[4] These gains reflected a wave of first-generation reforms: fiscal responsibility laws (Indonesia, 2003), medium-term expenditure frameworks (Viet Nam, 2016; Philippines, 2022), and broad expansion of Public Expenditure and Financial Accountability–assessed Public Financial Management systems (IMF 2016, 2023b; PEFA Secretariat 2022; World Bank 2008). However, progress has broadly plateaued since the mid-2010s. Country Policy and Institutional Assessment scores have remained flat or drifted marginally lower across most countries, and Public Expenditure and Financial Accountability assessments reveal persistent weaknesses in external audit effectiveness, legislative scrutiny, and multiyear fiscal planning.[5]

Technological change also affects the marginal cost of taxation and marginal benefit of spending. Electronic invoicing, digital tax filing, and third-party data reporting can expand the tax base while lowering enforcement costs. In Ethiopia, electronic cash registers increased VAT revenues by nearly half, and computerized VAT risk analysis in Pakistan reduced fraudulent refund claims by half (Mascagni et al. 2021; Okunogbe and Tourek 2024). On the spending side, digital project monitoring tools can improve transparency and reduce cost overruns in public infrastructure projects, as observed in Honduras and Thailand (CoST 2023; Straub et al. 2026).

Earmarking revenue to spending priorities and anchoring reforms in a credible fiscal framework

Even well-designed reforms can fail without credibility and public support. Tax increases are particularly difficult to implement because they have immediate and certain costs but diffuse and delayed benefits. When citizens do not trust the government to translate revenue into better services, they resist contributing—and that resistance is individually rational (Besley and Persson 2013). The collective outcome, however, is a low-level equilibrium trap: low revenues constrain service delivery, poor services erode trust and compliance, and depressed compliance further limits fiscal capacity. Breaking out requires mechanisms that make the tax-spending link observable and credible.

Three instruments are particularly effective. First, earmarking revenue to visible spending priorities—a VAT surcharge for health insurance or a fuel levy for road maintenance—converts abstract fiscal promises into verifiable commitments that citizens can monitor. Second, front-loading improvements in spending efficiency—demonstrating better service delivery before asking for more revenue—builds the compliance culture on which deeper fiscal capacity rests. Third, anchoring reforms in a medium-term fiscal framework moves policy beyond annual budgeting cycles, establishes multiyear revenue and expenditure targets, and allows the tax-spending link to become observable over time (Junquera-Varela et al. 2017).

Proactive communication is equally central. Incomplete information shapes public perceptions, and publishing distributional impact assessments—showing, for example, that energy subsidies disproportionately benefit higher-income households—can correct misperceptions and improve reform acceptability (Wai-Poi et al. 2025). In EAP, where public attitudes emphasize individual responsibility and economic opportunity, framing reforms around investment, job creation, and broad participation tends to be more effective than framing them as redistribution (Feng et al. 2022).

Notes

1. East Asian economies refer to Cambodia, China, Indonesia, Lao People's Democratic Republic, Malaysia, Mongolia, Myanmar, the Philippines, Thailand, Timor-Leste, and Viet Nam.
2. The World Bank EAP Pacific Island subregion includes Fiji, Kiribati, the Marshall Islands, the Federated States of Micronesia, Naoero, Palau, Papua New Guinea, Samoa, the Solomon Islands, Tonga, Tuvalu, and Vanuatu.
3. Government of Singapore Ministry of Finance, "GST Voucher: Overview," https://www.govbenefits.gov.sg/about-us/gst-voucher/overview/.
4. World Bank DataBank, "CPIA Efficiency of Revenue Mobilization Rating," https://data.worldbank.org/indicator/IQ.CPA.REVN.XQ; "CPIA Quality of Budgetary and Financial Management Rating," https://data.worldbank.org/indicator/IQ.CPA.FINQ.XQ.
5. Based on Public Expenditure and Financial Accountability, "Assessments," https://www.pefa.org/assessments, for the following assessment rounds: Cambodia, 2010, 2015, 2021; Indonesia, 2008, 2012, 2017; Myanmar, 2013, 2020; the Philippines, 2010, 2016; Thailand, 2009; and Viet Nam, 2011, 2024.

References

Acosta-Ormaechea, Santiago, and Atsuyoshi Morozumi. 2013. "Can a Government Enhance Long-Run Growth by Changing the Composition of Public Expenditure?" IMF Working Paper No. 13/162, International Monetary Fund. https://www.imf.org/external/pubs/ft/wp/2013/wp13162.pdf.

Afkar, Rythia, Tara Béteille, Mary E. Breeding, et al. 2023. *Fixing the Foundation: Teachers and Basic Education in East Asia and Pacific.* World Bank East Asia and Pacific Regional Report. World Bank. http://hdl.handle.net/10986/40332.

APO (Asian Productivity Organization). 2025. *APO Productivity Databook 2025.* APO. https://doi.org/10.61145/GENB1427.

Bachas, Pierre, Lucie Gadenne, and Anders Jensen. 2024. "Informality, Consumption Taxes, and Redistribution." *Review of Economic Studies* 91 (5): 2604–34. https://doi.org/10.1093/restud/rdad095.

Bai, Chong-En, Chang-Tai Hsieh, and Zheng Song. 2016. "The Long Shadow of China's Fiscal Expansion." *Brookings Papers on Economic Activity* Fall 2016: 129–81.

Bales, Sarah, Huong Lan Dao, Duyen Thi Thuy Nguyen, and Tran Tien Hung. 2022. "Potentially Preventable Hospitalizations in Vietnam: Analysis Using Health Insurance Claims Data (English)." Health, Nutrition, and Population (HNP) Discussion Paper, World Bank. http://documents.worldbank.org/curated/en/099447403132330753.

Barro, Robert J. 1990. "Government Spending in a Simple Model of Endogenous Growth." *Journal of Political Economy* 98 (5, Part 2): S103–25. https://doi.org/10.1086/261726.

Besley, Timothy, and Torsten Persson. 2013. *Pillars of Prosperity: The Political Economics of Development Clusters.* Princeton University Press.

Cebreiro-Gómez, Ana, Colin Clavey, Marcello Estevao, Jonathan Leigh-Pemberton, and Benjamin Stewart. 2022. "Digital Services Tax: Country Practice and Technical Challenges." Equitable Growth, Finance and Institutions Insight. World Bank. http://hdl.handle.net/10986/36840.

Chaloupka, Frank J., Alison Yurekli, and Geoffrey T. Fong. 2012. "Tobacco Taxes as a Tobacco Control Strategy." *Tobacco Control* 21 (2): 172–80. https://doi.org/10.1136/tobaccocontrol-2011-050417.

Chancel, Lucas, Thomas Piketty, Emmanuel Saez, and Gabriel Zucman. 2022. *World Inequality Report 2022.* World Inequality Lab. https://wir2022.wid.world/.

Chaudhuri, Shubham. 2003. "Assessing Vulnerability to Poverty: Concepts, Empirical Methods and Illustrative Examples." Department of Economics, Columbia University, New York.

CoST Infrastructure Transparency Initiative. 2023. *Thailand Programme Report 2023.* CoST Thailand. https://infrastructuretransparency.org/programme/cost-thailand.

Datt, Gaurav, and Martin Ravallion. 1992. "Growth and Redistribution Components of Changes in Poverty Measures: A Decomposition with Applications to Brazil and India in the 1980s." *Journal of Development Economics* 38 (2): 275–95. https://doi.org/10.1016/0304-3878(92)90001-P.

Debebe, Zelalem, Damien de Walque, Young Eun Kim, et al. 2026. *A Healthy Future: Primary Health Care and the Chronic Disease Epidemic in East Asia and Pacific.* East Asia and Pacific Development Studies. World Bank. https://doi.org/10.1596/978-1-4648-2284-1.

de Nicola, Francesca, Aaditya Mattoo, and Jonathan Timmis. 2025. *Firm Foundations of Growth: Productivity and Technology in East Asia and Pacific.* World Bank. https://doi.org/10.1596/978-1-4648-2200-1.

Eckstein, David, Vera Künzel, and Laura Schäfer. 2021. *Global Climate Risk Index 2021: Who Suffers Most from Extreme Weather Events? Weather-Related Loss Events in 2019 and 2000–2019.* Germanwatch e.V. https://www.germanwatch.org/en/19777.

Enache, Cristina. 2025. "Corporate Tax Rates Around the World, 2025." Tax Foundation, April 17. https://taxfoundation.org/data/all/global/corporate-tax-rates-by-country-2025/.

Feenstra, R. C., R. Inklaar, and M. P. Timmer. 2015. "The Next Generation of the Penn World Table." *American Economic Review* 105 (10): 3150–82. www.ggdc.net/pwt.

Feng, Shuaizhang, Jianguo Liu, and Yicheng Wang. 2022. "Public Support for Redistribution in East Asia." *Journal of East Asian Studies* 22 (1): 1–28.

Fuentes, Rodrigo, and Raimundo Soto. 2022. "A Counterfactual Appraisal of Fiscal Policy Under the Fiscal Rule." *SSRN Electronic Journal.* https://doi.org/10.2139/ssrn.4294845.

Huidrom, Raju, M. Ayhan Kose, Jamus J. Lim, and Franziska L. Ohnsorge. 2020. "Why Do Fiscal Multipliers Depend on Fiscal Positions?" *Journal of Monetary Economics* 114: 109–25. https://doi.org/10.1016/j.jmoneco.2019.03.004.

Ilzetzki, Ethan, Enrique G. Mendoza, and Carlos A. Végh. 2013. "How Big (Small?) Are Fiscal Multipliers?" *Journal of Monetary Economics* 60 (2): 239–54. https://doi.org/10.1016/j.jmoneco.2012.10.011.

IMF (International Monetary Fund). 2011. *Revenue Mobilization in Developing Countries.* International Monetary Fund.

IMF (International Monetary Fund). 2016. *Vietnam: 2016 Article IV Consultation.* IMF Country Report No. 16/240. International Monetary Fund. https://www.elibrary.imf.org/view/journals/002/2016/240/002.2016.issue-240-en.xml.

IMF (International Monetary Fund). 2023a. *Fiscal Monitor: On the Path to Policy Normalization.* International Monetary Fund, April. https://doi.org/10.5089/9798400234026.089.

IMF (International Monetary Fund). 2023b. "The Medium-Term Fiscal Framework for the Philippines." *Philippines: Selected Issues* 2023 (415). IMF Asia and Pacific Department. https://www.elibrary.imf.org/view/journals/002/2023/415/article-A002-en.xml.

Junquera-Varela, Raúl Félix, Marijn Verhoeven, et al. 2017. *Strengthening Domestic Resource Mobilization: Moving from Theory to Practice in Low- and Middle-Income Countries.* World Bank. https://doi.org/10.1596/978-1-4648-1073-2.

Krah, Kwabena, Veronica Sonia Montalva Talledo, and Sailesh Tiwari. 2026. "Striving for Economic Security: Emerging Middle Class in the East Asia and Pacific Region." Policy Research Working Paper 11301, World Bank. https://doi.org/10.60572/sy4m-nz07.

Kruk, Margaret E., Annie Danaei Gage, Nadia T. Joseph, Goodarz Danaei, Sebastián García-Saisó, and Joshua A. Salomon. 2018. "Mortality Due to Low-Quality Health

Systems in the Universal Health Coverage Era: A Systematic Analysis of Amenable Deaths in 137 Countries." *The Lancet* 392 (10160): 2203–12. https://doi.org/10.1016/S0140-6736(18)31668-4.

Mascagni, Giulia, Roel Dom, Fabrizio Santoro, and Denis Mukama. 2021. "The VAT in Practice: Equity, Enforcement and Complexity." *International Tax and Public Finance* 30: 525–63.

OECD (Organisation for Economic Co-operation and Development). 2010. *Tax Policy Reform and Economic Growth*. Tax Policy Studies No. 20. OECD Publishing. https://doi.org/10.1787/9789264091085-en.

OECD (Organisation for Economic Co-operation and Development). 2023. *PISA 2022 Results (Volume I): The State of Learning and Equity in Education*. OECD Publishing. https://doi.org/10.1787/53f23881-en.

OECD (Organisation for Economic Co-operation and Development). 2024. *Revenue Statistics 2024: Health Taxes in OECD Countries 1965–2023*. OECD Publishing. https://doi.org/10.1787/c87a3da5-en.

OECD (Organisation for Economic Co-operation and Development) and ADB (Asian Development Bank). 2022. *Revenue Statistics in Asia and the Pacific 2022: Strengthening Tax Revenues in Developing Asia 1990–2020*. OECD Publishing. https://www.oecd.org/content/dam/oecd/en/publications/reports/2022/07/revenue-statistics-in-asia-and-the-pacific-2022_c46a5310/db29f89a-en.pdf.

Okunogbe, Oyebola, and Gabriel Tourek. 2024. "How Can Lower-Income Countries Collect More Taxes? The Role of Technology, Tax Agents, and Politics." *Journal of Economic Perspectives* 38 (1): 81–106. https://doi.org/10.1257/jep.38.1.81.

PEFA (Public Expenditure and Financial Accountability) Secretariat. 2022. *Global Report on Public Financial Management 2022*. PEFA Secretariat. https://www.pefa.org/global-report-2022.

Riera-Crichton, Daniel, Carlos A. Végh, and Guillermo Vuletin. 2014. "Fiscal Multipliers in Recessions and Expansions: Does It Matter Whether Government Spending Is 'Bricks or Mortar'?" Policy Research Working Paper 6993, World Bank. https://doi.org/10.1596/1813-9450-6993.

Straub, Stéphane, He He, Yue Li, et al. 2026. *Infrastructure Foundations: From Current Assets to Future Growth*. Sustainable Infrastructure Series. World Bank. https://openknowledge.worldbank.org/entities/publication/c35564b6-20e5-4606-a9df-d5735f8481d3.

Tangcharoensathien, Viroj, Walaiporn Patcharanarumol, Phusit Prakongsai, Supon Limwattananon, Woranan Witthuta, and Kanjana Panichkriangkrai. 2011. "Health-Financing Reforms in Southeast Asia: Challenges in Achieving Universal Coverage." *The Lancet* 377(9768): 863–73.

UN DESA (United Nations, Department of Economic and Social Affairs, Population Division). 2022. *World Population Prospects 2022: Summary of Results*. UN DESA/POP/2022/TR/No. 3. United Nations.

Wai-Poi, Matthew, Mariano Sosa, and Pierre Bachas. 2025. *Taxes, Spending, and Equity: International Patterns and Lessons for Developing Countries*. Prosperity Insight Series. World Bank. https://doi.org/10.1596/44281.

World Bank. 2008. "Indonesia Public Expenditure Review: Spending for Development." World Bank. http://documents.worldbank.org/curated/en/370501468041427374.

World Bank. 2014. *Corporate Governance of State-Owned Enterprises: A Toolkit.* World Bank. http://documents.worldbank.org/curated/en/228331468169750340.

World Bank. 2015. *East Asia and Pacific Economic Update, October 2015: Staying the Course.* World Bank. https://openknowledge.worldbank.org/entities/publication/276374da-aaf2-51d4-9213-5e14c0f676ac.

World Bank. 2017a. *Doing Business 2017: Equal Opportunity for All.* World Bank. https://doi.org/10.1596/978-1-4648-0948-4.

World Bank. 2017b. *Pacific Possible: Long-Term Economic Opportunities and Challenges for Pacific Island Countries.* World Bank. https://doi.org/10.1596/28135.

World Bank. 2018a. *East Asia and Pacific Economic Update, April 2018: Enhancing Potential.* World Bank. https://doi.org/10.1596/978-1-4648-1283-5.

World Bank. 2018b. *Growing Smarter: Learning and Equitable Development in East Asia and Pacific.* World Bank. https://doi.org/10.1596/978-1-4648-1261-3.

World Bank. 2020. "Indonesia Public Expenditure Review 2020: Spending for Better Results." World Bank. https://www.worldbank.org/in/country/indonesia/publication/indonesia-public-expenditure-review1.

World Bank. 2021a. *East Asia and Pacific Economic Update, April 2021: Uneven Recovery.* World Bank. https://doi.org/10.1596/978-1-4648-1702-1.

World Bank. 2021b. *Indonesia Economic Prospects, December 2021: Boosting the Recovery.* World Bank. https://www.worldbank.org/en/country/indonesia/publication/indonesia-economic-prospects-iep-june-2021-boosting-the-recovery.

World Bank. 2022a. *East Asia and Pacific Economic Update, October 2022: Reforms for Recovery.* World Bank. https://doi.org/10.1596/978-1-4648-1921-6.

World Bank. 2022b. "From the Last Mile to the Next Mile—2022 Vietnam Poverty and Equity Assessment." World Bank. http://hdl.handle.net/10986/37952.

World Bank. 2022c. *Philippines Country Climate and Development Report.* CCDR Series. World Bank. https://doi.org/10.1596/38280.

World Bank. 2023a. *The Business of the State.* World Bank. https://doi.org/10.1596/978-1-4648-1998-8.

World Bank. 2023b. *Digital Progress and Trends Report 2023.* World Bank. https://doi.org/10.1596/978-1-4648-2049-6.

World Bank. 2023c. *East Asia and Pacific Economic Update, April 2023: Reviving Growth.* World Bank. http://hdl.handle.net/10986/39598.

World Bank. 2023d. "Raising the Tide, Lifting All Boats." Malaysia Economic Monitor (October), World Bank. http://documents.worldbank.org/curated/en/099100623063032359.

World Bank. 2023e. "Small States: Overlapping Crises, Multiple Challenges." In *Global Economic Prospects, January 2023.* World Bank. https://doi.org/10.1596/978-1-4648-1906-3.

World Bank. 2023f. "Thailand Public Revenue and Spending Assessment: Promoting an Inclusive and Sustainable Future." World Bank. https://www.worldbank.org/en/country/thailand/publication/th-prsa.

World Bank. 2023g. "Timor-Leste Public Expenditure Review." World Bank.

World Bank. 2024a. "Philippines—Land and Property Valuation: Case Study." World Bank.

World Bank. 2024b. *Poverty, Prosperity, and Planet Report 2024: Pathways Out of the Polycrisis*. World Bank. https://doi.org/10.1596/978-1-4648-2123-3.

World Bank. 2024c. *State and Trends of Carbon Pricing 2024*. World Bank. https://hdl.handle.net/10986/41544.

World Bank. 2025. *East Asia and Pacific Economic Update, April 2025: A Longer View*. World Bank. https://doi.org/10.1596/978-1-4648-2232-2.

World Bank Group and PwC. 2017. *Paying Taxes 2017*. PwC and World Bank Group. https://www.pwc.at/de/publikationen/steuern-und-recht/pwc-paying-taxes-2017-at.pdf.

World Health Organization. 2015. *WHO Report on the Global Tobacco Epidemic 2015*. World Health Organization.

Abbreviations

BLT	Bantuan Langsung Tunai (Indonesia)
CEQ	Commitment to Equity
CIT	corporate income tax
EAP	East Asia and Pacific
EMDEs	emerging market and developing economies
GDP	gross domestic product
GST	goods and services tax
HIC	high-income country
LIC	low-income country
LMIC	lower-middle-income country
MIC	middle-income country
MTFF	medium-term fiscal framework
NCD	noncommunicable disease
NDC	Nationally Determined Contribution
OECD	Organisation for Economic Co-operation and Development
PFFRA	Public Finance and Fiscal Responsibility Act (Malaysia)
PISA	Programme for International Student Assessment
PIT	personal income tax
PKH	Program Keluarga Harapan (Indonesia)
SOE	state-owned enterprise
UMIC	upper-middle-income country
VAT	value added tax
WEO	World Economic Outlook

From Growth-Enabling to Growth-Enhancing Fiscal Policy 1

Introduction

East Asia and Pacific (EAP) has grown faster than any other region over the past three decades. Between 1999 and 2019, East Asian economies averaged annual gross domestic product (GDP) growth of 5.6 percent—substantially faster than the 4.0 percent recorded across emerging market and developing economies (EMDEs) and more than double the 2.6 percent pace of advanced economies.[1] Hundreds of millions of people were lifted out of extreme poverty.

Fiscal policy played a central role in supporting economic growth. Most governments in East Asia pursued what this report calls a "growth-enabling" approach: keeping taxes low, holding operational spending in check, and directing scarce public resources to physical infrastructure. The logic was straightforward: low tax burdens would attract private capital, infrastructure investment would reduce the cost of doing business, and fiscal restraint would keep macroeconomic conditions stable.

Figure 1.1 illustrates the anatomy of this model. Three features stand out. First, East Asian governments are low tax collectors.[2] Government revenue as a share of GDP averages about 20.4 percent—below the middle-income country average of 25.0 percent and well below the high-income country average of 37.0 percent.

Second, overall spending is low. Primary government expenditure averages 14.1 percent of GDP, roughly two-thirds of the middle-income country average and less than half of the high-income country level. Third, public investment is high. At 6.5 percent of GDP, East Asia's average exceeds levels recorded in low-income countries (4.3 percent), middle-income countries (4.4 percent), and even high-income countries (4.6 percent). The growth-enabling approach represents, in essence, a deliberate trade-off: forgo revenue and consumption spending, prioritize investment, and let the private sector do the rest.

Most East Asian economies have adopted a low-revenue, low-spending model, while still prioritizing significant public investment. In contrast, Pacific Island countries tend to exhibit significantly higher revenue, spending, and public investment ratios.

FIGURE 1.1 Government revenue, spending, and public investment, EAP and comparators

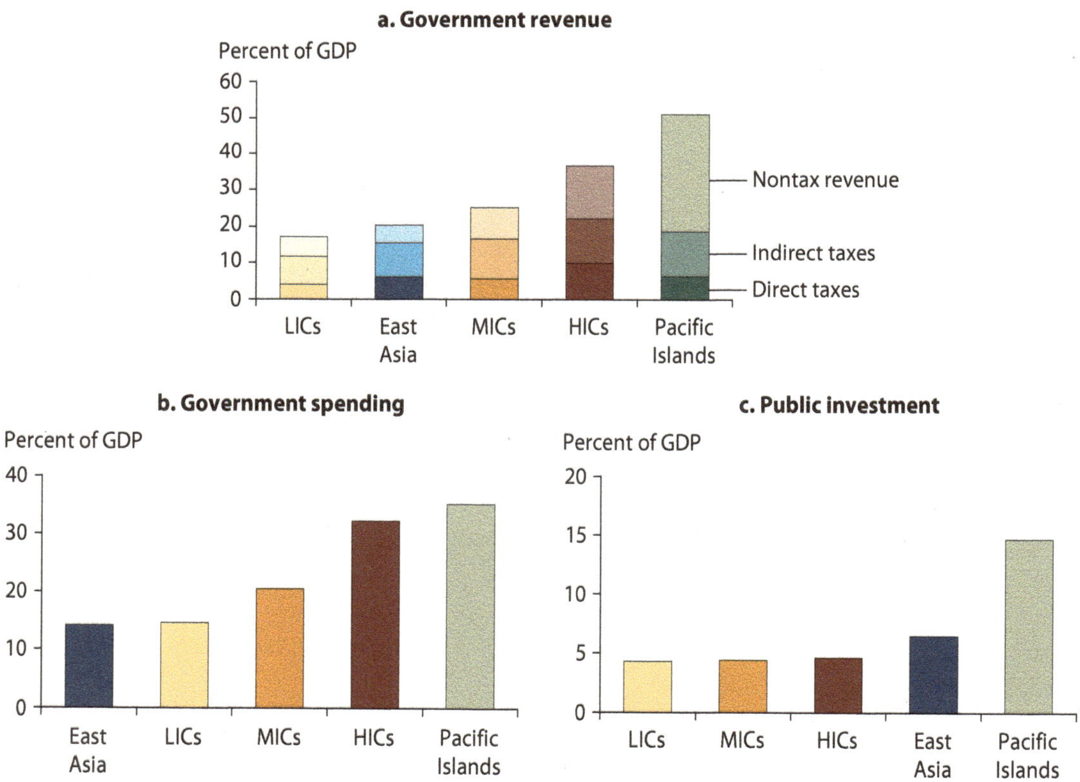

(continued)

FIGURE 1.1 Government revenue, spending, and public investment, EAP and comparators *(continued)*

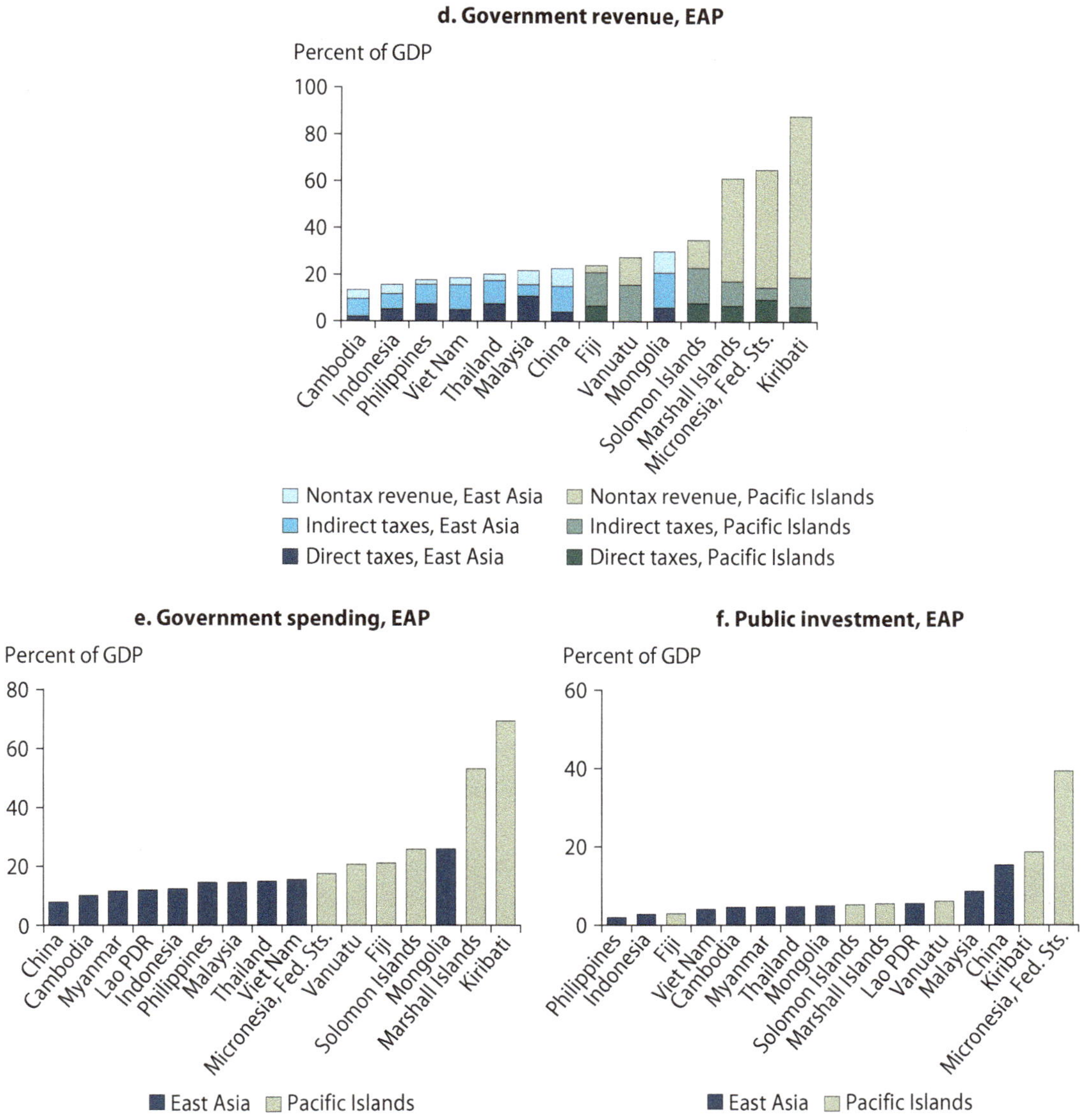

Sources: Original figure for this publication based on Government Finance Statistics, International Monetary Fund (IMF), https://data360.worldbank.org/en/int/dataset/IMF_GFSMAB; Investment and Capital Stock Dataset (ICSD), IMF, https://data.imf.org/Datasets/ICSD; World Economic Outlook (WEO) Database, IMF, https://www.imf.org/en/publications/sprolls/world-economic-outlook-databases; World Revenue Longitudinal Database, IMF, https://www.imf.org/en/topics/fiscal-policies/world-revenue-longitudinal-database.

Note: Revenue and spending show unweighted averages for 2000–22. Public investment shows unweighted averages for 2000–19. In panels a, b, and c, East Asia includes Cambodia, China, Indonesia, Malaysia, Mongolia, the Philippines, Thailand, and Viet Nam. Pacific Islands include Fiji, Kiribati, Marshall Islands, Federated States of Micronesia, Solomon Islands, and Vanuatu. Direct taxes include taxes on corporate and personal income; indirect taxes include taxes on goods and services, and trade; and nontax revenue includes revenue from social contributions and grants, and other revenue from property income, sales of goods and services, fines, penalties and forfeits, non-life insurance, and standardized guarantee schemes as well as current transfers. Government spending refers to total government spending excluding interest payment (WEO) and public investment (ICSD). Total government spending includes expenditure on government consumption, social benefits, grants, subsidies, and other transfers. EAP = East Asia and Pacific; HICs = high-income countries; LICs = low-income countries; MICs = middle-income countries.

The approach describes a broad tendency across the region's large middle-income economies (Indonesia, Malaysia, the Philippines, and Thailand) that have the fiscal and institutional potential to increase revenues. Smaller economies (Cambodia, the Lao People's Democratic Republic, and Myanmar) face more binding institutional and administrative constraints. Resource-dependent economies (Mongolia, Papua New Guinea, and Timor-Leste) have relied heavily on resource revenues without building robust domestic tax systems. Mongolia, for instance, drew over one-third of total revenue from mining in 2023 and supports a large public sector, including wages, pensions, and social assistance (World Bank 2024c, 2024d).

Pacific Island countries present a structurally distinct picture.[3] Their relatively high revenues and spending as a share of GDP reflect geography and exposure rather than policy choices: small and less diversified economies, geographic isolation, recurrent natural shocks, and high fixed costs of service delivery all inflate fiscal aggregates relative to GDP (World Bank 2017a, 2023e). In the Solomon Islands, natural disasters alone can cost between 5 and 7 percent of GDP per event (World Bank 2022a). Despite large budgets as a share of GDP, Pacific Island countries' spending needs exceed their revenues, leaving limited fiscal buffers and significant infrastructure gaps.

Public investment in infrastructure—such as transportation networks, ports, and energy systems—as well as government spending on human capital, can foster sustainable and inclusive growth (Barro 1990; Easterly and Rebelo 1993). Financing higher spending, however, requires greater revenue mobilization, which risks distorting economic incentives and discouraging private investment. In this context, low tax burdens, coupled with substantial public investment, can support private sector development and growth. However, low tax rates and generous tax incentives constrain revenue mobilization, potentially limiting governments' capacity to finance human capital investments, respond effectively to shocks, expand the provision of essential public services, and strengthen social protection systems.

Although no single solution exists for addressing this trade-off, fiscal policy in the region has traditionally combined low tax burdens, low operational spending, and comparatively high levels of public investment. This growth-enabling approach has served the region well, but its limits have become increasingly visible.

Governments that are too small to mobilize revenue are also too constrained to close persistent gaps in health, education, social protection, and climate resilience. Addressing these gaps while preserving macroeconomic stability is the central fiscal challenge facing the region today.

This chapter documents the key features of the growth-enabling approach—on both the revenue and the spending sides—and examines how it has shaped growth outcomes. The final section identifies where the approach is under strain and what the region's diverse economies need to do differently.

Government revenue in EAP

Government revenue in EAP is characterized by relatively low tax rates and the widespread use of tax incentives. Despite comparatively low statutory corporate income tax (CIT) rates, CIT revenues remain robust in many countries, reflecting strong investment and economic activity. In contrast, personal income tax (PIT) collections are generally modest, constrained by large informal sectors, narrow tax bases, and weaknesses in tax administration and enforcement. Revenues from taxes on goods and services are also low by international standards, reflecting both structural factors and policy choices. Together, these features have shaped a revenue model that has supported investment and growth but may face increasing pressure as countries seek to finance rising spending needs.

Low tax rates and generous incentives

East Asian economies have long used generous tax incentives to attract private investment and foster export-led growth. Statutory CIT rates fell from an average of about 40 percent in the 1980s to roughly 20–25 percent by the early 2020s; at the same time, the rest of the world moved in the same direction, contributing to a global race to the bottom (refer to figure 1.2, panel a). Tariffs tell a similar story: most East Asian economies have lower tariffs than the average for middle-income countries. Pacific Island countries maintain higher rates. Cambodia and Myanmar have rates on the higher side as well, exceeding those of middle-income countries (refer to figure 1.2, panel b).

Historically, EAP has had relatively low corporate tax and tariff rates.

FIGURE 1.2 Statutory CIT and effective tariff rates, EAP and comparators

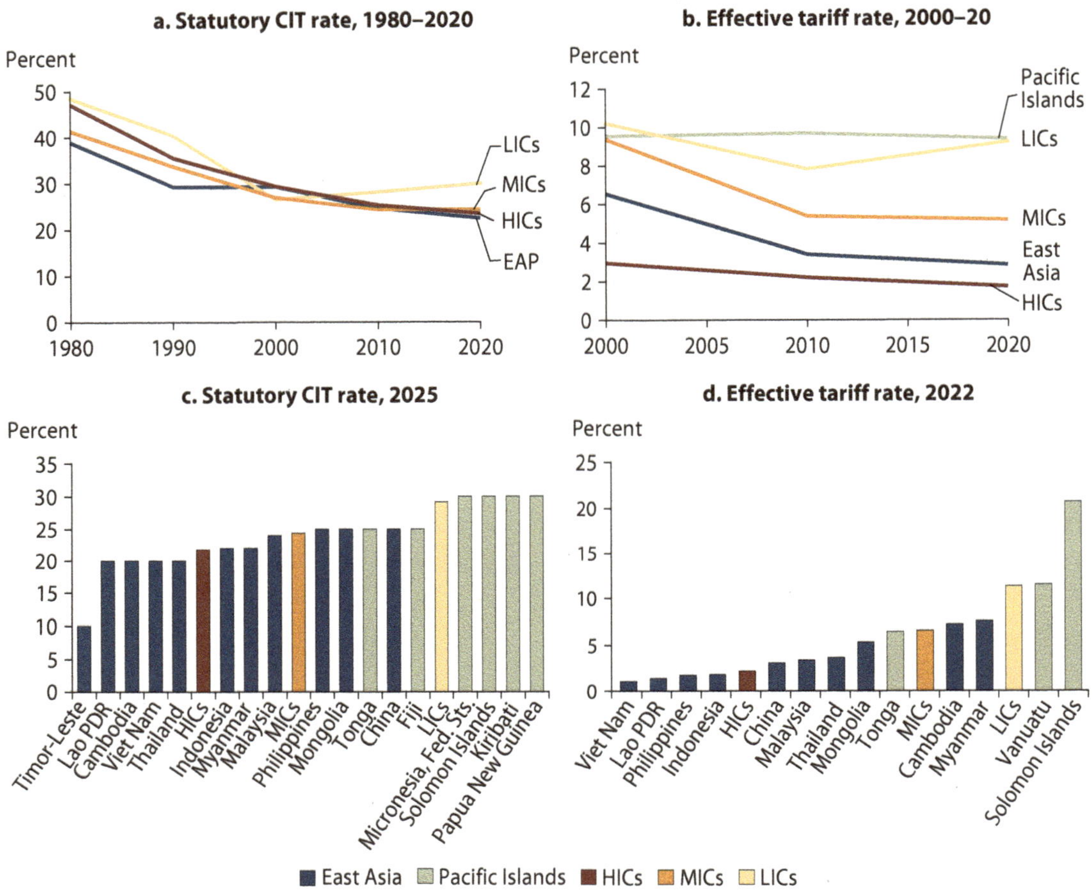

Sources: Original figure for this publication based on Enache 2025; World Development Indicators, World Bank, https://datatopics .worldbank.org/world-development-indicators/.

Note: In panels a and c, CIT rate refers to the standard top statutory corporate income tax rate. In panels b and d, tariff rate refers to the average of effectively applied rates weighted by the product import shares corresponding to each partner country. In panel a, available averages for Cambodia and Viet Nam start at 1990, and for Lao PDR at 2020. In panel b, East Asia includes Cambodia, Indonesia, Lao PDR, Malaysia, Myanmar, the Philippines, Thailand, Timor-Leste, and Viet Nam; Pacific Islands include Fiji, Papua New Guinea, Solomon Islands, Tonga, and Vanuatu. CIT = corporate income tax; EAP = East Asia and Pacific; HICs = high-income countries; LICs = low-income countries; MICs = middle-income countries.

EAP governments have gone beyond low statutory rates, layering on extensive tax incentives to attract investment. Tax holidays, preferential regimes, and special economic zone benefits are prevalent across the region (refer to figure 1.3). In several economies, including Indonesia, Lao PDR, Malaysia, and Thailand, corporate tax holidays can extend beyond 10 years. Pacific Island countries offer similarly generous arrangements: Fiji provides a 13-year tax holiday under its Tax Free Zone scheme, and the Solomon Islands structures individual holiday packages of up to 10 years for qualifying investors (World Bank 2015). In some cases, tax holidays can reach up to 30 years (refer to box 1.1).

These incentives come with a significant revenue cost. Across developing economies, forgone revenue from tax expenditures averages close to 4 percent of GDP and over 24 percent of tax revenues globally (World Bank 2024f). EAP's reliance on profit-based incentives—the least efficient form of tax subsidy—compounds the fiscal loss.[4] Large investors routinely negotiate between countries, driving holiday durations upward and eroding the fiscal base across the region (World Bank 2015). In Lao PDR, the CIT gap—the difference between taxes legally owed and taxes collected—stood at approximately 87 percent in 2020, meaning the government captured less than one-fifth of its potential corporate tax revenue (World Bank 2023c).

EAP economies offer generous corporate tax incentives.

FIGURE 1.3 Maximum corporate income tax holidays, selected EAP economies and comparators, 2022

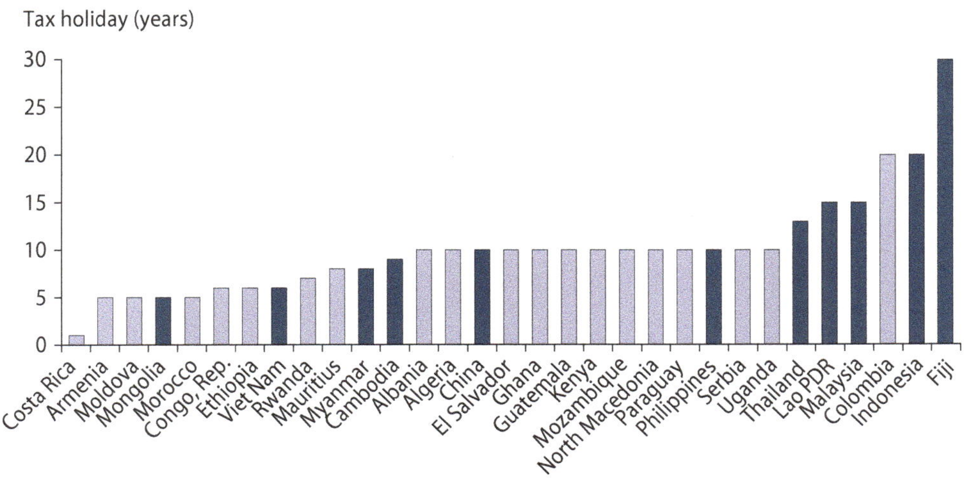

Sources: Original figure for this publication based on Global Tax Expenditures Database, Tax Expenditures Lab, https://gted.taxexpenditures.org; Redonda et al. 2025.
Note: EAP = East Asia and Pacific.

Box 1.1. Long corporate tax holidays: The case of Fiji

Pacific Island countries rely heavily on tax incentives to attract investment in sectors such as tourism, agriculture, and infrastructure. Fiji's investment framework, for example, includes corporate tax holidays that can be unusually long by international standards. Depending on the sector and the size of the investment, these tax holidays can range from about 5 to 20 years but, in some cases, last even longer (refer to table B1.1.1). For example, Fiji's incentive scheme for submarine network cable infrastructure provides a 30-year income tax holiday, one of the longest statutory corporate tax exemptions currently offered in the region (FRCS 2024).

TABLE B1.1.1 Duration and eligibility conditions of selected tax holidays in Fiji

Incentive scheme	Eligibility condition	Minimum investment	Tax holiday
Hotel Investment Incentive	New hotel construction	F$10 million–F$20 million	5 years
Hotel Investment Incentive	Large tourism projects	F$20 million–F$40 million	7–13 years
Hotel Investment Incentive	Major resort developments	Above F$40 million	20 years
Commercial Agriculture and Agro-processing	Approved commercial farming or agro-processing projects	Project approval required	Up to 20 years
ICT Infrastructure Incentive	Development of ICT infrastructure projects	Sector approval required	Up to 20 years
Recycling and Waste Management Incentive	Approved environmental investment projects	Sector approval required	Up to 20 years
Submarine Network Cable Infrastructure	Installation of international submarine cable systems	Strategic Infrastructure	30 years

Source: Original table for this publication based on FRCS 2024.
Note: ICT = information and communication technology.

Long tax holidays are typically justified as a way to offset structural disadvantages faced by Pacific Island countries, characterized by small domestic markets, geographic isolation, high transportation costs, and

(continued)

Box 1.1. Long corporate tax holidays: The case of Fiji *(continued)*

vulnerability to natural disasters. These factors increase the cost of doing business and can reduce expected returns on investment, making fiscal incentives a commonly used policy tool to attract private capital (IMF 2022).

The effectiveness of long tax holidays as investment promotion instruments is uncertain. Investment decisions are driven more strongly by economic fundamentals—political stability, infrastructure quality, market size, and regulatory certainty—than by marginal tax incentives (IMF et al. 2015; World Bank 2020b). Tax holidays exempt future profits rather than reduce up-front costs, meaning they typically benefit projects that would have been viable regardless, generating windfall gains rather than additional investment. Foregone tax revenues from Fiji's investment incentive regime are estimated at approximately F$127 million—roughly 0.9 percent of gross domestic product—without a clear return in the form of investment that would not otherwise have occurred (IMF 2022).

More targeted alternatives exist. Accelerated depreciation and investment tax credits directly reduce the cost of investment when it is made, preserving the tax base once projects become profitable. Greater transparency and periodic evaluation of incentive regimes can also improve the ratio of economic benefit to fiscal cost. Fiji's experience illustrates a broader regional challenge: tax incentives designed to offset structural disadvantages can impose substantial and poorly targeted fiscal costs. Instruments that are time-bound, transparent, and tied directly to new investment rather than to future profits offer a more fiscally sustainable path to the same objective (IMF et al. 2015).

Despite low CIT rates, EAP economies have relatively high statutory PIT rates, often matching or exceeding those in other middle-income country groups (refer to figure 1.4). Compared with a middle-income country average of about 28–31 percent, top marginal rates reach 30 percent in Malaysia; 35 percent in Indonesia, the Philippines, Thailand, and Viet Nam; and 42 percent in Papua New Guinea. China stands out at the top, with a statutory top rate of 45 percent—on par with the average for Organisation for Economic Co-operation and Development (OECD) countries (OECD and ADB 2022; World Bank 2021).

Many EAP economies have higher PIT rates than middle-income countries do.

FIGURE 1.4 Statutory PIT rates, EAP and comparators

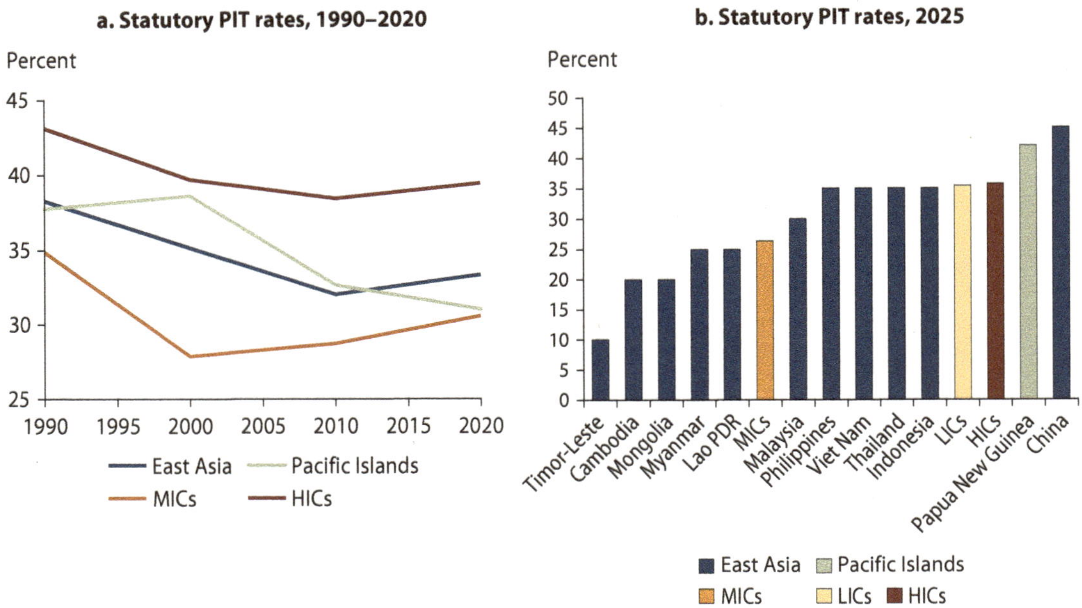

Sources: Original figure for this publication based on Worldwide Tax Summaries Online, PwC, https://taxsummaries.pwc.com; Végh and Vuletin 2015.

Note: East Asia includes Indonesia, Malaysia, the Philippines, Thailand, and Viet Nam; Pacific Island countries include Fiji and Papua New Guinea. PIT rate refers to highest marginal personal income tax rate. EAP = East Asia and Pacific; HICs = high-income countries; LICs = low-income countries; MICs = middle-income countries; PIT = personal income tax.

EAP economies have among the lowest value added tax (VAT) rates in the world. Cambodia, Lao PDR, Thailand, and Viet Nam all maintain rates at or below 10 percent—well below the middle-income country average of 15.8 percent and the high-income country average of 18.2 percent (refer to figure 1.5). The low rates reflect the region's growth-enabling philosophy. However, there is limited evidence that lower statutory tax rates by themselves are sufficient to generate higher long-run growth; tax design, tax efficiency, and the use of revenues appear to matter at least as much as tax rates (Acosta-Ormaechea and Morozumi 2013, 2021; Gemmell et al. 2014). Instead, low VAT rates leave substantial revenue on the table. VAT is among the most efficient tax available to governments (Mirrlees et al. 2011), and maintaining below-average rates constrains its yield without a clear growth return to show for it.

EAP has among the lowest VAT rates globally, with several economies maintaining rates at or below 10 percent.

FIGURE 1.5 VAT rates, EAP and comparators, 2025

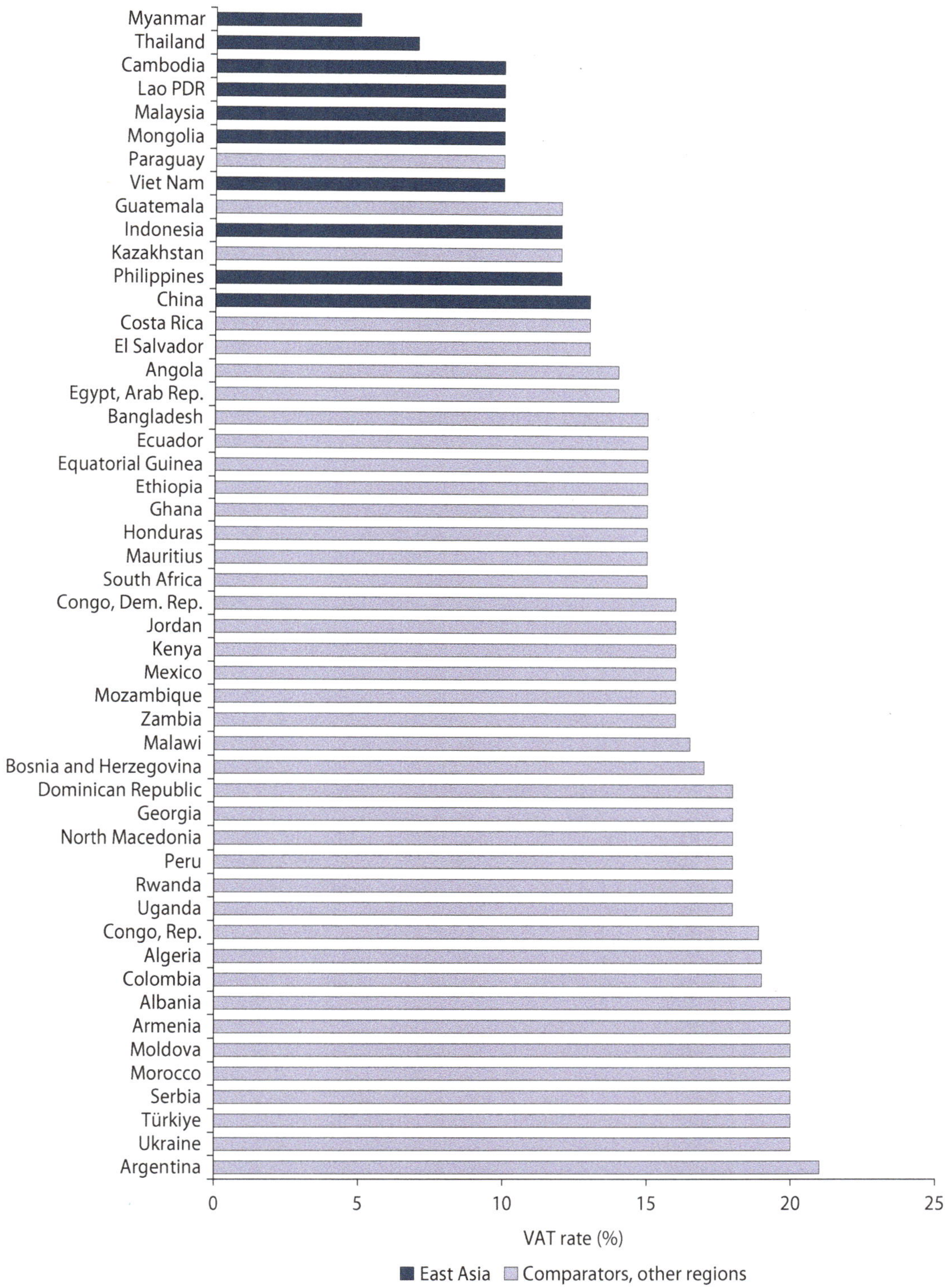

Source: Original figure for this publication based on Worldwide Tax Summaries Online, PwC, https://taxsummaries.pwc.com.
Note: EAP = East Asia and Pacific; VAT = value added tax.

Extensive exemptions and zero rates erode the base further. Viet Nam exempts 26 categories of goods from VAT entirely and applies a reduced 5 percent rate to another 15, narrowing the base well beyond what equity objectives would require (World Bank 2017b). A temporary rate reduction to 8 percent introduced in 2022 pushed VAT revenues down from 4.9 to 4.1 percent of GDP by 2024, eliminating an estimated 1 percent of GDP in annual revenue (World Bank 2025f). Cambodia's VAT C-efficiency—a measure of how much of the theoretical maximum the government collects—fell from 0.50 to 0.41 between 2019 and 2024, driven by slow refund processing and excessive domestic zero-rating (World Bank 2025a). Mongolia has among the lowest VAT rates globally (10 percent), compounded by exemptions on gold sales, and with two-thirds of VAT revenue now derived from mining-linked imports—leaving overall collection highly vulnerable to commodity price swings (World Bank 2025c).

Overall, most EAP economies have pursued the growth-enabling approach through relatively low tax rates and generous tax incentives, choices that supported an investment-friendly environment but eroded the tax base and limited governments' ability to mobilize revenue. Relatively low consumption tax rates reduce the revenue potential of one of the most efficient sources of taxation, without clear evidence of associated growth benefits.

High CIT revenue despite low tax rates

Between 2000 and 2022, EAP's total tax revenue averaged 14.3 percent of GDP—about 2 percentage points below the middle-income country average of 16.0 percent and 7 percentage points below the high-income country average of 21.2 percent. Revenue varies widely across the region, however (refer to figure 1.6). Cambodia, Indonesia, and Lao PDR collect between 9 and 12 percent of GDP, well below the middle-income country average. China, Malaysia, and the Philippines cluster around 14–16 percent. At the other end, Fiji, Mongolia, and the Solomon Islands exceed 20 percent, approaching high-income country levels. This dispersion reflects significant differences in tax capacity across the region.

Tax revenue remains below 15 percent of GDP—a common benchmark for EMDEs—in Cambodia, Indonesia, Lao PDR, Papua New Guinea, and Viet Nam.

FIGURE 1.6 Tax revenue, by type of tax, EAP and comparators, 2000–22

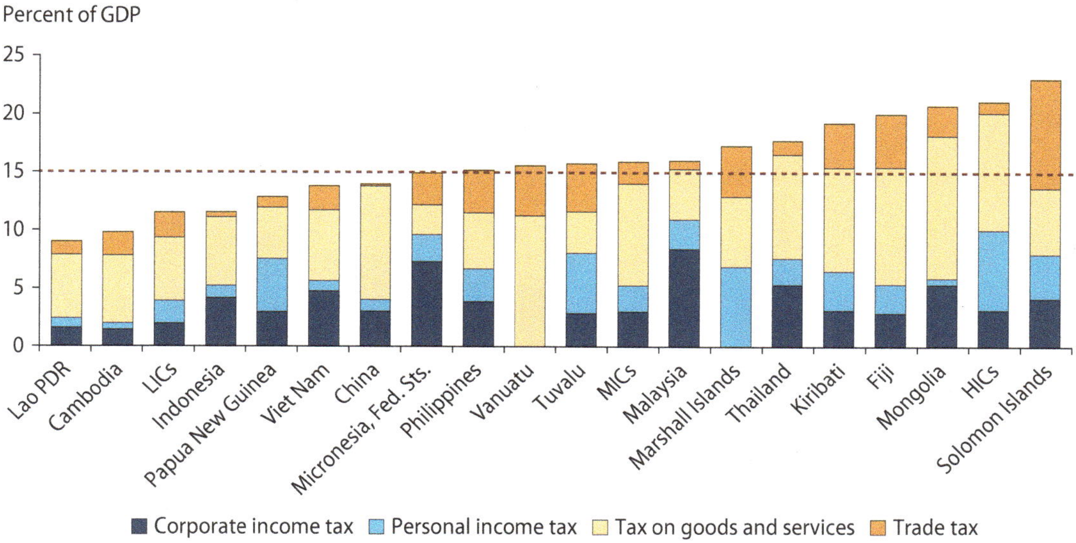

Sources: Original figure for this publication based on Government Finance Statistics, International Monetary Fund (IMF), https://data360.worldbank.org/en/int/dataset/IMF_GFSMAB; World Revenue Longitudinal Database (WoRLD), IMF, https://www.imf.org/en/topics/fiscal-policies/world-revenue-longitudinal-database.

Note: Data for Lao PDR, Papua New Guinea, Tuvalu, and Viet Nam come from WoRLD. EAP = East Asia and Pacific; EMDEs = emerging market and developing economies; HICs = high-income countries; LICs = low-income countries; MICs = middle-income countries.

Across tax instruments, EAP generates relatively low revenue, with one significant exception: CIT. Between 2000 and 2022, CIT revenue in East Asia averaged 4.3 percent of GDP, higher than both the middle-income country average of 3.1 percent and the high-income country average of 3.3 percent—meaning that many East Asian economies collect more corporate tax than OECD countries collect despite having lower statutory rates (refer to figure 1.7, panel a). This revenue reflects a relatively broad and formal corporate tax base, underpinned by a strong multinational enterprise presence (refer to figure 1.7, panel b).

CIT revenues have remained relatively high across the region despite declining statutory rates (refer to figure 1.8). However, the continued race to the bottom in CIT rates leaves limited scope to raise additional revenue through such taxes. Moreover, given the constraints on direct taxation in an environment of high capital and skill mobility, future revenue mobilization will likely need to rely more heavily on other tax instruments.

Despite relatively low statutory tax rates, several EAP economies collect more CIT revenue than high-income countries do, consistent with the strong presence of MNEs.

FIGURE 1.7 CIT revenue and presence of MNEs, EAP and comparators

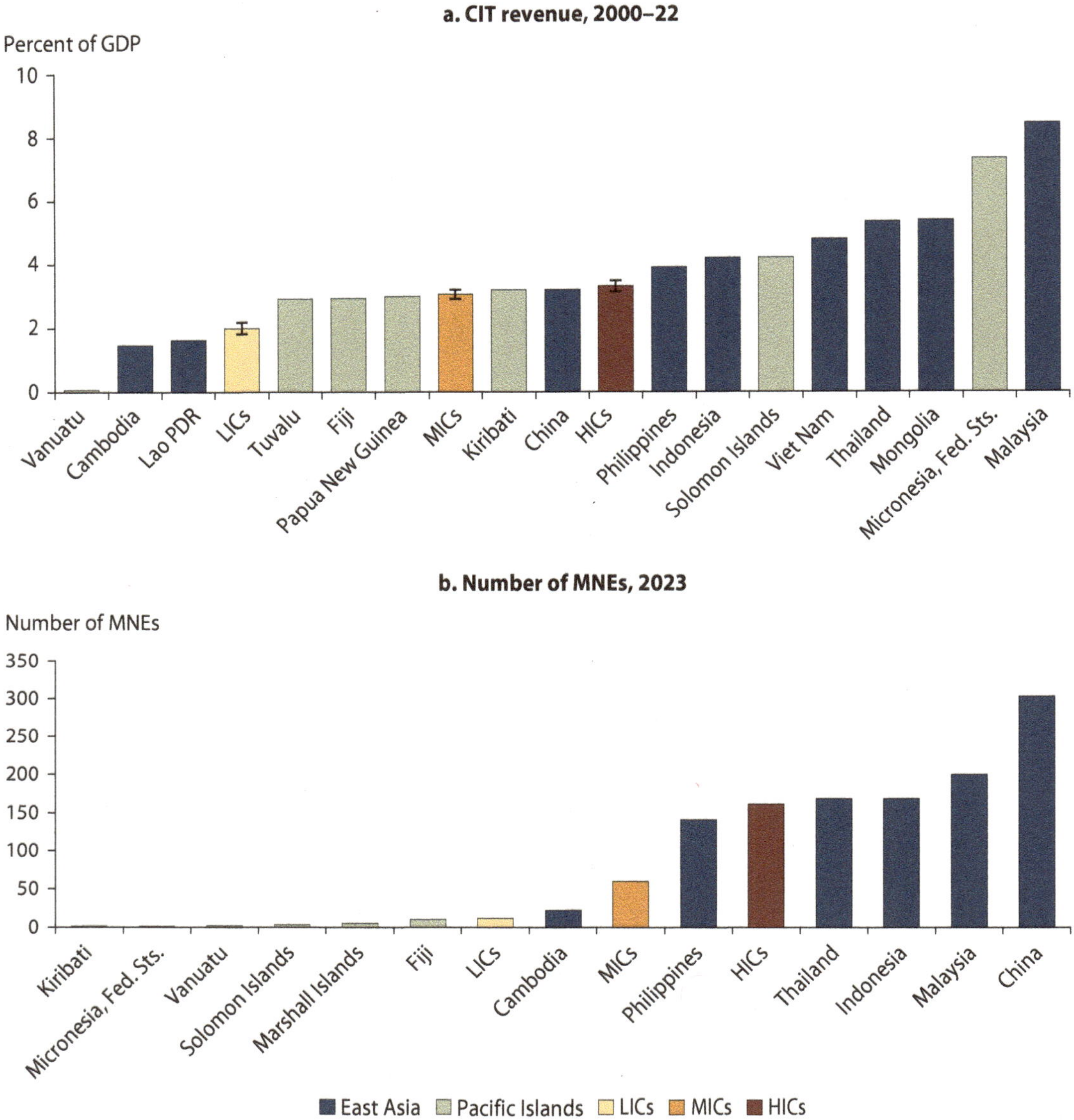

Sources: Original figure for this publication based on Government Finance Statistics, International Monetary Fund (IMF), https://data360.worldbank.org/en/int/dataset/IMF_GFSMAB; OECD-UNSD Multinational Enterprise Information Platform, Organisation for Economic Co-operation and Development and United Nations Statistics Division, https://www.oecd.org/en/data/dashboards/oecd-unsd-multinational-enterprise-information-platform.html; World Revenue Longitudinal Database WoRLD), IMF, https://www.imf.org/en/topics/fiscal-policies/world-revenue-longitudinal-database.

Note: Tax data for Lao PDR, Papua New Guinea, Tuvalu, and Viet Nam come from WoRLD. Error bars in panel a represent 90 percent confidence intervals around the mean. CIT = corporate income tax; EAP = East Asia and Pacific; HICs = high-income countries; LICs = low-income countries; MICs = middle-income countries; MNE = multinational enterprise.

CIT revenues in EAP remain strong despite falling statutory rates.

FIGURE 1.8 CIT rates and CIT revenues, selected EAP economies, 2000–07 vs. 2020–22

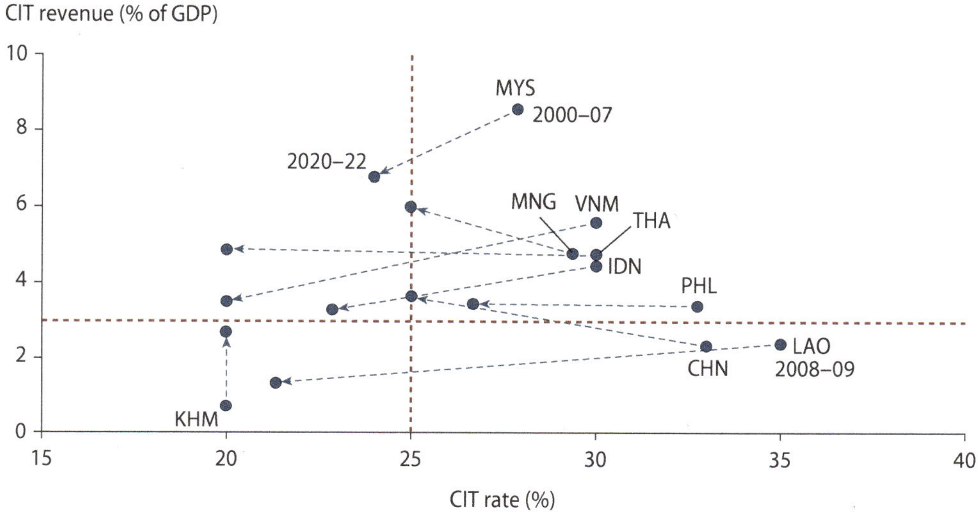

Sources: Original figure for this publication based on Enache 2022; Government Finance Statistics, International Monetary Fund (IMF), https://data360.worldbank.org/en/int/dataset/IMF_GFSMAB; World Revenue Longitudinal Database WoRLD), IMF, https://www.imf.org/en/topics/fiscal-policies/world-revenue-longitudinal-database.
Note: The plots show the average over two periods, 2000–07 and 2020–22 (Lao PDR starts at 2008–09 because of data availability). Each arrow shows how the CIT revenue has changed for a country. Dashed intersecting lines show the median in the period 2020–22. For a list of country codes, refer to https://www.iso.org/obp/ui/#search. CIT = corporate income tax; EAP = East Asia and Pacific.

Low PIT revenue driven by informality and weak tax enforcement

PIT revenues in most East Asian economies remain relatively low compared with other economies (refer to figure 1.9). Between 2000 and 2022, Cambodia, China, Indonesia, Lao PDR, Mongolia, and Viet Nam recorded some of the world's lowest ratios of PIT revenue to GDP, typically at or below 1 percent of GDP, compared to averages of about 2.0 percent and 2.2 percent in low-income and middle-income countries, respectively.

These low levels of PIT revenue, among the lowest in the world, occur despite moderate to relatively high statutory rates—a disconnect rooted in structural constraints: large informal sectors, limited administrative capacity, and an income base concentrated in hard-to-tax self-employment. Indonesia, the Philippines, and Viet Nam all maintain top marginal rates of 30–35 percent, broadly in line with the global average; however, ratios of PIT revenue to GDP remain low (refer to figure 1.10, panel a). Economies such as Indonesia and Viet Nam collect about 1.0–1.5 percent of GDP in PIT revenue, well below the average of about 2.5 percent observed in middle-income countries.

Most East Asian economies have notably low PIT revenues, but Malaysia, the Philippines, and Thailand have revenues on par with other middle-income countries. Meanwhile, Pacific Island countries collect some of the highest PIT revenues.

FIGURE 1.9 PIT revenue, EAP and comparators, 2000–22

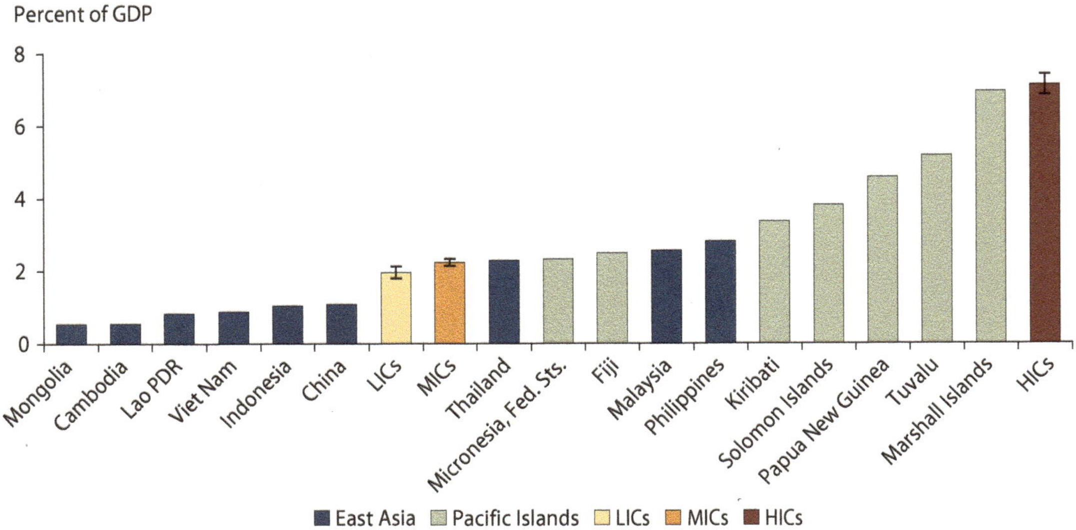

Sources: Original figure for this publication based on Government Finance Statistics, International Monetary Fund (IMF), https://data360.worldbank.org/en/int/dataset/IMF_GFSMAB; World Revenue Longitudinal Database WoRLD), IMF, https://www.imf.org/en/topics/fiscal-policies/world-revenue-longitudinal-database.

Note: Tax data for Lao PDR, Papua New Guinea, Tuvalu, and Viet Nam come from WoRLD. Error bars represent 90 percent confidence intervals around the mean. EAP = East Asia and Pacific; HICs = high-income countries; LICs = low-income countries; MICs = middle-income countries; PIT = personal income tax.

Most EAP economies combine high levels of informality with very low PIT revenue, reflecting the difficulty of taxing income outside formal employment and reporting systems (refer to figure 1.10, panel b). Economies such as Cambodia and Lao PDR exhibit informality rates above 80 percent and collect close to zero PIT revenue as a share of GDP.[5] In Lao PDR, the PIT productivity ratio—actual collection divided by the top statutory rate—stands at just 0.035, the lowest in the region, reflecting a base confined almost entirely to formal payroll (World Bank 2023c). Indonesia and Viet Nam have informality rates above 60 percent,[6] limiting the share of workers that can be effectively taxed and contributing to PIT revenues of about only 1 percent of GDP. Economies with lower informality rates, such as Malaysia and Thailand, have correspondingly higher PIT revenues, reaching about 2.0–2.5 percent of GDP and closer to the average for middle-income countries. Limited administrative capacity further constrains enforcement, particularly when tax administrations face difficulties monitoring self-employment income and small businesses (World Bank 2020c).

Among EAP economies, PIT revenue remains low even when statutory rates are relatively high; higher informality is associated with lower PIT collection.

FIGURE 1.10 PIT revenue, PIT rate, and informality rate, EAP economies

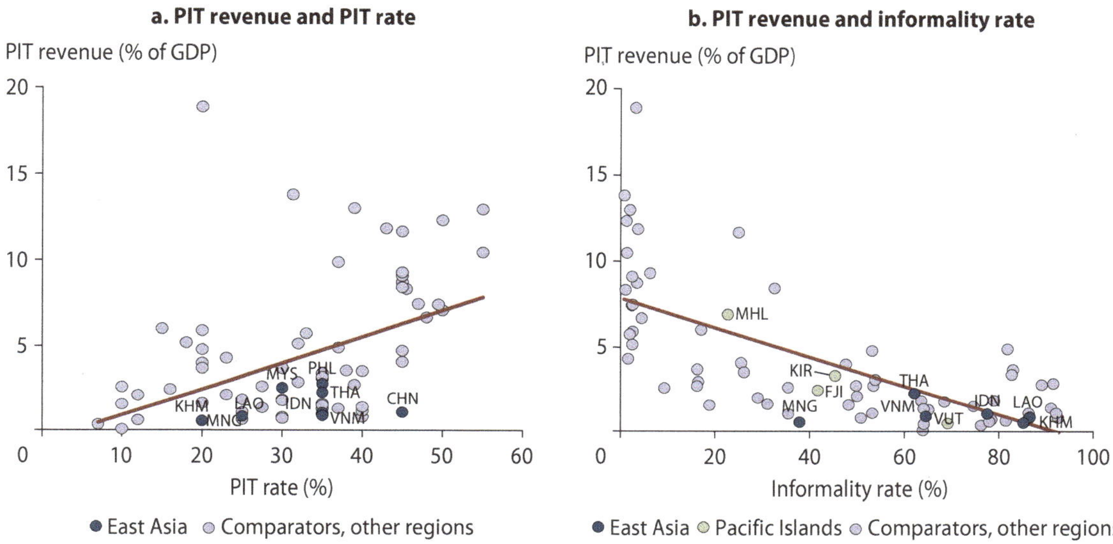

Sources: Original figure for this publication based on Government Finance Statistics (GFS), International Monetary Fund (IMF), https://data360.worldbank.org/en/int/dataset/IMF_GFSMAB; ILOSTAT, International Labour Organization, https://ilostat.ilo.org/data/?cat_mode=subject; World Revenue Longitudinal Database (WoRLD), IMF, https://www.imf.org/en/topics/fiscal-policies/world-revenue-longitudinal-database; Worldwide Tax Summaries Online, PwC, https://taxsummaries.pwc.com.

Note: PIT revenue corresponds to the 2000–22 average based on GFS. PIT revenue data for Lao PDR and Viet Nam come from WoRLD. Panel a uses the latest available statutory PIT rates reported by PwC as of January 2025. Panel b uses the latest estimates of informality available from ILOSTAT. EAP = East Asia and Pacific; PIT = personal income tax.

Low goods and services tax revenue driven by structural and policy factors

Goods and services taxes (GSTs) generate relatively low revenue across EAP. Between 2000 and 2022, GST revenue averaged 5.9 percent of GDP—nearly 3 percentage points below the middle-income country average of 8.8 percent and more than 4 points below the high-income country average of 10.1 percent (refer to figure 1.11). Two distinct sets of factors explain this underperformance: structural constraints that narrow the effective base, and policy design choices that further erode it.

On the structural side, large informal sectors, small firms operating outside the tax net, and limited administrative capacity all reduce what governments can collect. In Indonesia, for instance, low revenue collection reflects both the size of the informal sector and weak compliance, with VAT compliance estimated at only 56.6 percent (World Bank 2020b). In the Philippines, retail activity is dominated by micro and small enterprises, including neighborhood retailers such as sari-sari stores, many of which

GST revenue collection in most EAP economies remains low relative to other middle-income economies.

FIGURE 1.11 GST revenue in EAP, 2000–22

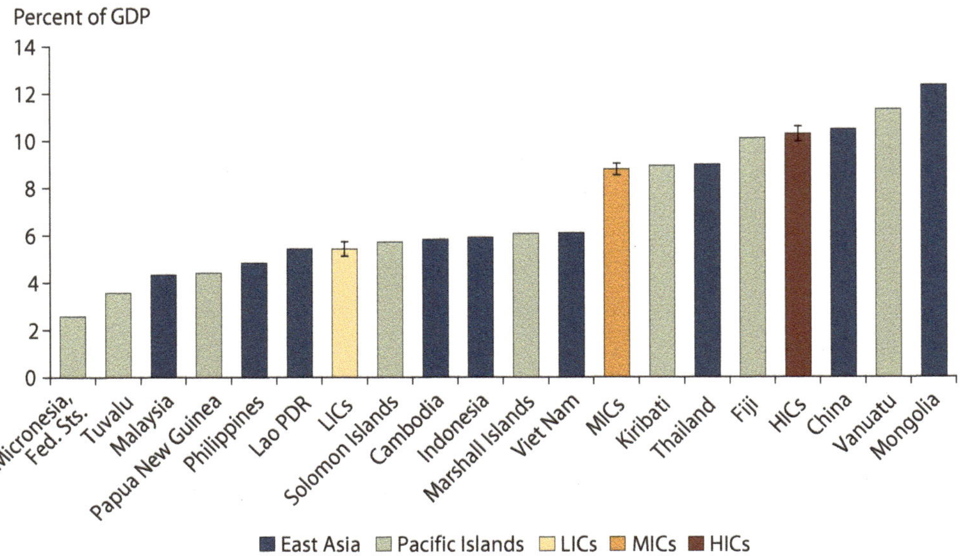

Sources: Original figure for this publication based on Government Finance Statistics, International Monetary Fund (IMF), https://data360.worldbank.org/en/int/dataset/IMF_GFSMAB; World Revenue Longitudinal Database (WoRLD), IMF, https://www.imf.org/en/topics/fiscal-policies/world-revenue-longitudinal-database.
Note: Tax data for Lao PDR, Papua New Guinea, Tuvalu, and Viet Nam come from WoRLD. Error bars represent 90 percent confidence intervals around the mean. EAP = East Asia and Pacific; GST = goods and services tax.

operate outside the formal tax system (World Bank 2011). Finally, Cambodia illustrates the region's limited administrative capacity, with only 0.10 tax staff per 1,000 inhabitants compared with an international average of about 0.65, and each staff member managing only 28 active taxpayers compared with about 676 in comparable countries (World Bank 2019). These structural factors tend to evolve only gradually as economies develop, making improvements in the GST base largely a long-term process.

Policy design compounds the problem. As discussed earlier, relatively low statutory VAT rates and extensive exemptions have already narrowed the tax base in several EAP economies. In addition, relatively high VAT registration thresholds exclude many smaller firms from the tax system. In Indonesia, for example, the VAT registration threshold set at Rp 4.8 billion in annual turnover (about US$300,000) allows many micro and small enterprises to remain outside the VAT system and weakens the VAT credit chain. Evidence from VAT gap analysis further highlights the role of both policy design and enforcement. In Indonesia, the VAT compliance gap averaged 43.9 percent of potential VAT liability between 2016 and 2021, equivalent to about 2.6 percent of GDP (World Bank 2025c).

Cross-country tax capacity analysis suggests that EAP economies could raise about 2 percent of GDP in additional GST revenue (refer to box 1.2). Although overall tax capacity in the region is broadly comparable with that of other middle-income economies, GST revenues in several EAP economies remain well below their estimated potential. Mongolia and Thailand stand out as notable exceptions.

Box 1.2. Estimating tax capacity and revenue gaps in East Asia and Pacific

Ratios of tax to gross domestic product (GDP) provide a useful snapshot of observed revenue performance but do not capture how much revenue countries could realistically mobilize. To address this limitation, the literature has developed the concept of tax capacity, the level of revenue a country can feasibly raise given its underlying characteristics.[a]

This box extends the regression-based tax capacity framework by estimating tax capacity both in aggregate and by tax type, with a particular focus on goods and services taxes (GSTs).[b] Using a panel of 112 developing and high-income countries over 2000–22, the analysis models tax revenue outcomes as a function of structural and institutional determinants commonly identified in the literature, including income per capita, trade openness, the share of agriculture in GDP, population growth, and corruption. To better capture factors relevant to specific tax instruments, the analysis also incorporates controls for self-employment, informal output, and consumption, which proxy informality and demand-side dynamics.[c] The regression results across different tax instruments are broadly consistent with theoretical expectations.[d]

Tax capacity in the region has increased over time and is broadly comparable to that of middle-income countries (refer to figure B1.2.1). Most East Asia and Pacific (EAP) economies cluster around estimated tax capacity levels of about 15–17 percent of GDP, close to the commonly cited benchmark of 15 percent of GDP for developing economies. Indonesia shows one of the largest increases in estimated tax capacity, reflecting improvements in institutional quality that supports revenue mobilization. Pacific Island countries appear to have comparatively higher estimated tax capacity; however, these estimates should be interpreted with caution: because of data limitations, the specification for Pacific Island countries excludes some control variables.[e]

(continued)

Box 1.2. Estimating tax capacity and revenue gaps in East Asia and Pacific *(continued)*

Tax capacity in most East Asian economies aligns broadly with middle-income countries and the widely cited 15 percent benchmark for developing economies.

FIGURE B1.2.1 Tax capacity, EAP and comparators, 2000–07 vs. 2010–19

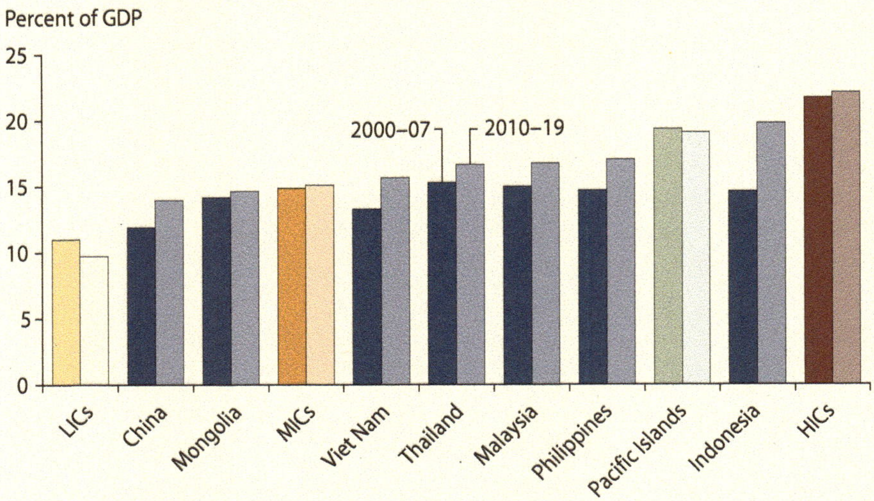

Sources: Original figure for this publication based on Government Finance Statistics, International Monetary Fund (IMF), https://data360.worldbank.org/en/int/dataset/IMF_GFSMAB; International Country Risk Guide data set, PRS Group, https://www.prsgroup.com/explore-our-products/icrg/; World Development Indicators, World Bank, https://datatopics.worldbank.org/world-development-indicators/; World Economic Outlook (WEO) Database, IMF, https://www.imf.org/en/publications/sprolls/world-economic-outlook-databases; World Revenue Longitudinal Database, IMF, https://www.imf.org/en/topics/fiscal-policies/world-revenue-longitudinal-database.

Note: The predicted tax revenue is obtained from the ordinary least squares estimation of the following equation: Tax revenue/GDP$_{it}$ = $\alpha + \beta_1$. GDPPC$_{it}$ + β_2. AGR$_{it}$ + β_3. Corruption$_{it}$ + β_4. Population$_{it}$ + β_5. Trade$_{it}$ + regional dummies + time dummies + ε. Because of data availability, the predicted revenue for Pacific Island countries is obtained from the following equation: Tax revenue/GDP$_{it}$ = $\alpha + \beta_1$. GDPPC$_{it}$ + β_2. AGR$_{it}$ + β_3. Population$_{it}$ + β_4. Trade$_{it}$ + regional dummies + time dummies + ε. In the equation, i = country; t = year; GDPPC = log GDP per capita; AGR = agricultural share of GDP; Corruption = the degree of political corruption; Population = population growth rate; Trade = sum of exports and imports as share of GDP; α = constant term; $\beta_1 - \beta_5$ = estimated coefficients; regional dummies = binary controlling for fixed differences across regions; time dummies = binary controlling for common shocks or trends across all countries in a given year; ε = the error term. EAP = East Asia and Pacific; HICs=high-income countries; LICs=-low-income countries; MICs = middle-income countries.

The resulting estimates indicate that GST revenue collection in several EAP economies falls significantly short of its estimated capacity, with gaps of about 2 percent of GDP in economies such as Indonesia, Malaysia, the Philippines, and Viet Nam (refer to figure B1.2.2). In contrast, GST revenue in middle-income countries aligns broadly with estimated capacity.

(continued)

Box 1.2. Estimating tax capacity and revenue gaps in East Asia and Pacific *(continued)*

Regarding other tax instruments, estimated revenue gaps appear more limited. Personal income tax revenues in most EAP economies align broadly with estimated capacity; Indonesia stands out, with an estimated personal income tax gap of about 2 percent of GDP.

GST revenue in most East Asian economies falls short of estimated capacity, pointing to significant untapped revenue potential of about 2 percent of GDP.

FIGURE B1.2.2 GST revenue and capacity, EAP and comparators, 2000–20

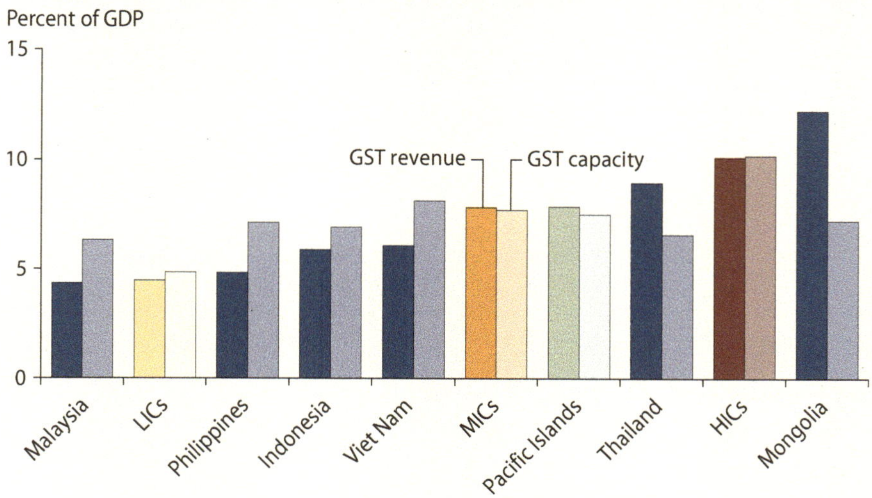

Sources: Original figure for this publication based on Government Finance Statistics, International Monetary Fund (IMF); https://data360.worldbank.org/en/int/dataset/IMF_GFSMAB; Informal Economy Database, World Bank, https://www.worldbank.org/en/research/brief/informal-economy-database; International Country Risk Guide data set, PRS Group, https://www.prsgroup.com/explore-our-products/icrg/; World Development Indicators, World Bank, https://datatopics.worldbank.org/world-development-indicators/; World Economic Outlook (WEO) Database, IMF, https://www.imf.org/en/publications/sprolls/world-economic-outlook-databases; World Revenue Longitudinal Database, IMF, https://www.imf.org/en/topics/fiscal-policies/world-revenue-longitudinal-database.

Note: GST revenue refers to the GST revenue collected; GST capacity refers to the predicted GST revenue that could be collected. GST capacity is the predicted GST revenue obtained from the OLS estimation of the following equation, $GST/GDP_{it} = \alpha + \beta_1 . GDPPC_{it} + \beta_2 . AGR_{it} + \beta_3 . Corruption_{it} + \beta_4 . Population_{it} + \beta_5 . Trade_{it} + \beta_6 . Informal\ output_{it} + \beta_7 . Consumption_{it}$ + regional dummies + time dummies + ε. In the equation, i = country; t = year; GDPPC = log GDP per capita; AGR = agricultural share of GDP; Corruption = the degree of political corruption; Population = population growth rate; Trade = sum of exports and imports as share of GDP; Informal output = estimated size of informal output as share of actual GDP; Consumption: expenditure on goods and services by households and governments as share GDP; α = constant term; $\beta_1 - \beta_7$ = estimated coefficients; regional dummies = binary controlling for fixed differences across regions; time dummies = binary controlling for common shocks or trends across all countries in a given year; ε = the error term. Because of data availability, the estimation for Pacific Island countries excludes corruption, informal output, and consumption. EAP = East Asia and Pacific; GST = goods and services tax; HICs = high-income countries; LICs = low-income countries; MICs = middle-income countries.

(continued)

Box 1.2. Estimating tax capacity and revenue gaps in East Asia and Pacific *(continued)*

The policy implication is clear: EAP's remaining revenue headroom lies primarily in GSTs. Several economies have scope for substantial additional GST mobilization through VAT policy reform and administrative improvement—without new tax instruments or higher statutory rates.

a. The empirical literature has proposed several approaches to estimating tax capacity. Early contributions relied on cross-country regression frameworks linking tax revenue to structural determinants such as income levels, economic structure, trade openness, and institutional quality (for example, Tanzi 1992). More recent studies have expanded these approaches by incorporating measures of institutional quality and demographic factors—such as corruption, informality, and population growth (Le et al. 2012; Sen Gupta 2007)—or by applying stochastic frontier methods to distinguish between structural capacity and revenue effort (Fenochietto and Pessino 2013; Mawejje and Sebudde 2019).

b. Most existing benchmarks estimate tax capacity in aggregate, obscuring important differences across tax instruments, which can have distinct implications for growth and may offer varying degrees of revenue headroom.

c. Refer to annex 1A for methodological details.

d. Higher income per capita and consumption are associated with higher tax capacity; a larger agricultural sector, faster population growth, higher informality, and weaker institutional quality tend to reduce revenue potential. Meanwhile, trade openness, although expected to increase revenue potential, has mixed effects across specifications.

e. Because of data availability limitations, the tax capacity estimation for Pacific Island countries excludes several control variables used in the baseline specification, including corruption, self-employment, informal output, and consumption. Consequently, estimates for these economies are based on a reduced specification and should be interpreted with caution.

In Thailand, a relatively broad tax base and strong compliance among registered taxpayers support VAT productivity. Thailand has among the region's highest filing and payment compliance rates, and base erosion from exemptions and preferential treatments remains comparatively limited (World Bank 2023f). Consequently, Thailand collects a large share of its potential VAT revenue despite maintaining a relatively low statutory VAT rate of 7 percent (refer to figure 1.12).

Both cases demonstrate that administrative and design improvements can deliver substantial revenue gains without raising statutory rates.

Thailand collects a large share of potential VAT revenue despite maintaining a low statutory VAT rate.

FIGURE 1.12 Observed and potential VAT revenue, Thailand, EAP, and comparators, 2018

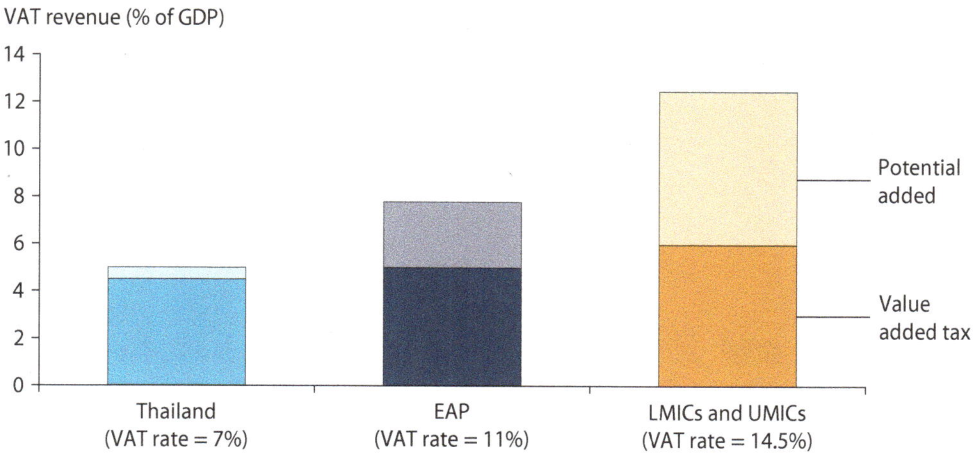

Source: Original figure for this publication based on World Bank 2023f.
Note: EAP = East Asia and Pacific; LMICs = lower-middle-income countries; UMICs = upper-middle-income countries; VAT = value added tax.

Reduced reliance on trade taxes

Trade tax revenue varies significantly across East Asia. Indonesia, Malaysia, and Thailand collect relatively little from trade taxes, whereas Cambodia and the Philippines rely more heavily on them. Cambodia collected 1.9 percent of GDP and the Philippines 4.7 percent from trade taxes in 2020–22 (refer to figure 1.13). This pattern is consistent with global trends: as countries have liberalized trade and reduced tariffs, reliance on trade taxes has declined in middle- and high-income countries but persists in lower-income countries.

In most East Asian economies, tariff reductions and trade liberalization have driven trade tax revenues down even as trade volumes expanded (refer to figure 1.14). Geopolitical pressures may partially reverse this trend in some economies, but higher tariffs are unlikely to restore trade taxes as a primary revenue instrument: they risk reducing trade volumes and create long-run uncertainty around revenue, whereas a shift to domestic taxation has proven a more effective and durable path to revenue mobilization (Acosta-Ormaechea and Yoo 2012; Baunsgaard and Keen 2010).

International trade tax revenue varies widely across East Asian economies, with lower-income economies relying more heavily on it—a pattern also observed globally.

FIGURE 1.13 Trade tax revenue, East Asia and comparators, 2020–22

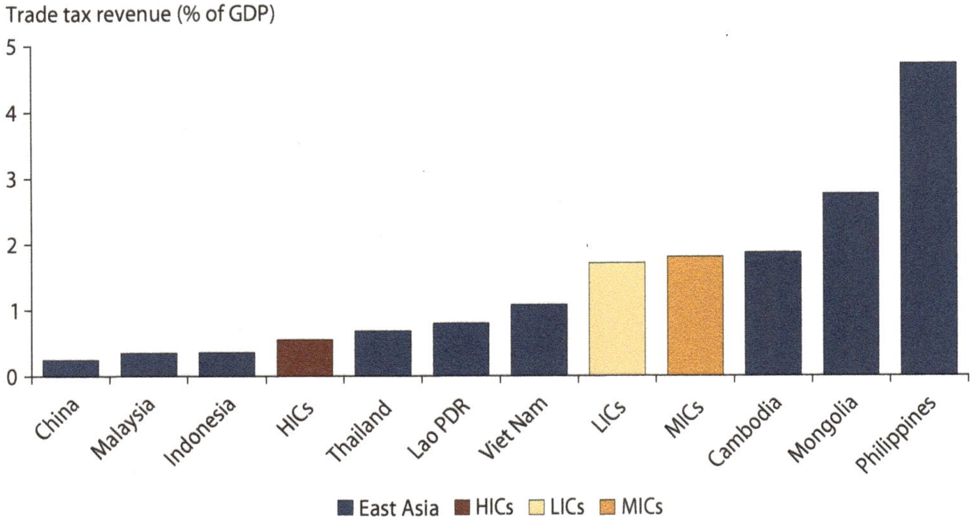

Sources: Original figure for this publication based on Government Finance Statistics, International Monetary Fund (IMF), https://data360.worldbank.org/en/int/dataset/IMF_GFSMAB; World Revenue Longitudinal Dataset, IMF, https://www.imf.org/en/topics/fiscal-policies/world-revenue-longitudinal-database.
Note: HICs = high-income countries; LICs = low-income countries; MICs = middle-income countries.

The Philippines appears an outlier, with trade tax revenue increasing despite tariff reductions and declining trade openness. Two factors explain this difference. First, the Bureau of Customs collects VAT on imported goods at the standard 12 percent rate applied to the full landed cost; however, some data sets classify this import VAT under trade taxes rather than under GST, overstating trade tax revenue relative to tariffs alone. Second, the Philippines retains high statutory tariffs of 20–50 percent on sensitive agricultural products (rice, poultry, pork, and sugar) as protection for domestic producers (OECD 2025).[7]

Overall, EAP has uneven revenue performance across instruments. CIT continues to generate significant revenues but offers limited scope for further gains given rate convergence globally. PIT remains underutilized, constrained by informality and administrative capacity. GST systems underperform relative to peers and represent the largest addressable revenue gap. Trade taxes are declining with development and are not a viable instrument for sustained revenue growth. Strengthening domestic revenue mobilization will require shifting to broader and more efficient tax bases, particularly GST, while improving income tax enforcement and preserving the pro-growth features of the existing framework.

International trade tax revenue has declined in most East Asian economies because of tariff cuts and trade liberalization, even as trade expanded in some cases.

FIGURE 1.14 Tariffs, tax revenue, and trade, East Asia, 2000–07 vs. 2020–22

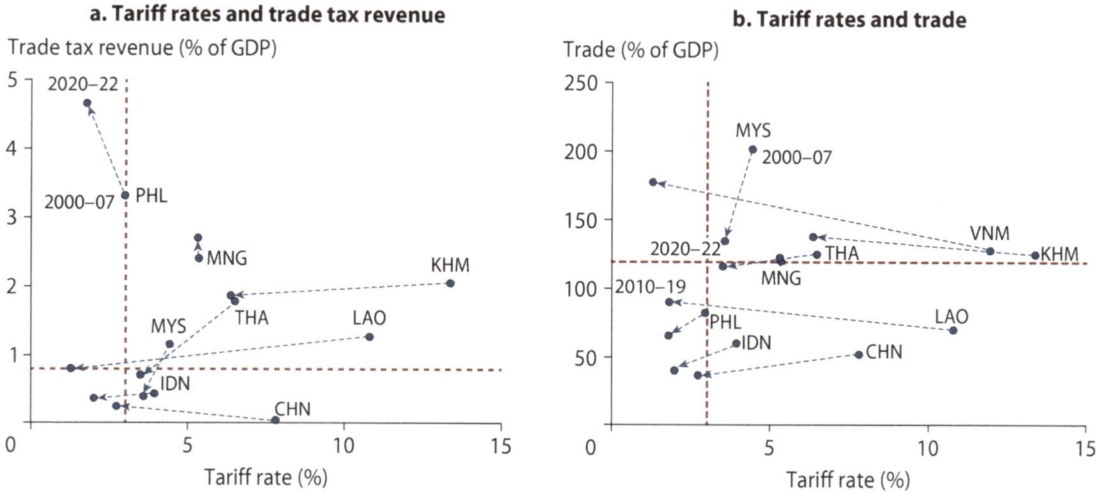

Sources: Original figure for this publication based on Government Finance Statistics, International Monetary Fund (IMF), https://data360.worldbank.org/en/int/dataset/IMF_GFSMAB; World Development Indicators, World Bank, https://datatopics.worldbank.org/world-development-indicators/; World Revenue Longitudinal Database (WoRLD), IMF, https://www.imf.org/en/topics/fiscal-policies/world-revenue-longitudinal-database.

Note: Tax data for Lao PDR and Viet Nam come from WoRLD. Dots represent averages for the 2000–07 and 2020–22 periods. For Lao PDR, the endpoint represents the 2010–19 period average due to limited data availability. The intersecting dashed lines indicate the medians for the respective variables over the later period. For a list of country codes, refer to https://www.iso.org/obp/ui/#search.

Government spending in EAP

Government spending in EAP is characterized by relatively low expenditure levels; however, public investment remains comparatively high, reflecting the region's longstanding emphasis on infrastructure development. In contrast, government consumption has remained low and broadly stable over time, consistent with a preference for lean public sectors. Comparatively modest expenditures on social protection and human capital limit the capacity of fiscal policy to reduce vulnerability and address inequality. At the same time, subsidies continue to absorb a sizable share of public resources in several economies such as Indonesia and Malaysia.

Prioritizing public investment despite low government spending

Government spending in most East Asian economies remains well below the average for middle-income countries, and well below what some current theories would predict (refer to annex 1B). Wagner's Law predicts that public spending rises with income: as economies grow, citizens demand more and better public services (Wagner 1883). Rodrik (1998) adds that open economies tend toward larger governments, using public spending as insurance against the external risks that come with trade integration.

East Asian economies are among the fastest-growing and most trade-integrated economies in the world, yet their governments remain small. They often show a large gap between predicted and actual spending: Indonesia's government spending stood at 15.4 percent of GDP in 2022 against a predicted 27.4 percent—a shortfall of 12 percentage points. Malaysia's gap is 8.5 points, Cambodia's 8.4 points, and Thailand's 5.7 points (refer to figure 1.15, panel a). China and Mongolia, the main exceptions, have spending closer to what income and openness would predict (refer to figure 1.15, panel b).

Neither Wagner's Law nor Rodrik's conjecture can fully explain the relatively small size of government observed in most East Asian economies.

FIGURE 1.15 Government spending vs. income and trade, EAP and comparators, 2000–22

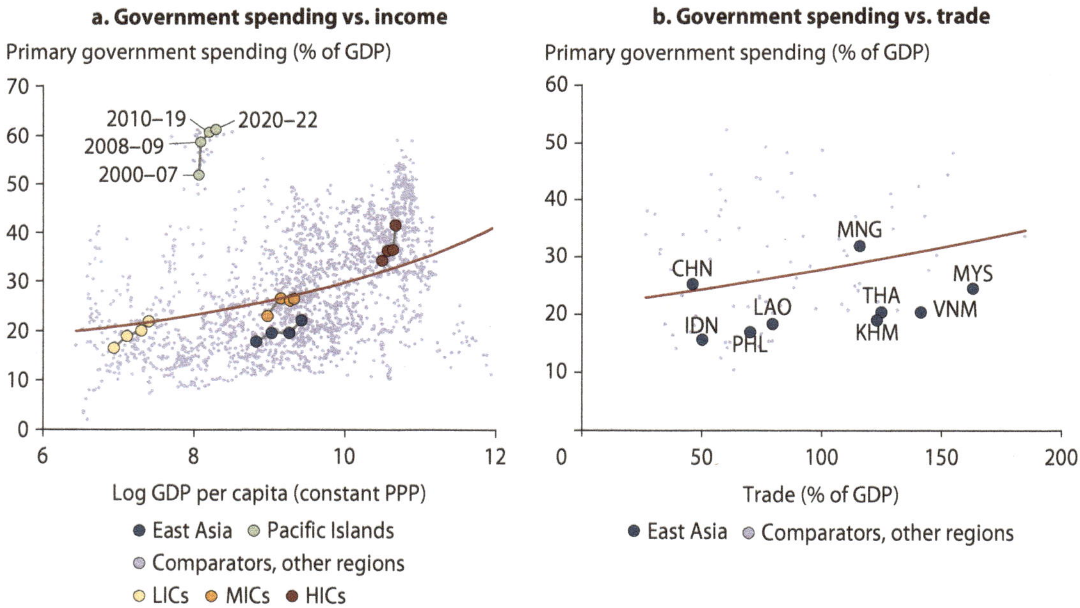

Sources: Original figure for this publication based on Government Finance Statistics, International Monetary Fund (IMF), https://data360.worldbank.org/en/int/dataset/IMF_GFSMAB; Investment and Capital Stock Dataset, IMF, https://data.imf.org/Datasets/ICSD; World Development Indicators, World Bank, https://datatopics.worldbank.org/world-development-indicators/; World Economic Outlook (WEO), IMF, https://www.imf.org/en/publications/sprolls/world-economic-outlook-databases.

Note: In panel a, primary government spending is government expenditure minus interest payments. Spending data for Pacific Island countries come from WEO because of data availability. The sample excludes outliers defined as being outside of 2 standard deviations from the world average. In panel b, the sample includes HICs, LICs, and MICs. HICs = high-income countries; LICs = low-income countries; MICs = middle-income countries; PPP = purchasing power parity.

Within this constrained spending envelope, most East Asian governments have prioritized public investment, including the construction of roads, bridges, hospitals, power plants, and other physical assets. On average, the ratio of public investment to GDP in the region stood at 6.5 percent during the 2000–19 period. The Philippines represents a notable exception, with public investment averaging about 2.2 percent of GDP over the same period, well below the regional average.

Indonesia illustrates how infrastructure investment can advance even under limited fiscal space. Despite relatively moderate levels of public investment, Indonesia has supported private capital formation through strong macroeconomic anchors, prudent fiscal management, and the active mobilization of private participation via public-private partnerships (refer to box 1.3). Institutional innovations in project preparation, risk-sharing mechanisms, and guarantee frameworks have helped crowd in private investment, underscoring that the effectiveness of public investment depends not only on its scale but also on governance, credibility, and the ability to leverage private capital.

Box 1.3. Infrastructure investment under limited fiscal space: Lessons from Indonesia

The growth-enabling fiscal approach in Indonesia has constrained fiscal space for infrastructure investment; however, the country has sustained infrastructure development by adopting alternative financing models. A central pillar of this approach has been the use of state-owned enterprises (SOEs) as off-budget investors (World Bank 2020c). SOEs in sectors such as transportation, energy, and construction have undertaken large infrastructure projects financed through a combination of borrowing, retained earnings, and government capital injections, allowing Indonesia to scale up infrastructure investment while limiting direct budgetary outlays.

In parallel, Indonesia has developed a comprehensive public-private partnership framework to mobilize private capital at scale. This framework includes dedicated institutions for project preparation, mechanisms for viability gap funding, and a structured pipeline of projects. Strengthening the public-private partnership framework—including pricing, regulation, and project selection—has been identified as critical to attract private investment (World Bank 2024b).

A defining feature of this model is the government's role as a risk manager rather than a direct financier. Through guarantees and co-financing arrangements, the government absorbs specific risks that would otherwise

(continued)

Box 1.3. Infrastructure investment under limited fiscal space: Lessons from Indonesia *(continued)*

deter private investment, improving project bankability. In this way, the state uses its balance sheet to crowd in private capital.

Although this approach can accelerate project delivery, spread costs over time, and leverage private sector expertise, it also creates important fiscal risks. SOE borrowing and government guarantees give rise to contingent liabilities, which may materialize as government obligations if projects underperform or if SOEs face financial distress. In Indonesia, explicit guarantees alone amount to about 2–3 percent of gross domestic product, but broader exposure through SOE borrowing is significantly larger (World Bank 2020c, 2024b). Moreover, for projects executed outside the central government budget, weak oversight can increase the risk of misallocation of resources, cost overruns, and corruption.

Indonesia's experience illustrates how countries can finance infrastructure under a growth-enabling fiscal approach with low revenue. Although its public investment remains relatively low, Indonesia has sustained infrastructure investment by mobilizing private capital and leveraging public balance sheets. At the same time, the effectiveness and sustainability of this model depend critically on strong institutions, transparent governance, and robust oversight frameworks to manage fiscal and governance risks.

In contrast, Pacific Island countries tend to exhibit significantly higher revenue and expenditure ratios because of structural factors. Small economic size, geographic isolation, exposure to recurrent shocks, and high fixed costs of service delivery mechanically raise fiscal aggregates relative to GDP. Consequently, relatively high revenue-to-GDP ratios coexist with elevated spending levels, including on infrastructure, but they remain insufficient to meet large spending needs, build fiscal buffers, and close persistent infrastructure gaps.

Lower-middle-income economies in East Asia seeking to expand foundational infrastructure have had particularly high public investment. Viet Nam provides a prominent example, with public investment averaging close to 8 percent of GDP during the 2000s (World Bank 2017b). Cambodia has also maintained elevated public investment levels, averaging about 7 percent of GDP during the 2010s as the country expanded road connectivity, electricity access, and irrigation systems (World Bank 2019). Lao PDR has had even higher public investment during some periods, exceeding

8 percent of GDP as the government financed large energy and transportation projects aimed at strengthening regional connectivity (World Bank 2023c). These levels are well above the public investment ratios typically observed across emerging market and developing economies, where government investment generally ranges between 3 and 5 percent of GDP.

As countries become richer, governments increasingly rely on private sector participation—rather than expanding public investment as a share of GDP—to finance infrastructure (Francois et al. 2026). This pattern is visible within the region. Upper-middle-income economies such as Malaysia and Thailand have gradually reduced public investment levels, whereas lower-middle-income countries such as Cambodia and the Philippines have expanded public investment as they continue to address infrastructure gaps (refer to figure 1.16). Despite these efforts, infrastructure needs across the region remain substantial and vary depending on the level of economic development.

Whereas Malaysia and Thailand have reduced public investment, Cambodia and the Philippines have increased it in recent decades, reflecting a broader shift to greater reliance on the private sector for infrastructure provision as economies develop.

FIGURE 1.16 Public investment and income, EAP and selected East Asian economies, 2000–19

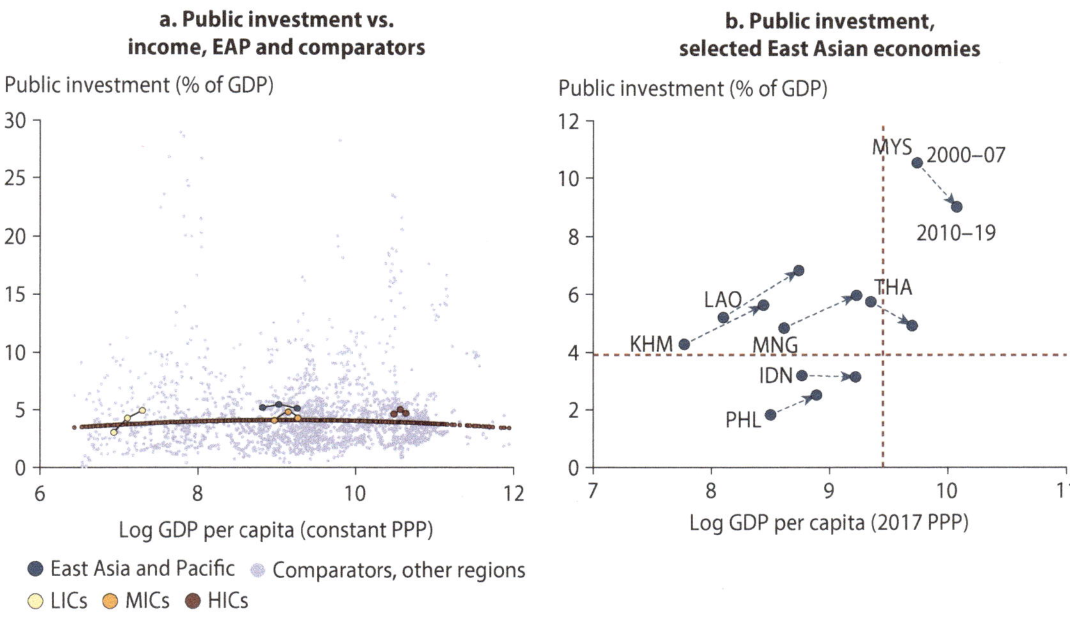

Sources: Original figure for this publication based on Investment and Capital Stock Dataset (ICSD), IMF, https://data.imf.org/Datasets/ICSD; World Economic Outlook (WEO) Database, IMF, https://www.imf.org/en/publications/sprolls/world-economic-outlook-databases.
Note: EAP includes Cambodia, Indonesia, Malaysia, the Philippines, and Thailand. In panel a, the dots represent averages for the following periods: 2000–07, 2008–09, and 2010–19. In panel b, the dots represent averages for the following periods: 2000–07 and 2010–19. The intersecting dashed lines indicate the medians for the respective variables over the 2010–19 period. For a list of country codes, refer to https://www.iso.org/obp/ui/#search. EAP = East Asia and Pacific; HICs = high-income countries; LICs = low-income countries; MICs = middle-income countries; PPP = purchasing power parity.

Low and stable government consumption

Government spending can be classified either by economic category or by function. The former refers to what governments spend on, such as wages, goods and services, social benefits, grants, subsidies, other transfers, and public investment.[8] The latter refers to what governments spend for, such as education, health, social protection, and other government functions.

According to the economic classification of government spending, government consumption is one of the main components explaining the relatively small size of governments in the EAP region (refer to figure 1.17). Between 2000 and 2022, the ratio of government consumption to GDP in East Asia averaged 9.7 percent, close to the level observed in middle-income countries (10.9 percent) and roughly two-thirds that of high-income countries (14.8 percent).

Low public consumption and limited social benefits have largely contributed to small governments in the region.

FIGURE 1.17 Economic classification of government spending, East Asia and comparators, 2000–22

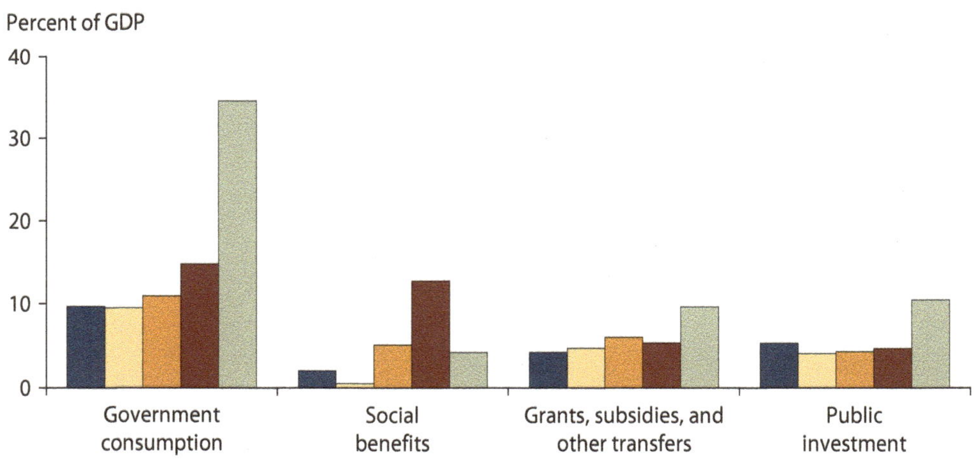

Sources: Original figure for this publication based on Government Finance Statistics, International Monetary Fund (IMF), https://data360.worldbank.org/en/int/dataset/IMF_GFSMAB; World Economic Outlook (WEO), IMF, https://www.imf.org/en/publications/sprolls/world-economic-outlook-databases.

Note: The East Asia average includes Cambodia, Indonesia, Lao PDR, Malaysia, Mongolia, the Philippines, and Thailand. Pacific Islands include Fiji and Kiribati. For Kiribati, public investment is obtained by taking the difference between WEO's primary expenditure and the operational expenditure at the general government level. Consumption refers to compensation of employees and the use of goods and services by the government. HICs = high-income countries; LICs = low-income countries; MICs = middle-income countries.

Government consumption tends to increase only modestly with income, suggesting that a large expansion of the public sector has not accompanied the region's economic development (refer to figure 1.18). Across the global sample, the relationship between income and government consumption is relatively weak, with the fitted trend showing only a gradual increase in consumption as economies become richer. At comparable levels of income, East Asian economies tend to have lower government consumption than many other countries.

Patterns within the region also reflect different stages of development. In lower-income economies such as Cambodia, government consumption increased between the 2000–07 and 2010–19 periods, rising from about 7.9 percent to roughly 10.5 percent of GDP as governments expanded the provision of basic

Government consumption increases only modestly with income and remains contained in many East Asian economies, despite rising income levels.

FIGURE 1.18 Government consumption and income, East Asian economies and comparators

a. Government consumption vs. income, East Asia and Pacific and comparators, 2000–22

b. Government consumption, East Asia, 2000–19

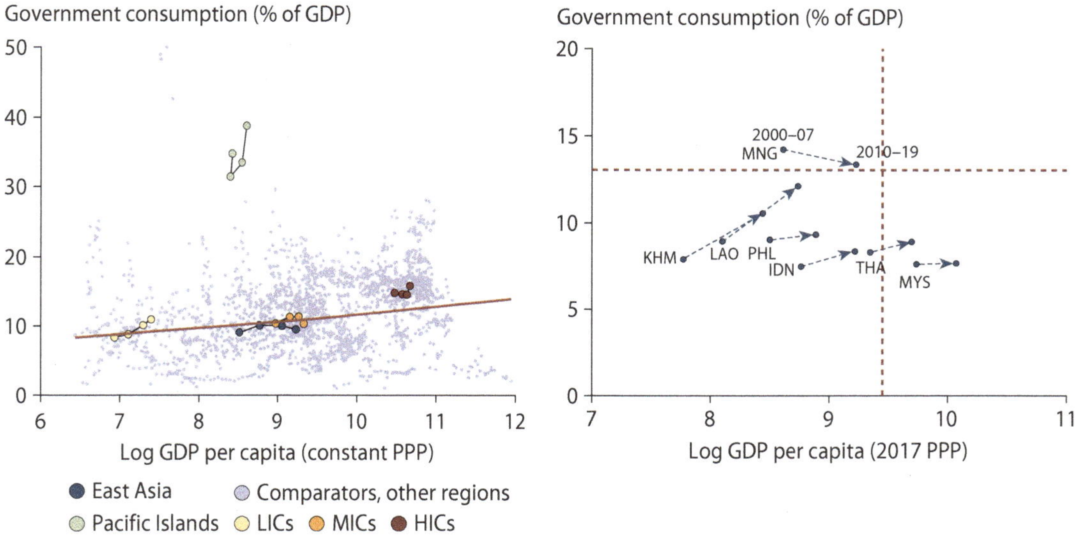

Sources: Original figure for this publication based on Government Finance Statistics, International Monetary Fund (IMF), https://data360.worldbank.org/en/int/dataset/IMF_GFSMAB; World Economic Outlook, IMF, https://www.imf.org/en/publications/sprolls/world-economic-outlook-databases.

Note: Government consumption includes compensation of employees and the use of goods and services. East Asia average includes Cambodia, Indonesia, Lao PDR, Malaysia, Mongolia, the Philippines, and Thailand. HICs = high-income countries; LICs = low-income countries; MICs = middle-income countries; PPP = purchasing power parity.

public services. In contrast, in more advanced economies such as Malaysia, government consumption has remained broadly stable as a share of GDP (about 7 percent) over the same period, despite rising income levels. Other upper-middle-income countries show similar patterns, suggesting that many governments have deliberately contained the expansion of government consumption despite rising income levels.

Low government consumption reflects deliberate efforts to contain recurrent spending. In many economies, governments have sought to limit the expansion of administrative expenditures and the public wage bill while maintaining fiscal discipline and prioritizing investment in infrastructure and other growth-enhancing areas. This pattern is consistent with what this report refers to as a growth-enabling approach, whereby relatively small governments seek to support economic development by focusing public resources on investment while keeping recurrent spending contained.

Limited spending on social protection and human capital

Social benefits are extremely limited in the region and represent one of the main factors explaining the relatively small size of the government (refer to figure 1.19). Between 2000 and 2022, East Asia averaged just 1.8 percent of GDP in social benefit spending—less than half the middle-income country average of 4.8 percent, and less than one-seventh of the 12.7 percent recorded in high-income countries. No other spending category shows a gap of this magnitude relative to income peers.

The region also shows wide variation in social benefits. Mongolia stands apart, with a comprehensive social protection system—including near-universal pensions, child money transfers, and disability benefits—that reflects the legacy of a Soviet-era welfare state sustained by mining revenues (World Bank 2025d). Although social protection systems in other countries, including Cambodia, Indonesia, the Philippines, Thailand, and Viet Nam, have expanded significantly over the past decade, they remain modest relative to the scale of informality and vulnerability in each country. Consequently, social protection systems in several countries still play a relatively limited role in mitigating income shocks and supporting inclusive growth (World Bank 2021, 2023b, 2025b).

Social benefits in East Asia remain significantly lower than in high- and middle-income countries.

FIGURE 1.19 Government spending on social benefits: East Asia, the Pacific Islands, and comparators, 2000–22

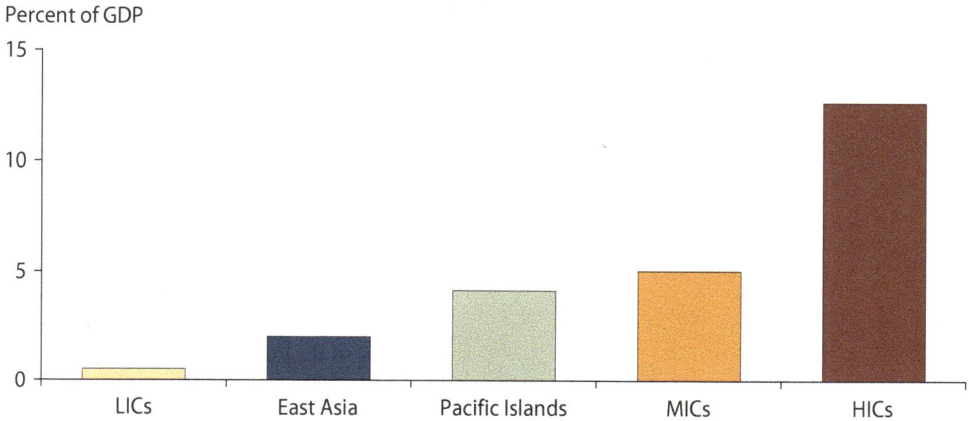

Sources: Original figure for this publication based on Government Finance Statistics, International Monetary Fund (IMF), https://data360.worldbank.org/en/int/dataset/IMF_GFSMAB; World Economic Outlook, IMF, https://www.imf.org/en/publications/sprolls/world-economic-outlook-databases.
Note: HICs = high-income countries; LICs = low-income countries; MICs = middle-income countries.

Human capital spending also remains relatively low across much of the region, particularly in East Asian economies, where expenditures on education and health lag those of middle- and high-income countries (refer to figure 1.20). Malaysia leads East Asian economies, spending close to 8 percent of GDP on health and education combined; Cambodia and Indonesia sit at the bottom, allocating just 2–3 percent of GDP. Viet Nam has invested heavily in education, raising its education budget from 3.3 percent of GDP in 2000 to 5.7 percent in 2013, moving it close to meeting its statutory target of allocating 20 percent of total government spending to education (Afkar et al. 2023; World Bank 2022b). The Philippines spends about 4.0 percent of GDP on education and 4.4 percent on health—above the regional average—yet records a Human Capital Index of just 0.52, pointing to deep efficiency and governance challenges rather than a simple resource gap (World Bank 2024e).

The "growth-enabling" fiscal approach in East Asia has come at the cost of lower investment in human capital, whereas structural factors in Pacific Island countries mean that they continue to face significant human capital spending needs despite relatively large public spending.

FIGURE 1.20 Spending on human capital, EAP and comparators, 2000–22

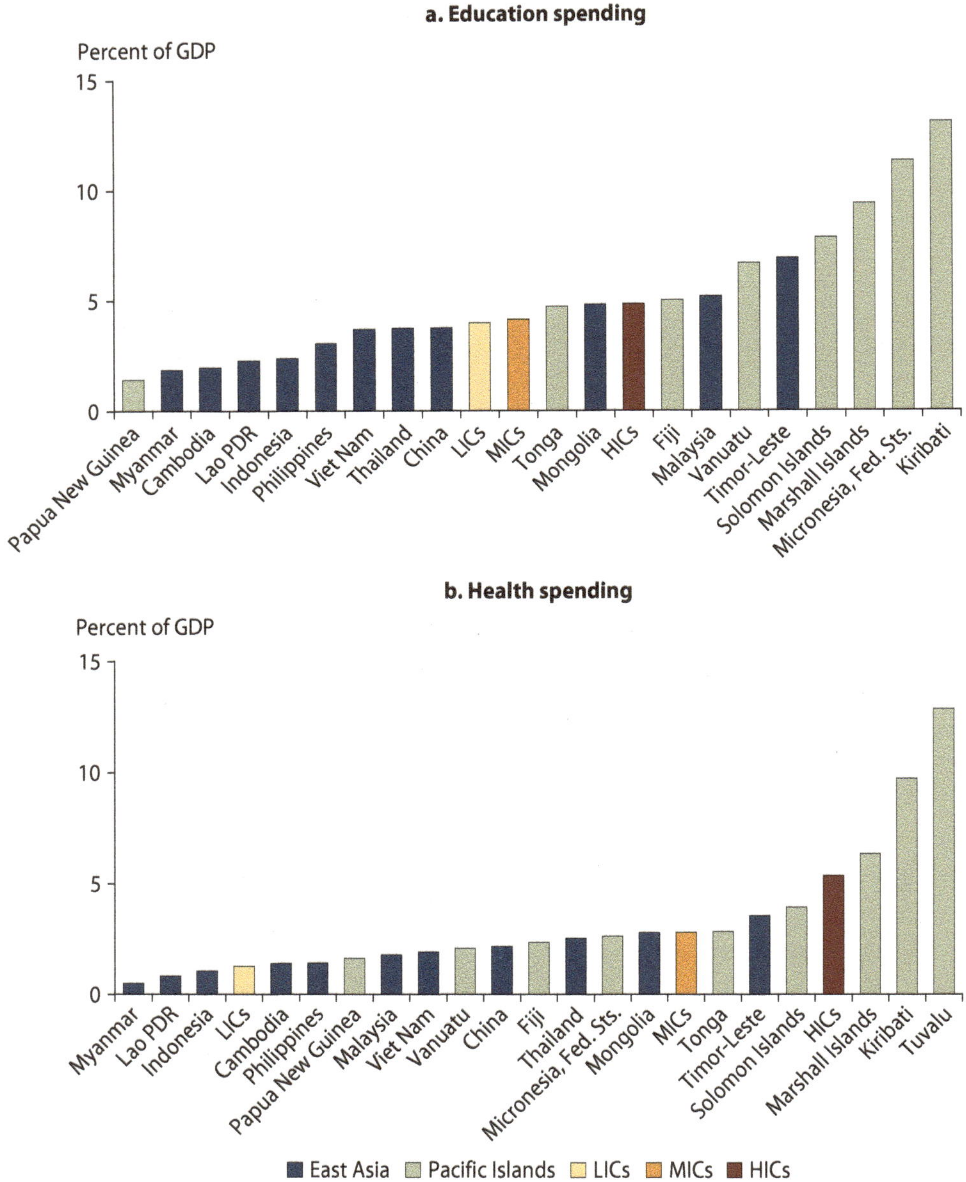

Source: Original figure for this publication based on World Development Indicators, World Bank, https://datatopics.worldbank.org/world-development-indicators/.

Note: EAP = East Asia and Pacific; HICs = high-income countries; LICs = low-income countries; MICs = middle-income countries.

Spending on health and social protection has gradually increased across EAP, but education spending has declined as a share of GDP in many economies (refer to figure 1.21). Health spending has edged upward, rising from 1.4 percent of GDP in 2000–07 to 1.6 percent in 2010–19. Social protection has also grown modestly, from 1.2 to 1.3 percent of GDP over the same period. Spending on education, however, has moved in the opposite direction. The regional average fell from 3.6 percent of GDP in 2000–07 to 3.2 percent in 2010–19, a decline that widened EAP's already significant gap relative to the global average of 4.5 percent. During the COVID-19 pandemic, the pressure intensified: education budgets declined as a share of GDP in half of EAP countries between 2017–19 and 2020–21, with Fiji, Myanmar, and Tuvalu recording the sharpest contractions (World Bank 2023b).

Whereas government spending on health and social protection has increased over time in EAP, government spending on education has declined.

FIGURE 1.21 Evolution of government spending, by function, EAP, 2000–22

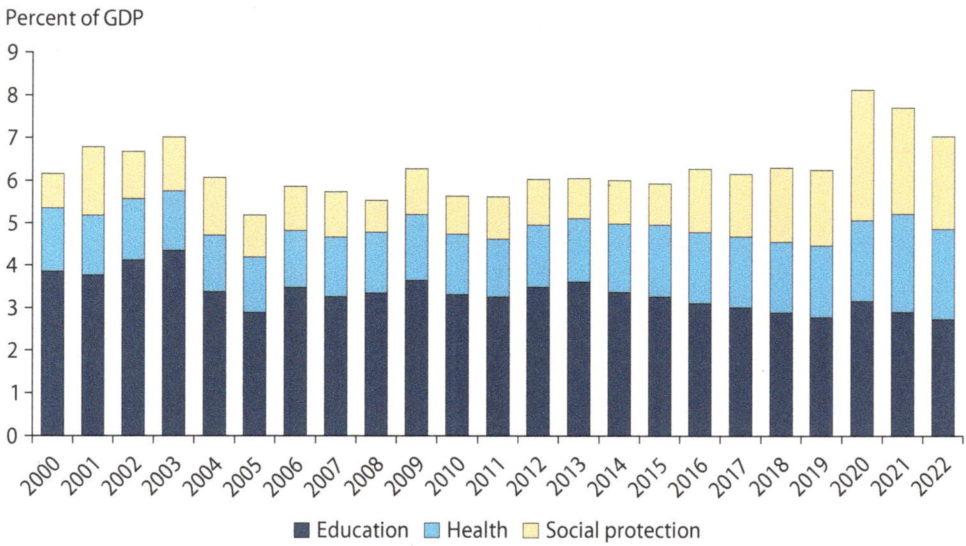

Sources: Original figure for this publication based on Government Finance Statistics (GFS), International Monetary Fund (IMF), https://data360.worldbank.org/en/int/dataset/IMF_GFSMAB; World Development Indicators (WDI), World Bank, https://datatopics.worldbank.org/world-development-indicators/.

Note: Health and education spending data come from WDI; social protection data come from GFS. Average includes Cambodia, Indonesia, Lao PDR, Malaysia, Mongolia, Myanmar, the Philippines, Thailand, and Viet Nam. Because of data availability, social protection average includes only Indonesia, the Philippines, and Thailand. EAP = East Asia and Pacific.

Most economies in the region continue to spend less on health and education than countries at similar income levels, diverging from the global pattern in which human capital investment rises with income (refer to figure 1.22). Consequently, a child born in developing EAP is expected to be only 52 percent as productive as one with full education and health, below the averages in developing Europe and Central Asia and in Latin America and the Caribbean (World Bank 2020a).

Overall, relatively low levels of public spending on health, education, and social protection have important implications for growth in the region. Even as spending on health and social protection has increased in recent decades, overall investment in human capital remains below that observed in countries at comparable income levels. Limited investment in these areas can slow the accumulation of human capital and constrain productivity gains over the long term. As EAP economies continue to grow

Although government spending on health and education has risen with income, most EAP countries continue to lag in human capital investment.

FIGURE 1.22 Human capital and income, EAP and comparators, 2000–22

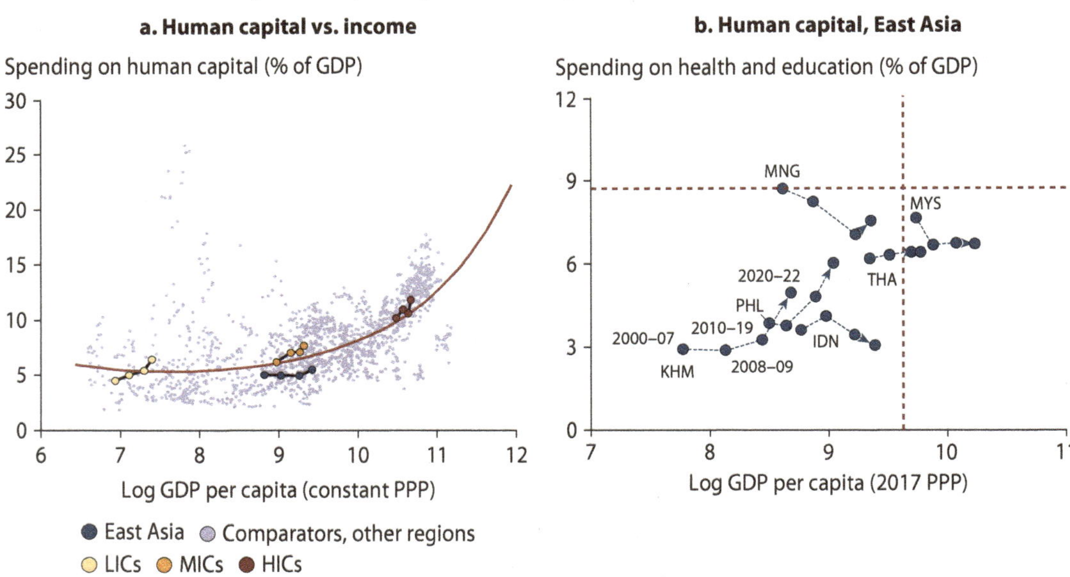

Sources: Original figure for this publication based on World Development Indicators, World Bank, https://datatopics.worldbank.org/world-development-indicators/; World Economic Outlook Database, International Monetary Fund, https://www.imf.org/en/publications/sprolls/world-economic-outlook-databases.

Note: Human capital refers to health and education spending. The sample includes LICs, MICs, and HICs. EAP includes Cambodia, Indonesia, Malaysia, the Philippines, and Thailand. In panels a and b, the dots represent averages for the following periods: 2000–07, 2008–09, 2010–19, and 2020–22. The intersecting dashed lines in panel b indicate the medians for the respective variables over the last period. For a list of country codes, refer to https://www.iso.org/obp/ui/#search. EAP = East Asia and Pacific; HICs = high-income countries; LICs = low-income countries; MICs = middle-income countries; PPP = purchasing power parity.

and transition to more skill-intensive production structures, strengthening investment in human capital and social protection will become increasingly important to support sustained productivity growth.

High and often inefficient subsidies

Governments often use subsidies to address market failures, support specific sectors, or protect vulnerable households. In practice, however, subsidies are often poorly targeted and can disproportionately benefit higher-income households. Universal price subsidies for energy, food, or transportation tend to allocate a large share of their benefits to wealthier households that consume more of the subsidized goods. Consequently, subsidies frequently deliver limited progressivity while absorbing significant fiscal resources.

In the region, subsidies represent a nonnegligible share of public spending, further limiting fiscal space for productive spending. Indonesia and Malaysia have higher subsidy outlays than most regional peers, reflecting the prominence of energy and fuel support schemes. By contrast, in economies such as Cambodia, the Philippines, and Thailand, subsidy spending remains comparatively lower and more contained (refer to figure 1.23). As discussed in chapter 3, these subsidies are often inefficient, with their distributional incidence frequently skewed to higher-income households.

Once introduced, subsidies tend to become permanent and fiscally costly. Governments adopt many subsidies in response to temporary shocks such as increases in food or energy prices, but political economy constraints can make removing subsidies challenging once they are in place. Over time, this persistence can generate significant fiscal costs, especially when subsidies reduce the price of goods or services for a broad share of the population. These expenditures limit fiscal space that could otherwise be directed to more productive spending priorities.

Several EAP economies have both fiscally costly and highly inefficient subsidy programs. In 2022, blanket fuel subsidies alone in Malaysia amounted to RM 52 billion, equivalent to about 2.9 percent of GDP and accounting for 56 percent of total subsidy spending. These subsidies are highly regressive, with the richest 20 percent of households receiving about 53 percent of the benefits (World Bank 2023e). Indonesia spent, on average, 2.3 percent of GDP on subsidies between 2000 and 2022. Evidence also suggests that subsidy programs have suffered from weak targeting. For example, reforms to electricity subsidies removed 19.4 million non-poor households from the list of beneficiaries, indicating that a large share of benefits had previously accrued to households outside the intended target group (World Bank 2020c).

In EAP, subsidies account for a relatively large share of GDP, particularly in Indonesia and Malaysia.

FIGURE 1.23 Subsidies as a share of GDP, selected EAP economies and comparators, 2000–22

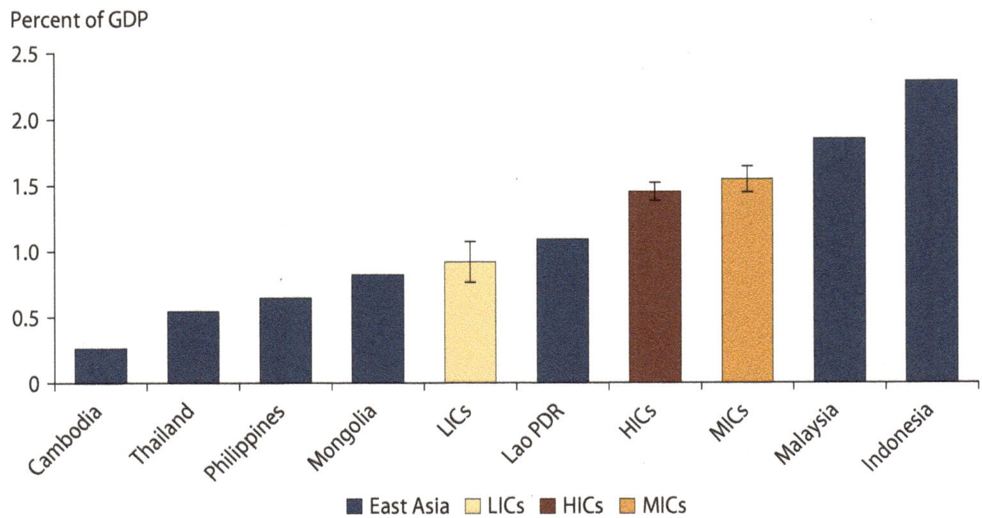

Source: Original figure for this publication based on Government Finance Statistics, International Monetary Fund, https://data360.worldbank.org/en/int/dataset/IMF_GFSMAB.
Note: Error bars represent 90 percent confidence intervals around the mean. EAP = East Asia and Pacific; HICs = high-income countries; LICs = low-income countries; MICs = middle-income countries.

Subsidies often distort economic incentives by modifying relative prices. When governments subsidize a particular good, input, or sector, they reduce its relative price and encourage higher consumption or production than would otherwise occur. Doing so can lead to inefficient allocation of resources and shift economic activity to subsidized uses rather than those with the highest productivity. Evidence from the Philippines illustrates these distortions in agriculture. Although rice accounts for about 20 percent of the value of agricultural production, public support for rice represented about 57 percent of the budget of major agricultural programs and roughly 22 percent of the total budget of the Department of Agriculture in 2022 (World Bank 2023d).

Taken together, these examples illustrate a fiscal trap: subsidy programs absorb substantial resources, deliver limited distributional benefits, distort economic incentives, and crowd out more productive spending, yet they are politically difficult to unwind once in place. Reforming subsidies can therefore play an important role in improving the efficiency and equity of public spending while creating fiscal space for more productive investments. In practice, subsidy reform can take several forms, including repurposing subsidies to more effective objectives, reforming them to improve targeting, replacing them with more efficient policy instruments such as targeted transfers, or removing them altogether when they no longer serve a clear policy purpose (refer to chapter 4).

Although EAP governments generally spend less as a share of GDP relative to economies at comparable income levels in other regions, the footprint of the state in the region's economies extends well beyond the fiscal budget. State-owned enterprises (SOEs)—and, in some countries, local government financing vehicles and other quasi-fiscal entities—represent a substantial share of economic activity.[9] Viet Nam has among the highest SOE revenues relative to GDP in the world, equivalent to approximately 38 percent of GDP, with SOEs holding near-monopoly positions in sectors such as fertilizer, cement, and energy (de Nicola et al. 2025; World Bank 2023a). In China, SOEs' share of industrial assets declined from nearly 69 percent in 1998 to about 42 percent in the early 2010s, but SOEs still play a central role in electricity, petroleum, aviation, banking, and telecommunications (World Bank 2014a). Off-budget entities, including local government financing vehicles and extrabudgetary funds, add a further layer of state presence. In Indonesia, approximately 150 SOEs—but primarily the 22 largest—contribute an estimated 15–40 percent of GDP (World Bank 2023a). In Malaysia and Singapore, state holding companies (Khazanah Nasional and Temasek, respectively) maintain controlling stakes in several state-linked corporations, with Temasek-linked firms representing about 12 percent of Singapore's GDP and 20 percent of its stock exchange market capitalization (OECD 2011). This broader presence of the state falls outside the analytical scope of this report but is an important complement to the fiscal picture.

From growth enabling to growth enhancing: What needs to change

The case for change rests on three converging pressures: the productivity imperative, mounting human capital deficits, and forward-looking investment needs in infrastructure, climate resilience, and demographic adaptation. Each reflects a gap that the growth-enabling approach did not close and that the region's next development stage cannot afford to leave open.

The growth-enabling approach, investment, and growth

The growth-enabling approach rests on two reinforcing pillars: low tax burdens and substantial public investment. Both shape private investment and long-term growth, but they do so through different channels and with different empirical implications. On the one hand, corporate taxation affects growth by influencing firms' investment and employment decisions and by shaping firm entry and formality, with stronger effects in EMDEs, which have high tax sensitivity and informality (refer to box 1.4). On the other hand, public investment supports growth by crowding in private investment, with stronger effects in countries with larger capital gaps and better institutions (Francois et al. 2026).

Box 1.4. Corporate taxation and firms' behavior in emerging market and developing economies

Corporate taxation affects firms along two margins: how much they invest, hire, and produce (the intensive margin) and whether they operate formally at all (the extensive margin). On the intensive margin, higher corporate taxes raise production costs and reduce expected returns, inducing firms to scale back employment, wages, and capital spending. Evidence from Chile suggests that the labor-demand response is significantly stronger among large corporations and that capital demand is more responsive among small firms (Cerda and Larrain 2010). Because large firms account for a disproportionate share of formal employment and value added, stronger labor responses among these firms can translate into sizable aggregate effects on job creation, productivity, and growth.

Firms in emerging market and developing economies are generally more responsive to corporate taxation than firms in advanced economies. Estimated taxable profit elasticities for Organisation for Economic Co-operation and Development economies are relatively low; by contrast, Bachas and Soto (2021) estimate elasticities of 3–5 for Costa Rica, and Garriga and Scot (2023) and Lediga et al. (2019) report elasticities of approximately 7.4 for Lithuania and 1.3 for South Africa.

On the extensive margin, higher taxes can render formal operation unprofitable for marginal firms, inducing informality or exit and discouraging new firm entry (Waseem 2018). In East Asia and Pacific, where informality already constrains personal income tax and value added tax performance, this effect has particular relevance: policies that push marginal firms out of the formal sector narrow the tax base precisely where it is already thin.

Taxation and growth

The evidence suggests a negative impact of taxation on investment and growth.[10] On average, tax increases equivalent to 1 percent of GDP reduce output by approximately 2–3 percent over three years, with larger effects in EMDEs (refer to table 1.1); however, this aggregate result masks important heterogeneity across tax instruments. Increases in direct taxes, particularly in CITs, are associated with meaningful declines in investment, firm entry, and foreign direct investment inflows. A 10-percentage-point increase in the effective CIT rate reduces the investment-to-GDP ratio by roughly 2 percentage points (Djankov et al. 2010), with the effect amplified among financially constrained firms and in economies with weaker institutions. By contrast, indirect tax increases have a considerably smaller growth cost. A 1-percentage-point increase in VAT rates is associated with a negligible—and in some specifications, near-zero or slightly positive—effect on GDP per capita growth (refer to figure 1.24).

TABLE 1.1 Empirical evidence on taxation, private investment, and growth

Paper	Methodology	Identification strategy	Main quantitative result
Romer and Romer (2010)	Narrative time-series (United States)	Historical classification of legislated tax changes by motivation; isolates exogenous tax shocks	A tax increase of 1% of GDP reduces real GDP by about 2–3% over three years; investment declines substantially.
Cloyne (2013)	Narrative time-series (United Kingdom)	Historical classification of discretionary tax changes by motivation; isolates exogenous tax shocks	A tax increase of 1% of GDP reduces output by roughly 2–3% at peak, with sizable declines in consumption and investment.
Dabla-Norris and Lima (2018)	Multicountry narrative panel (OECD)	Narrative identification of exogenous tax rate and base changes during fiscal consolidations	Tax increases reduce output and private investment, with larger effects during economic downturns.
Djankov et al. (2010)	Cross-country firm-level data set (85 countries)	Variation in effective corporate tax rates across countries; controls for institutional and macro factors	A 10-percentage-point increase in the effective corporate tax rate reduces the investment-to-GDP ratio by roughly 2 percentage points and lowers business entry.
Klemm and Van Parys (2012)	Cross-country panel (Latin America and the Caribbean, Sub-Saharan Africa)	Variation in statutory CIT rates and tax holidays; country and time fixed effects	Lower CIT rates and longer tax holidays are associated with higher FDI inflows, though fiscal costs are significant.
Cevik and Miryugin (2018)	Cross-country firm-level dataset (five ASEAN countries)	Within-firm variation in effective corporate tax rates; firm and country controls	Moderate levels of taxation do not appear to constrain business investment, but the relationship becomes negative as tax burdens rise.

Source: Original table for this publication.
Note: ASEAN = Association of Southeast Asian Nations; CIT = corporate income tax; FDI = foreign direct investment; OECD = Organisation for Economic Co-Operation and Development.

Low tax rates and generous tax incentives are associated with stronger FDI inflows; increases in VAT rates have a negligible effect on growth.

FIGURE 1.24 Impacts of taxation on FDI and growth

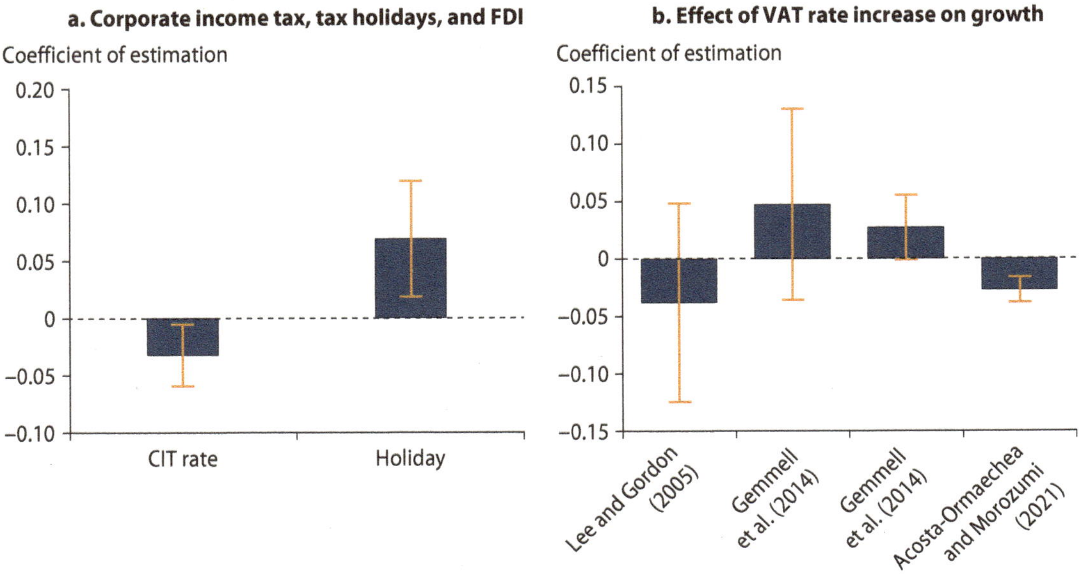

Sources: Original figure for this publication based on Acosta-Ormaechea and Morozumi 2021; Gemmell et al. 2014; Klemm and Van Parys 2012; Lee and Gordon 2005.

Note: In panel a, the first bar indicates that a 10-percentage-point increase in the CIT rate decreases FDI by 0.32 percentage point; the second bar shows that increasing tax holidays by 10 years increases FDI by 0.7 percentage point of GDP. In panel b, the first bar indicates that a 1-percentage-point increase in the VAT rate reduces GDP per capita growth by 0.04 percentage point; the second and third bars indicate that a 1-percentage-point increase in the VAT rate increases growth by 0.05 and 0.03 percentage point, respectively; the last bar shows that a 1-percentage-point increase in the VAT rate reduces GDP per capita growth by 0.03 percentage point. CIT = corporate income tax; FDI = foreign direct investment; VAT = value added tax.

The experience of individual EAP economies reflects these patterns. In upper-middle-income economies such as Indonesia, Malaysia, and Thailand, moderate and predictable corporate tax burdens have been consistent with sustained private investment (Cevik and Miryugin 2018). In Cambodia and Viet Nam, strong investment performance has also been shaped by export-oriented industrialization and integration into global value chains, alongside targeted fiscal incentives. By contrast, in economies facing deeper structural constraints—such as Lao PDR, Mongolia, Myanmar, and Pacific Island countries—investment outcomes are shaped more by institutional capacity, macroeconomic stability, and geographic factors than by tax policy alone. The Philippines' recent corporate tax reform, reducing the headline CIT rate while rationalizing incentives, illustrates how shifting a distortionary tax structure to a more enabling one can improve the investment environment even as the overall revenue effort rises.

Evidence from other regions points to a similar conclusion. In Latin America and the Caribbean, lower CIT rates and longer tax holidays are associated with higher foreign direct investment inflows, whereas comparable incentives appear to have little effect in Sub-Saharan Africa. This contrast suggests that the effectiveness of tax incentives depends critically on the broader investment environment, including infrastructure quality, institutional capacity, and macroeconomic stability (Klemm and Van Parys 2012).

Public investment and growth

Recent evidence shows that public investment crowds in private investment. On average, an additional dollar of public investment is associated with US$1.60 in additional private investment across EMDEs (Francois et al. 2026). The crowding-in effect is strongest in countries with larger capital gaps and more robust institutions, underscoring that the growth dividend of public investment depends critically on governance quality. A public investment shock equivalent to 1 percent of GDP is associated with an increase in real GDP of about 1.2 percent over a five-year horizon, with larger effects during recessions and in economies with greater fiscal space (Adarov et al. 2024; Furceri and Li 2017; Miyamoto et al. 2018). Moreover, the effects appear larger in countries with wider infrastructure gaps, consistent with higher marginal returns to public capital where infrastructure stocks remain relatively underdeveloped (Barro 1990).

Overall, the evidence suggests that low tax burdens, combined with sustained public investment in infrastructure, have played an important role in supporting job creation, crowding in private investment, and sustaining long-term growth in EAP economies with strong fundamentals. The experience of several upper-middle-income economies in East Asia illustrates how infrastructure investment, anchored in macroeconomic stability and relatively strong state capacity, can foster private sector dynamism and durable growth. By contrast, in lower-middle-income economies and Pacific Island countries, infrastructure gaps remain substantially larger, implying potentially higher marginal returns to additional public investment, provided it is accompanied by strengthened institutional capacity, sound public investment management, and fiscal sustainability.

But crowding in private capital is not the same as raising productivity—and it is the productivity gap, not the infrastructure gap, that now poses the binding constraint on the region's long-term growth.

The productivity imperative

EAP's growth has been driven overwhelmingly by factor accumulation, not productivity gains. In EAP excluding China, capital accumulation has contributed

2–4 percentage points to output growth throughout the past five decades (refer to figure 1.25). The contribution of total factor productivity has been declining and remains modest: from 1.3 percentage points in 2000–05, it fell to just 0.1 percentage point in 2010–15 before recovering slightly to 0.4 percentage point in 2015–23. The contribution of hours worked has also diminished as populations age, from 1.4 percentage points in 1970–75 to 0.4 percentage point in 2015–23.

China has had a more dynamic productivity trajectory. Total factor productivity contributed 1.6 percentage points to output growth in 2015–23, which nonetheless represents a significant decline from averages above 3 percentage points during 1980–2010. Information and communication technology capital accumulation has contributed more in China (0.6 percentage point) than in the rest of the region (0.1 percentage point), reflecting China's more advanced digital economy. China now faces a shrinking labor force, however, with employment deducting 0.3 percentage point from output growth. Across the region, as capital deepening matures and labor supply tightens, sustaining growth will require the productivity improvements that have remained elusive.

A longer view: Capital accumulation, not productivity improvements, has driven recent growth in the region excluding China.

FIGURE 1.25 Drivers of GDP growth, EAP and China, 1970–2023

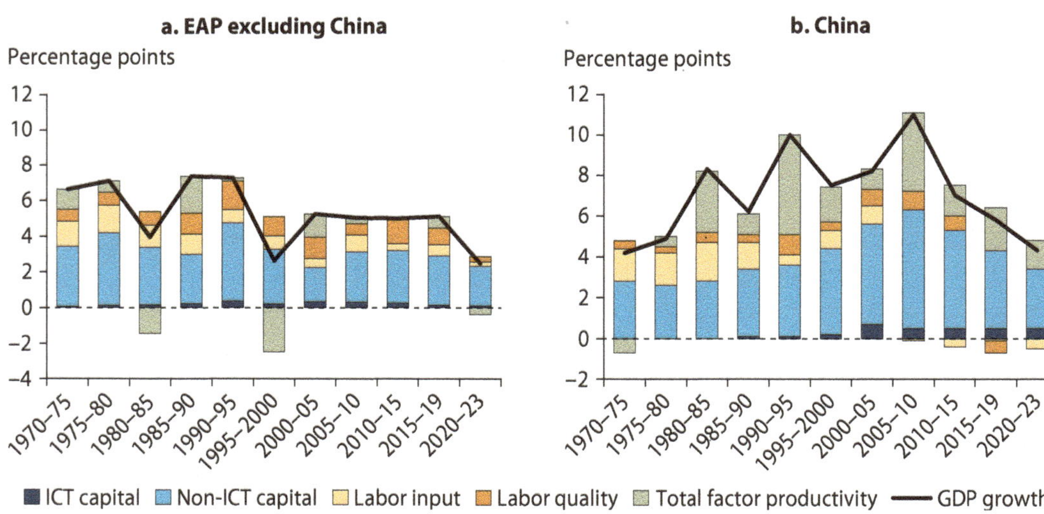

Source: Original figure for this publication based on APO 2025.

Note: Regional aggregates use APO (2025) GDP-weighted averages. EAP = East Asia and Pacific; ICT = information and communication technology.

The structural shift under way compounds the challenge. Jobs are no longer moving from agriculture to manufacturing but into low-productivity services, and firms in the digital economy are falling behind the global frontier. Raising productivity requires more than physical capital: it requires a workforce with foundational skills, higher-order cognitive capabilities, and good health. Fiscal policy that prioritizes infrastructure while underinvesting in education, health, and early childhood development cannot sustain the productivity-driven growth the region now needs.

Uneven human capital development

EAP has uneven human capital performance across countries and components. China, Malaysia, Mongolia, Thailand, and Viet Nam score relatively high on the World Bank Human Capital Index compared to other middle-income countries, whereas most other EAP economies, especially Pacific Island countries, score well below income-level expectations, pointing to large room for improvement (refer to figure 1.26, panel a). Learning outcomes tell a similar story: except for China and Viet Nam, EAP economies perform below the levels predicted by income per capita (refer to figure 1.26, panel b).

EAP's human capital edge lies in education, whereas the region trails on health (refer to figure 1.27). For example, Mongolia and Viet Nam overperform on education but underperform on health. Malaysia and Thailand show similar imbalances. Most other EAP economies underperform on both dimensions (refer to bottom-left quadrant of figure 1.27). Cambodia, Lao PDR, Myanmar, Papua New Guinea, and Timor-Leste are among the weakest, and Indonesia and the Philippines fare relatively worse in education than in health. China's Human Capital Index stands out, with both education and health outcomes approaching high-income benchmarks.

Notwithstanding the relative edge in education, absolute endowments remain weak in many economies. For example, Viet Nam's high performance in primary and secondary education contrasts with the relative weakness of its tertiary education. In other EAP economies, the low quality of basic education, which results in weak foundational skills, also constrains the contribution of education to human capital. In 14 of the region's 22 middle-income economies, more than half of 10-year-olds cannot read and understand age-appropriate reading material (Afkar et al. 2023). Even in Malaysia and the Philippines, only 24 percent and 16 percent of 15-year-olds, respectively, leave high school with basic literacy and numeracy skills (OECD 2023).[11] Moreover, although many EAP economies have stepped up their efforts to expand tertiary education over the last two decades, the college-educated workforce shares remain below one-third, with an even lower share of graduates in science, technology, engineering, and mathematics fields (World Bank 2025e).

EAP economies generally lag on human capital and score below other countries at similar income levels on learning outcomes. China and Viet Nam lead the region; Malaysia, Mongolia, and Thailand are catching up but face a wider gap.

FIGURE 1.26 Human capital outcomes, EAP economies and comparators

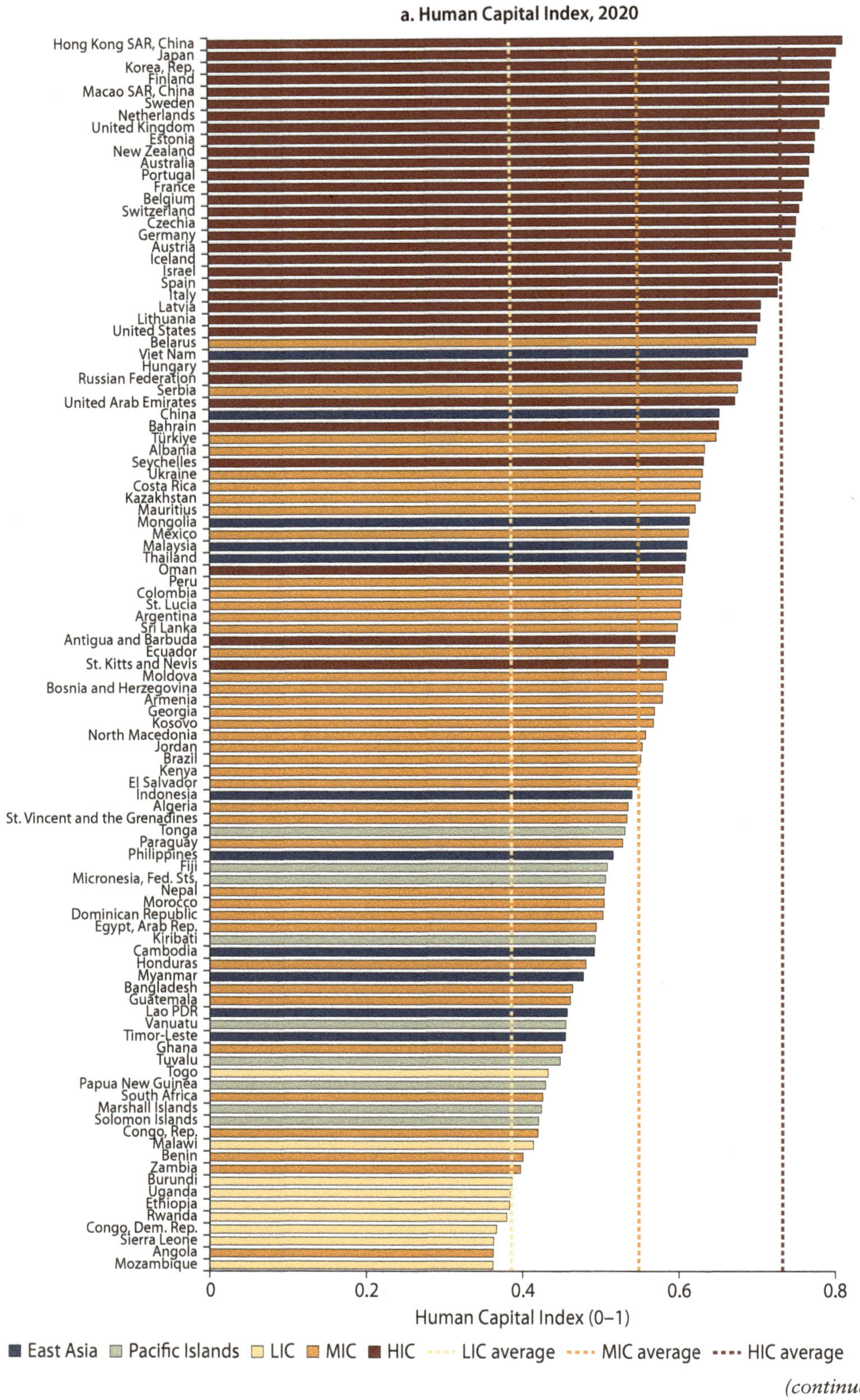

(continued)

FIGURE 1.26 Human capital outcomes, EAP economies and comparators *(continued)*

b. PISA scores vs. income, 2018

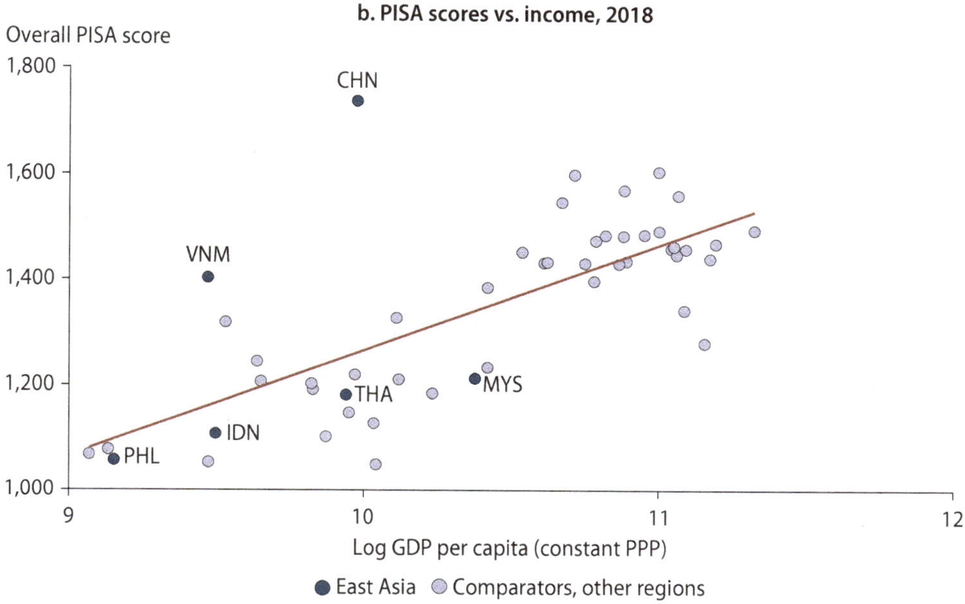

Sources: Original figure for this publication based on Education Statistics, World Bank, https://datatopics.worldbank.org/education/; World Economic Outlook Database, Intenational Monetary Fund, https://www.imf.org/en/publications/sprolls/world-economic-outlook-databases.

Note: The Human Capital Index measures how productive a child born today will be as a future worker relative to the benchmark full health and complete education. For a list of country codes, refer to https://www.iso.org/obp/ui/#search. EAP = East Asia and Pacific; PISA = Programme for International Student Assessment; PPP = purchasing power parity.

In health, EAP faces a two-dimensional challenge that prevents people from preserving their human capital while living longer and healthier lives (Debebe et al. 2026). First, although most economies in the region have achieved significant progress in maternal and child health and nutrition outcomes, some still struggle. In Cambodia, Lao PDR, Timor-Leste, and most Pacific Island countries, the levels of child and maternal mortality remain elevated relative to comparator economies. Second, all EAP economies face an increasing burden of noncommunicable diseases (NCDs) such as hypertension, diabetes, and cardiovascular disease among the adult population. The likelihood of premature death (at ages 30–70) due to NCDs exceeds 30 percent in some EAP economies. The NCD burden affects economies like Mongolia and some Pacific Island countries (such as Fiji and Tonga) more severely than others like China and Thailand. Poor quality of health care accounts for one-third of avoidable mortality in EAP, with low quality of primary care leading to poor management of NCD conditions and high rates of preventable hospitalization (Bales et al. 2022; Kruk et al. 2018).

EAP economies have uneven human capital outcomes, with some economies such as Mongolia and Viet Nam overperforming in education but lagging in health, others underperforming in both, and China approaching high-income standards in both dimensions.

FIGURE 1.27 Education and health components of the Human Capital Index Plus, EAP and comparators, circa 2024

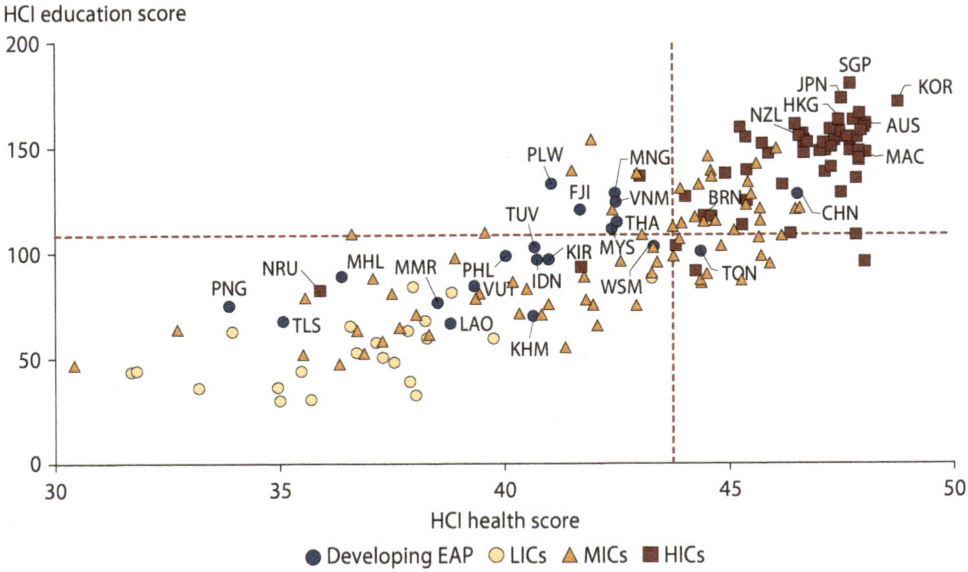

Sources: Original figure for this publication based on Human Capital Index Plus, World Bank, https://humancapital.worldbank.org/hciplus/.

Note: Education refers to years of schooling a child can expect to complete by age 18, quality of schooling captured by Harmonized Learning Outcomes, and the share of people ages 25–29 who complete tertiary education. Health refers to adult survival rate, ages 15–60, and the fraction of children under 5 who are not stunted. Both are components of the Human Capital Index Plus (HCI+), which combines 11 outcomes on health, education, and on-the-job learning (omitted from the figure) and how each of these outcomes affects earnings. Improvements in the HCI+ can be directly interpreted as improvements in lifetime earnings of workers and long-run GDP. In panel a, each component is weighted by its contribution to a total potential score of 238. A score of 0 reflects conditions under which human capital cannot develop: universal stunting, no schooling, and no employment prospects. For methodological details of the estimation, refer to HCI+ Methodology, World Bank, https://humancapital.worldbank.org/hciplus/methodology/. EAP = East Asia and Pacific; HCI = Human Capital Index; HICs = high-income countries; LICs = low-income countries; MICs = middle-income countries.

The link between human capital and long-run productivity is one of the most robust findings in development economics (refer to annex 1C). Endogenous growth models show that skill accumulation, knowledge creation, and innovation generate sustained productivity gains, and cross-country evidence links both educational attainment and cognitive skills to higher long-run growth rates. Micro-level studies further demonstrate strong causal returns to schooling in terms of individual earnings and productivity, providing a foundation for the macroeconomic relationship between human capital, technological upgrading, and structural transformation.

Consistent with that evidence, expanding the supply of skills can enable a transition to higher value-added manufacturing and services, and raise productivity. This dynamic has underpinned the successful transformations of high-income EAP economies such as the Republic of Korea and Singapore. In China, for example, the rapid expansion of tertiary education since the early 2000s has boosted firm productivity, exports, and innovation in skill-intensive sectors. Across the region, however, progress has been uneven; and, for many economies, the scale of underinvestment means the human capital gap will widen rather than close under current spending trajectories.

Looking ahead: Investment needs in EAP

The gaps in the current fiscal approach are not hypothetical. They take concrete form in four interconnected investment deficits—infrastructure, human capital, climate resilience, and demographic adaptation—each of which creates fiscal pressure and each of which the region is currently underprepared to meet.

Infrastructure

Physical connectivity gaps remain significant across the region and are holding back the next stage of growth. Paved road density in most EAP countries remains well below levels in developed economies, particularly outside major metropolitan corridors (refer to map 1.1). Limited road connectivity raises logistics costs and constrains firms' ability to access larger markets—consistent with a broad literature showing that infrastructure supports growth both by expanding productive capacity and by improving the spatial allocation of economic activity (Heblich et al. 2020). In Indonesia, infrastructure deficiencies contribute to logistics costs of about 15 percent of firms' total expenditure (Kasyanenko et al. 2023). In the Philippines, transportation and trade infrastructure weaknesses continue to limit competitiveness despite recent improvements.

Digital infrastructure gaps compound the physical ones. Mobile connectivity has expanded rapidly across the region, but disparities in broadband quality and connection speeds remain pronounced both within and across countries (refer to figure 1.28). Data center density—increasingly critical for cloud computing, digital services, and data-driven economic activity—remains low in most EAP economies relative to the demands of a modern digital economy.

EAP economies lag well behind advanced economies on paved roads per capita.

MAP 1.1 Global distribution of paved roads per capita

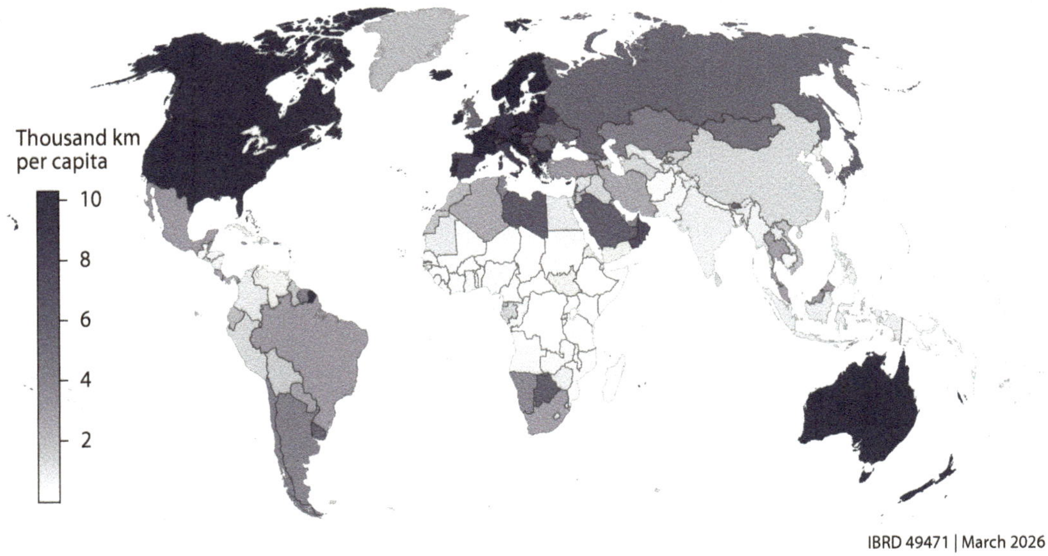

Source: Straub et al. 2026, map 2.2, panel a.

The returns to closing these gaps are high. Benefit-cost ratios for investments in energy and transportation exceed 1 in almost all EAP economies, meaning that additional investment passes a basic social rate-of-return threshold across virtually every economy in the region (refer to figure 1.29; Straub et al. 2026). Over 2016–30, baseline infrastructure investment needs remain substantial, at about 5 percent of GDP annually in East Asia and considerably higher in many Pacific Island countries, dominated by power and transportation (refer to figure 1.30; ADB 2017).

Infrastructure priorities vary across income levels (refer to figure 1.31). Lower-middle-income economies (Cambodia and Lao PDR) focus on expanding basic connectivity to integrate markets and reduce geographic disparities. Upper-middle-income countries (Malaysia) shift to network upgrading to support more integrated value chains, public transportation, and renewable energy. Pacific Island countries face a distinct challenge: geographic dispersion and climate vulnerability make connectivity, energy reliability, and climate-resilient design central to lowering trade costs and supporting private sector activity.

High-speed broadband is unevenly available within and across EAP countries.

FIGURE 1.28 Fixed and mobile broadband, EAP

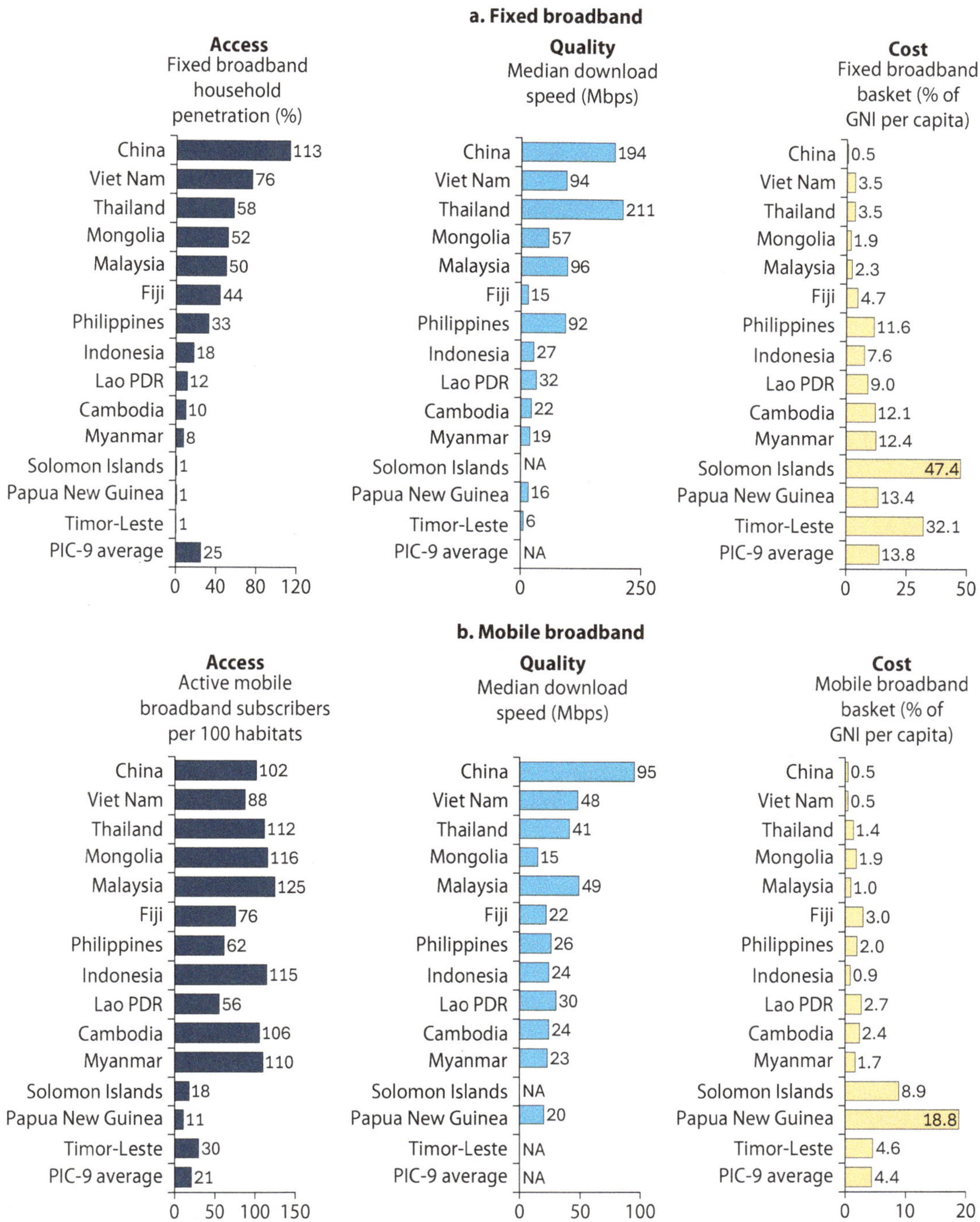

Source: World Bank 2025g, figure II.43.
Note: PIC-9 shows simple average of Kiribati, the Marshall Islands, the Federated States of Micronesia, Naoero, Palau, Samoa, Tonga, Tuvalu, and Vanuatu. GNI = gross national income; Mbps = megabits per second; NA = not available.

The benefits of further investments in energy and transportation exceed their costs in almost all EAP economies.

FIGURE 1.29 Benefit-cost ratios for investments in energy and transportation, selected EAP economies

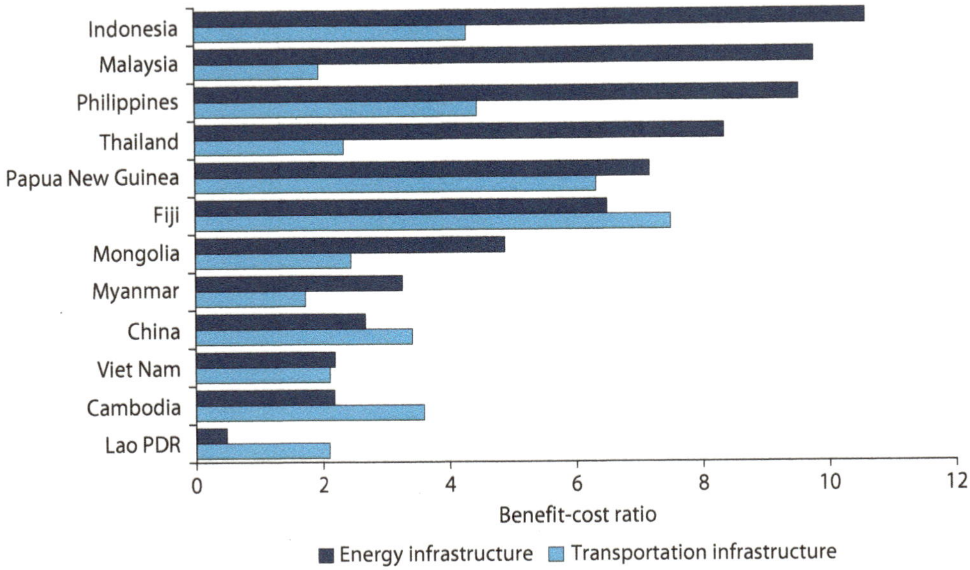

Source: Original figure for this publication based on Straub et al. 2026.
Note: Benefit-cost ratio, termed infrastructure efficiency ratio in Straub et al. (2026), denotes the social rates of return to investment divided by the country-specific borrowing costs and country-sector-specific depreciation. An efficiency ratio above 1 indicates additional investment is warranted, because it passes a basic benefit-cost threshold.

EAP economies have significant infrastructure investment needs.

FIGURE 1.30 Climate-adjusted estimated infrastructure investment needs

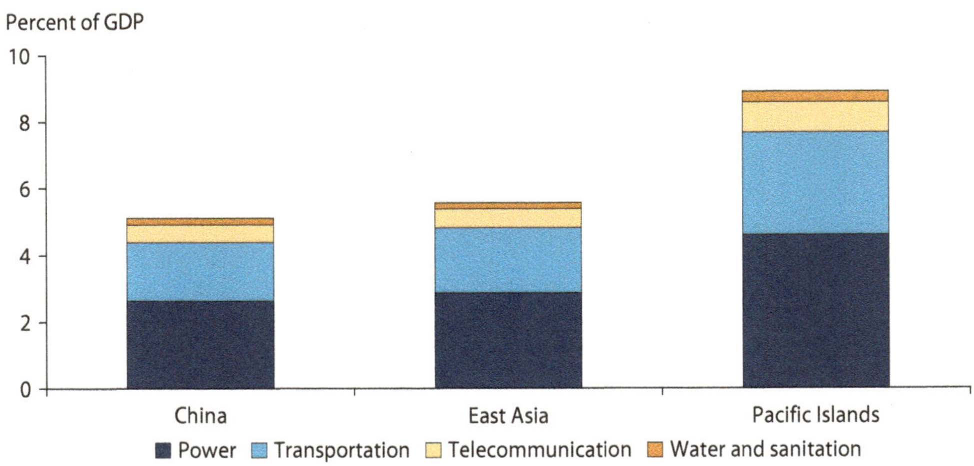

Source: Original figure for this publication based on Kasyanenko et al. 2023.
Note: Climate-adjusted estimated infrastructure investment needs.

As economies develop, infrastructure priorities shift from expanding access to upgrading networks and boosting productivity.

FIGURE 1.31 Infrastructure priorities

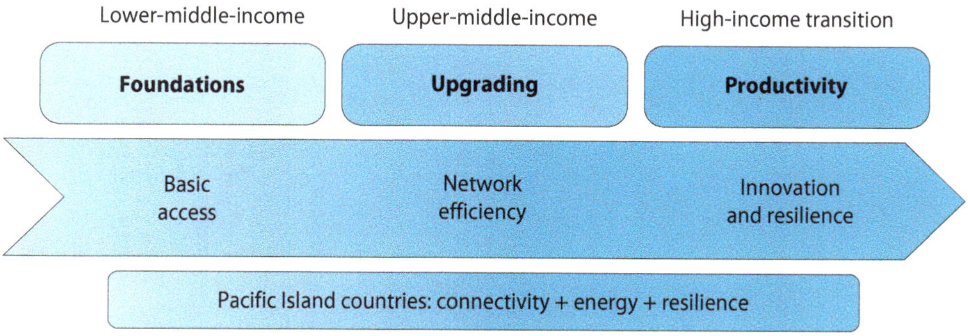

Source: Original figure for this publication.

Human capital

Human capital investment needs differ substantially across the region's income groups (refer to figure 1.32). In lower-middle-income economies (Cambodia, Lao PDR, Myanmar, the Philippines, and Timor-Leste) the priority is foundational: strengthening basic literacy and numeracy, improving teacher effectiveness, expanding early childhood development, and reinforcing primary health care. Although enrollment rates have risen substantially, learning poverty remains widespread, and COVID-19-related learning losses have not been fully recovered (Afkar et al. 2023). Viet Nam illustrates that strong foundational outcomes are achievable at lower income levels. Before the pandemic, Vietnamese students performed near the OECD average in mathematics and science despite income levels well below the OECD mean, reflecting sustained commitment to universal basic education, coherent curriculum standards, and teacher quality.

In upper-middle-income economies (China, Indonesia, Malaysia, and Thailand), the priority shifts to quality at secondary and tertiary levels, technical and vocational training, and the skills mismatches that constrain productivity upgrading. Despite near-universal basic enrollment, graduates' skills frequently diverge from labor market needs. Sustained investment in curriculum reform, university-industry linkages, digital skills, and lifelong learning will be critical as demographic transitions accelerate.

As economies develop, human capital investment must shift from building foundations to continuous skills upgrading.

FIGURE 1.32 Human capital investment priorities

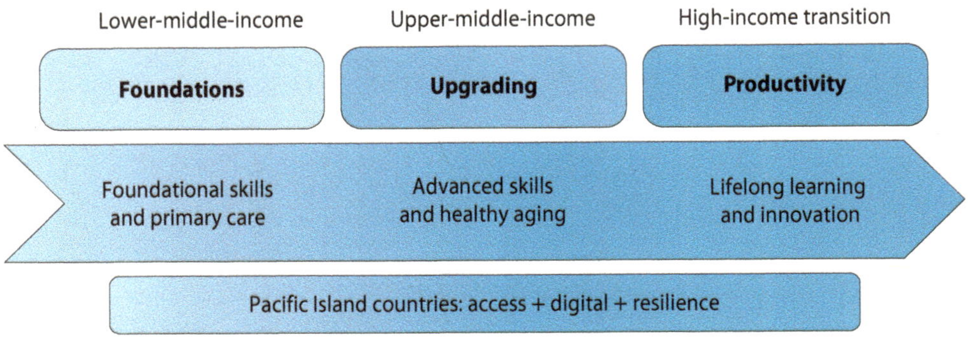

Source: Original figure for this publication.

In Pacific Island countries, foundational learning remains the priority, but investment needs are shaped by geographic dispersion—for example, in ensuring that qualified teachers are deployed and supported across outer islands, and that digital and distance learning platforms maintain schooling continuity during climate-related disruptions.

Across income groups, meeting these needs will require both additional fiscal space and improvements in spending efficiency. Within a framework historically characterized by low revenue mobilization and constrained social spending, sustaining higher human capital investment will require stronger domestic revenue collection and expenditure reprioritization.

Climate adaptation

Climate change introduces a macro-fiscal challenge largely absent from the traditional growth-enabling approach. The EAP region is particularly exposed, with more than half of annual global losses from natural disasters occurring there (refer to map 1.2; Eckstein et al. 2021). Without major adaptation efforts, coastal, river, and chronic flooding alone could generate GDP losses of 5–20 percent by 2100 in China, Indonesia, the Philippines, and Viet Nam. The stakes are highest for Pacific Island countries, where natural disasters already cost over 2 percent of GDP annually and sea level rise threatens the territorial existence of Kiribati, the Marshall Islands, and Tuvalu.

EAP countries are highly exposed to climate change impacts.

MAP 1.2 Climate Risk Index ranking, 1999–2019

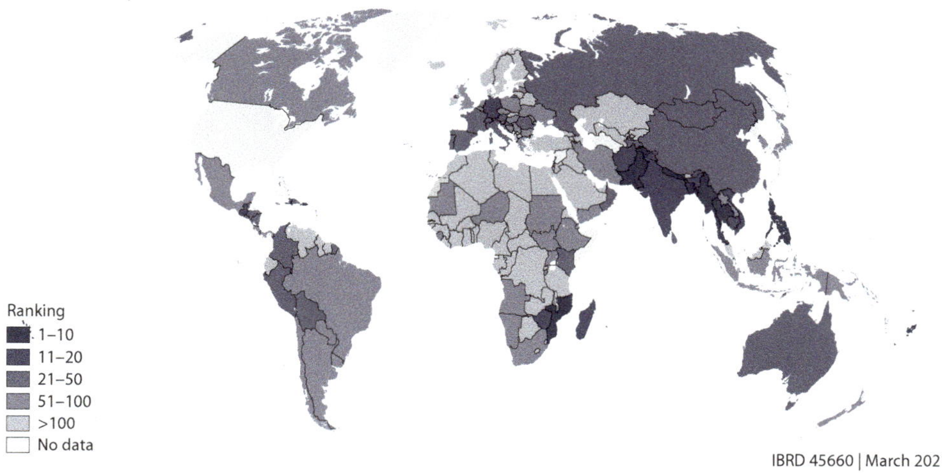

Source: Original map for this publication based on Eckstein et al. 2021.

Climate adaptation has two pillars. The first is risk reduction: ex ante infrastructure investments, land use regulation that keeps development out of flood-prone areas, and protection of ecosystems that shield cities from storm surges. The second is risk management: early warning systems, sovereign insurance, and shock-responsive social safety nets. Inherent in how governments assess these options is incorporating measures to incentivize private sector cost-sharing to the extent possible.

Globally and in EAP, there is underinvestment in climate adaptation. Recent more detailed analysis of a range of adaptation investments shows that the returns on investment in adaptation can be much greater than simply the avoided losses. This analysis, referred to as the triple dividends, uses cost-benefit analysis to properly estimate avoided losses (first dividend), induced economic or development benefits (second dividend), and additional social and environmental benefits (third dividend) of adaptation actions (refer to figure 1.33).

Empirical analysis of adaptation investments shows that each dividend is often significant. Recent analysis of seven different projects targeting six different categories of climate change impacts—forests and wildfires, urban flooding and drainage, stormwater management, coastal flooding, urban heat islands, and drought—shows that, in all cases, valuing the three dividend types makes a significant difference in assessing total project benefits (refer to table 1.2).

Investing in adaptation will deliver a triple dividend.

FIGURE 1.33 Triple dividends of climate adaptation

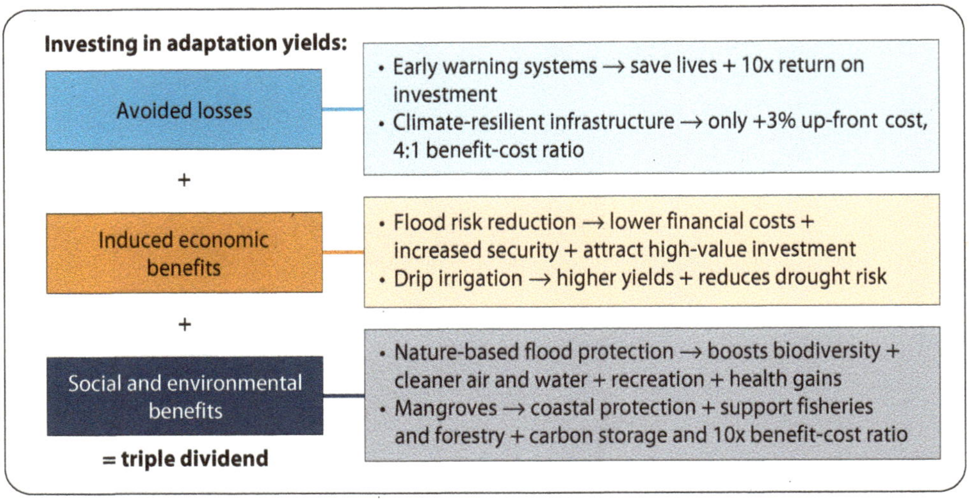

Source: World Bank 2023g, figure O21.

TABLE 1.2 Returns on investment of different adaptation investments

	Forests and wildfires	Urban flooding and drainage	Stormwater management	Coastal flooding	Urban heat islands (Two US cities in one study)		Drought
	Tahoe National Forest (United States)	Kunshan Forest Park (China)	Princes Park (Australia)	Felixstowe (United Kingdom)	Washington, DC	Philadelphia	Ningxia (China)
Project cost (US$, millions)	4	1.2	6.7	20.3	838	2,380	1,970
Project benefits (US$, millions)	22.9	59.7	12.7	644.9	5,750	10,780	11,050
Benefit-cost ratio	5.7	49.6	1.9	31.8	6.9	4.5	5.6

Source: World Bank 2023g, table O1.

At the sector and macro levels, adaptation investments have clear benefits. For example, in Samoa, investing an additional 2 percent of GDP in adaptation for the next five years would save about 4.5 percent of 2021 GDP in output losses. In the Philippines, all sectors would benefit from climate adaptation measures: investments of less than 1 percent of GDP would avoid losses of 1–2 percent of GDP in many sectors (refer to figure 1.34).

Unlike human capital investment, adaptation needs are not monotonic in income level. Upper-middle-income countries with large stocks of high-value infrastructure in climate-exposed areas can face substantial adaptation requirements. Thailand's 2011 floods, associated with losses of about 10 percent of GDP and major disruptions to global supply chains, illustrate that adaptation needs remain large even at higher development levels. Adaptation investment priorities can be organized along two dimensions: exposure to natural hazards and fiscal and institutional capacity (refer to figure 1.35).

In the Philippines, all sectors would benefit from adaptation investments.

FIGURE 1.34 Sectoral benefits of climate adaptation, the Philippines, by 2030 and 2040

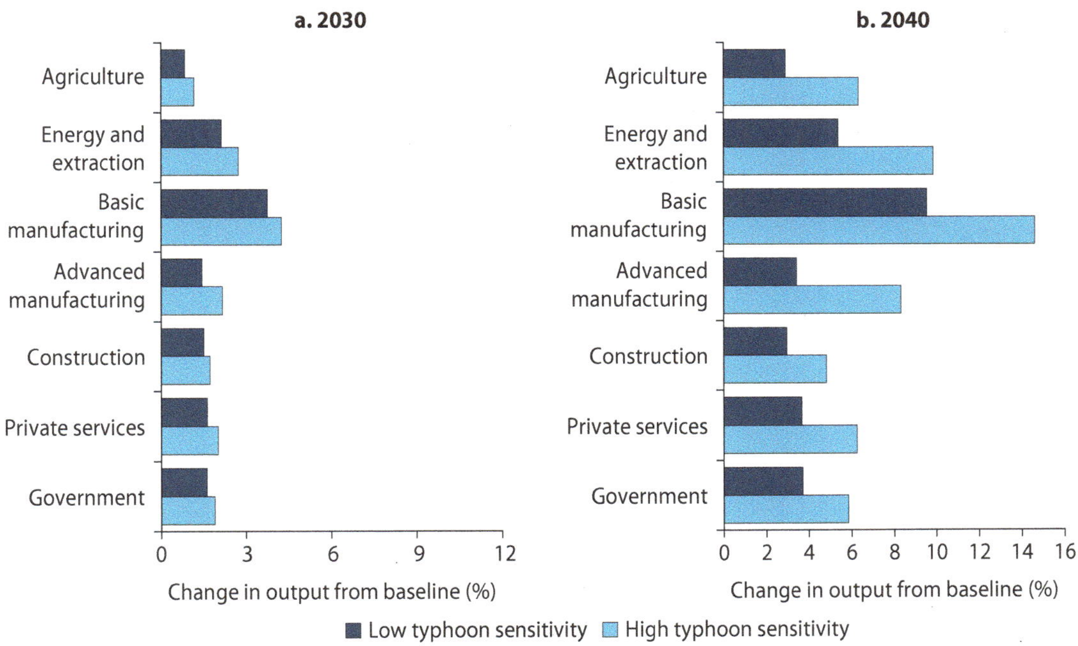

Source: World Bank 2023g, figure O22.

Climate adaptation needs vary with exposure and capacity, requiring differentiated fiscal strategies across EAP economies.

FIGURE 1.35 Priorities for climate adaptation, by exposure and capacity level

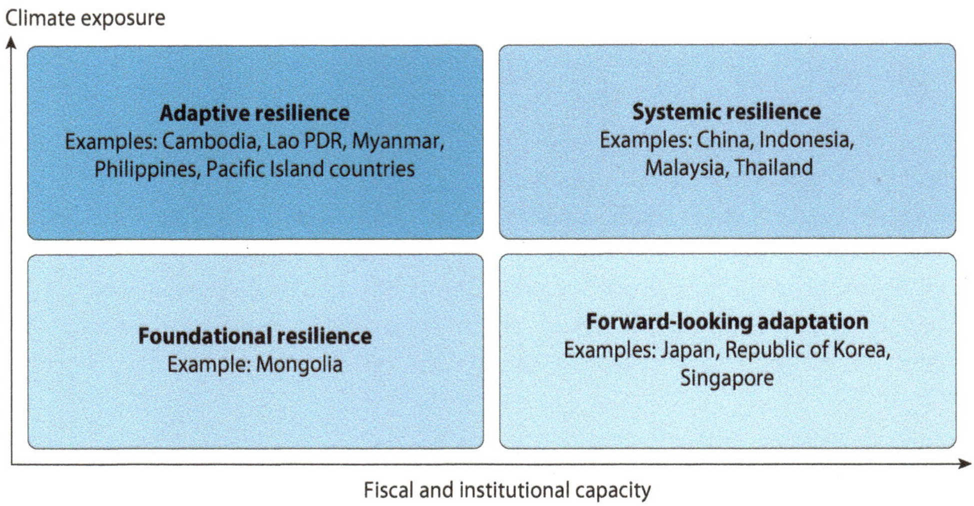

Source: Original figure for this publication.
Note: EAP = East Asia and Pacific.

In highly exposed economies with limited capacity—Cambodia, Lao PDR, Myanmar, the Philippines, and most Pacific Island countries —the priority is adaptive resilience: protecting basic services, climate-resilient infrastructure, and shock-responsive social protection. In highly exposed economies with stronger capacity—China, Indonesia, Malaysia, and Thailand—the priority shifts to systemic resilience: integrating climate risks into investment planning, infrastructure standards, and land use decisions. Across all contexts, scaling up adaptation requires additional fiscal space supported by stronger domestic revenue mobilization and integration of climate risk into fiscal frameworks.

Aging

The EAP region is aging faster and at lower levels of income than the currently richer and older countries in Europe and Central Asia and OECD. The transition from aging to aged societies (that is, growth of the age 65 and older cohort from 7 percent to 14 percent of the total population) has taken only 20–25 years for most EAP economies, in contrast to 50–100 years or more in those other countries. EAP economies are also becoming aged societies at far lower income levels than their OECD counterparts, with purchasing power parity per capita GDP at peak working age between 10 percent and 40 percent of the level in the United States at the same point in demographic transition (refer to figure 1.36). The region is getting old before it gets rich.

EAP countries are aging faster than rich countries did, and the working-age population will peak at lower levels of income per capita.

FIGURE 1.36 Population aging and per capita income, selected EAP economies and comparators

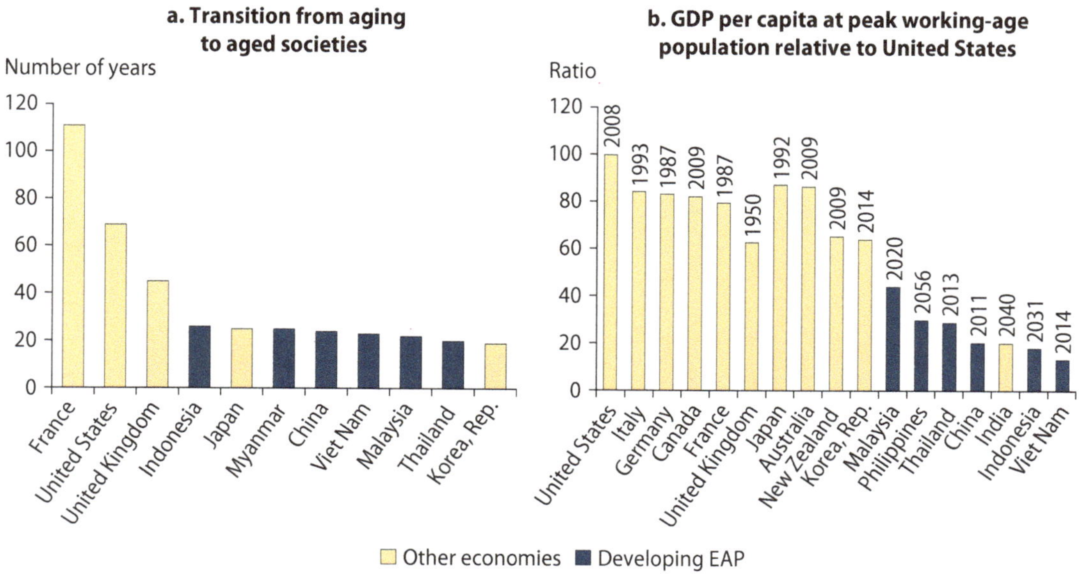

Source: Original figure for this publication based on UN DESA 2022.
Note: In panel a, bars denote years realized or projected for the age 65 and older share of the population to go from 7 percent to 14 percent of the total population. In panel b, bars denote realized or projected GDP per capita relative to the United States when the working-age population (ages 15–65) reaches peak (in the year above each country's bar). EAP = East Asia and Pacific.

Population aging may affect economic growth through the decline in the share of the working-age population, typically defined as the population ages 15–64 (refer to figure 1.37). However, measures to encourage and help older people to work could lessen the adverse impact.

Population aging could also strain fiscal balances on both the expenditure and revenue sides. On the expenditure side, the pressures on public finances will come from rising pension costs and health and long-term care spending, with the first the most pronounced. On the revenue side, the declining size of the working-age population will shrink the contribution base from which several major economies in the region finance pension, unemployment, and health insurance systems. To address this situation, economies could increase current contribution rates and bring them closer to actuarially fair rates (refer to figure 1.38).

Aging could reduce the share of the conventionally defined working-age population, unless older people (especially women) continue to work.

FIGURE 1.37 **Working-age population and share of people working beyond working age, EAP and comparators**

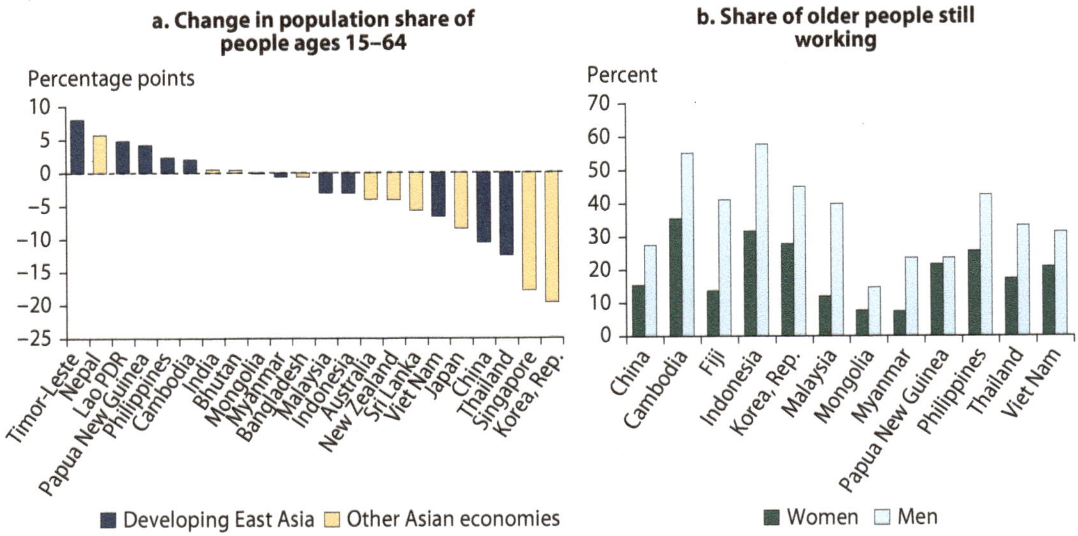

Sources: Original figure for this publication based on ILOSTAT database, International Labour Organization, https://ilostat.ilo.org/data/?cat_mode=subject (panel a); Global Health Observatory, World Health Organization, https://www.who.int/data/gho (panel b).

Aging will increase spending on pensions and requires bridging the gap between actual and actuarially fair contribution rates.

FIGURE 1.38 **Pension spending and contribution rates, selected EAP economies**

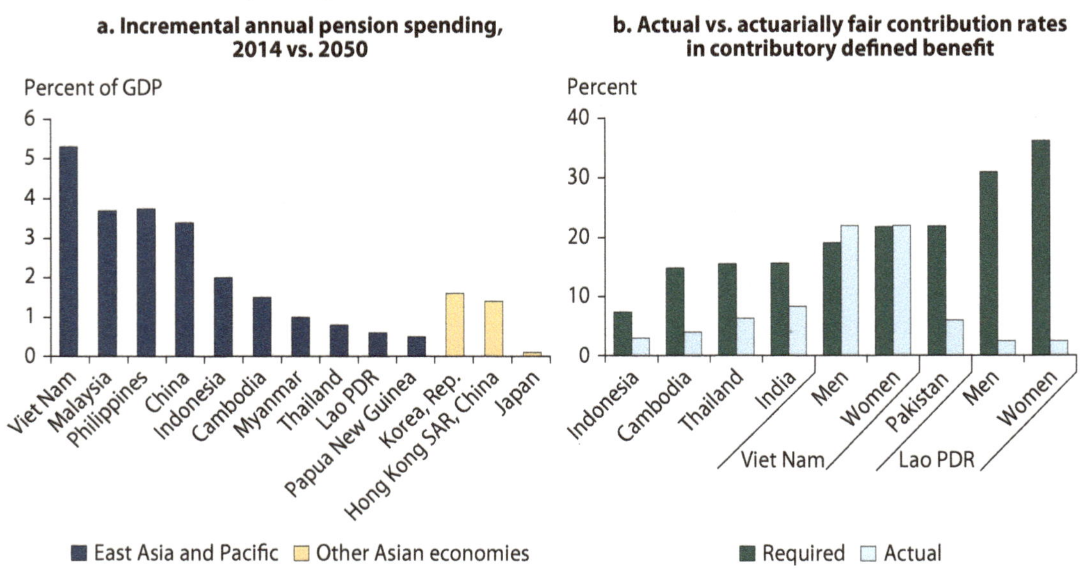

Source: Original figure for this publication based on World Bank 2023g.
Note: EAP = East Asia and Pacific.

Aging will also likely drive up health and aged-care spending over time but with public spending impacts, because aging is a less significant driver of health care costs. However, aging populations with higher NCD prevalence and higher comorbidities will accelerate the epidemiological transition, leading to the fiscal cost of inadequate preventive health care compounding over time as populations age. The health sector will require structural reforms to better prevent, control, and manage NCDs across the life cycle.

Conclusion

The region's development record over the past three decades is one of the most remarkable in economic history, and fiscal policy played a part in making that record possible. Most EAP governments pursued a distinctive fiscal strategy. They kept taxes low to attract private capital. They used generous incentives to draw foreign investment. Within tight budgets, they directed scarce public resources to physical infrastructure rather than social spending. This approach worked: low corporate tax burdens supported firm entry and investment, infrastructure spending crowded in private capital, and fiscal discipline kept debt moderate and borrowing costs low.

The model, however, rested on a deliberate trade-off. By keeping taxes low and operational spending lean, governments preserved space for infrastructure investment and maintained the macroeconomic stability that anchored private sector confidence. The strategy delivered, but it also left persistent gaps—in human capital, social protection, and climate resilience—that now act as binding constraints on the region's next growth phase.

Skill-intensive, climate-resilient, and inclusive growth requires broader revenue bases, more balanced spending, and stronger institutions than the current approach has built. Spending on building human capital, increasing social protection, and adapting to climate risks will require ensuring that social returns exceed private returns to investment, even after implementation of the relevant regulatory reforms (refer to box 1.5). The good news is that the region starts from a position of relative fiscal strength, with moderate debt, generally sound macroeconomic frameworks, and a track record of reform when political conditions align. The task is not to abandon what worked. Instead, it is to evolve—deliberately, strategically, and with the urgency that the region's rising pressures demand.

Box 1.5. When should the state spend? Public vs. private provision in health, education, and climate adaptation

The case for public spending rests not on a preference for state action but on the economics of market failure. The standard framework—rooted in the welfare theorems of Arrow (1951), Pigou (1932), and Samuelson (1954) and elaborated in World Bank operational guidance (Devarajan and Hammer 1998; Pradhan 1996)—identifies three conditions under which markets systematically underprovide: when goods are nonexcludable or nonrivalrous (pure public goods), when private returns fall short of social returns (positive externalities), and when information asymmetries prevent efficient private contracting. When none of these conditions hold, the presumption should favor private provision—not because governments cannot deliver but because public spending risks crowding out private investment and misallocating scarce fiscal resources.

The social-private return gap as the operational test

The key diagnostic is the gap between social and private returns. Public spending is warranted, and most productive, when this gap is largest. When private returns are high and social returns are not materially different, markets will supply the good, and public provision risks fiscal waste or crowding out. Table B1.5.1 applies this logic across a spectrum of goods relevant to East Asia and Pacific (refer also to figure B1.5.1).

TABLE B1.5.1 Private returns, social returns, and the optimal role for the state

Sector/activity	Private return	Social return	Market failure	Optimal role for the state
Vector control, sanitation	Very low	Very high	Nonexcludable public good	Full public provision and financing
Immunization, communicable disease control	Low–moderate	Very high	Large positive externalities	Public financing; mixed provision
Primary education	Moderate	High	Externalities + credit market failure	Public financing; mixed provision
Coastal protection, early warning systems	Low (private)	Very high	Nonexcludable, systemic risk	Full public provision
Climate adaptation infrastructure	Moderate	High	Coordination failures, long horizons	Public investment + regulatory framework

Source: Original table for this publication.

(continued)

Box 1.5. When should the state spend? Public vs. private provision in health, education, and climate adaptation *(continued)*

The implication—often lost in debates about spending levels—is that the composition of public spending matters at least as much as its volume. Research finds that rates of return to public goods in education, health, and infrastructure consistently exceed those to subsidies for private goods or nonsocial transfers, and that countries spending more on public goods grow faster and reduce poverty more rapidly than those directing equivalent resources to private subsidies (López et al. 2008; Pradhan 1996).

The case for public spending is strongest when social returns systematically exceed private returns.

FIGURE B1.5.1 Public vs. private goods: A framework for public spending

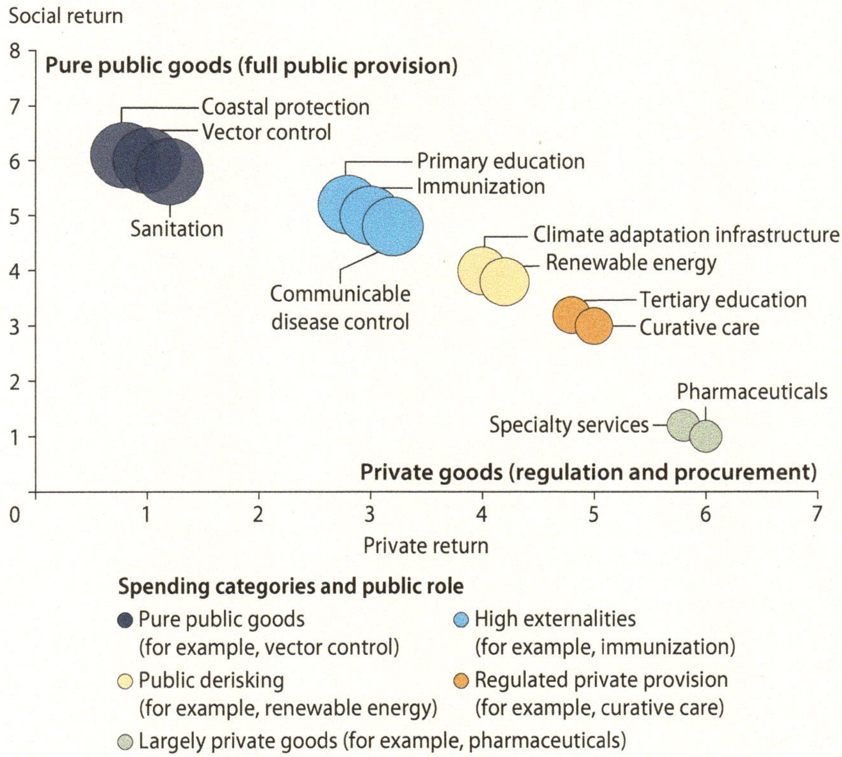

Source: Original figure for this publication.

(continued)

Box 1.5. When should the state spend? Public vs. private provision in health, education, and climate adaptation *(continued)*

Country examples

The distinction plays out clearly in East Asia and Pacific. Malaysia's early investments in rural immunization and primary schooling, both high-externality activities, produced strong human capital outcomes at modest fiscal cost, whereas government spending on secondary hospitals had no detectable impact on infant mortality, because it crowded out private provision without adding net services (Devarajan and Hammer 1998; Hammer et al. 1995). Malaysia's later move toward regulated private provision of specialist hospital care—with government retaining a financing and standard-setting role—improved both access and efficiency, illustrating that the optimal boundary between public and private shifts as markets deepen.

Thailand's Universal Health Coverage reform offers a complementary lesson. By shifting to capitation-based provider payments and centralized pharmaceutical procurement, Thailand achieved large efficiency gains without sacrificing coverage. The government retained a financing role but deliberately opened provision to a mix of public hospitals and contracted private providers.

On climate adaptation, the market failure logic is particularly stark. Coastal flood defenses, early warning systems, and watershed management generate benefits that are inherently nonexcludable—a sea wall protects all coastal residents regardless of who pays—and involve coordination failures that no individual firm can resolve (Hallegatte et al. 2016; Pigato 2019). Private capital will systematically underinvest because it cannot capture the full social return. The appropriate public role here is not merely financing but de-risking and coordinating—establishing regulatory and pricing frameworks, including carbon pricing and nature-based investment standards, that allow private capital to flow toward adaptation at scale.

The government failure caveat

Market failure justifies public intervention but does not guarantee its success. Governments, too, can fail through political capture, misallocation to visible but low-return inputs, and the entrenchment of subsidies (Devarajan and Hammer 1998; World Bank 1996). For governments in East Asia and Pacific operating with small fiscal envelopes, the cost of government failure is especially high: resources misallocated to low-return activities are unavailable for the high-externality investments such as primary health, early childhood education, and climate resilience, which carry the greatest social return to public spending.

Annex 1A. Methodology for tax capacity estimation

Data

The analysis draws on panel data for 112 countries over the period 2000–22. Key data sources include the following:

- Government Finance Statistics, International Monetary Fund, https://data360.worldbank.org/en/int/dataset/IMF_GFSMAB (for tax revenue data)
- Informal Economy Database, World Bank, https://data360.worldbank.org/en/dataset/WB_INFECDB (for informal output data)
- International Country Risk Guide data set, PRS Group, https://www.prsgroup.com/explore-our-products/icrg/ (corruption index data)
- World Development Indicators, World Bank, https://datatopics.worldbank.org/world-development-indicators/ (for trade, population growth, agriculture value added, and consumption data)
- World Economic Outlook (WEO) Database, International Monetary Fund, https://www.imf.org/en/publications/sprolls/world-economic-outlook-databases (for GDP per capita data)

Estimation approach

Tax capacity is estimated using ordinary least squares regression with regional and time fixed effects, following the framework of Le et al. (2012). Fitted values from the regression represent tax capacity.

Model specifications

Total tax revenue. Capacity is estimated using the following baseline equation:

$$\text{Tax revenue/GDP}_{it} = \alpha + \beta_1 .\ \text{GDPPC}_{it} + \beta_2 .\ \text{AGR}_{it} + \beta_3 .\ \text{Corruption}_{it} + \beta_4 .\ \text{Population}_{it} + \beta_5 .\ \text{Trade}_{it} + \text{regional dummies} + \text{time dummies} + \varepsilon$$

where *i* is the country; *t* is the year; GDPPC is log GDP per capita; AGR is agricultural share of GDP; Corruption is the degree of political corruption; Population is the population growth rate; Trade is the sum of exports and imports as a share of GDP; α represents the constant term; $\beta_1 - \beta_5$ are estimated coefficients; regional dummies are binary controlling for fixed differences across regions; time dummies are binary controlling for common shocks or trends across all countries in a given year; and ε is the error term.

Goods and services tax. GST capacity is estimated using the baseline equation and extended to include informal output as a share of GDP and total consumption as a share of GDP, reflecting their distinct effects on indirect tax bases. Multicollinearity was checked across all specifications, and no concerning issues were found:

$$GST/GDP_{it} = \alpha + \beta_1 .\ GDPPC_{it} + \beta_2 .\ AGR_{it} + \beta_3 .\ Corruption_{it} + \beta_4 .\ Population_{it} + \beta_5 .\ Trade_{it} + \beta_6 .\ Informal\ output_{it} + \beta_7 .\ Consumption_{it} + regional\ dummies + time\ dummies + \varepsilon$$

where i is the country; t is the year; GDPPC is log GDP per capita; AGR is agricultural share of GDP; Corruption is the degree of political corruption; Population is population growth rate; Trade is the sum of exports and imports as share of GDP; Informal output is the estimated size of informal output as share of actual GDP; Consumption is the expenditure on goods and services by households and governments as share GDP; α represents the constant term; $\beta_1 - \beta_7$ are estimated coefficients; regional dummies are binary controlling for fixed differences across regions; time dummies are binary controlling for common shocks or trends across all countries in a given year; and ε is the error term.

Table 1A.1 describes the expected relationships of the variables and the rationales for those relationships.

TABLE 1A.1 Expected coefficient signs

Variable	Expected relationship	Rationale
GDP per capita	Positive	Higher development increases tax capacity and demand for public goods.
Agriculture value added	Negative	Agricultural sectors are harder to tax and more informal.
Trade openness	Mixed	Trade liberalization expands the economic base but reduces tariff rates and revenues.
Population growth	Negative	Faster growth lowers the productive labor share.
Corruption	Negative	Higher corruption reduces tax administration efficiency.
Informal output	Negative	Informality reduces the formal, taxable income base.
Total consumption	Positive	Higher consumption expands the indirect tax base.

Source: Original table for this publication.

Note on Pacific Island countries

Because of data availability constraints, corruption data are unavailable for Pacific Island countries. Equations were therefore reestimated without the corruption, informal output, and consumption variables for this group. Consequently, results for these economies should be interpreted with that limitation in mind.

Annex 1B. Explaining the size of government: A summary of theoretical perspectives

What explains why some governments are larger than others as a share of gross domestic product? A wide body of theory identifies both demand-side drivers—economic, demographic, and social conditions that shape the appetite for public goods and redistribution—and supply-side factors rooted in political institutions (refer to table 1B.1; refer also to Facchini 2018 and Shelton 2007).

On the demand side, five mechanisms stand out.

- *Trade openness.* More open economies face greater external risk and use public spending—through social protection in advanced economies, and public employment in developing ones—as insurance (Cameron 1978; Rodrik 1998).
- *Income (Wagner's Law).* As countries grow richer, demand rises for regulatory functions and public services; empirical support is mixed across time-series but broadly consistent in cross-section (Henrekson 1993; Ram 1987; Wagner 1883).
- *Country size.* Smaller countries tend toward larger governments, because nonrival public goods are more efficiently spread across small populations and because small states depend more on trade (Alesina and Wacziarg 1998).
- *Ethnic fragmentation.* Because of conflicting preferences, diverse societies spend less on shared public goods but may spend more on targeted programs, reducing efficiency (Alesina et al. 1999; Easterly and Levine 1997).
- *Income inequality.* Greater inequality shifts the median voter's calculus to redistribution, though observed effects are typically smaller than theory predicts, constrained by political institutions (Meltzer and Richard 1981).

On the supply side, political systems mediate what is delivered:

- Electoral rules shape what kind of spending is prioritized. Majoritarian systems favor geographically targeted goods, whereas proportional systems favor transfers (Milesi-Ferretti et al. 2002; Persson and Tabellini 1999).

- Government type matters. Presidential systems, with separated powers, tend toward smaller and more efficient government; parliamentary systems, through coalition-building, tend toward higher spending (Persson and Tabellini 1999).
- Federalism shapes decentralization, with ambiguous net effects on aggregate size.

A wide range of country-specific factors—geography (for example, island or landlocked), colonial history, cultural norms, and corruption—can also influence spending patterns, often interacting with the variables above. For instance, corruption may distort spending toward categories more prone to rent extraction (Mauro 1998). Although important, these factors are difficult to model systematically and are often excluded in favor of variables with well-documented first-order effects.

TABLE 1B.1 Summary of key theories and mechanisms influencing government size

Theory	Key variable	Mechanism	Main reference(s)
Trade openness	Openness to trade	Insurance against external risk	Cameron (1978); Rodrik (1998)
Country size	Population	Economies of scale; preference heterogeneity	Alesina and Wacziarg (1998)
Wagner's Law	Per capita income	Increased complexity and luxury goods demand	Henrekson (1993); Ram (1987); Wagner (1883)
Ethnic fragmentation	Ethnic diversity	Disagreement on public goods provision	Alesina et al. (1999); Easterly and Levine (1997)
Income inequality	Mean-to-median income ratio	Median voter preferences for redistribution	Meltzer and Richard (1981)
Political rights	Suffrage and participation	Extent of redistribution possible	Benabou (1996); Lott and Kenny (1999)
Electoral rules	Majoritarian vs. proportional	Targeting of public goods vs. transfers	Milesi-Ferretti et al. (2002); Persson and Tabellini (1999)
Government type	Presidential vs. parliamentary	Separation of powers vs. logrolling	Persson and Tabellini (1999)
Federalism	Federal system dummy	Decentralization effects on expenditure	Oates (1972, 1999)

Source: Original table for this publication.

Annex 1C. Human capital and growth: Theory and evidence

Endogenous growth theory places human capital at the core of long-run productivity dynamics (refer to table 1C.1). Lucas (1988) shows that skill accumulation generates externalities that sustain persistent growth. Romer (1990) links human capital to idea production, generating increasing returns through knowledge. Aghion and Howitt (1992) show that skilled labor enables continuous technological upgrading through creative destruction.

The empirical macro literature confirms that both quantity and quality of human capital matter. Mankiw et al. (1992) show that schooling helps explain cross-country income differences and conditional convergence. Barro (1991) finds a positive association between schooling and subsequent growth; Benhabib and Spiegel (1994) show that the effect operates primarily through technology adoption and total factor productivity rather than as a direct production factor. Hanushek and Woessmann (2012) demonstrate that cognitive skills, not years of schooling alone, are strongly related to long-run growth rates, suggesting that education quality is the binding link between human capital and productivity.

Finally, the empirical micro literature provides strong evidence that human capital accumulation raises individual earnings and productivity. Mincer (1974) formalized the schooling-earnings relationship. Causal studies exploiting natural experiments consistently find positive returns, with global meta-analyses estimating average private returns of 8–10 percent per year of schooling (Psacharopoulos and Patrinos 2018). More recent work confirms that education quality and cognitive skills are stronger predictors of individual productivity than years of schooling alone (Hanushek and Woessmann 2008).

TABLE 1C.1 Human capital and growth: Theory and empirical evidence

Paper	Type	Approach	Main contribution/key finding
Lucas (1988)	Theory	Endogenous growth model with human capital accumulation and externalities	Human capital accumulation via education or learning can generate spillovers that sustain long-run growth.
Romer (1990)	Theory	Endogenous technological change (ideas; knowledge production)	Human capital is a key input into idea production; knowledge generates increasing returns and sustained growth.

(continued)

TABLE 1C.1 Human capital and growth: Theory and empirical evidence *(continued)*

Paper	Type	Approach	Main contribution/key finding
Aghion and Howitt (1992)	Theory	Creative destruction; innovation-driven growth	Skilled labor supports R&D and innovation; growth arises from continuous technological upgrading.
Mankiw et al. (1992)	Empirical (macro)	Cross-country regressions (augmented Solow growth model)	Schooling helps explain income differences and conditional convergence.
Barro (1991)	Empirical (macro)	Cross-country growth regressions	A positive association exists between schooling and subsequent growth (sensitive to specification).
Benhabib and Spiegel (1994)	Empirical (macro)	Cross-country evidence	Human capital may matter more through technology adoption or TFP than as a direct production factor.
Hanushek and Woessmann (2012)	Empirical (macro)	Cross-country with test scores	Cognitive skills are strongly related to long-run growth rates.
Angrist and Krueger (1991)	Empirical (micro)	IV using compulsory schooling/quarter of birth	Causal returns to schooling: additional schooling raises earnings.
Psacharopoulos and Patrinos (2018)	Empirical (micro)	Global meta-analysis	Average private returns to schooling are approximately 8–10% with heterogeneity.

Source: Original table for this publication.
Note: IV = instrumental variable; R&D = research and development; TFP = total factor productivity.

Notes

1. East Asian economies refer to Cambodia, China, Indonesia, the Lao People's Democratic Republic, Malaysia, Mongolia, Myanmar, the Philippines, Thailand, Timor-Leste, and Viet Nam.
2. Direct taxes comprise corporate income tax, personal income tax, and property taxes. This chapter discusses the first two in detail but does not discuss the latter because most EAP economies have very low or nonexistent property taxes. Chapter 4 returns to the issue of property taxes.
3. The World Bank EAP Pacific Island subregion includes Fiji, Kiribati, the Marshall Islands, the Federated States of Micronesia, Naoero, Palau, Papua New Guinea, Samoa, the Solomon Islands, Tonga, Tuvalu, and Vanuatu.

4. Developing economies, including in EAP, rely predominantly on profit-based CIT incentives, such as tax holidays and reduced rates, whereas developed countries favor expenditure-based instruments like investment tax credits, research and development credits, and superdeductions (James 2013). Profit-based incentives are widely used for their visibility to investors and administrative simplicity, but empirical evidence finds them largely ineffective at generating new investment; expenditure-based incentives, by contrast, are better targeted and more reliably stimulate additional investment activity.
5. In Cambodia, informality in nonagricultural activity remains above 83 percent, and the country has no comprehensive PIT system; it relies instead on a fragmented salary tax (World Bank 2025a).
6. International Labour Organization, ILOSTAT database, https://ilostat.ilo.org/data/?cat_mode=subject.
7. Refer also to PwC Worldwide Tax Summaries, "Philippines: Corporate—Other Taxes," https://taxsummaries.pwc.com/philippines/corporate/other-taxes.
8. The International Monetary Fund's Government Finance Statistics (https://www.imf.org/external/pubs/ft/gfs/manual/gfs.htm) defines grants as noncompulsory transfers, in cash or in kind, paid to another general government unit or an international organization; subsidies as current transfers paid by government units to enterprises based on their production levels or the quantities or values of goods and services they produce, sell, or import; and other transfers as current transfers to nonprofit institutions serving households, capital transfers other than capital grants, and non-life insurance premiums and claims.
9. Significant data gaps and definitional inconsistencies across countries complicate the measurement of the state footprint through SOEs. Definitions vary in terms of ownership thresholds, inclusion of financial versus nonfinancial entities, and treatment of indirect subsidiaries and subnational entities. Cross-country comparisons should therefore be interpreted with caution (World Bank 2020d, 2023a).
10. Identifying causal effects is difficult: tax changes are typically endogenous to macroeconomic conditions, and reforms rarely occur in isolation. Two main approaches in the literature attempt to address this challenge. One strand of the literature has built a narrative historical record of tax changes, classifying them according to their motivation and isolating those that are exogenous to current macroeconomic conditions (Cloyne 2013; Dabla-Norris and Lima 2018; Romer and Romer 2010). Another strand exploits cross-country variation in effective corporate tax rates and tax incentives, using panel methods and firm-level data to mitigate endogeneity concerns (Cevik and Miryugin 2018; Djankov et al. 2010; Klemm and Van Parys 2012).
11. Available data on adult skills suggest that gaps in foundational skills carry over to the workforce (OECD 2016; World Bank 2014b, 2024a).

References

Acosta-Ormaechea, Santiago, and Atsuyoshi Morozumi. 2013. "Can a Government Enhance Long-Run Growth by Changing the Composition of Public Expenditure?" IMF Working Paper No. 13/162, International Monetary Fund. https://www.imf.org/external/pubs/ft/wp/2013/wp13162.pdf.

Acosta-Ormaechea, Santiago, and Atsuyoshi Morozumi. 2021. "The Value-Added Tax and Growth: Design Matters." *International Tax and Public Finance* 28 (5): 1211–41.

Acosta-Ormaechea, Santiago, and Jiae Yoo. 2012. "Tax Composition and Growth: A Broad Cross-Country Perspective." IMF Working Paper No. 12/257, International Monetary Fund. https://www.imf.org/external/pubs/ft/wp/2012/wp12257.pdf.

Adarov, Amat, Benedict Clements, and João Tovar Jalles. 2024. "Revisiting Public Investment Multipliers: Nonlinear Effects of the Business Cycle, Fiscal Space, Efficiency, and Capital Stock." Policy Research Working Paper 10954, World Bank. https://doi.org/10.1596/1813-9450-10954.

ADB (Asian Development Bank). 2017. *Meeting Asia's Infrastructure Needs.* Asian Development Bank. https://www.adb.org/publications/asia-infrastructure-needs.

Afkar, Rythia, Tara Béteille, Mary E. Breeding, et al. 2023. *Fixing the Foundation: Teachers and Basic Education in East Asia and Pacific.* World Bank East Asia and Pacific Regional Report. World Bank. http://hdl.handle.net/10986/40332.

Aghion, Philippe, and Peter Howitt. 1992. "A Model of Growth Through Creative Destruction." *Econometrica* 60 (2): 323–51.

Alesina, Alberto, Reza Baqir, and William Easterly. 1999. "Public Goods and Ethnic Divisions." *The Quarterly Journal of Economics* 114 (4): 1243–84. https://doi.org/10.1162/003355399556269.

Alesina, Alberto, and Romain Wacziarg. 1998. "Openness, Country Size and Government." *Journal of Public Economics* 69 (3): 305–21.

Angrist, Joshua D., and Alan B. Krueger. 1991. "Does Compulsory School Attendance Affect Schooling and Earnings?" *Quarterly Journal of Economics* 106 (4): 979–1014.

APO (Asian Productivity Organization). 2025. *APO Productivity Databook 2025.* APO. https://doi.org/10.61145/GENB1427.

Arrow, Kenneth. J. 1951. *Social Choice and Individual Values.* Wiley.

Bachas, Pierre, and Mauricio Soto. 2021. "Corporate Taxation Under Weak Enforcement." *American Economic Journal: Economic Policy* 13 (4): 36–71.

Bales, Sarah, Dao Lan Huong, Nguyen Thi Thuy Duyen, and Tran Tien Hung. 2022. "Potentially Preventable Hospitalizations in Vietnam: Analysis Using Health Insurance Claims Data" [English]. Health, Nutrition, and Population (HNP) Discussion Paper. World Bank. http://documents.worldbank.org/curated/en/099447403132330753.

Barro, Robert J. 1990. "Government Spending in a Simple Model of Endogenous Growth." *Journal of Political Economy* 98 (S5): 103–25.

Barro, Robert J. 1991. "Economic Growth in a Cross Section of Countries." *Quarterly Journal of Economics* 106 (2): 407–43.

Baunsgaard, Thomas, and Michael Keen. 2010. "Tax Revenue and (or?) Trade Liberalization." *Journal of Public Economics* 94 (9–10): 563–77.

Benabou, Roland. 1996. "Inequality and Growth." *NBER Macroeconomics Annual* 11: 11–74.

Benhabib, Jess, and Mark M. Spiegel. 1994. "The Role of Human Capital in Economic Development: Evidence from Aggregate Cross-Country Data." *Journal of Monetary Economics* 34 (2): 143–73.

Cameron, David R. 1978. "The Expansion of the Public Economy: A Comparative Analysis." *American Political Science Review* 72 (4): 1243–61.

Cerda, Rodrigo A., and Felipe Larrain. 2010. "Corporate Taxes and the Demand for Labor and Capital in Developing Countries." *Small Business Economics* 34 (2): 187–201.

Cevik, Serhan, and Fedor Miryugin. 2018. "Does Taxation Stifle Corporate Investment? Firm-Level Evidence from ASEAN Countries." *Australian Economic Review* 51 (3): 351–67.

Cloyne, James. 2013. "Discretionary Tax Changes and the Macroeconomy: New Narrative Evidence from the United Kingdom." *American Economic Review* 103 (4): 1507–28.

Dabla-Norris, Era, and Frederico Lima. 2018. "Macroeconomic Effects of Tax Rate and Base Changes: Evidence from Fiscal Consolidations." *IMF Working Papers* 2018 (220). https://doi.org/10.5089/9781484377451.001.

Debebe, Zelalem, Damien de Walque, Young Eun Kim, et al. 2026. *A Healthy Future: Primary Health Care and the Chronic Disease Epidemic in East Asia and Pacific.* East Asia and Pacific Development Studies. World Bank. https://doi.org/10.1596/978-1-4648-2284-1.

de Nicola, Francesca, Aaditya Mattoo, and Jonathan Timmis. 2025. *Firm Foundations of Growth: Productivity and Technology in East Asia and Pacific.* World Bank. https://doi.org/10.1596/978-1-4648-2200-1.

Devarajan, Shantayanan, and Jeffrey S. Hammer. 1998. "Risk Reduction and Public Spending." Policy Research Working Paper 1869, World Bank. http://documents.worldbank.org/curated/en/539401468739468826.

Djankov, Simeon, Tim Ganser, Caralee McLiesh, Rita Ramalho, and Andrei Shleifer. 2010. "The Effect of Corporate Taxes on Investment and Entrepreneurship." *American Economic Journal: Macroeconomics* 2 (3): 31–64.

Easterly, William, and Ross Levine. 1997. "Africa's Growth Tragedy: Policies and Ethnic Divisions." *Quarterly Journal of Economics* 112 (4): 1203–50.

Easterly, William, and Sergio Rebelo. 1993. "Fiscal Policy and Economic Growth: An Empirical Investigation." *Journal of Monetary Economics* 32 (3): 417–58.

Eckstein, David, Vera Künzel, and Laura Schäfer. 2021. *Global Climate Risk Index 2021: Who Suffers Most from Extreme Weather Events? Weather-Related Loss Events in 2019 and 2000–2019.* Germanwatch e.V. https://www.germanwatch.org/en/19777.

Enache, Cristina. 2022. "Corporate Tax Rates Around the World, 2022." Tax Foundation, December 13. https://taxfoundation.org/data/all/global/corporate-tax-rates-by-country-2022/.

Enache, Cristina. 2025. "Corporate Tax Rates Around the World, 2025." Tax Foundation, April 17. https://taxfoundation.org/data/all/global/corporate-tax-rates-by-country-2025/.

Facchini, François. 2018. "What Are the Determinants of Public Spending? An Overview of the Literature." *Atlantic Economic Journal* 46 (4): 419–39. https://doi.org/10.1007/s11293-018-9603-9.

Fenochietto, Ricardo, and Carola Pessino. 2013. "Understanding Countries' Tax Effort." IMF Working Paper WP/13/244, International Monetary Fund. https://www.imf.org/external/pubs/ft/wp/2013/wp13244.pdf.

Francois, John Nana, Maty Konte, and Franz Ulrich Ruch. 2026. "'Crowding In' Effect of Public Investment on Private Investment Revisited." *Journal of International Money and Finance* 164: 103567.

FRCS (Fiji Revenue and Customs Service). 2024. "Fiji Tax and Customs Incentives." FRCS. https://frcs.org.fj/incentives/.

Furceri, Davide, and Bin Grace Li. 2017. "The Macroeconomic (and Distributional) Effects of Public Investment in Developing Economies." IMF Working Paper No. 17/217, International Monetary Fund. https://doi.org/10.5089/9781484320709.001.

Garriga, Pablo, and Thiago Scot. 2023. "Corporate Responses to Size-Based Tax Rates in Lithuania." Policy Research Working Paper 10500, World Bank. https://documents1.worldbank.org/curated/en/099313106262317603/pdf/IDU0e3c1b6c300a6c045390bb860c3c2931a384f.pdf.

Gemmell, Norman, Richard Kneller, and Ismael Sanz. 2014. "The Growth Effects of Tax Rates in the OECD." *Canadian Journal of Economics* 47 (4): 1217–55.

Hallegatte, Stéphane, Mook Bangalore, Laura Bonzanigo, et al. 2016. *Shock Waves: Managing the Impacts of Climate Change on Poverty.* Climate Change and Development Series. World Bank. http://hdl.handle.net/10986/22787.

Hammer, Jeffrey S., Ijaz Nabi, and James A. Cercone. 1995. "Distributional Effects of Social Sector Expenditures in Malaysia, 1974 to 1989." In *Public Spending and the Poor: Theory and Evidence*, edited by Dominique van de Walle and Kimberly Nead, 521–54. Johns Hopkins University Press for the World Bank.

Hanushek, Eric A., and Ludger Woessmann. 2008. "The Role of Cognitive Skills in Economic Development." *Journal of Economic Literature* 46 (3): 607–68.

Hanushek, Eric A., and Ludger Woessmann. 2012. "Do Better Schools Lead to More Growth? Cognitive Skills, Economic Outcomes, and Causation." *Journal of Economic Growth* 17 (4): 267–321.

Heblich, Stephan, Stephen J. Redding, and Daniel M. Sturm. 2020. "The Making of the Modern Metropolis: Evidence from London." *Quarterly Journal of Economics* 135 (4): 2059–133.

Henrekson, Magnus. 1993. "Wagner's Law: A Spurious Relationship?" *Public Finance* 48 (3): 406–15.

IMF (International Monetary Fund). 2022. *Fiscal Monitor: Fiscal Policy from Pandemic to War*. IMF. http://imf.org/en/Publications/FM/Issues/2022/04/12/fiscal-monitor-april-2022.

IMF (International Monetary Fund), Organisation for Economic Co-operation and Development, United Nations, and World Bank. 2015. "Options for Low Income Countries' Effective and Efficient Use of Tax Incentives for Investment: A Report to the G-20 Development Working Group by the IMF, OECD, UN and World Bank." October 2015, IMF. http://imf.org/external/np/g20/pdf/101515.pdf.

James, Sebastian. 2013. "Effectiveness of Tax and Non-Tax Incentives and Investments: Evidence and Policy Implications." SSRN. https://ssrn.com/abstract=2401905 or http://dx.doi.org/10.2139/ssrn.2401905.

Kasyanenko, Sergiy, Philip George Kenworthy, Franz Ulrich Ruch, Ekaterine T. Vashakmadze, Dana Lauren Vorisek, and Collette Mari Wheeler. 2023. "Investment in Emerging Market and Developing Economy Regions: Trends, Prospects, and Policy Options." Policy

Research Working Paper 10369, World Bank. http://documents.worldbank.org/curated/en/099542403162311587.

Klemm, Alexander, and Stefan Van Parys. 2012. "Empirical Evidence on the Effects of Tax Incentives." *International Tax and Public Finance* 19 (3): 393–423.

Kruk, Margaret E., Anna D. Gage, Naima T. Joseph, Goodarz Danaei, Sebastián García-Saisó, and Joshua A. Salomon. 2018. "Mortality Due to Low-Quality Health Systems in the Universal Health Coverage Era: A Systematic Analysis of Amenable Deaths in 137 Countries." *The Lancet* 392 (10160): 2203–12.

Le, Tuan Minh, Blanca Moreno-Dodson, and Nihal Bayraktar. 2012. "Tax Capacity and Tax Effort: Extended Cross-Country Analysis from 1994 to 2009." Policy Research Working Paper 6252, World Bank. http://hdl.handle.net/10986/12094.

Lediga, Collen, Nadine Riedel, and Kristina Strohmaier. 2019. "The Elasticity of Corporate Taxable Income: Evidence from South Africa." *Economics Letters* 175 (February): 43–46.

Lee, Young, and Roger H. Gordon. 2005. "Tax Structure and Economic Growth." *Journal of Public Economics* 89 (5–6): 1027–43.

López, Ramón E., Vinod Thomas, and Yan Wang. 2008. "The Quality of Growth: Fiscal Policies for Better Results." IEG Working Paper 2008/6, World Bank. http://documents.worldbank.org/curated/en/254571468339912673.

Lott, John R., Jr., and Lawrence W. Kenny. 1999. "Did Women's Suffrage Change the Size and Scope of Government?" *Journal of Political Economy* 107 (6): 1163–98.

Lucas, Robert E., Jr. 1988. "On the Mechanics of Economic Development." *Journal of Monetary Economics* 22 (1): 3–42.

Mankiw, N. Gregory, David Romer, and David N. Weil. 1992. "A Contribution to the Empirics of Economic Growth." *Quarterly Journal of Economics* 107 (2): 407–37.

Mauro, Paolo. 1998. "Corruption and the Composition of Government Expenditure." *Journal of Public Economics* 69 (2): 263–79.

Mawejje, Joseph, and Rachel K. Sebudde. 2019. "Tax Revenue Potential and Effort: Worldwide Estimates Using a New Dataset." *Economic Analysis and Policy* 63: 119–129.

Meltzer, Allan H., and Scott F. Richard. 1981. "A Rational Theory of the Size of Government." *Journal of Political Economy* 89 (5): 914–27.

Milesi-Ferretti, Gian Maria, Roberto Perotti, and Massimo Rostagno. 2002. "Electoral Systems and Public Spending." *Quarterly Journal of Economics* 117 (2): 609–57.

Mincer, Jacob. 1974. *Schooling, Experience, and Earnings*. National Bureau of Economic Research and Columbia University Press.

Mirrlees, James, Stuart Adam, Timothy Besley, et al. 2011. *Tax by Design: The Mirrlees Review*. Oxford University Press.

Miyamoto, Wataru, Thuy Lan Nguyen, and Dmitriy Sergeyev. 2018. "Government Spending Multipliers Under the Zero Lower Bound: Evidence from Japan." *American Economic Journal: Macroeconomics* 10 (3): 247–77.

Oates, Wallace E. 1972. *Fiscal Federalism*. Harcourt Brace Jovanovich.

Oates, Wallace E. 1999. "An Essay on Fiscal Federalism." *Journal of Economic Literature* 37 (3): 1120–49. https://www.aeaweb.org/articles?id=10.1257/jel.37.3.1120.

OECD (Organisation for Economic Co-operation and Development). 2011. *Reform Priorities in Asia: Taking Corporate Governance to a Higher Level.* OECD Publishing. http://dx.doi.org/10.1787/9789264204416-en.

OECD (Organisation for Economic Co-operation and Development). 2016. *Skills Matter: Further Results from the Survey of Adult Skills.* OECD Skills Studies. OECD Publishing. http://doi.org/10.1787/9789264258051-en.

OECD (Organisation for Economic Co-operation and Development). 2023. *PISA 2022 Results (Volume I): The State of Learning and Equity in Education.* OECD Publishing. https://doi.org/10.1787/53f23881-en.

OECD (Organisation for Economic Co-operation and Development). 2025. "Philippines." In *Agricultural Policy Monitoring and Evaluation 2025: Making the Most of the Trade and Environment Nexus in Agriculture.* OECD Publishing. https://www.oecd.org/en/publications/2025/10/agricultural-policy-monitoring-and-evaluation-2025_354e7040/full-report/philippines_6571bcaf.html#chapter-d1e120152-b18e248f8d.

OECD (Organisation for Economic Co-operation and Development) and ADB (Asian Development Bank). 2022. *Revenue Statistics in Asia and the Pacific: Strengthening Tax Revenues in Developing Asia 1990–2020.* OECD Publishing. https://www.oecd.org/content/dam/oecd/en/publications/reports/2022/07/revenue-statistics-in-asia-and-the-pacific-2022_c46a5310/db29f89a-en.pdf.

Persson, Torsten, and Guido Tabellini. 1999. "The Size and Scope of Government: Comparative Politics with Rational Politicians." *European Economic Review* 43 (4–6): 699–735.

Pigato, Miria A., ed. 2019. *Fiscal Policies for Development and Climate Action.* International Development in Focus. World Bank. https://doi.org/10.1596/978-1-4648-1358-0.

Pigou, A. C. 1932. *The Economics of Welfare.* 4th ed. Macmillan.

Pradhan, Sanjay. 1996. "Evaluating Public Spending: A Framework for Public Expenditure Reviews." Discussion Paper 323, World Bank. http://documents.worldbank.org/curated/en/509221468740209997.

Psacharopoulos, George, and Harry Anthony Patrinos. 2018. "Returns to Investment in Education: A Decennial Review of the Global Literature." *Education Economics* 26 (5): 445–58.

Ram, Rati. 1987. "Wagner's Hypothesis in Time-Series and Cross-Section Perspectives: Evidence from 'Real' Data for 115 Countries." *Review of Economics and Statistics* 69 (2): 194–204.

Redonda, Augustin, Christian von Haldenwang, and Flurim Aliu. 2025. "Global Tax Expenditures Database (GTED) (1.3.2) [Data set]." Tax Expenditures Lab. https://doi.org/10.5281/zenodo.17312217.

Rodrik, Dani. 1998. "Why Do More Open Economies Have Bigger Governments?" *Journal of Political Economy* 106 (5): 997–1032.

Romer, Christina, and David H. Romer. 2010. "The Macroeconomic Effects of Tax Changes: Estimates Based on a New Measure of Fiscal Shocks." *American Economic Review* 100 (3): 763–801.

Romer, Paul M. 1990. "Endogenous Technological Change." *Journal of Political Economy* 98 (5): S71–S102.

Samuelson, Paul A. 1954. "The Pure Theory of Public Expenditure." *Review of Economics and Statistics* 36 (4): 387–9.

Sen Gupta, Abhijit. 2007. "Determinants of Tax Revenue Efforts in Developing Countries." IMF Working Paper 07/184, International Monetary Fund. https://www.imf.org/external/pubs/ft/wp/2007/wp07184.pdf.

Shelton, Cameron A. 2007. "The Size and Composition of Government Expenditure." *Journal of Public Economics* 91 (11–12): 2230–60. http://www.sciencedirect.com/science/article/pii/S0047-2727(07)00007-2.

Straub, Stéphane, He He, Yue Li, et al. 2026. *Infrastructure Foundations: From Current Assets to Future Growth*. Sustainable Infrastructure Series. World Bank. https://openknowledge.worldbank.org/entities/publication/c35564b6-20e5-4606-a9df-d5735f8481d3.

Tanzi, Vito. 1992. "Structural Factors and Tax Revenue in Developing Countries: A Decade of Evidence." In *Open Economies: Structural Adjustment and Agriculture*, edited by Ian Goldin and L. Alan Winters. Cambridge University Press.

UN DESA (United Nations, Department of Economic and Social Affairs, Population Division). 2022. *World Population Prospects 2022: Summary of Results*. UN DESA/POP/2022/TR/No. 3. United Nations.

Végh, Carlos A., and Guillermo Vuletin. 2015. "How Is Tax Policy Conducted over the Business Cycle?" *American Economic Journal: Economic Policy* 7 (3): 327–70.

Wagner, Adolph. 1883. *Finanzwissenschaft*. 2nd ed. C. F. Winter'sche Verlagshandlung.

Waseem, Mazhar. 2018. "Taxes, Informality and Income Shifting: Evidence from a Recent Pakistani Tax Reform." *Journal of Public Economics* 157 (January): 41–77.

World Bank. 1996. *World Development Report 1996: From Plan to Market*. Oxford University Press. http://hdl.handle.net/10986/5979.

World Bank. 2011. *Philippines: Public Expenditure Review—Strengthening Public Finance for More Inclusive Growth*. Report 55695-PH. World Bank.

World Bank. 2014a. *Corporate Governance of State-Owned Enterprises: A Toolkit*. World Bank. http://documents.worldbank.org/curated/en/228331468169750340.

World Bank. 2014b. *Skilling Up Vietnam: Preparing the Workforce for a Modern Market Economy*. Vietnam Development Report 2014. World Bank. http://documents.worldbank.org/curated/en/729391468126891915.

World Bank. 2015. *East Asia and Pacific Economic Update, October 2015: Staying the Course*. World Bank. https://doi.org/10.1596/978-1-4648-0733-6.

World Bank. 2017a. *Pacific Possible: Long-Term Economic Opportunities and Challenges for Pacific Island Countries*. World Bank. https://doi.org/10.1596/28135.

World Bank. 2017b. "Taking Stock: An Update on Vietnam's Recent Economic Developments—Special Focus: Towards a High-Quality Fiscal Consolidation (Vietnamese)." World Bank. http://documents.worldbank.org/curated/en/530061500266807981.

World Bank. 2019. *Improving the Effectiveness of Public Finance: Cambodia Public Expenditure Review*. World Bank. http://hdl.handle.net/10986/32034.

World Bank 2020a. *East Asia and Pacific Economic Update, October 2020: From Containment to Recovery*. World Bank. http://hdl.handle.net/10986/34497.

World Bank. 2020b. *Global Investment Competitiveness Report 2019/2020: Rebuilding Investor Confidence in Times of Uncertainty*. World Bank. http://hdl.handle.net/10986/33808.

World Bank. 2020c. "Indonesia Public Expenditure Review 2020: Spending for Better Results." World Bank. http://documents.worldbank.org/curated/en/611541588612447572.

World Bank. 2020d. "State Your Business! An Evaluation of World Bank Group Support to the Reform of State-Owned Enterprises, FY08–18." Independent Evaluation Group, World Bank Group. http://ieg.worldbankgroup.org/evaluations/state-your-business.

World Bank. 2021. *East Asia and Pacific Economic Update, April 2021: Uneven Recovery.* http://hdl.handle.net/10986/35272.

World Bank. 2022a. "Solomon Islands Public Expenditure Review: Fiscal Reform and the Path to Debt Sustainability." World Bank. https://doi.org/10.1596/38362.

World Bank. 2022b. "Vibrant Vietnam: Forging the Foundation of a High-Income Economy—Background Papers." World Bank. http://documents.worldbank.org/curated/en/099107106102226523.

World Bank. 2023a. *The Business of the State*. World Bank. https://doi.org/10.1596/978-1-4648-1998-8.

World Bank. 2023b. "Crisis and Recovery: Learning from COVID-19's Economic Impacts and Policy Responses in East Asia." World Bank. https://doi.org/10.1596/39977.

World Bank. 2023c. "Forging Ahead: Restoring Stability and Boosting Prosperity." Lao PDR Public Finance Review. World Bank. https://doi.org/10.1596/40861.

World Bank. 2023d. "Philippines—Agriculture Public Expenditures Review: With a Special Focus on the Implications of the Mandanas Ruling for the Agri-food System." World Bank. https://documents.worldbank.org/pt/publication/documents-reports/documentdetail/099170002212314528.

World Bank. 2023e. "Small States: Overlapping Crises, Multiple Challenges." In *Global Economic Prospects, January 2023*. World Bank. https://doi.org/10.1596/978-1-4648-1906-3.

World Bank. 2023f. "Thailand Public Revenue and Spending Assessment: Promoting an Inclusive and Sustainable Future." World Bank. http://documents.worldbank.org/curated/en/099052523201510112.

World Bank. 2023g. *World Bank East Asia and the Pacific Economic Update, April 2023: Reviving Growth*. World Bank. http://hdl.handle.net/10986/39598.

World Bank 2024a. "Fostering Foundational Skills in Thailand: From a Skills Crisis to a Learning Society (English)." World Bank. http://documents.worldbank.org/curated/en/099021424061519032.

World Bank. 2024b. "Indonesia Economic Prospects: Funding Indonesia's Vision 2045." World Bank. http://documents.worldbank.org/curated/en/099121324112039917.

World Bank 2024c. "Mongolia Economic Update, May 2024." World Bank. https://doi.org/10.1596/41540.

World Bank. 2024d. "Mongolia Economic Update, November 2024: Sustaining the Gains—Special Focus: Distributional Impacts of Mongolia's Fiscal System." World Bank. https://doi.org/10.1596/42544.

World Bank. 2024e. "The Philippines Human Capital Review: Investing in the Early Years to Boost Human Potential." World Bank. https://documents1.worldbank.org/curated/en/099062024032533487/pdf/P18060313496220b71b50416ae4e2822cf2.pdf.

World Bank. 2024f. *Tax Expenditure Manual.* World Bank. http://documents.worldbank.org/curated/en/099062724151636908.

World Bank. 2025a. "Cambodia Economic Update, June 2025: Navigating Uncertainty: Strengthening Revenues for Cambodia's Future." World Bank. http://hdl.handle.net/10986/43470.

World Bank. 2025b. *East Asia and Pacific Economic Update, April 2025: A Longer View.* World Bank. https://doi.org/10.1596/978-1-4648-2232-2.

World Bank. 2025c. "Estimating Value Added Tax (VAT) and Corporate Income Tax (CIT) Gaps in Indonesia." Prosperity Insight Series, World Bank. http://hdl.handle.net/10986/42959.

World Bank. 2025d. "Mongolia Public Finance Review: Making This Time Different—Fiscal Reforms for Stable, Sustainable, and Inclusive Development." World Bank. http://hdl.handle.net/10986/43650.

World Bank. 2025e. *Services Unbound: Digital Technologies and Policy Reform in East Asia and Pacific.* East Asia and Pacific Development Series. World Bank. http://hdl.handle.net/10986/42486.

World Bank. 2025f. "Viet Nam Rising: Pathways to a High-Income Future." World Bank. http://hdl.handle.net/10986/43481.

World Bank. 2025g. "World Bank East Asia and Pacific Economic Update, October 2025: Jobs." World Bank. http://hdl.handle.net/10986/43739.

Fiscal Policy for Macroeconomic Stability

2

Introduction

Macroeconomic stability is a necessary condition for sustainable growth. Economies that avoid deep recessions accumulate more capital, attract more private investment, and give households and firms the confidence to plan ahead. Volatility disrupts investment in innovation and human capital, depressing the long-run growth rate through channels that go beyond simple demand effects (Aghion and Banerjee 2005).

Cross-country evidence shows significant and negative correlation between output volatility and long-run growth—that is, countries with more volatile output grow more slowly, with the strongest correlation in developing economies (Hnatkovska and Loayza 2005; Ramey and Ramey 1995). For instance, figure 2.1, panel a, plots output volatility against average gross domestic product (GDP) growth across a broad sample of economies over 2000–2023. The largest economies in East Asia and Pacific (EAP)—China, Malaysia, Thailand, and Viet Nam—cluster in the low-volatility, high-growth quadrant. The region's outliers—economies with higher commodity dependence, weaker institutions, or limited market access—sit farther up the volatility axis, and their growth records reflect it. The implication is direct: policies that reduce output volatility not only smooth the business cycle but also raise the long-run level of economic development.

Macroeconomic stability is associated with higher growth, whereas countercyclical government spending is associated with lower volatility.

FIGURE 2.1 Volatility, growth, and cyclicality of government spending, 2000–22

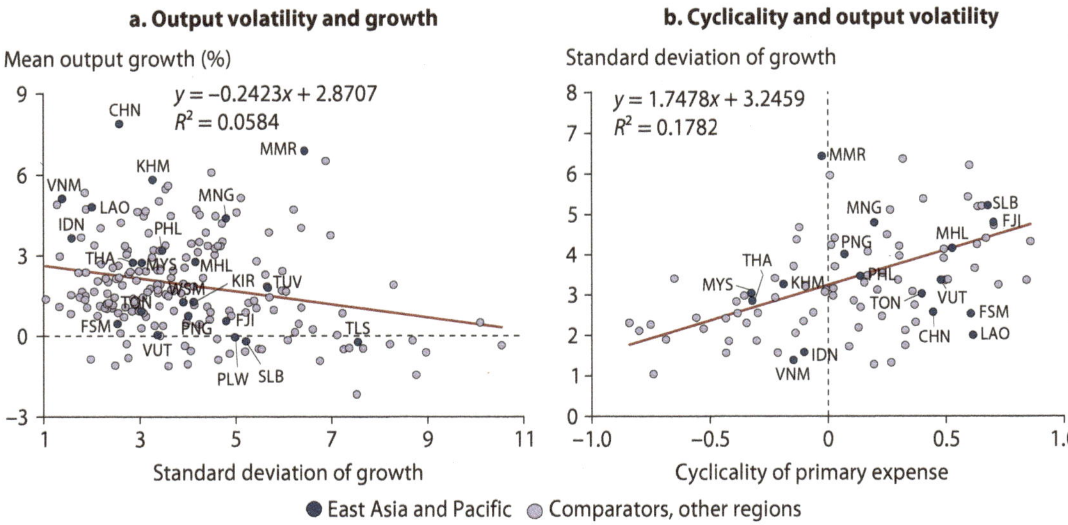

Source: Original figure for this publication based on World Economic Outlook Database, International Monetary Fund, https://www.imf.org/en/publications/sprolls/world-economic-outlook-databases.
Note: Cyclicality of government expenditure is calculated as the correlation between the cyclical component of real government expenditure and real GDP. The cyclical component has been estimated using the Hodrick-Prescott filter. Sample (excluding China and East Asia and Pacific) includes 66 developing and transition economies, and 22 industrial economies. For a list of country codes, refer to https://www.iso.org/obp/ui/#search.

Fiscal policy offers one of the most powerful tools governments have to promote macroeconomic stability. It does so primarily through countercyclical policy—that is, expanding the fiscal stance during downturns to support demand and tightening it during expansions to rebuild buffers (refer to figure 2.1, panel b). When the economy contracts, tax revenues fall and social spending rises simultaneously; both move to cushion the shock, and their combined effect on the fiscal balance determines how much automatic stabilization the government provides.

Effective stabilization requires adequate fiscal space. Governments that enter a recession with high debt, large deficits, and limited access to financing cannot borrow to support demand—even with a compelling economic case—and instead must cut spending or raise taxes precisely when the economy needs the opposite. Procyclical austerity in downturns is therefore not typically a policy choice but a symptom of insufficient fiscal buffers. This constraint reflects underlying fundamentals: debt levels, financing conditions, and institutional credibility. Governments with lower debt, access to long-term domestic financing, and stronger fiscal frameworks can borrow at lower cost and sustain countercyclical policy.

The chapter is organized as follows. It first examines EAP's record on fiscal cyclicality—that is, how governments in the region have managed the spending-revenue interaction over the business cycle and where the heterogeneity lies. It then assesses the current state of fiscal space across the region, with attention to debt levels, debt structure, and emerging sources of fiscal risk. Finally, it asks what institutional reforms—fiscal rules, medium-term frameworks, and disaster risk financing mechanisms—the region needs to rebuild buffers and sustain its track record of macroeconomic stabilization.

Fiscal policy over the business cycle in EAP

Fiscal policy in the region's economies has played a stabilizing role over the business cycle. Most East Asian economies have adopted a countercyclical or, at minimum, an acyclical fiscal policy stance, supporting activity in downturns while rebuilding fiscal buffers in expansions. Pacific Island countries, by contrast, remain largely procyclical, reflecting volatile revenues, limited financing options, and high exposure to shocks. Social transfers have been mostly countercyclical across the region. The effectiveness of fiscal policy, however, has depended on preexisting fiscal space: countries that entered crises with stronger fiscal positions, lower debt levels, and more credible fiscal frameworks could better maintain countercyclical spending when they most needed it.

Countercyclical capacity in East Asia versus structural procyclicality in Pacific Island countries

Procyclical fiscal policy is the norm in developing economies. Governments tend to spend more during booms and cut back during downturns, amplifying rather than smoothing economic fluctuations—with the pattern well documented across countries, time periods, and methodologies (Alesina et al. 2008; Frankel et al. 2013; Gavin and Perotti 1997; Ilzetzki and Végh 2008; Mendoza and Oviedo 2006; Talvi and Végh 2005; Tornell and Lane 1999). Tax policy shows a similar pattern: developing economies typically reduce taxes during booms and increase them during downturns, whereas taxes remain broadly acyclical in advanced economies (Végh and Vuletin 2015).

The cyclicality of fiscal policy in EAP is bifurcated. On one side, a core of relatively disciplined middle-income economies with some fiscal space can conduct countercyclical or broadly acyclical policy. On the other side, fiscal policy remains highly procyclical in a periphery of smaller, more vulnerable states with limited fiscal space, such as the Lao People's Democratic Republic and most Pacific Island countries.

Cambodia, Malaysia, Thailand, Viet Nam, and, to some extent, Indonesia, Myanmar, and the Philippines have been able to deploy less procyclical spending to support macroeconomic stabilization, despite having small governments (refer to figure 2.2). On average, the correlation between the cyclical components of government spending and GDP in East Asia is approximately –0.10, compared to 0.30 in other emerging market and developing economies (EMDEs).[1] Moreover, 89 percent of East Asian economies exhibit acyclical or countercyclical spending patterns—similar to the 91 percent observed in advanced economies and far above the 41 percent seen in other EMDEs.[2]

Most Pacific Island countries exhibit highly procyclical government spending. These economies face significantly higher macroeconomic volatility because of

Despite the relatively small size of government, spending in East Asia is less procyclical than in other EMDEs; by contrast, it remains highly procyclical in Pacific Island countries.

FIGURE 2.2 Cyclicality and size of government: East Asian economies, Pacific Island countries, and comparators, 2000–22

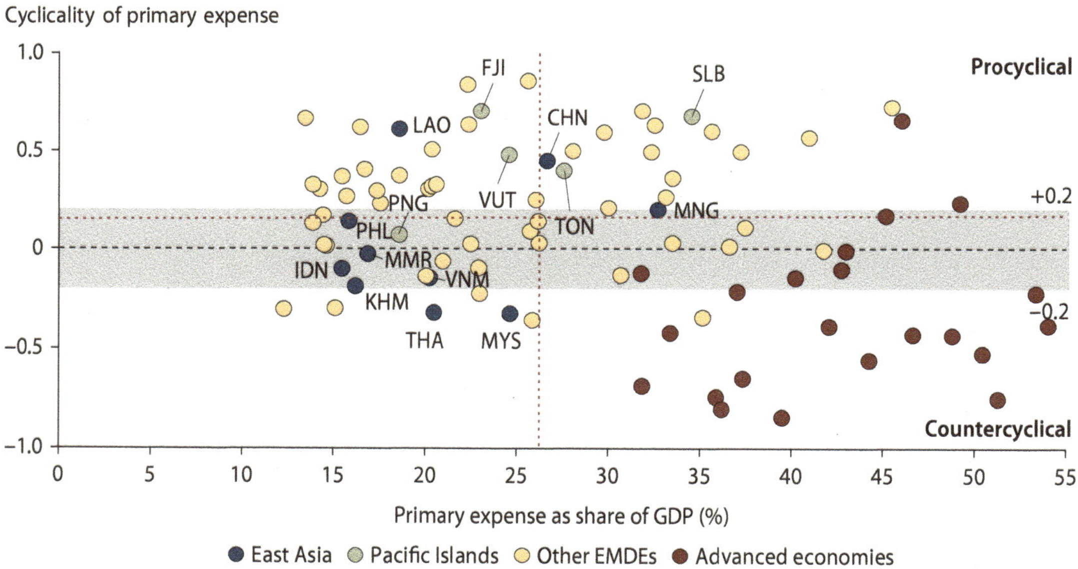

Source: Original figure for this publication based on World Economic Outlook Database, International Monetary Fund, https://www.imf.org/en/publications/sprolls/world-economic-outlook-databases.

Note: Cyclicality of government expenditure is calculated as the correlation between the cyclical component of real government expenditure and real GDP. The cyclical component has been estimated using the Hodrick-Prescott filter. Sample (excluding China and East Asia and Pacific) includes 66 developing and transition economies, and 22 industrial economies. For a list of country codes, refer to https://www.iso.org/obp/ui/#search. EMDEs = emerging market and developing economies.

their small size, limited economic diversification, and high exposure to external and climate shocks. At the same time, narrow and volatile tax bases, limited access to international capital markets, and frequent natural disasters constrain governments' ability to borrow or accumulate fiscal buffers. Consequently, fiscal policy has limited capacity to smooth economic fluctuations and often becomes highly procyclical (refer to box 2.1).

China presents a different and important case. At the national level, the government has deployed substantial countercyclical stimulus during major downturns—most visibly during the global financial crisis of 2008–09 and again during the COVID-19 pandemic. However, expenditure by local governments accounts for a significant share of public spending in China, and local government revenues are closely tied to local economic activity, particularly land sales, real estate taxes, and investment-linked receipts. These revenue sources surge during booms and collapse during downturns, creating a built-in procyclical dynamic at the subnational level (refer to box 2.2).

On the revenue side, Végh and Vuletin (2015) measure tax policy cyclicality by correlating changes in tax rates with real GDP growth. A negative correlation indicates procyclical policy—that is, tax rates rise in downturns and fall during booms—whereas a positive correlation reflects countercyclical policy. In this context, tax policy in East Asia appears less procyclical than in other EMDEs, mainly because of corporate income taxes (CITs) (refer to figure 2.3, panel a).

Between 2000 and 2022, East Asian economies enacted 17 CIT rate changes—16 of them cuts (refer to figure 2.3, panels b and c). Malaysia and Viet Nam reduced CIT rates four times, Indonesia and the Philippines three times, and Thailand twice. Of the 16 cuts, four occurred during the global financial crisis and two during the COVID-19 pandemic. These trends suggest that East Asian economies have used CIT cuts as a key fiscal tool, often deploying them during downturns.

In contrast, Pacific Island countries have highly procyclical tax policy. Tax instruments exhibit a negative correlation with the business cycle, particularly for corporate and personal income tax, indicating that tax rates tend to decline during expansions and rise during downturns. This pattern suggests that tax policy in Pacific Island countries amplifies economic fluctuations by raising tax burdens during downturns and easing them during expansions.

Box 2.1. Cyclicality and fiscal resilience in Pacific Island countries

Pacific Island countries are among the most volatile economies in the world (refer to figure B2.1.1). Their small size, limited diversification, geographic remoteness, and deep exposure to climate and external shocks combine to produce lower and more variable growth outcomes than in the rest of East Asia and Pacific and in other emerging market and developing economies. Since 2000, Pacific Island countries have had average annual growth of about 3.3 percent—more than 2 percentage points below the 5.6 percent recorded in other East Asian economies—and substantially higher growth volatility.

Pacific Island countries have had both lower and more volatile growth than the rest of EAP and other EMDEs.

FIGURE B2.1.1 GDP growth and growth volatility, Pacific Island countries and comparators, 2000–19

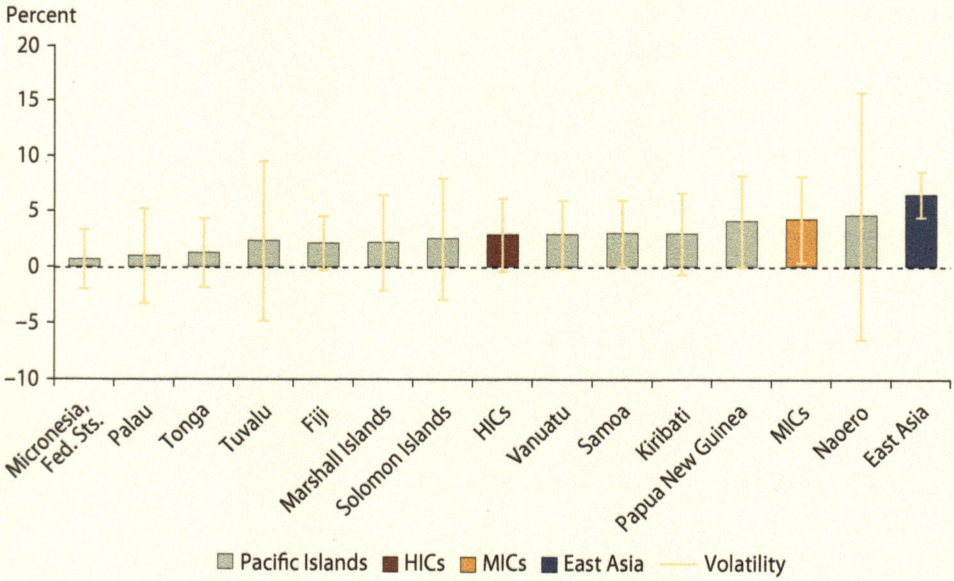

Source: Original figure for this publication based on World Economic Outlook Database, International Monetary Fund, https://www.imf.org/en/publications/sprolls/world-economic-outlook-databases.

Note: Bar height shows average annual growth rate; whiskers show average standard deviation over the period. EAP = East Asia and Pacific; EMDEs = emerging market and developing economies; HICs = high-income countries; MICs = middle-income countries.

(continued)

Box 2.1. Cyclicality and fiscal resilience in Pacific Island countries ***(continued)***

In this environment, fiscal policy should in principle play a larger stabilizing role than in more resilient economies. Unfortunately, the same structural features that make Pacific Island countries volatile also make countercyclical fiscal policy exceptionally hard to deliver: Narrow and volatile revenue bases leave little room to maneuver. Economic activity in most Pacific Island countries is concentrated in a handful of sectors—tourism, fisheries, and in some cases resource extraction—all highly sensitive to external shocks. When a cyclone strikes or global tourist arrivals fall, revenues collapse. These countries have no large, diversified tax base to cushion the blow. At the same time, small population size and geographic dispersion make the unit cost of delivering public services—infrastructure, health, education, and administration—structurally high. These factors limit governments' ability to adjust fiscal policy in response to economic fluctuations, often resulting in procyclical fiscal outcomes.

Pacific Island countries have severely constrained market access. Advanced economies and larger emerging market and developing economies can borrow their way through downturns. Most Pacific Island countries cannot. They do not issue sovereign debt in international capital markets. Financing comes primarily from multilateral and bilateral concessional lenders—a slower, more conditional, and less flexible channel than market borrowing (refer to figure B2.1.2).

Natural disasters compound the challenges. Climate shocks in Pacific Island countries are not rare tail events but recurring features of the fiscal calendar. A major cyclone or flood simultaneously reduces economic activity, destroys the revenue base, and generates large emergency spending needs for reconstruction and recovery. Each shock erodes the buffers that took years to accumulate. For many Pacific Island countries, the question is not whether to conduct countercyclical policy but whether enough remains in reserve to respond at all by the time the next shock arrives.

Pacific Island countries must therefore strengthen fiscal resilience. Well-designed fiscal frameworks, including fiscal rules, medium-term fiscal frameworks, and sovereign wealth or stabilization funds, can help governments build fiscal buffers during good times and create fiscal space to respond more effectively when shocks occur. For example, trust funds such as Kiribati's Revenue Equalization Reserve Fund and the Tuvalu Trust Fund have helped smooth fiscal revenues over time and provide resources during downturns. In addition, disaster risk financing mechanisms such as contingency funds, insurance schemes, or contingent credit lines can provide rapid liquidity following natural disasters, helping governments finance emergency response and reconstruction while preserving fiscal sustainability.

(continued)

Box 2.1. Cyclicality and fiscal resilience in Pacific Island countries *(continued)*

Pacific Island countries rely heavily on concessional public debt.

FIGURE B2.1.2 Reliance on concessional public debt, EAP and comparators, 2015–19

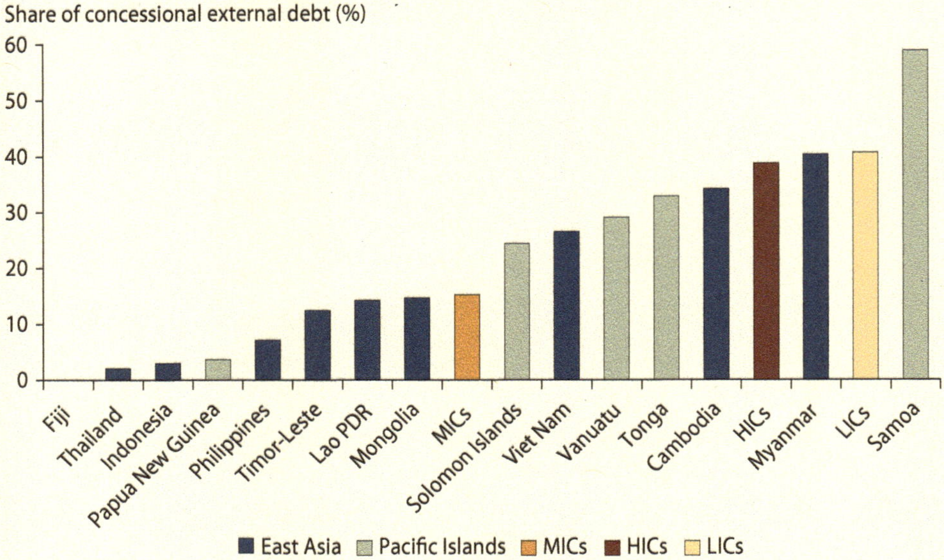

Source: Original figure for this publication based on World Development Indicators, World Bank, https://datatopics.worldbank.org/world-development-indicators/.

Note: Concessional debt is expressed as a share of total external debt. Values are averages over 2015–19. EAP = East Asia and Pacific; HICs = high-income countries; LICs = low-income countries; MICs = middle-income countries.

Box 2.2. Fiscal decentralization and procyclical spending in developing economies

The procyclicality of fiscal policy in emerging market and developing economies (EMDEs) is well-documented. Gavin and Perotti (1997) show that government spending in EMDEs tends to amplify rather than smooth the business cycle, driven by imperfect access to international credit markets and political economy pressures to spend during good times. Ilzetzki and Végh (2008) and Talvi and Végh (2005) reinforce that finding, establishing a robust empirical link between output and government consumption in EMDEs.

(continued)

Box 2.2. Fiscal decentralization and procyclical spending in developing economies *(continued)*

A less explored but important dimension of this phenomenon is the role of subnational governments. Rodden and Wibbels (2010) show that subnational revenues are strongly procyclical across both advanced and developing economies, with the degree of procyclicality driven by the income elasticity of the local tax base and the extent to which intergovernmental transfers can offset revenue shortfalls. Fardoust et al. (2012) note that, because of largely decentralized public service responsibilities in China, government expenditures are structurally prone to procyclicality. A World Bank comparative study of Brazil, China, and India argues that, when subnational governments face revenue shortfalls and constrained borrowing, as in Brazil, their fiscal response is likely to be procyclical, dampening national efforts to stabilize demand (Fardoust and Ravishankar 2013).

Figure B2.2.1, panel a, illustrates this correlation across a sample of EMDEs for which consistent data for central and local government spending are available. Countries where local governments account for a larger share of total public expenditure tend to exhibit more procyclical fiscal policy—spending rises during booms and falls during downturns, amplifying rather than dampening economic fluctuations. China, with the highest share of local spending in the sample (over 90 percent), sits at the far right of the distribution. The R^2 is modest (0.18), consistent with the broader literature's recognition that multiple factors drive fiscal cyclicality, but the direction of the relationship is clear.

Panel b of figure B2.2.1 further shows that across EMDEs general government spending declines when output is below trend and expands when it is above trend—a procyclical pattern that contrasts with advanced economies, where spending moves in the opposite direction to stabilize demand. This procyclicality is substantially more pronounced for local government spending than for central government spending. In EMDEs, local spending falls more compared to its trend during downturns than central government spending does, and it rises more during booms. Advanced economies display the reverse pattern: both central and local spending are mildly countercyclical, with local governments contributing little to cyclical volatility.

Together, these findings align with the broader literature and suggest that fiscal decentralization—particularly where subnational revenues are tied to volatile sources such as land sales, real estate transactions, and investment-linked receipts—can be an important structural driver of procyclical fiscal policy in EMDEs.

(continued)

Box 2.2. Fiscal decentralization and procyclical spending in developing economies *(continued)*

The procyclicality of government spending in developing economies is more pronounced for local government spending than for central government spending.

FIGURE B2.2.1 Local government spending and procyclicality

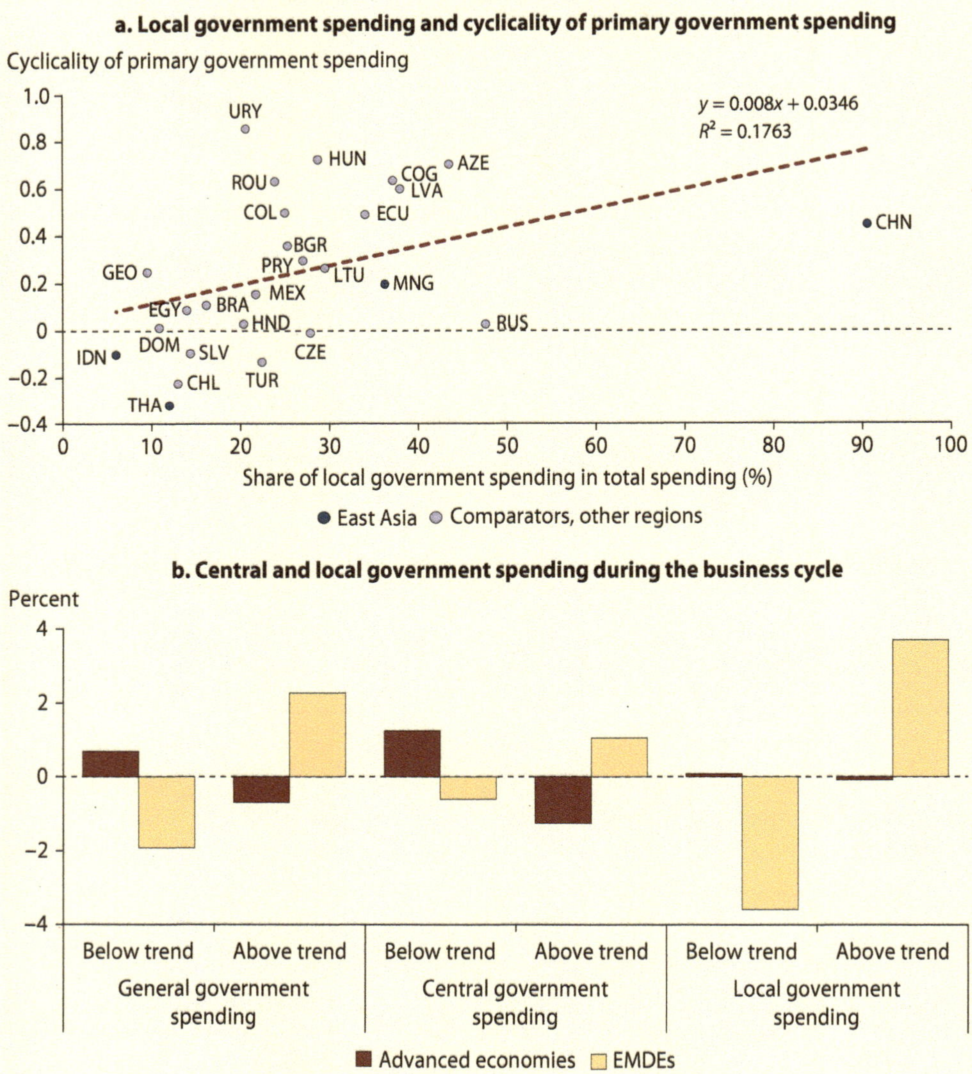

Source: Original figure for this publication based on Government Finance Statistics, International Monetary Fund, https://data360.worldbank.org/en/int/dataset/IMF_GFSMAB.

Note: Cyclicality of government expenditure is calculated as the correlation between the cyclical component of real government expenditure and real GDP. The cyclical component has been estimated using the Hodrick-Prescott filter. For a list of country codes, refer to https://www.iso.org/obp/ui/#search. EMDEs = emerging market and developing economies.

East Asian economies have less procyclical tax policy than other EMDEs have, mainly because of cuts in CIT rates. Out of 17 changes in CITs in East Asia between 2000 and 2022, 16 were reductions.

FIGURE 2.3 Tax rate changes and real GDP: East Asian economies, Pacific Island countries, and comparators, 2000–22

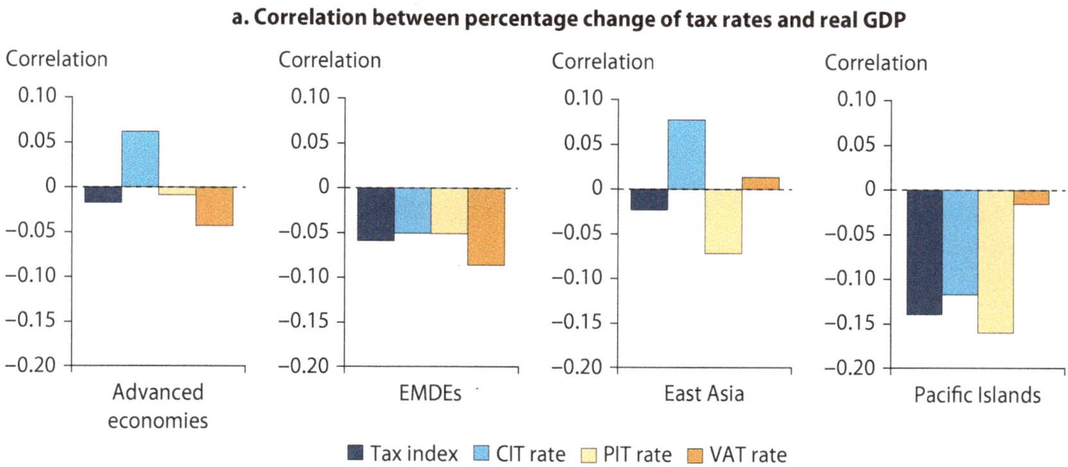

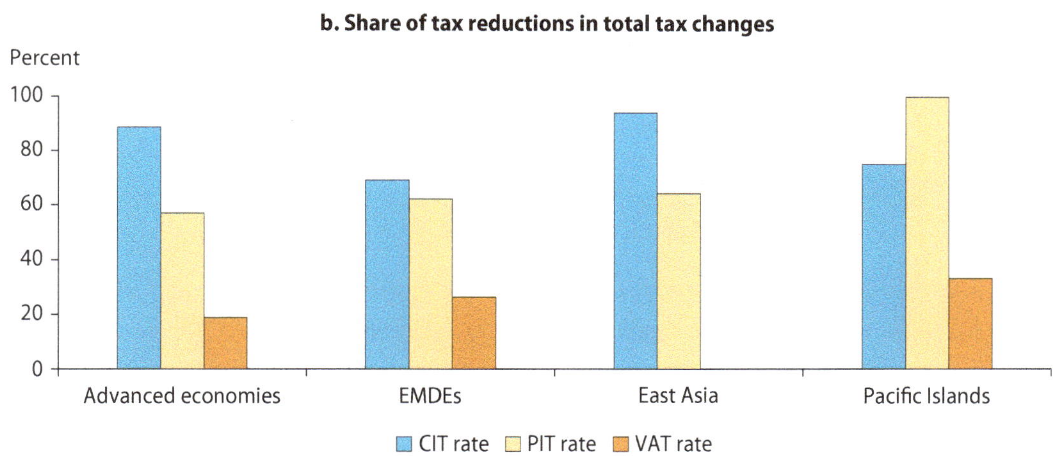

(continued)

FIGURE 2.3 Tax rate changes and real GDP, East Asian economies, Pacific Island countries, and comparators, 2000–22 *(continued)*

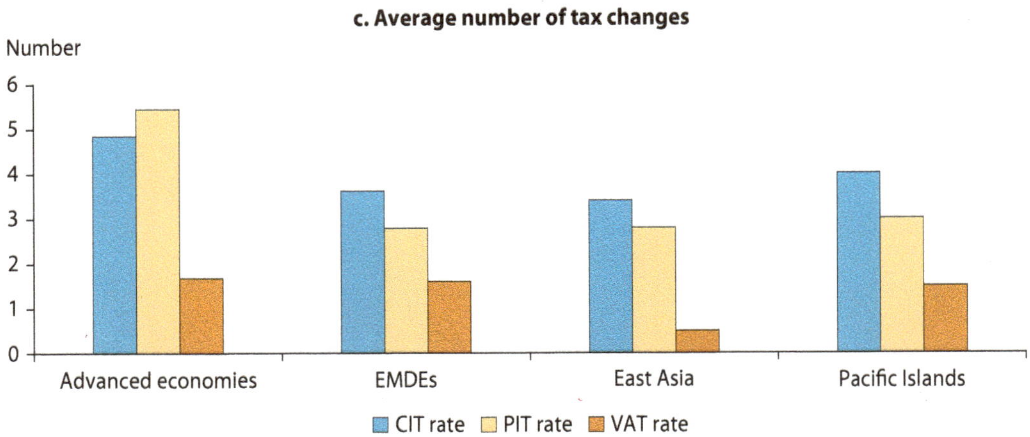

Sources: Original figure for this publication based on Global Revenue Statistics Database, Organisation for Economic Co-operation and Development, https://www.oecd.org/en/data/datasets/global-revenue-statistics-database.html; Végh and Vuletin 2025; World Economic Outlook Database, International Monetary Fund, https://www.imf.org/en/publications/sprolls/world-economic-outlook-databases.

Note: Panel a reports the cyclicality of CIT, PIT, and VAT as well as a composite tax index that weights the three individual tax rates by base period total tax revenue and aggregates them into a single index. Calculation of cyclicality of tax rates follows Végh and Vuletin (2015). Specifically, it reports country correlations between the percentage change in tax rates and percentage change in real GDP. Sample for subcomponents of the tax index (excluding China and East Asia and Pacific) includes 34 developing and transition economies and 20 industrial economies; the sample for the tax index itself includes 28 developing and transition economies and 20 industrial economies. The discrepancy between sample sizes exists because tax revenue data used to construct the weighted index are not available for all countries. In all panels, East Asia includes Indonesia, Malaysia, the Philippines, Thailand, and Viet Nam. Pacific Islands includes Fiji and Papua New Guinea. CIT = corporate income tax; EMDEs = emerging market and developing economies; PIT = personal income tax; VAT = value added tax.

What explains these differences? Three factors stand out. First, borrowing constraints determine whether governments can borrow when they need to. A government that can issue debt at reasonable cost during a downturn has the option to sustain spending even as revenues fall. One that cannot—because markets are closed, spreads have spiked, or debt is already at its limit—has no such option. The link between borrowing constraints and procyclicality is well established: when credit dries up, fiscal policy tightens whether policy makers want it to or not (Gavin and Perotti 1997; Kaminsky et al. 2004). The depth and liquidity of domestic bond markets determine whether a country can borrow in local currency, from a stable domestic investor base, and at long maturities, which in turn make the fiscal policy less susceptible to external financing conditions.

Institutional quality is the second driver. Strong fiscal frameworks allow governments to plan across the cycle rather than react to each year's revenue outturn. Credible fiscal rules anchor market expectations, keeping borrowing costs contained during downturns. Strong fiscal management capacity ensures that, when spending is authorized, it is executed quickly and reaches its intended target. In cases of weak capacities, the gap between fiscal intention and fiscal outcome is large and the stabilization effect of any given policy decision is smaller (Alesina et al. 2008; Frankel et al. 2013).

Political economy is the third and most persistent pressure. Booms generate revenue windfalls, and windfalls generate spending demands. Governments face powerful incentives—from legislators, constituencies, and coalition partners—to accommodate those demands. Accumulating buffers during expansions requires resisting such pressures, which is politically costly. A well-documented asymmetry results: spending rises easily in good times and falls only when forced by necessity in bad ones (Frankel et al. 2013; Talvi and Végh 2005). Breaking this asymmetry requires institutions that build buffers automatically and make spending restraint credible through well-designed fiscal rules.

Malaysia and Thailand stand out for their ability to implement countercyclical fiscal policy, supported by favorable financing conditions and relatively strong fiscal institutions. Both economies have deep domestic bond markets. Their governments can issue local currency debt across a range of maturities even during periods of stress, a capacity that proved decisive during the global financial crisis and again during COVID-19. Their fiscal frameworks have remained credible enough to keep sovereign spreads contained, preserving market access when most needed. Consequently, they have a spending cyclicality profile that resembles advanced economies more than developing country peers (World Bank 2023b). Lao PDR illustrates the opposite case: High public debt, limited financing options, and declining revenues have severely eroded fiscal space. As debt service obligations increased, fiscal adjustment relied largely on expenditure compression, reducing the resources available for critical public spending (World Bank 2023a).

Importantly, countercyclical fiscal policy does not necessarily translate into effective fiscal stabilization. Although many East Asian economies have increased spending during downturns, the small size of government often constrains the magnitude, composition, and persistence of these responses. Effective stabilization therefore requires not only countercyclical spending but also higher levels of spending, which in turn require greater fiscal space.

Social transfers as the main countercyclical instrument

In East Asia, on average, social benefits and other transfers represent the most countercyclical components of government spending (refer to figure 2.4, panel a). Social benefits play a critical role in stabilizing household income and consumption during economic downturns (Islamaj and Rothert 2024; Michaud and Rothert 2018). By cushioning consumption when private demand weakens, social benefits help limit deeper contractions in output and employment. Other transfers play a complementary role by supporting nonprofit institutions serving households and providing insurance-related transfers that help households cope with economic shocks.[3]

The behavior of these other spending components, however, exhibits considerable heterogeneity across EAP economies (refer to figure 2.4, panel b). In most cases, social benefits and other transfers are countercyclical. By contrast, public investment, grants, and subsidies tend to be procyclical across several economies. A few exceptions emerge. In Malaysia, for example, public investment has at times played a stabilizing role, consistent with the country's relatively strong access to domestic financing, which allows it to sustain capital spending during downturns.

Social transfers are an important source of countercyclicality in advanced economies and East Asia. Social benefits contribute to countercyclicality in most countries, except in Fiji, the Solomon Islands, and Vanuatu.

FIGURE 2.4 Cyclicality, by government expenditure subcomponent, 2000–22

a. Cyclicality, by expenditure subcomponent

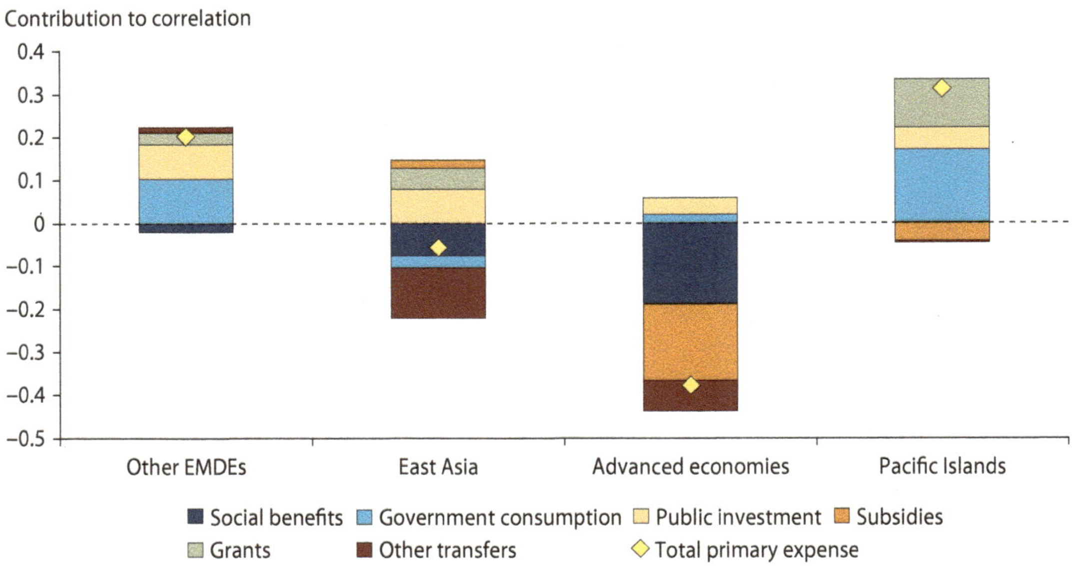

(continued)

FIGURE 2.4 Cyclicality, by government expenditure subcomponent, 2000–22 *(continued)*

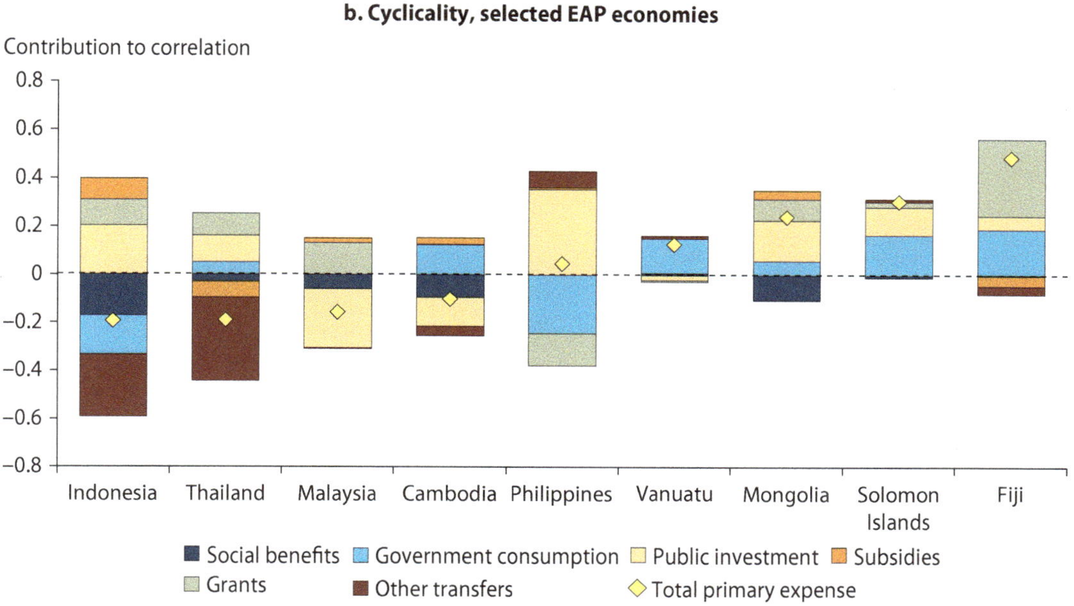

Sources: Original figure for this publication based on Government Finance Statistics, International Monetary Fund (IMF), https://data360.worldbank.org/en/int/dataset/IMF_GFSMAB; World Economic Outlook Database, IMF, https://www.imf.org/en/publications/sprolls/world-economic-outlook-databases.

Note: East Asia includes Cambodia, Indonesia, Malaysia, Mongolia, the Philippines, and Thailand; Pacific Islands include Fiji, the Solomon Islands, and Vanuatu; the sample also includes 34 EMDEs, and 16 advanced economies. Cyclical components estimated using the Hodrick-Prescott filter. Government consumption is calculated as the sum of compensation of employees and use of goods and services. Reported values for country groupings are weighted averages of country-level correlations over time, weighted by the number of years a given country appears in the sample. This calculation of cyclicality (with cyclicality calculated as the correlation between real GDP growth and real primary expense growth) differs slightly from that in figure 2.2, in which cyclicality of government expense is calculated as the correlation between the cyclical components of real GDP and real primary government expense. This methodology, consistent with the broad literature, allows decomposition of the correlation of total primary expense into additive subcomponents. Although the methodologies yield different magnitudes of cyclicality for most economies, the signs of the correlations remain broadly consistent across countries (industrial economies show strong countercyclicality, and East Asian economies are less procyclical than EMDEs). EAP = East Asia and Pacific; EMDEs = emerging market and developing economies.

East Asian economies have effectively scaled up social benefit expenditure during economic downturns (refer to figure 2.5, panel a). On average, social benefits, as a share of GDP, are approximately 7 percent above trend during downturns and about 6 percent below trend during economic upswings. This countercyclical pattern stands in sharp contrast to other EMDEs, including the Pacific Islands, where social benefit expenditure is typically above trend during economic booms and below trend during downturns.

Social benefits and other transfers in East Asia typically expand during economic downturns and decline during economic upswings.

FIGURE 2.5 Social benefits during the economic cycle, EAP and comparators

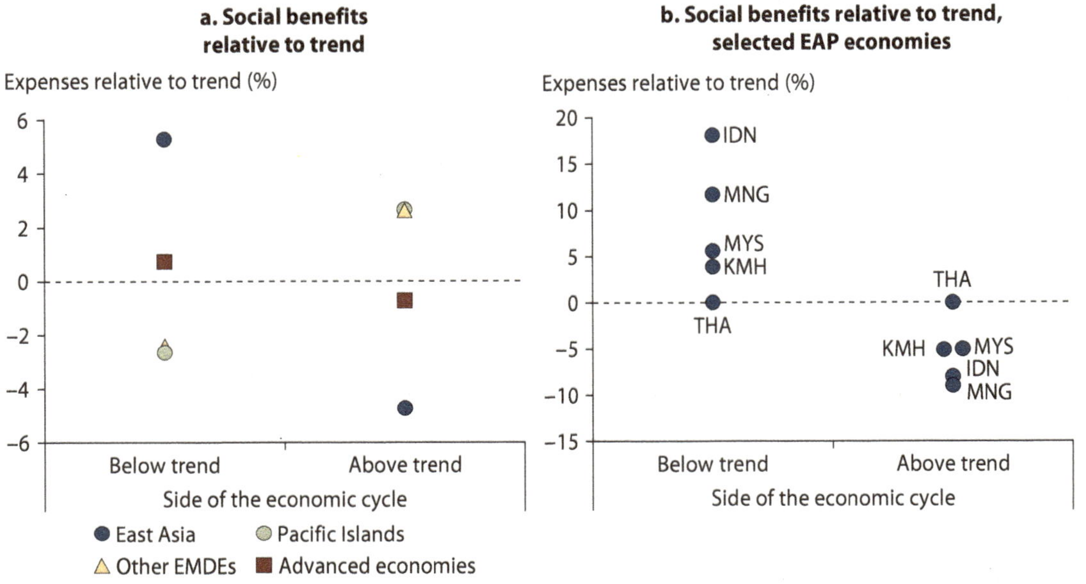

Sources: Original figure for this publication based on Government Finance Statistics, International Monetary Fund (IMF), https://data360.worldbank.org/en/int/dataset/IMF_GFSMAB; World Economic Outlook Database, IMF, https://www.imf.org/en/publications/sprolls/world-economic-outlook-databases.

Note: Dots and other shapes represent, for each country group, the median percentage change in social benefits across all country-episode observations classified as below trend or above trend during 2000–22. For a list of country codes, refer to https://www.iso.org/obp/ui/#search. EAP = East Asia and Pacific; EMDEs = emerging market and developing economies.

Despite the broad countercyclicality of social benefits in East Asia, the pattern is uneven across economies and largely absent in Pacific Island countries (refer to figure 2.5, panel b). Indonesia and Mongolia show a particularly strong response, with social benefit expenditure rising by close to 18 percent and 12 percent above trend during downturns, respectively, compared to much smaller or even negligible responses in other EMDEs. Cambodia and Malaysia exhibit a more moderate response, and social spending in Thailand remains broadly acyclical. In contrast, Pacific Island countries show weak or even procyclical patterns, with social spending increasing during upswings in Fiji and remaining close to trend in the Solomon Islands and Vanuatu.

The COVID-19 pandemic provides a clear illustration of the region's capacity to scale up spending. Although the countercyclicality of social benefits in East Asia remains robust even after excluding the COVID-19 period, the pandemic shows how economies in the region can rapidly scale up spending in times of need. Specifically, the fiscal response to COVID-19 in most EAP economies, except Lao PDR, Myanmar, Papua New Guinea, and Viet Nam, was close to the world average (5.9 percent of GDP). More important, the response was the largest relative to the predicted value based on the size of government (refer to box 2.3).

Despite the region's low levels of social spending (documented in chapter 1), the countercyclicality of social transfers highlights East Asia's relatively greater fiscal space and its capacity to deliver timely fiscal responses. First, by containing expenditures and maintaining low deficits during economic upswings, many economies in the region have preserved the fiscal space needed to respond forcefully to adverse shocks. Second, even limited but timely social transfers have supported macroeconomic stabilization in some of the region's economies during downturns. Chapter 3 argues that the effectiveness of social transfers could be further strengthened by larger and better-targeted social protection systems.

Box 2.3. Fiscal response during COVID-19

Governments responded to the COVID-19 crisis through fiscal measures that either increased spending (for example, through direct grants, wage subsidies, and expanded social protection) or reduced revenue (for example, through tax deferrals and cancellations). These interventions were essential to contain the health emergency, support health systems, and protect the incomes of households and firms, thereby mitigating the economic impact of the pandemic.

Although large fiscal responses are typically expected in high-income countries, the East Asia and Pacific region stands out with notably larger fiscal responses than in other developing regions (refer to figure B2.3.1, panel a). Responses within the region, however, varied considerably: most countries clustered around the global average (about 5.9 percent of GDP), but some—such as the Lao People's Democratic Republic, Myanmar, and Viet Nam—fell significantly below it (refer to figure B2.3.1, panel b). In contrast, Pacific Island countries exceeded not only the global average but also that of high-income countries, with particularly large responses in the Marshall Islands and the Federated States of Micronesia.

East Asia and Pacific also had the largest fiscal response relative to expectations given its macro-fiscal conditions. Predicted fiscal response is obtained from a regression controlling for government revenue, public debt, gross domestic product per capita, and number of COVID-19 cases. Overall, governments in the region mounted a strong and largely countercyclical fiscal response, with actual fiscal response averaging 3.9 and 2.7 percentage points higher than predicted in East Asian economies and the Pacific Islands, respectively (refer to figure B2.3.2, panel a), with significant variation across countries (refer to figure B2.3.2, panel b).

(continued)

Box 2.3. Fiscal response during COVID-19 *(continued)*

Fiscal response to COVID-19 in most East Asian economies was close to the world average; meanwhile, Pacific Island countries, especially the Marshall Islands and the Federated States of Micronesia, exceeded not only the global average but also that of high-income countries.

FIGURE B2.3.1 Fiscal response to COVID-19, by region and in EAP

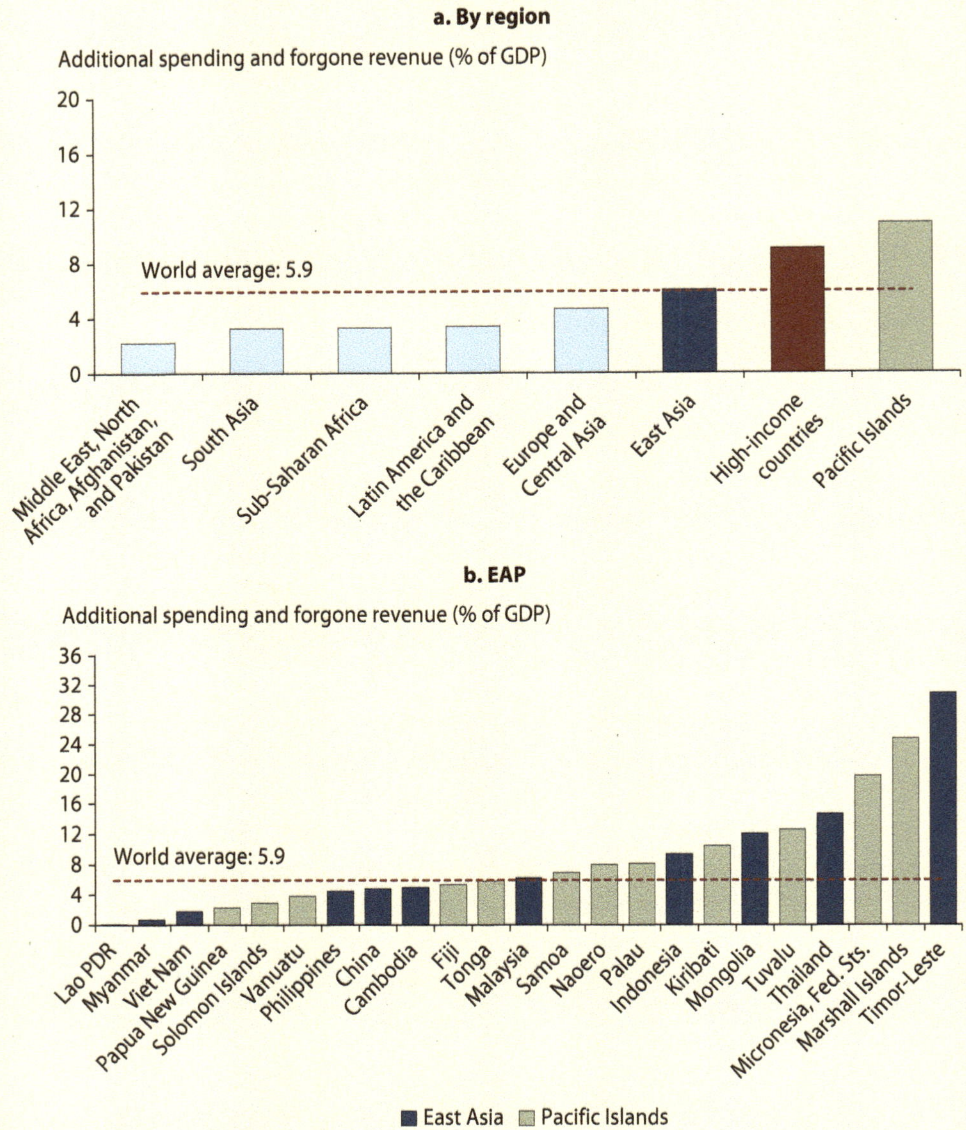

Source: Original figure for this publication based on Database of Fiscal Policy Responses to COVID-19, International Monetary Fund, https://www.imf.org/en/topics/imf-and-covid19/fiscal-policies-database-in-response-to-covid-19.
Note: Estimates as of October 2021. Fiscal spending includes all the fiscal tools implemented in response to the COVID-19 crisis (excluding government guarantees): deferred and canceled taxes, strengthening the social safety net, direct grants, wage subsidies, money transfers, and income support. EAP = East Asia and Pacific.

(continued)

Box 2.3. Fiscal response during COVID-19 *(continued)*

During COVID-19, EAP had the largest fiscal response relative to predicted value, illustrating the capacity of many EAP governments to finance countercyclical fiscal policy.

FIGURE B2.3.2 Difference between observed and predicted fiscal response to COVID-19, by region and in EAP

a. By region

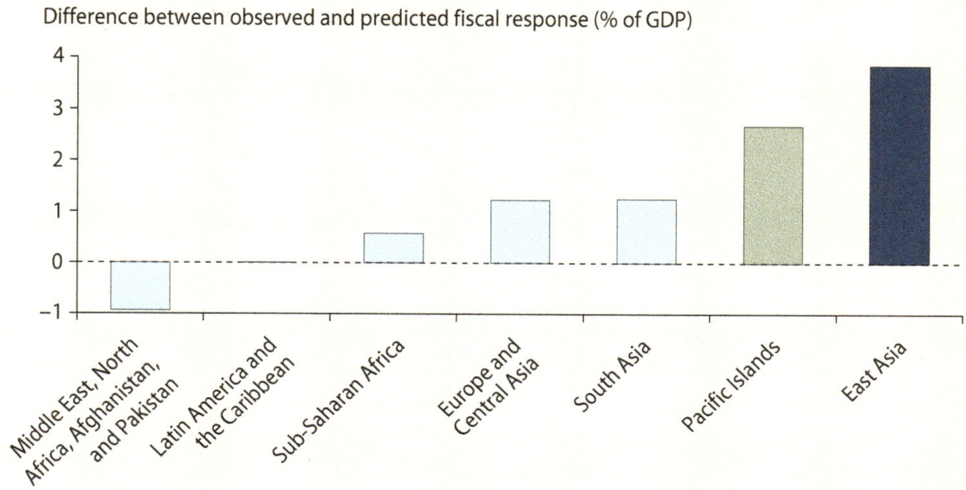

b. EAP

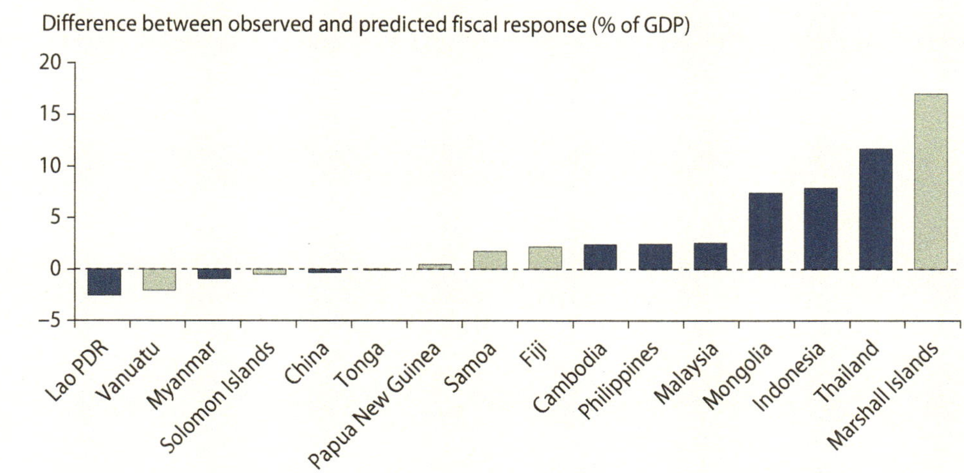

Sources: Original figure for this publication based on Database of Fiscal Policy Responses to COVID-19, International Monetary Fund (IMF), https://www.imf.org/en/topics/imf-and-covid19/fiscal-policies-database-in-response-to-covid-19; World Development Indicators, World Bank, https://datatopics.worldbank.org/world-development-indicators/; World Economic Outlook Database, IMF, https://www.imf.org/en/publications/sprolls/world-economic-outlook-databases.

Note: Estimates as of October 2021. Fiscal spending includes all the fiscal tools implemented in response to the COVID-19 crisis (excluding government guarantees): deferred and canceled taxes, strengthening the social safety net, direct grants, wage subsidies, money transfers, and income support. Bars represent the difference between the observed fiscal response and the predicted fiscal response after controlling for government revenue, public debt, GDP per capita, and number of COVID-19 cases. EAP = East Asia and Pacific.

(continued)

Box 2.3. Fiscal response during COVID-19 *(continued)*

Although crucial to mitigate the long-term effects of the pandemic, these measures may leave a legacy of elevated debt levels, which pose significant sustainability risks. Moving forward, governments need to actively seek to reduce deficits and improve policies to rebuild fiscal buffers, so they can respond effectively to future economic shocks.

Fiscal discipline as an enabler of countercyclical spending

The region's ability to deploy countercyclical government spending reflects a defining feature of fiscal policy in East Asia: strong fiscal discipline. This discipline reinforces the three drivers of cyclicality. First, it mitigates borrowing constraints by building fiscal space during good times, preserving market access when downturns hit. Second, it strengthens institutional effectiveness by narrowing the gap between fiscal plans and outcomes, ensuring that approved spending is executed quickly and predictably when needed. Third, it helps counter political economy pressures, allowing governments to accumulate buffers rather than spend windfalls.

During 2010–19, East Asia's median primary deficit stood at approximately 0.5 percent of GDP, compared to 1.4 percent for the developing economy benchmark (refer to figure 2.6). This low deficit reflects relatively prudent fiscal positions across most economies in the region, with several economies maintaining primary surpluses and others running only moderate deficits. Consequently, East Asia entered recent shocks with stronger fiscal buffers than other EMDEs. In contrast, most Pacific Island countries have been unable to deploy countercyclical government spending despite recording a median primary balance of 1.1 percent of GDP, reflecting the structural constraints discussed earlier.

By containing expenditures and maintaining relatively low deficits and debt levels during economic upswings, several EAP economies have built fiscal space over time. This fiscal discipline has also contributed to stronger credibility and more favorable financing conditions during economic downturns. Consistent with this pattern, primary balance pressures in East Asia tend to lessen during economic expansions and rise during downturns, as governments allow deficits to widen to support countercyclical fiscal policy; however, the pattern is much less evident in Pacific Island countries and other EMDEs (refer to figure 2.7, panel a).

East Asian economies have typically exhibited stronger fiscal discipline than other EMDEs, as reflected in relatively low primary deficits and moderate debt levels.

FIGURE 2.6 Primary balance, selected East Asian economies and comparators, 2010–19

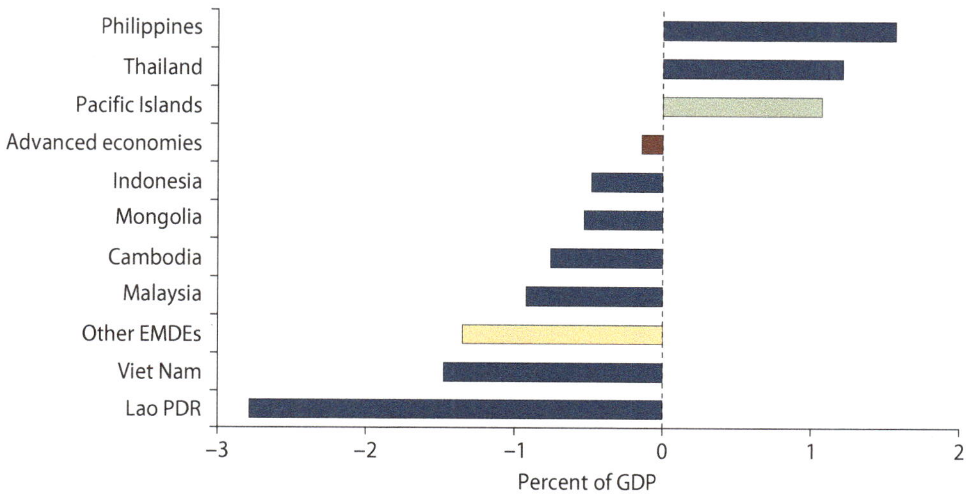

Source: Original figure for this publication based on World Economic Outlook Database, International Monetary Fund, https://www.imf.org/en/publications/sprolls/world-economic-outlook-databases.

Note: Bars show the median primary balance during 2010–19. The sample includes 25 advanced economies and 63 developing economies (excluding East Asia and Pacific). Pacific Islands include Fiji, the Marshall Islands, Micronesia, Papua New Guinea, the Solomon Islands, Tonga, and Vanuatu. EMDEs = emerging market and developing economies.

Among East Asian economies illustrating this pattern, Cambodia, Thailand, and Viet Nam provide the clearest examples over 2000–23 (refer to figure 2.7, panel b). Cambodia moves from near balance during upswings to a deficit of approximately 3.0 percent during downturns. Thailand shifts from a median primary surplus of approximately 1.4 percent of GDP during upswings to a median deficit of about 0.8 percent during downturns, and Viet Nam shifts from a median surplus of 0.4 percent to a median deficit of 1.5 percent. The Philippines has a similar but more muted countercyclical pattern. Malaysia, despite exhibiting countercyclical behavior, continues to run primary deficits even during upswings. Mongolia shows little variation in its primary balance over the cycle, pointing to limited cyclical adjustment. Lao PDR exhibits a strongly procyclical pattern. In Pacific Island countries, fiscal positions also show limited variation over the business cycle and do not show a systematic adjustment between upswings and downturns.

By containing primary deficits and debt accumulation during upswings, many East Asian economies have preserved the fiscal space needed to respond effectively to shocks.

FIGURE 2.7 Primary balance over the cycle: EAP, comparators, and selected EAP economies, 2000–23

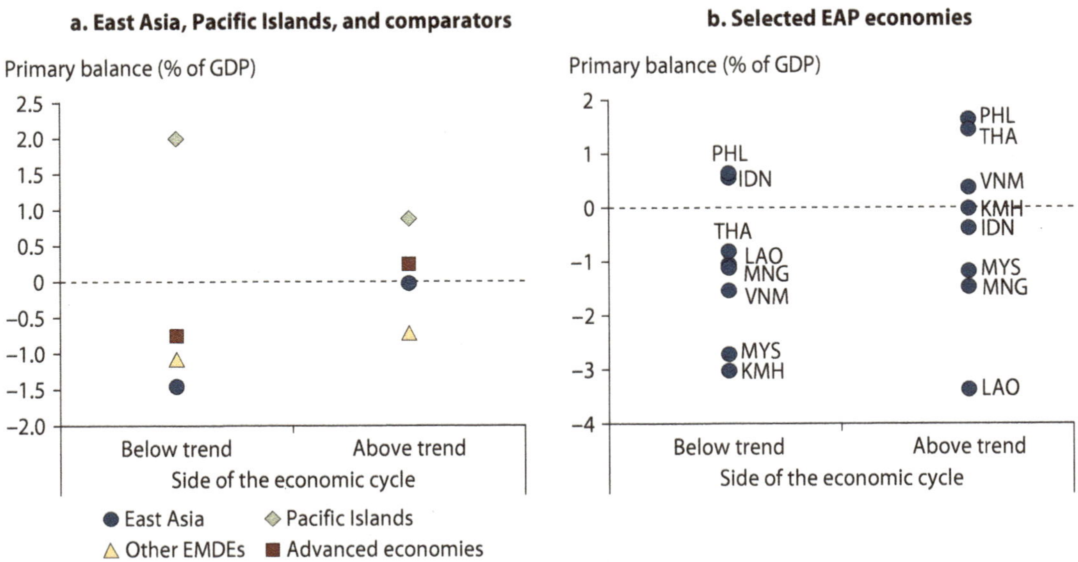

Source: Original figure for this publication based on World Economic Outlook Database, International Monetary Fund, https://www.imf.org/en/publications/sprolls/world-economic-outlook-databases.

Note: Dots and other shapes represent, for each country group, the median primary balance across all country-episode observations classified as below trend or above trend during 2000–22. The sample includes 25 advanced economies and 63 developing economies (excluding EAP). East Asia includes Cambodia, Indonesia, Lao PDR, Malaysia, Mongolia, the Philippines, Thailand, and Viet Nam. Pacific Islands include Fiji, the Marshall Islands, Micronesia, Papua New Guinea, the Solomon Islands, Tonga, and Vanuatu. For a list of country codes, refer to https://www.iso.org/obp/ui/#search. EAP = East Asia and Pacific; EMDEs = emerging market and developing economies.

Empirical evidence suggests that fiscal discipline plays an important role in shaping the cyclicality of fiscal policy (refer to box 2.4). Using deviations of realized primary balances from World Economic Outlook forecasts as a proxy, analysis for this chapter finds that countries that consistently outperform their fiscal projections, running smaller deficits than planned, tend to conduct more countercyclical spending.[4] Notably, EAP economies systematically outperform their fiscal forecasts relative to both advanced economies and other developing countries, pointing to stronger discipline in execution. This relationship is robust to standard controls, highlighting the role of de facto discipline: countries that deliver better fiscal outcomes than projected are more likely to build fiscal space over time, enabling them to expand spending during downturns.

Box 2.4. Fiscal discipline and the cyclicality of fiscal policy: An empirical analysis

To assess the role of fiscal discipline in shaping the cyclicality of government spending, a panel regression is estimated using data for 95 countries over 2012–23.[a]

Although fiscal discipline is often proxied by the primary balance or public debt, these measures are not well-suited for isolating the relationship between fiscal discipline and cyclicality. The primary balance is mechanically linked to government spending and moves with the business cycle, creating simultaneity and reverse causality concerns. Public debt reflects not only past fiscal outcomes but also financing conditions and market access (Gavin and Perotti 1997; Kaminsky et al. 2004), making it a limited proxy for fiscal discipline. The related literature has instead relied on proxies such as fiscal rules (Debrun and Kumar 2007; Frankel et al. 2013) and institutional quality (Alesina et al. 2008; Frankel et al. 2013), but these proxies capture de jure constraints rather than the actual exercise of discipline.

The analysis measures fiscal discipline using deviations of realized primary balances from one-year-ahead World Economic Outlook (WEO) forecasts.[b] Countries that consistently outperform their projected primary deficit, running smaller deficits than forecast, signal stronger fiscal discipline and, as shown here, tend to conduct more countercyclical fiscal policy. This pattern is consistent with these countries' building fiscal space over time, which in turn allows them to raise spending when a downturn arrives without hitting a financing constraint or breaching a debt threshold.[c]

Figure B2.4.1 plots average deviations of realized primary deficits from one-year-ahead WEO forecasts over 2011–23. A negative value indicates that, on average, economies ran smaller deficits than projected. The majority of East Asia and Pacific economies outperformed their fiscal projections during the sample period, whereas benchmarks for both advanced and other emerging market and developing economies underperform, showing slight positive deviations on average. This pattern suggests that fiscal discipline in implementation is a distinguishing feature of the region.

(continued)

Box 2.4. Fiscal discipline and the cyclicality of fiscal policy: An empirical analysis *(continued)*

Primary deficits in most EAP economies typically outperform forecasts, reflecting more prudent fiscal management than in other EMDEs.

FIGURE B2.4.1 Average deviation from primary deficit forecasts, selected EAP economies and comparators, 2011–23

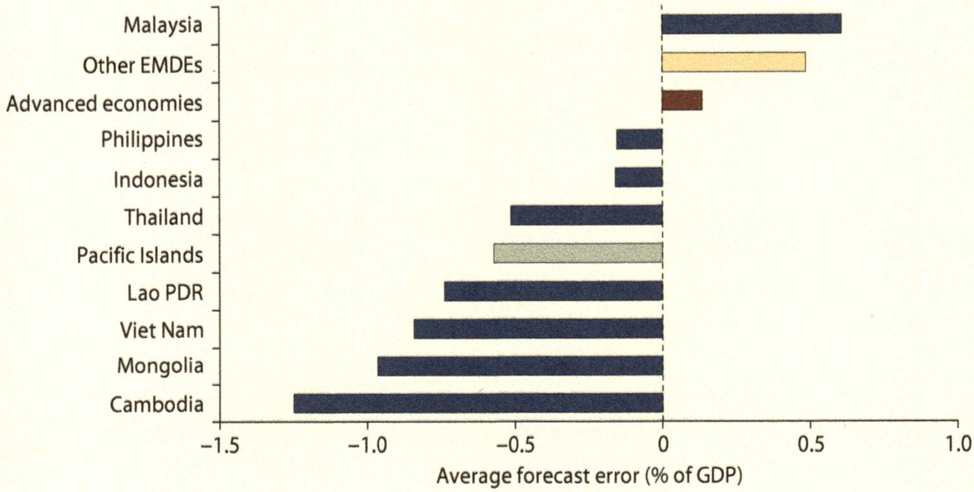

Source: Original figure for this publication based on World Economic Outlook Database, International Monetary Fund, https://www.imf.org/en/publications/sprolls/world-economic-outlook-databases.
Note: EAP = East Asia and Pacific; EMDEs = emerging market and developing economies.

The determinants of the cyclicality of government spending are formally examined by estimating the equation in note a. Beyond primary deficit forecast error, additional controls include measures of institutional quality, financial openness, interest rate volatility, and the existence of fiscal rules and fiscal councils.[d]

Table B2.4.1 presents the baseline results. Columns (2) and (3) show that positive forecast error (running a larger deficit than projected) is significantly associated with more procyclical spending (coefficients –0.098 and –0.093, respectively), consistent with the central hypothesis. Columns (4) and (5) replicate the specification using a two-year lag, and the result holds with comparable magnitude (–0.083 and –0.090), providing further evidence against a reverse causality interpretation. Financial openness and institutional quality are both significantly

(continued)

Box 2.4. Fiscal discipline and the cyclicality of fiscal policy: An empirical analysis *(continued)*

associated with more countercyclical policy, consistent with Frankel et al. (2013). Fiscal rules are not statistically significant, consistent with the broader finding that the type of rule matters for cyclicality (refer to the later subsection on fiscal rules to support discipline and help rebuild fiscal space). These results suggest that fiscal discipline in implementation, proxied by deviations of realized primary balances from WEO forecasts, may be an important determinant of countercyclical government spending.

TABLE B2.4.1 Determinants of the cyclicality of fiscal policy, 2012–23
Dependent variable: cyclical component of real government expenditure

Variable	(1)	(2)	(3)	(4)	(5)
GDP cycle	0.227**	0.199**	1.144***	0.182*	1.198***
	(0.096)	(0.089)	(0.429)	(0.097)	(0.431)
GDP cycle × Forecast error (*t*–1)	—	−0.098***	−0.093***	—	—
		(0.023)	(0.028)		
GDP cycle × Forecast error (*t*–2)	—	—	—	−0.083***	−0.090***
				(0.031)	(0.029)
GDP cycle × Gov't effectiveness	—	—	−0.013*	—	−0.010
			(0.007)		(0.007)
GDP cycle × Financial openness	—	—	−0.510	—	−0.563*
			(0.316)		(0.305)
GDP cycle × Fiscal rule	—	—	0.180	—	−0.083
			(0.233)		(0.246)
GDP cycle × Fiscal council	—	—	−0.074	—	−0.005
			(0.299)		(0.307)
Observations	950	950	938	852	841

(continued)

(continued)

Box 2.4. Fiscal discipline and the cyclicality of fiscal policy: An empirical analysis *(continued)*

TABLE B2.4.1 Determinants of the cyclicality of fiscal policy, 2012–23 *(continued)*

Variable	(1)	(2)	(3)	(4)	(5)
Countries	92	92	91	92	91
Within R^2	0.013	0.064	0.093	0.026	0.057

Sources: Original table for this publication based on Alonso et al. 2025a, 2025b; Chinn-Ito Index (Chinn and Ito 2006); World Economic Outlook (WEO) Database, International Monetary Fund, https://www.imf.org/en/publications/sprolls/world-economic-outlook-databases; Worldwide Governance Indicators, World Bank, https://www.worldbank.org/en/publication/worldwide-governance-indicators.

Note: Country fixed effects throughout. All interaction variables lagged one period. Sample restricted to 2012–23 because of fiscal risk data availability (WEO errors). Columns (1)–(3) use one-year lag of forecast error; columns (4) and (5) use two-year lag. Forecast error is the deviation of the realized primary balance from one-year-ahead WEO forecasts. The forecast error measure is not significantly correlated with government effectiveness ($r = 0.04$, $p = 0.19$) or rule of law ($r = 0.04$, $p = 0.24$), supporting its interpretation as a distinct dimension of fiscal discipline. Standard errors in parentheses, clustered at the country level. — = not applicable.

*$p < .10$ **$p < .05$ ***$p < .01$

a. Following Frankel et al. (2013), the analysis regresses the cyclical component of real government expenditure on the cyclical component of real gross domestic product (GDP) and its interactions with various factors identified in the literature as determinants of fiscal policy cyclicality. Specifically, it estimates the following equation:

$$g_{it} = \alpha_i + \alpha_2 y_{it} + \sum_K \alpha_{3k}\left(y_{it} \times X_{kit}\right) + \sum_K \alpha_{4k} X_{kit} + \varepsilon_{it}$$

where g_{it} is the cyclical component of real government expenditure, and y_{it} is the cyclical component of real GDP for country i in year t. X_{kit} denotes the k-th control variable, which enters both as a standalone term and interacted with the GDP cycle. The estimation is primarily interested in the coefficient of the interaction term, a_{3k}, which captures the marginal effect of a given control variable on the cyclicality of government spending: a negative value indicates that higher values of X_{kit} are associated with countercyclical fiscal policy. All controls enter with a one-period lag to address endogeneity concerns. Standard errors are clustered at the country level, and country fixed effects are included across all specifications.

b. World Economic Outlook Database, International Monetary Fund, https://www.imf.org/en/publications/sprolls/world-economic-outlook-databases.

c. To minimize the influence of data revisions, outturns are taken from the earliest available WEO vintage following the reference year, ensuring the measure reflects fiscal execution as initially recorded rather than subsequent methodological revisions. A potential concern is that forecast errors may proxy for institutional quality rather than a distinct dimension of discipline. However, the measure is not significantly correlated with either government effectiveness ($r = 0.04$) or rule of law ($r = 0.04$) across the sample (refer to annex 2A), indicating that forecast outperformance captures something closer to execution capacity and political commitment to stated targets, orthogonal to the broader institutional environment already controlled for in the regression.

d. Institutional quality is measured using the Worldwide Governance Indicators index of government effectiveness, which ranges from 0 to 100. Financial openness is captured by the Chinn-Ito KAOPEN index (Chinn and Ito 2006), which measures the degree of capital account openness on a scale from 0 to 1. Interest rate volatility is computed as the standard deviation of each economy's real interest rate. Fiscal rules are identified using the International Monetary Fund's Fiscal Rules Dataset (Alonso et al. 2025b), which contains information on the use and design of national and supranational fiscal rules from 1985 to 2024. Similarly, fiscal councils are identified using the Fiscal Councils Dataset (Alonso et al. 2025a).

Fiscal space and debt sustainability in EAP

Fiscal space in EAP has narrowed in recent years. Many economies entered the pandemic with relatively sound fiscal positions, but successive shocks—COVID-19, slower global growth, tighter financial conditions, and climate-related disasters—have driven public debt up, eroding the capacity for countercyclical fiscal policy. Looking ahead, the region faces a more challenging environment characterized by higher debt burdens and greater exposure to external, financial, and climate shocks. Importantly, fiscal space depends not only on the level of public debt but also on how it is financed. Countries with longer debt maturities, domestic currency issuance, and diversified investor bases face lower refinancing risks and retain greater flexibility to respond to future shocks.

Rising debt levels and shrinking fiscal space

Fiscal space in EAP has narrowed in recent years, as reflected in increasing public debt levels, resulting in a reduced capacity to respond to future shocks. Although the region's economies entered the COVID-19 crisis with relatively strong fiscal positions, the shock accelerated an upward trend in public debt that began after the global financial crisis of 2008–09. In developing EAP excluding China, the ratio of public debt-to-GDP increased from about 35 percent in 2008 to 45 percent in 2019, and further to 54 percent in 2024 (refer to figure 2.8, panel a). Debt increased across most EAP economies, with particularly sharp increases in Lao PDR, Papua New Guinea, the Philippines, and Thailand. Looking ahead, public debt in EAP excluding China is projected to remain elevated over 2025–27. In China, debt rose more sharply, with the ratio increasing from about 27 percent in 2008 to 59 percent in 2019 and 88 percent in 2024, and it is expected to continue increasing in the coming years (refer to figure 2.8, panel b).

Primary deficits have become a key driver of debt accumulation in EAP and are expected to add about 0.4 percentage point per year to the debt-to-GDP ratio during 2025–27. A debt dynamics decomposition shows that primary deficits contributed an average of 0.5 percentage point per year to debt accumulation during 2010–19 (refer to annex 2B). This contribution increased sharply during the COVID-19 pandemic, reaching 3.3 percentage points per year, before moderating to 0.2 percentage point per year in 2023–24 as fiscal consolidation efforts resumed (refer to figure 2.9). In China, the contribution of primary deficits is expected to increase from 1.6 percentage points per year in 2010–19 to 6.9 percentage points in 2025–27. At the same time, the reduction in debt ratios driven by real interest rates below GDP growth is diminishing, weakening a key offset to debt accumulation.

The COVID-19 shock accelerated an upward trend in the ratio of public debt-to-GDP observed in most developing EAP economies since the global financial crisis of 2008–09.

FIGURE 2.8 Public debt accumulation, EAP and China, 2000–27

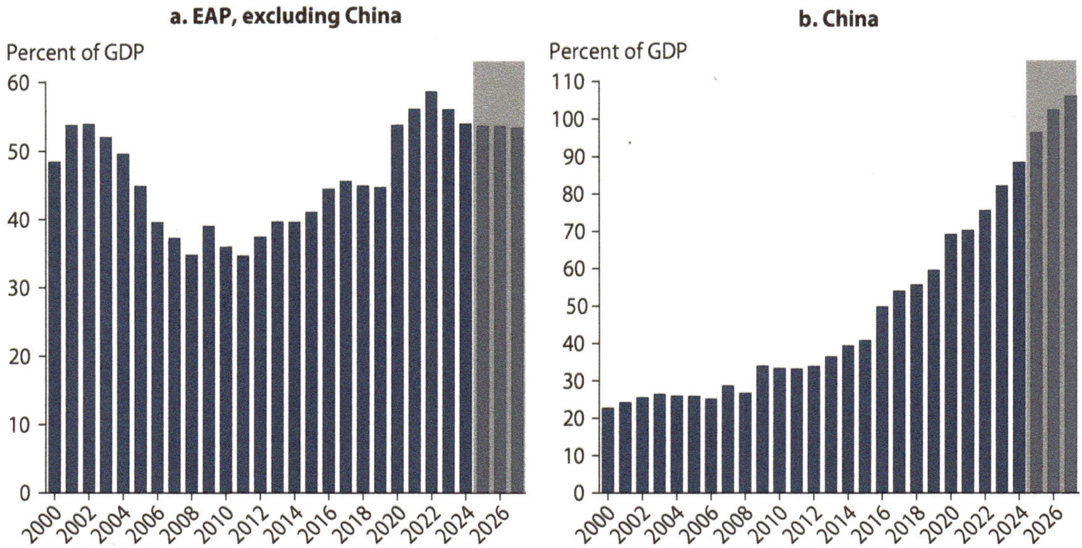

Source: Original figure for this publication based on World Economic Outlook Database, International Monetary Fund, https://www.imf.org/en/publications/sprolls/world-economic-outlook-databases.

Note: In panel a, EAP includes Cambodia, Indonesia, Lao PDR, Malaysia, Mongolia, Papua New Guinea, the Philippines, Thailand, and Viet Nam. Results for 2025–27 are projections. EAP = East Asia and Pacific.

In some EAP economies, rising public debt reflects persistently high primary deficits rather than temporary shocks. Malaysia offers an example, with the ratio of public debt-to-GDP increasing from about 39 percent in 2008 to 57 percent in 2019 and 70 percent in 2024, alongside primary deficits in every year over the past two decades, averaging about 2.3 percent of GDP (refer to box 2.5). Similar patterns are observed in Fiji, as well as in China, where primary deficits have also contributed to rising debt over time. Unlike in countries where public debt increased in response to the COVID-19 pandemic, these deficits reflect structural fiscal imbalances that require sustained and comprehensive fiscal adjustments.

Public debt as a share of GDP will likely remain elevated, driven by higher primary deficits, rising interest rates, and weaker growth.

FIGURE 2.9 Drivers of debt accumulation, EAP and China, 2000–27

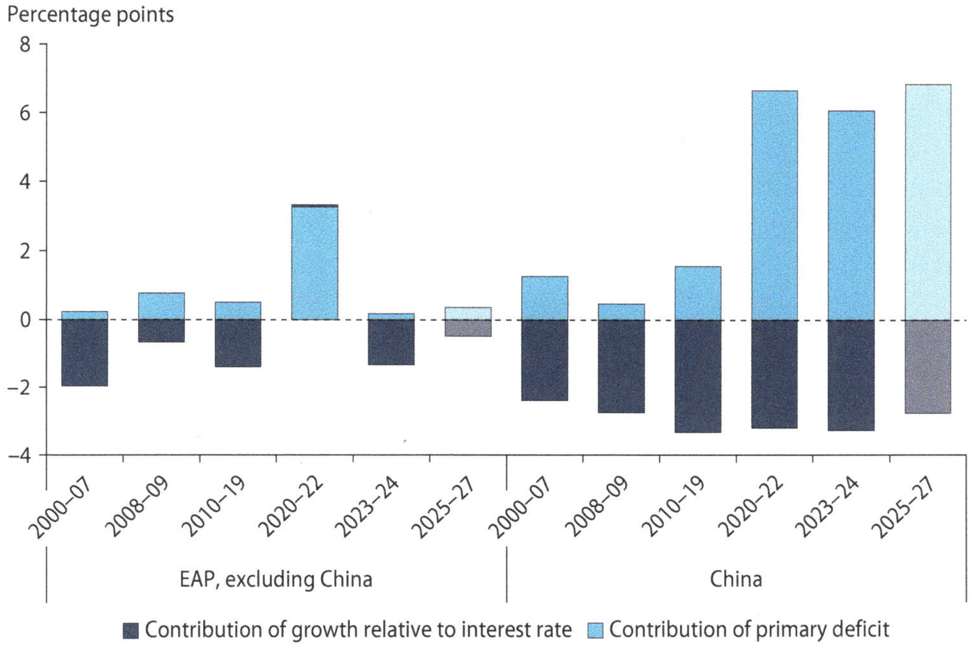

Source: Original figure for this publication based on World Economic Outlook Database, International Monetary Fund, https://www.imf.org/en/publications/sprolls/world-economic-outlook-databases.
Note: Using standard debt dynamic accounting decomposition, changes in the ratio of public debt-to-GDP in any given year can be decomposed into changes in the primary fiscal deficit (defined as revenues minus expenditures net of interest payments), growth rates, interest payments, inflation rates, exchange rate depreciations, and a residual that can be explained by factors such as privatization or the realization of contingent liabilities. EAP excluding China includes Cambodia, Indonesia, Lao PDR, Malaysia, Mongolia, Papua New Guinea, the Philippines, Thailand, and Viet Nam. Lighter bars show projections for 2025, 2026, and 2027. EAP = East Asia and Pacific.

Box 2.5. Persistent deficits and contribution to public debt: The case of Malaysia

Malaysia provides a clear example of how persistent fiscal deficits contribute to increases in public debt. Over the past two decades, Malaysia has recorded primary deficits in most years, with public debt rising from about 39 percent of gross domestic product (GDP) in 2008 to 57 percent in 2019 and 70 percent in 2024. This sustained pattern contrasts with other economies in the region whose debt increased primarily in response to temporary shocks, such as the COVID-19 pandemic.

(continued)

Box 2.5. Persistent deficits and contribution to public debt: The case of Malaysia *(continued)*

The persistence of primary deficits reflects a sustained imbalance, with expenditures consistently outpacing revenues (refer to figure B2.5.1). Government spending in Malaysia, including public investment, decreased from nearly 30 percent of GDP in 2009 to 21.6 percent in 2019 and remained at about 21.9 percent in 2024. At the same time, revenue mobilization declined, with government revenue falling from about 23.5 percent of GDP in 2008 to 21.6 percent in 2019 and further decreasing to 19.9 percent in 2024. Consequently, primary deficits averaged about 2.3 percent of GDP over the past two decades.

Public debt has remained manageable largely because of favorable financing conditions. Following the global financial crisis of 2008–09, global interest rates declined and remained low for an extended period, reducing borrowing costs (refer to figure B2.5.2, panel a). At the same time, a large domestic investor base has allowed the government to finance most of its debt locally, limiting exposure to external financing pressures (refer to figure B2.5.2, panel b). Taken together, these factors have been reflected in an effective interest rate on government debt of about 2.9 percent during the 2010–19 period.

Primary deficits in Malaysia averaged about 2.3 percent of GDP over the past two decades, with government spending consistently outpacing revenue for most of the period.

FIGURE B2.5.1 Primary government spending and government revenue, Malaysia, 2000–24

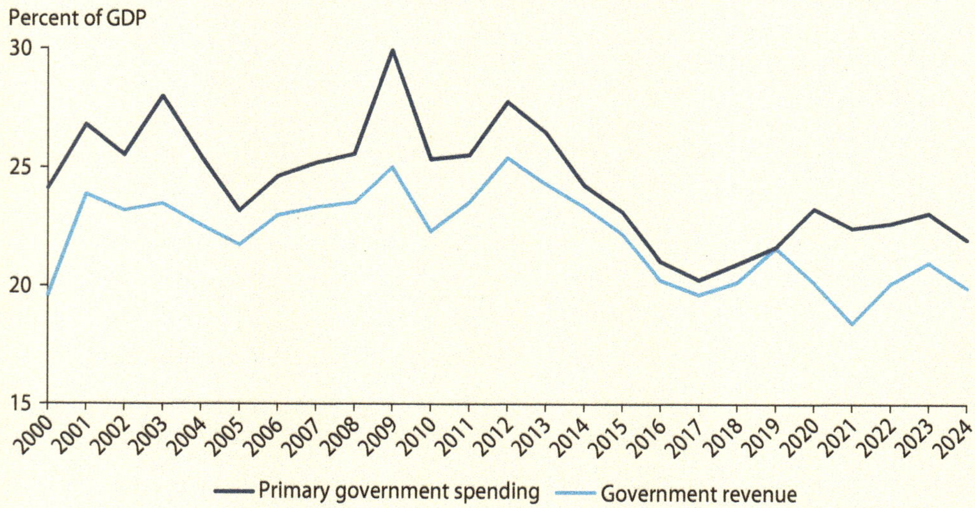

Source: Original figure for this publication based on World Economic Outlook Database, IMF, https://www.imf.org/en/publications/sprolls/world-economic-outlook-databases.
Note: Primary government spending is total government spending less interest payments.

(continued)

Box 2.5. Persistent deficits and contribution to public debt: The case of Malaysia *(continued)*

Relatively low global interest rates and a high share of domestic financing have helped keep public debt manageable despite rising levels.

FIGURE B2.5.2 US 10-year Treasury interest rate and drivers of debt in Malaysia

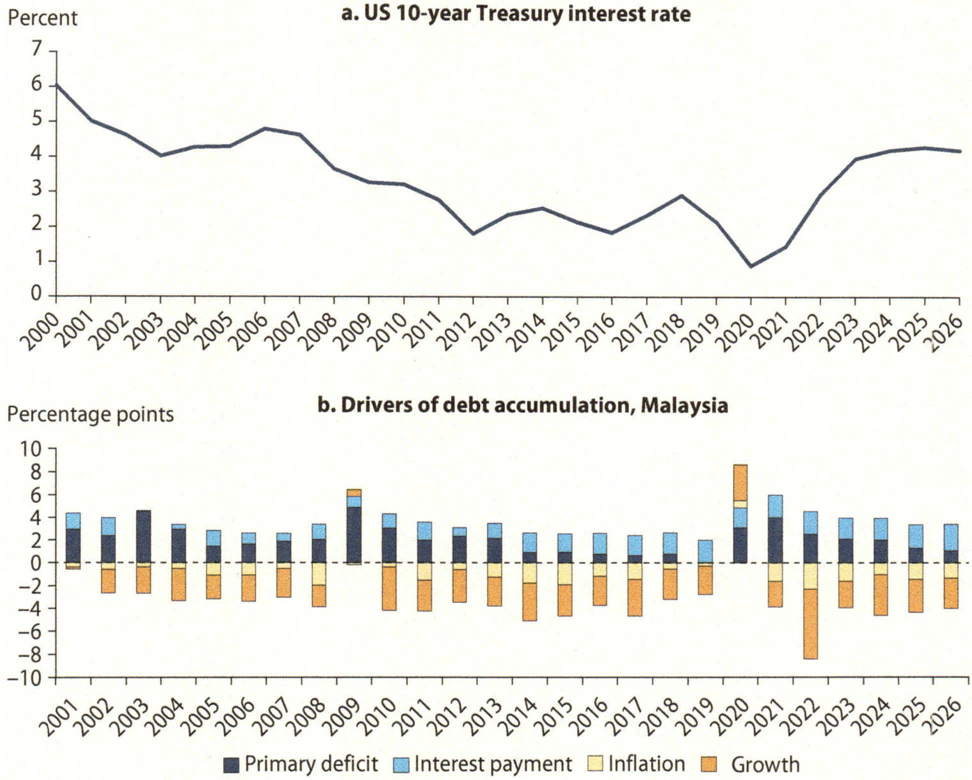

Sources: Original figure for this publication based on FRED Data, Federal Reserve Bank of St. Louis, https://fred.stlouisfed.org; World Economic Outlook Database, International Monetary Fund, https://www.imf.org/en/publications/sprolls/world-economic-outlook-databases.

Global interest rates have increased in recent years and remain higher than in the period after the global financial crisis. The effective interest rate on government debt has remained constant from about 2.9 percent in 2010–19 to 2.8 percent in 2020–24 (refer to figure B2.5.3, panel a). At the same time, interest payments have risen from about 1.6 percent of GDP in 2010–19 to 1.9 percent in 2020–24 (refer to figure B2.5.3, panel b). This rise reflects higher borrowing costs, a larger debt stock, and moderating growth, all of which increase the fiscal burden of debt servicing.

(continued)

Box 2.5. Persistent deficits and contribution to public debt: The case of Malaysia *(continued)*

Despite stable borrowing costs, larger debt stocks and moderating growth have increased the fiscal burden of debt servicing.

FIGURE B2.5.3 Effective interest rates and interest payments, Malaysia, 2000–24

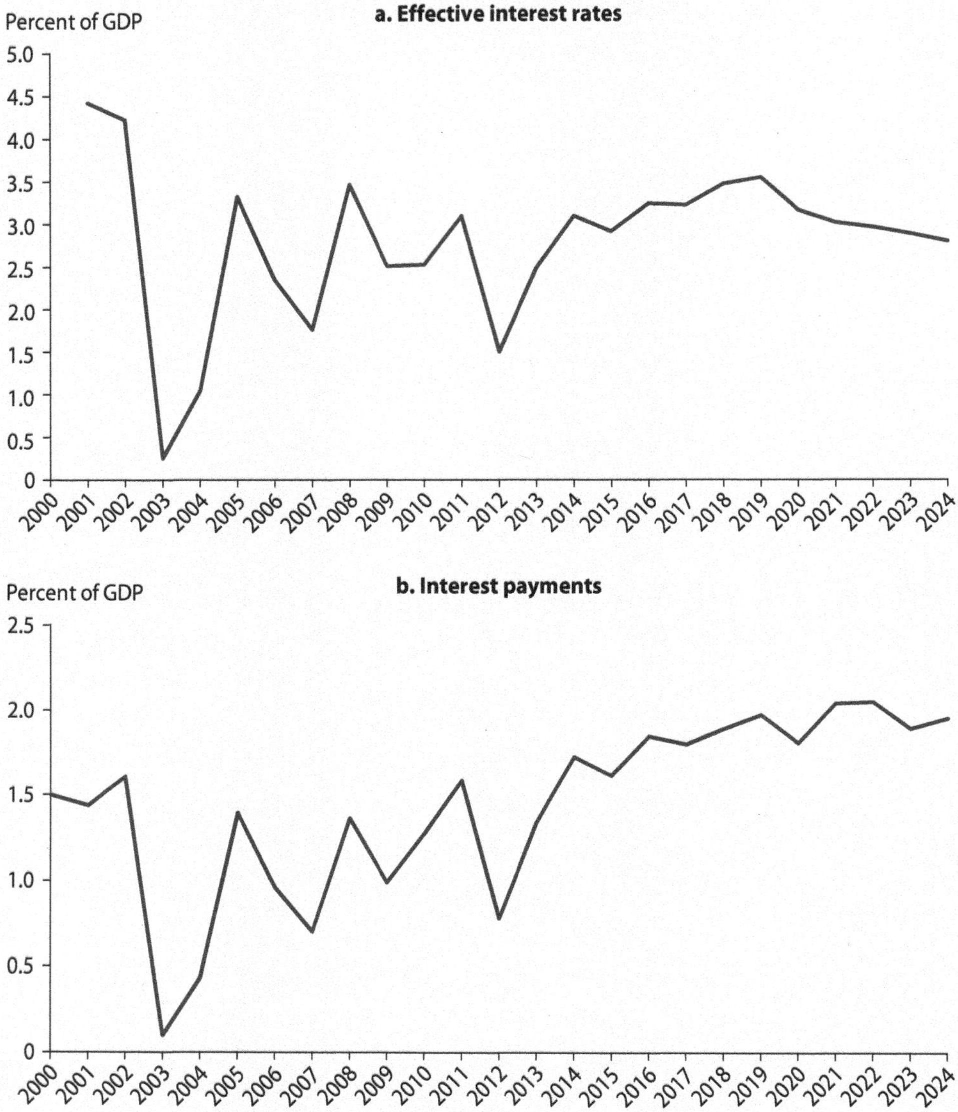

Source: Original figure for this publication based on World Economic Outlook Database, IMF, https://www.imf.org/en/publications/sprolls/world-economic-outlook-databases.
Note: The effective interest rate is defined as interest payments over total public debt in the previous year.

Malaysia's experience shows how persistent deficits can remain manageable under favorable financing conditions but become increasingly costly as those conditions reverse. At the same time, reliance on domestic financing may crowd out private investment, reinforcing the need to address underlying fiscal imbalances.

Rising debt levels create conditions for faster debt accumulation, further constraining fiscal space. Although real interest rates have remained below growth in EAP, higher debt is associated with higher interest rates and lower growth (refer to figure 2.10, panel a). Favorable macroeconomic conditions have kept deficits sustainable in the past, but this situation can change. Higher interest rates and lower growth can accelerate debt accumulation (refer to figure 2.10, panel b), which can increase the burden of interest payments, particularly in Fiji, Lao PDR, and Malaysia, raising vulnerabilities and tightening financing conditions. Looking ahead, EAP economies are unlikely to be able to rely on low interest rates, strong growth, or inflation to reduce debt-to-GDP ratios. Consequently, financing conditions and debt dynamics will play a more central role in shaping fiscal space.

Even though interest rates are expected to remain below growth rates, increasing debt could push up the former and lower the latter.

FIGURE 2.10 Debt, interest rates, and economic growth

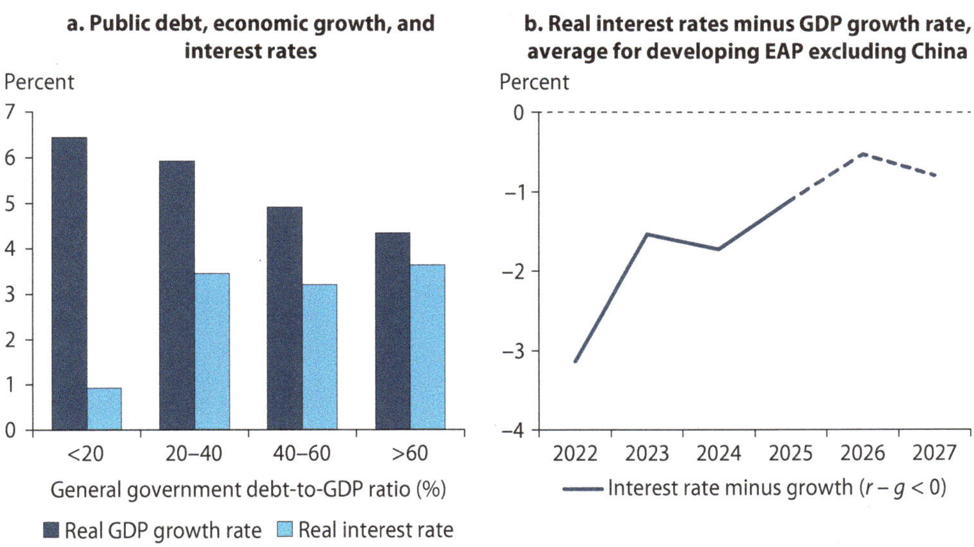

Sources: Original figure for this publication based on International Finance Statistics, International Monetary Fund, https://data360.worldbank.org/en/int/dataset/IMF_IFS; World Development Indicators, World Bank, https://datatopics.worldbank.org/world-development-indicators/; World Economic Outlook Database, International Monetary Fund, https://www.imf.org/en/publications/sprolls/world-economic-outlook-databases.

Note: Panel a plots the average real GDP growth and real long-term interest rates for different levels of the ratio of public debt-to-GDP (*x*-axis). The sample includes 50 developing economies (including 10 in EAP) with at least 10 observations on $r - g$ and public debt over GDP over the period 2000–19. In panel b, r refers to real interest rates and g to GDP growth rate. Values for 2026 and 2027 are estimates. EAP = East Asia and Pacific.

Public debt and increasing fiscal risks

Looking ahead, EAP economies face a more challenging macroeconomic environment, characterized by higher debt levels and increased exposure to shocks. Compared to the prepandemic period, governments now enter potential downturns with reduced fiscal buffers and face higher global interest rates and weaker growth prospects. In this context, fiscal outcomes will likely become more sensitive to adverse shocks.

On average, a 1-percentage-point increase in interest rates raises the debt-to-GDP ratio by about 0.8 and 0.6 percentage point per year in East Asian economies and Pacific Island countries, respectively. This risk is particularly relevant given that global interest rates remain about 1.9 percentage points above their 2010–19 averages and are expected to remain elevated over 2026–30. The fiscal impact is larger in countries with higher debt levels such as Fiji and Malaysia, where a 1-percentage-point increase in interest rates would raise the debt-to-GDP ratio by approximately 1.2 percentage points and 1.0 percentage point per year, respectively (refer to figure 2.11).

Public debt in EAP will likely continue rising, with even moderate shocks leading to significantly higher debt trajectories, as seen in the examples of Fiji and Malaysia.

FIGURE 2.11 Projected debt under different interest rate scenarios, Fiji and Malaysia, 2026–30

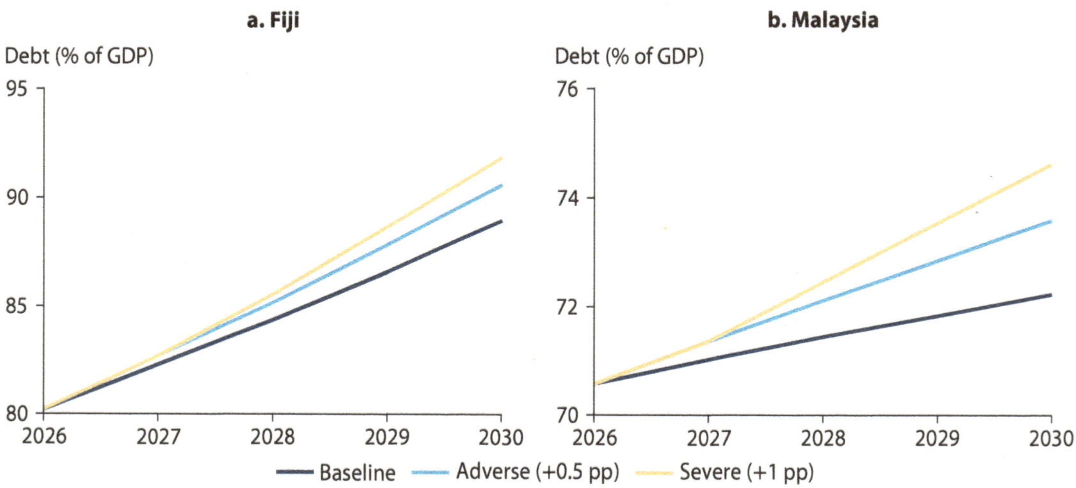

Source: Original figure for this publication based on World Economic Outlook Database, International Monetary Fund, https://www.imf.org/en/publications/sprolls/world-economic-outlook-databases.

Note: Scenarios assume alternative paths for US interest rates over 2026–30: baseline assumes rates remain at current levels; adverse scenario assumes an increase of 0.5 percentage point in 2027, remaining elevated thereafter; and severe assumes a cumulative increase of 1 percentage point, implemented in two steps of 0.5 percentage point in 2027 and 2028, and remaining at that level through 2030. EAP = East Asia and Pacific; pp = percentage point.

On average, a 1-percentage-point decline in growth increases the debt-to-GDP ratio by about 1.6 and 1.1 percentage points per year in East Asian economies and Pacific Island countries, respectively. World Economic Outlook projections indicate that growth in EAP will average about 4.0 percent over 2026–30, down from about 6.3 percent during 2010–19.[5] In recent years, growth has made a limited contribution to reducing debt ratios, lowering debt by only about 2.7 percentage points over 2022–24 in China and Thailand, which highlights the challenges to stabilizing debt dynamics under current projections (refer to figure 2.12).

Taken together, these results suggest that public debt in EAP is unlikely to decline under current global conditions and could increase further in the absence of policy adjustment. Elevated interest rates and weaker growth prospects imply that debt dynamics are becoming less favorable. In this context, even moderate adverse shocks could lead to further increases in debt, underscoring the need for fiscal measures to rebuild buffers and stabilize debt trajectories.

A 1-percentage-point decline in growth increases debt-to-GDP ratios by 0.9 and 0.6 percentage point per year in China and Thailand, respectively.

FIGURE 2.12 Projected debt under different growth scenarios, China and Thailand, 2026–30

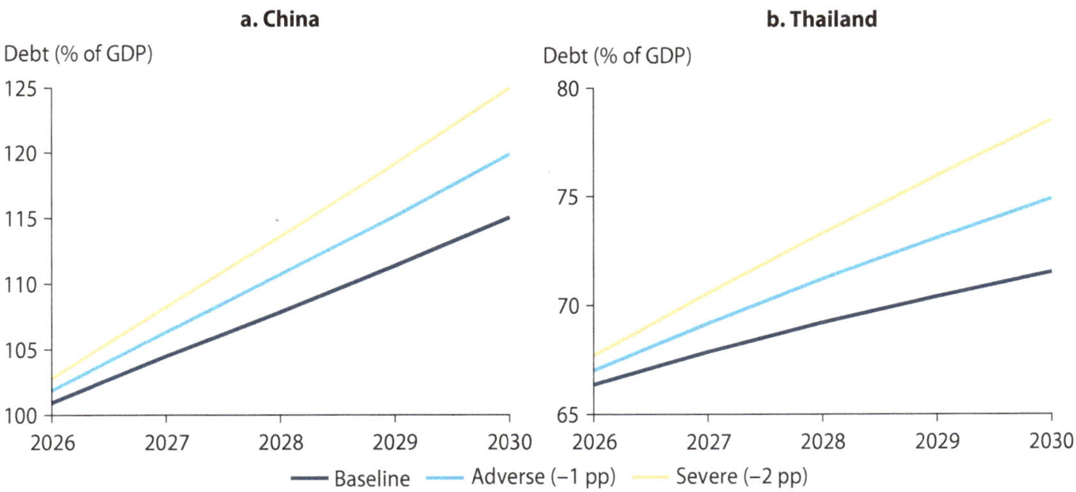

Sources: Original figure for this publication based on World Economic Outlook (WEO) Database, International Monetary Fund, https://www.imf.org/en/publications/sprolls/world-economic-outlook-databases.

Note: Scenarios assume alternative growth paths over 2026–30: baseline follows WEO projections for each country; adverse assumes growth is 1 percentage point lower than the baseline in each year over 2026–30, consistent with typical cyclical slowdowns in the region; and severe assumes growth is 2 percentage points lower than the baseline in each year over the same period, broadly in line with more pronounced downturns observed in past episodes. pp = percentage point.

Debt structure and composition

The implications of rising public debt also depend on how debt is financed and structured. Countries with longer maturities, domestic currency issuance, and diversified investor bases face lower rollover risks and retain greater room for countercyclical policy. For instance, Mexico's 1994–95 Tequila Crisis was driven less by high debt levels than by the government's inability to roll over large volumes of short-term debt (Cole and Kehoe 2000).

Long maturities and a predominance of domestic currency debt characterize the debt structure in East Asia, particularly among its upper-middle-income economies. China, Malaysia, and Thailand have increasingly relied on domestic government bond markets, issuing debt largely in local currency and at longer maturities (refer to figure 2.13, panels a and b). This structure has reduced rollover risks and limited exposure to exchange rate shocks. The development of domestic institutional investors and deeper local capital markets has supported this shift, allowing governments to smooth financing needs over time.

In contrast, lower-middle-income economies in East Asia tend to exhibit more vulnerable debt structures, with a higher reliance on debt denominated in foreign currency. In Cambodia, Lao PDR, and Mongolia, for example, such debt accounts for 100, 91.7, and 98.7 percent of total public debt, respectively. This situation increases exposure to exchange rate depreciations and external financing conditions, raising debt-servicing costs during periods of stress. Although some economies have made progress in developing domestic debt markets, limited market depth and investor bases continue to constrain local currency issuance at longer maturities. Consequently, rollover risks and exchange rate vulnerabilities remain more pronounced, reducing the scope for countercyclical fiscal responses.

In Pacific Island countries, limited access to debt markets results in a heavy reliance on concessional external financing (refer to figure 2.14). Although concessional loans typically carry lower interest rates and longer maturities, they are predominantly denominated in foreign currency and provided by a narrow set of official creditors. As such, they expose governments to exchange rate risk and creditor concentration. At the same time, the limited availability of concessional loans relative to growing financing needs constrains the ability to scale up financing in response to shocks.

As economies develop, debt structures shift toward longer maturities and issuance of domestic currency.

FIGURE 2.13 Debt composition and maturity, selected EAP economies and comparators

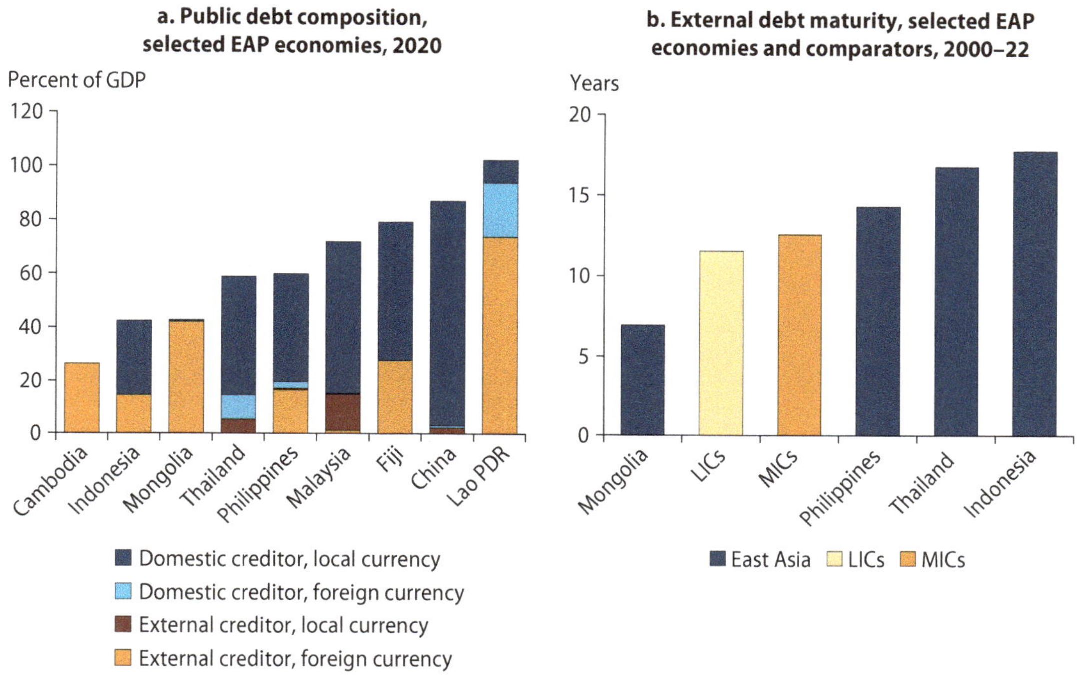

Source: Original figure for this publication based on International Debt Statistics, World Bank, https://databank.worldbank.org/source/international-debt-statistics.

Note: In panel b, debt refers to all external public and public guaranteed debt. Private creditors include bonds (publicly or privately issued), commercial banks, other private financial institutions, and private export credits. EAP = East Asia and Pacific; LICs = low-income countries; MICs = middle-income countries.

These patterns show that the implications of rising public debt in EAP depend not only on its level but also on its structure and financing. Upper-middle-income economies have reduced rollover and exchange rate risks through longer maturities and greater reliance on domestic currency issuance. By contrast, lower-middle-income economies and Pacific Island countries remain more exposed because of higher reliance on foreign currency borrowing, concessional financing, and more limited market depth. These factors constrain fiscal space and make it more sensitive to shifts in global financial conditions.

Limited access to debt markets in Pacific Island countries results in heavy reliance on concessional external financing.

FIGURE 2.14 Reliance on concessional public debt: East Asian economies, Pacific Island countries, and comparators, 2015–19

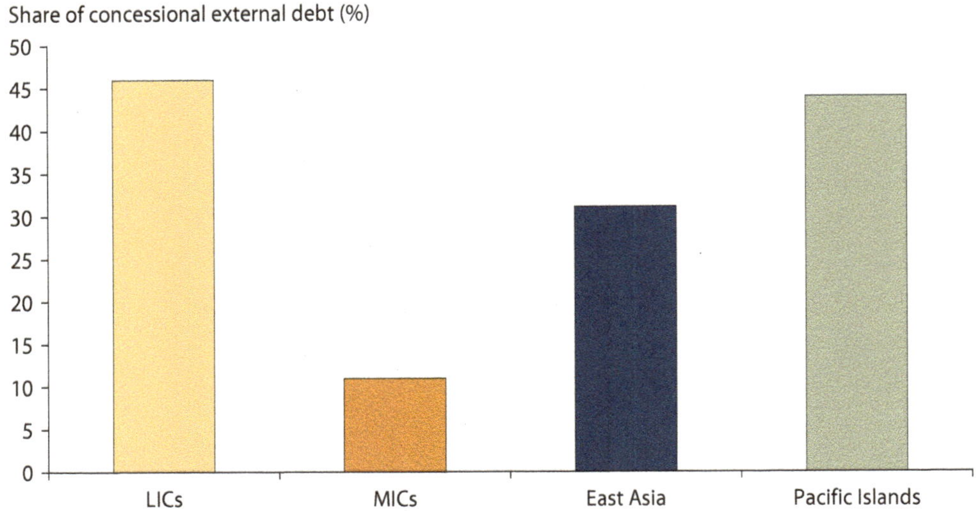

Source: Original figure for this publication based on World Economic Outlook Database, International Monetary Fund, https://www.imf.org/en/publications/sprolls/world-economic-outlook-databases.
Note: Concessional debt is expressed as a share of total public and publicly guaranteed external debt. Values are averages over 2015–19. Country groups follow World Bank income classifications. LICs = low-income countries; MICs = middle-income countries.

Rebuilding fiscal space in EAP: Institutions, rules, and buffers

Rebuilding fiscal space in EAP will require stronger fiscal institutions, credible policy commitments, and better shock-management mechanisms. Medium-term fiscal frameworks (MTFFs) can help align revenue and spending decisions with fiscal objectives, and fiscal rules strengthen discipline, anchor expectations, and reduce the risk of policy slippages. In a region exposed to frequent economic, financial, and climate shocks, however, discipline alone is often insufficient. Liquidity buffers, such as stabilization funds, contingency reserves, and other readily available financing instruments, can help governments absorb shocks without resorting to disruptive spending cuts or costly borrowing. Together, these tools can help rebuild fiscal space by improving fiscal sustainability, strengthening credibility, and enhancing resilience.

Linking revenue and spending to help rebuild fiscal space

The preceding analysis points to a clear conclusion: the region's ability to conduct countercyclical fiscal policy depends on sufficient fiscal space, which is increasingly constrained by tighter financing conditions, rising debt, and greater exposure to shocks. Rebuilding fiscal space therefore requires institutional mechanisms that strengthen fiscal discipline, anchor expectations, and ensure access to financing during downturns. MTFFs, fiscal rules, and liquidity buffers form a mutually reinforcing system that restores countercyclical capacity (refer to figure 2.15). Rules without MTFFs lack an operational anchor; MTFFs without buffers leave governments unable to respond when shocks materialize; and buffers without rules risk premature depletion.

MTFFs anchor government spending and revenue in a multiyear plan based on realistic macroeconomic and fiscal projections. By moving beyond annual budgets, MTFFs promote more consistent and forward-looking fiscal policy, aligning revenue mobilization with spending priorities and reducing the likelihood of deficits without a clear financing path. In turn, this alignment helps contain persistent imbalances and supports more sustainable debt dynamics over time.

Importantly, MTFFs can also shape the composition of fiscal policy over the cycle. As shown in the earlier section on social transfers and countercyclicality, public investment is highly procyclical in most EAP economies. Embedding guidance on the cyclicality of spending within MTFFs—including protecting a baseline level of public investment during downturns—can help preserve growth-enhancing expenditures and reduce the tendency for investments to amplify economic fluctuations.

Medium-term fiscal frameworks, fiscal rules, and liquidity buffers rebuild fiscal space by aligning revenues and spending, strengthening discipline, and ensuring liquidity during downturns.

FIGURE 2.15 Rebuilding fiscal space: Planning, commitment, and resilience

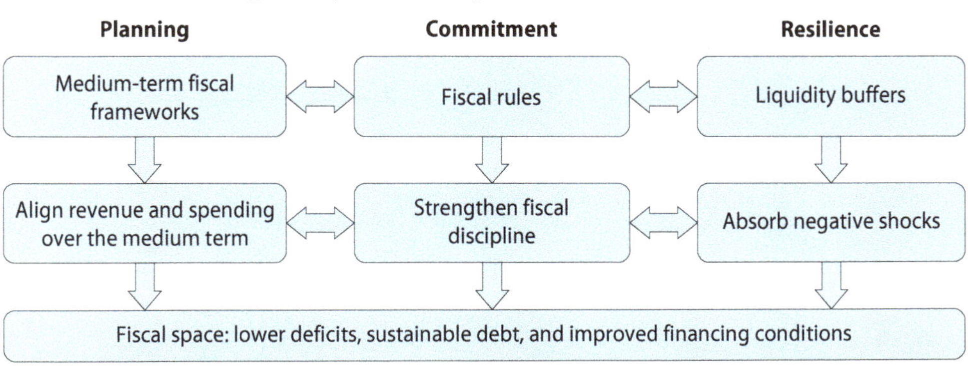

Source: Original figure for this publication.

Although most EAP economies have adopted MTFFs, coverage and effectiveness vary widely (refer to table 2.1). In many cases, economies do not use MTFFs consistently to guide budget decisions, which limits their role as a fiscal anchor. This heterogeneity suggests that the challenge is not adoption but strengthening coverage and integration with the budget process so that MTFFs can effectively guide fiscal policy. Doing so will require translating medium-term targets into effective budget constraints and applying them consistently throughout the budget process.

The effectiveness of MTFFs depends on their design, enforcement, and credibility (refer to box 2.6 for a salient example from Malaysia). International experience shows that MTFFs strengthen fiscal discipline, particularly when combined with well-designed fiscal rules and independent oversight. In Peru, for example, a four-year MTFF reinforced by fiscal rules and supported by an independent

TABLE 2.1 Coverage, anchoring, and key issues of medium-term fiscal frameworks in EAP

Economy	Coverage	Anchoring	Key issue
Cambodia	Central government	None	MTFF is not approved and not used in budget decisions.
Indonesia	General government	Partial	Budget decisions often bypass MTFF across levels of government.
Lao PDR	Central government	Partial	MTFF is not consistently used to guide budget decisions.
Malaysia	General government	Strong	MTFF is integrated in budget, but enforcement varies.
Mongolia	General government	Partial	Frequent revisions weaken adherence to medium-term plans.
Myanmar	Central government	None	MTFF is used for projections, not for budget allocations.
Philippines	General government	Strong	Medium-term targets consistently guide budgets.
Thailand	General government	Partial	MTFF is not consistently used to guide budget decisions.
Viet Nam	General government	Partial	Weak link exists between medium-term plans and annual budgets.
Pacific Islands	Central government	None	Budgeting is largely annual with limited multiyear planning.

Sources: Original table for this publication based on Chowdhury et al. 2024; Government of Malaysia 2023; Government of the Philippines 2022; World Bank 2017a, 2017b, 2020, 2023c, 2024a, 2024b, 2025.

Note: Coverage refers to whether the MTFF applies to the central government or general government. Anchoring reflects the extent to which MTFFs shape budget decisions: *None* indicates that the MTFF is not adopted or used in budgeting (that is, it is used only for projections); *Partial* indicates that the MTFF exists and informs fiscal planning but is not consistently used to guide budget decisions; and *Strong* indicates that medium-term targets are systematically used to guide annual budget preparation and fiscal outcomes. EAP = East Asia and Pacific; MTFF = medium-term fiscal framework.

fiscal council has helped integrate medium-term projections with expenditure planning and guiding budget decisions. Similarly, in Jamaica, a fiscal responsibility framework combining binding targets, clearly defined escape clauses, and strong institutional oversight contributed to halving the ratio of public debt-to-GDP within a decade (Arslanalp et al. 2024).

Box 2.6. Public Finance and Fiscal Responsibility Act in Malaysia

Malaysia's Public Finance and Fiscal Responsibility Act (PFFRA), enacted in 2023, represents a landmark step toward strengthening the fiscal framework and integrating medium-term targets into the budget process; however, its effectiveness hinges on credible implementation.

PFFRA's credibility depends on its enforcement. Fiscal rules are effective only when consistently enforced. Over time, enforcement strengthens credibility by making future policy paths more predictable. In the absence of enforcement, rules risk being ignored or circumvented, weakening their ability to discipline fiscal policy. Consequently, PFFRA's contribution to rebuilding fiscal space depends on its ability to ensure sustained compliance.

Having too many rules can, in principle, undermine the credibility of PFFRA. The current design relies on multiple numerical limits to pursue a single objective of fiscal discipline (refer to table B2.6.1), making the act harder to monitor and enforce. Rather than strengthening discipline, excessive rules can create confusion, generate loopholes, and weaken compliance. A more effective approach would rely on a smaller number of well-defined rules.

There is a gap between the fiscal balance and debt limits stipulated by PFFRA and Malaysia's recent fiscal averages. Aligning the rules more closely with historical benchmarks would strengthen both credibility and enforceability.

Credibility also depends on the framework's ability to accommodate shocks without undermining compliance. This ability requires escape clauses that clearly specify when rules may be temporarily suspended, as well as the mechanisms and timelines for returning to compliance. Without clear return paths, temporary deviations risk becoming permanent, underscoring the importance of well-defined mechanisms that ensure a gradual and predictable return.

(continued)

Box 2.6. Public Finance and Fiscal Responsibility Act in Malaysia *(continued)*

TABLE B2.6.1 Numerical rules under Malaysia's Fiscal Responsibility Act
Percent of GDP

	2000–07	2008–09	2010–19	2020–22	2023–24
Annual development expenditure ≥ 3%	7	6	4	4	5
Fiscal balance ≤ −3%	−4	−5	−3	−5	−4
Debt level ≤ 60%	39	45	55	67	70
Financial guarantee ≤ 25%	—	—	16	20	18

Sources: Original table for this publication based on Monthly Highlights & Statistics February 2026, National Summary Data Page for Malaysia, Central Bank Malaysia, https://www.bnm.gov.my/-/monthly-highlights-statistics-in-february-2026; World Economic Outlook Database, International Monetary Fund, https://www.imf.org/en/publications/sprolls/world-economic-outlook-databases.

Note: Financial Guarantee data start from 2012 and include only guaranteed debt under Loans Guarantee (Bodies Corporate) Act 1965 [Act 96]. The historical amount under the Financial Procedure Act 1957 [Act 61] is not available and thus not included. The outstanding amount under [Act 61] for June 2024 was 3.9 percent of GDP (Ministry of Finance Malaysia 2024). — = not available.

Malaysia could further strengthen the credibility of the PFFRA by establishing a fiscal council to monitor compliance, assess fiscal projections, and enhance transparency. Experiences from countries such as Chile and Peru suggest that fiscal councils can reinforce the credibility and accountability of fiscal frameworks.

Fiscal rules to support discipline and help rebuild fiscal space

Fiscal rules have become widely used tools to support fiscal discipline and preserve fiscal space. Over the past three decades, their adoption has expanded rapidly across countries. For instance, the number of countries with at least one fiscal rule increased from 49 in 2000 to 122 in 2024. Although high-income countries were early adopters, recent growth has been driven largely by low- and middle-income economies (refer to figure 2.16, panel a). Across countries, budget balance and debt rules are the most widely used instruments (refer to figure 2.16, panel b). In EAP, most economies have adopted at least one fiscal rule (refer to table 2.2).

Well-designed fiscal rules strengthen fiscal discipline and improve macroeconomic outcomes. They have been shown to reduce deficits and debt-to-GDP ratios (Caselli and Reynaud 2020; Hallerberg et al. 2007; Heinemann et al. 2018).

By anchoring expectations about future fiscal paths, fiscal rules can lower sovereign risk premium and borrowing costs (Badinger and Reuter 2017; Heinemann et al. 2018; Iara and Wolff 2014; Islamaj et al. 2024). They have also proven effective during episodes of fiscal consolidation (Aaskoven and Wiese 2022; Ardanaz et al. 2021; World Bank 2026). In addition, fiscal rules can support private capital accumulation and long-term growth (Esquivel and Samano 2026).

In recent decades, low- and middle-income countries have widely adopted fiscal rules—particularly debt and budget balance rules.

FIGURE 2.16 Fiscal rules, by country income group and type of rule, 1985–2024

a. Adoption of fiscal rules, by country income group

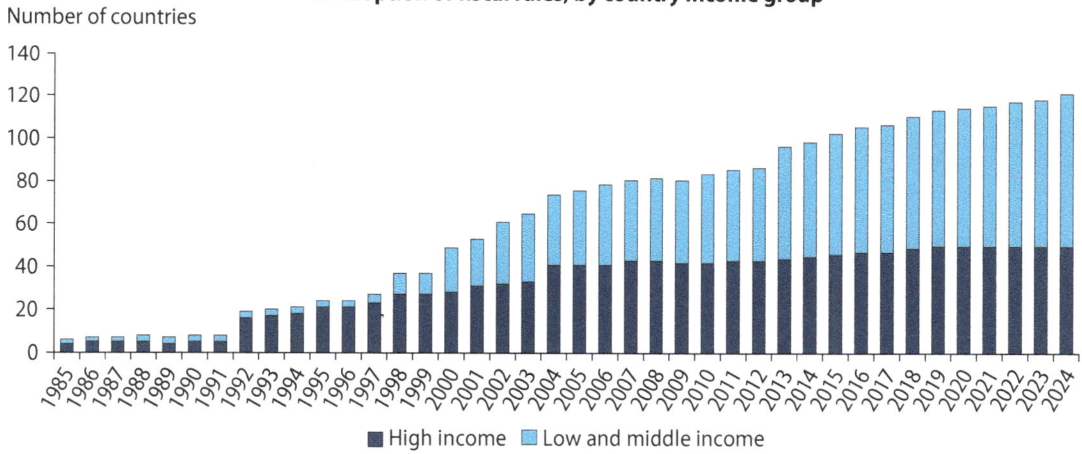

b. Fiscal rules, by type, low- and middle-income countries

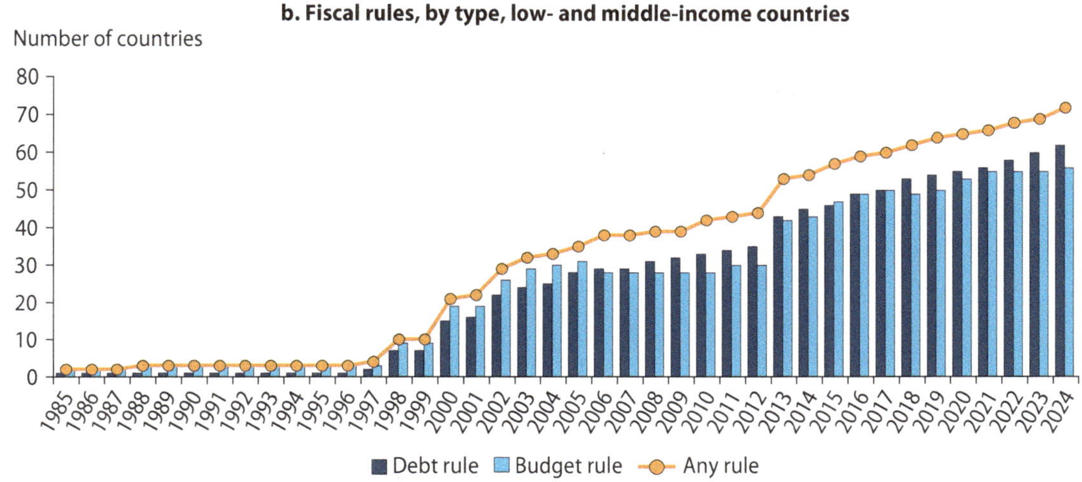

Source: Original figure for this publication based on Alonso et al. 2025c.

TABLE 2.2 Adoption of fiscal rules, by type, selected EAP economies, as of 2025

Country	Type(s) of rule	Years fiscal rule in place	Notes
East Asia			
Cambodia	Budget balance rule; Debt rule	2019 (BBR); 2024 (DR)	BBR revised in 2024
Indonesia	Budget balance rule; Debt rule	1967 (BBR); 2004 (DR)	BBR suspended between 2020 and 2022
Malaysia	Budget balance rule; Debt rule; Expenditure rule	1959 (BBR); 1959 (DR); 2023 (ER)	BBR revised in 2021 and 2023; DR revised multiple times
Mongolia	Budget balance rule; Debt rule; Expenditure rule	2013 (BBR); 2014 (DR); 2013 (ER)	BBR and DR revised multiple times
Thailand	Debt rule; Expenditure rule	2018 (DR); 2018 (ER)	DR revised in 2021
Timor-Leste	Debt rule; Revenue rule	2015 (DR); 2015 (RR)	—
Viet Nam	Budget balance rule; Debt rule; Revenue rule	2016 (BBR); 2016 (DR); 2016 (RR)	BBR, DR, and RR revised in 2021
Pacific Islands			
Marshall Islands	Budget balance rule	2021 (BBR)	—
Papua New Guinea	Debt rule	2006 (DR)	Debt ceiling revised multiple times
Solomon Islands	Budget balance rule; Debt rule	2013 (BBR); 2012 (DR)	BBR suspended between 2020 and 2021
Tonga	Debt rule; Revenue rule; Expenditure rule	2018 (DR); 2018 (RR); 2018 (ER)	—
Vanuatu	Budget balance rule; Debt rule	1998 (BBR); 2015 (DR)	DR revised in 2019

Source: Original table for this publication based on Alonso et al. 2025c.
Note: BBR = budget balance rule; DR = debt rule; ER = expenditure rule; RR = revenue rule; — = not applicable.

Nonetheless, the extent to which fiscal rules reduce the procyclicality of government spending remains inconclusive, because their effectiveness depends on rule design. Expenditure and budget balance rules are more likely to support countercyclical policy because they directly constrain annual fiscal decisions, whereas debt rules target a slow-moving stock and have little effect on cyclical policy (Guerguil et al. 2017). Similarly, investment-friendly rules are associated with stronger countercyclicality, because they protect capital spending from procyclical cuts. Compliance is also critical: deviations weaken these constraints and tend to reinforce procyclical behavior (Larch et al. 2021).

Consistent with the literature, fiscal rule adoption in EAP is associated with stronger primary balances over the 2000–23 period. Event study estimates suggest that, on average, rule adoption is linked to an improvement in the primary balance of about 2 percent of GDP in the year of adoption and up to 3 percent of GDP two years later, relative to countries that did not adopt rules (refer to figure 2.17). Importantly, no evidence exists to show a pre-trend in fiscal balances before adoption, suggesting that the observed improvements are not driven by underlying trends. The adjustment materializes rapidly following adoption. A transitory softening emerges around three years postadoption, attributable primarily to Mongolia's 2016 debt crisis (refer to box 2.7), after which the effect recovers and strengthens into a pronounced positive by the five-year mark.

These findings are broadly consistent with World Bank (2026), which uses local projection regressions on a large sample of EMDEs and advanced economies and finds that improvements in the cyclically adjusted primary balance build gradually, soften in the medium term, and peak about five years after adoption. The pattern observed in East Asia closely mirrors these dynamics, although with larger estimated magnitudes. Although that approach relies on local projections in a global setting, the interaction-weighted estimator used for this chapter is better suited to the smaller, staggered EAP sample, because it avoids the contaminated control problem that arises when already-treated units serve as controls for later adopters.[6]

Experiences in the region, however, show that fiscal rules are neither necessary nor sufficient to ensure fiscal discipline. Mongolia experienced a debt crisis in 2016 despite adopting fiscal rules in 2013–14, showing that rules alone cannot ensure discipline. By contrast, the Philippines achieved sustained fiscal discipline without a formal rule during 2000–19, supported instead by strong medium-term fiscal planning (refer to box 2.8).

Although fiscal rules are associated with stronger primary balances in East Asian economies, their effect on the cyclicality of government spending is less clear. To examine this effect, the same panel specification as in box 2.4 is estimated, restricting the sample to East Asia and regressing the cyclical component of real government expenditure on the cyclical component of real GDP, interacted with fiscal rules and institutional quality. Table 2.3 presents three specifications. Column (1) shows that fiscal rules are associated with more countercyclical spending in the absence of controls. Column (2) adds controls for government effectiveness and financial openness; the rule effect loses significance, consistent with the presence of stronger institutions in rule-adopting countries, which absorb much of the baseline effect. Column (3) interacts fiscal rules with an indicator of low government effectiveness, defined as the sample mean, and shows that the rule effect is concentrated in

Recent fiscal rule adoption in East Asia is associated with stronger primary balances.

FIGURE 2.17 Association between primary balance and fiscal rule adoption, East Asia

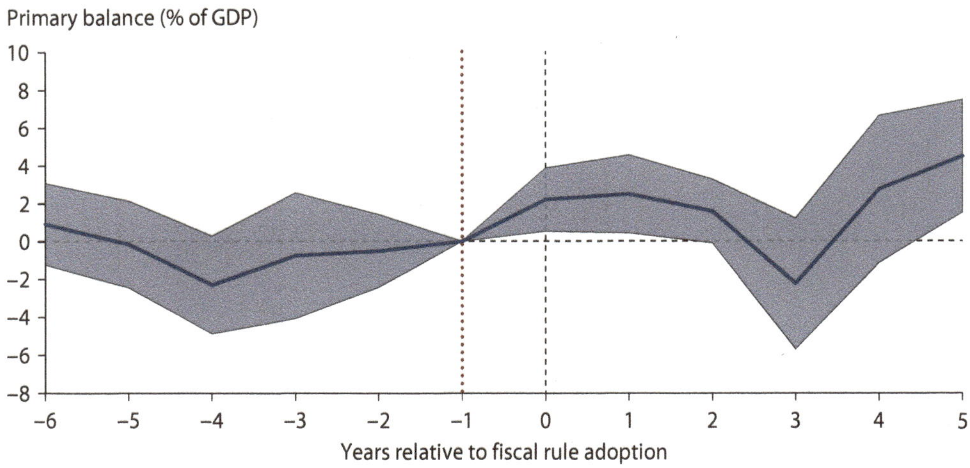

Source: Original figure for this publication based on Alonso et al. 2025c.

Note: The figure shows interaction-weighted difference-in-differences estimates of the effect of fiscal rule adoption on primary balances for East Asian economies (2000–23), following Wooldridge (2021). The plotted blue line shows average treatment effect on the treated estimates; the shaded band shows 90 percent confidence intervals. The dotted vertical line marks treatment onset ($t = 0$); estimates are normalized to zero in the year before adoption ($t = -1$). Cambodia, Indonesia, Mongolia, Thailand, and Viet Nam adopted fiscal rules during the sample period, whereas Lao PDR, Myanmar, and the Philippines have never adopted rules. For Indonesia, adoption is dated to 2004, corresponding to the introduction of binding numerical debt limits; earlier fiscal provisions are treated as part of the preadoption period.

countries above this threshold. In countries with weaker institutions, fiscal rules are not associated with more countercyclical spending. Overall, the results suggest that fiscal rules support countercyclical policy in East Asia only where institutional quality exceeds a minimum threshold, consistent with Bergman and Hutchison (2015).

Overall, fiscal rules have contributed to maintaining fiscal space in East Asia and have supported more countercyclical fiscal policy, particularly in economies with stronger institutions. Their effectiveness depends importantly on design: rules must be simple, flexible, and enforceable, which shapes their credibility and how strongly they guide fiscal decisions. Chapter 4 discusses these dimensions further and outlines how fiscal rules in the region can be strengthened.

Box 2.7. Fiscal rules and Mongolia's debt distress of 2016

During 2015–16, Mongolia's economy contracted because of a sharp decline in commodity prices and weakened demand from China (World Bank 2018). Government revenue, highly dependent on the mining sector, fell sharply, leading to large fiscal deficits and rapid debt accumulation. Mongolia's reliance on debt denominated in US dollars compounded these pressures, amplifying debt burdens as the dollar appreciated. Public debt rose rapidly, reaching about 90 percent of gross domestic product and triggering a loss of market confidence (IMF 2017).

Mongolia's fiscal rules, introduced in 2013–14, did little to mitigate these shocks. Both the structural balance and expenditure rules relied on overly optimistic assumptions about commodity prices (World Bank 2018). The structural balance rule used a 16-year moving average of mineral prices, which overstated revenues when prices fell, masking fiscal deterioration and delaying adjustment. Because the expenditure rule was tied to these same estimates, it allowed spending to remain elevated even as actual revenues declined.

Enforcement of fiscal rules was also weak. Fiscal targets were repeatedly revised upward beginning in 2015, eroding the credibility of the rules and weakening their role as commitment devices. At the same time, the debt rule focused on aggregate levels but did not properly account for composition risks. By not accounting for the currency denomination of debt, the rule failed to constrain debt dynamics as exchange rate depreciation increased the local currency value of foreign currency liabilities, leaving the country highly exposed to external shocks.

Mongolia's experience highlights three key lessons. First, the effectiveness of fiscal rules depends critically on realistic assumptions, particularly in commodity-dependent economies. Second, credibility and enforcement are as important as formal adoption; rules that are frequently revised fail to anchor expectations. Third, rule design must account for underlying fiscal risks, including debt composition and exposure to external shocks.

Mongolia has made some progress since 2016, including rebuilding some fiscal buffers and restoring fiscal rules; however, effectiveness of buffers depends on the scale of potential shocks. Strengthening fiscal resilience therefore requires improving the realism of projections—potentially supported by stronger technical capacity and independent oversight—reinforcing enforcement, and more consistently accumulating liquidity buffers to absorb shocks and support countercyclical policy.

Box 2.8. Fiscal discipline without a formal rule: The case of the Philippines

Between 2000 and 2019, the Philippines consistently maintained primary surpluses (refer to figure B2.8.1), illustrating the possibility of achieving fiscal discipline even in the absence of formal fiscal rules. The Philippines sustained fiscal discipline through the consistent use of medium-term fiscal planning. Fiscal aggregates defined in the medium-term fiscal framework effectively guided budget preparation, ensuring that annual allocations remained aligned with the intended fiscal path. Implementation of fiscal plans with limited revisions and strong expenditure control helped prevent ad hoc expansions and reinforce discipline through the budget process (Mueller et al. 2015).

This approach relies on credible assumptions and strong budget execution. In the Philippines, the Development Budget Coordination Committee sets macroeconomic assumptions and fiscal targets, which the Department of Budget and Management uses to guide budget preparation and issue ceilings to line agencies. This process helps ensure that plans are realistic and implemented as approved, with fiscal outcomes that closely align with projections (refer to figure B2.4.1 in box 2.4).

The Philippines has demonstrated strong fiscal discipline, as reflected in sustained primary surpluses between 2000 and 2019.

FIGURE B2.8.1 Primary balance, the Philippines, 2000–19

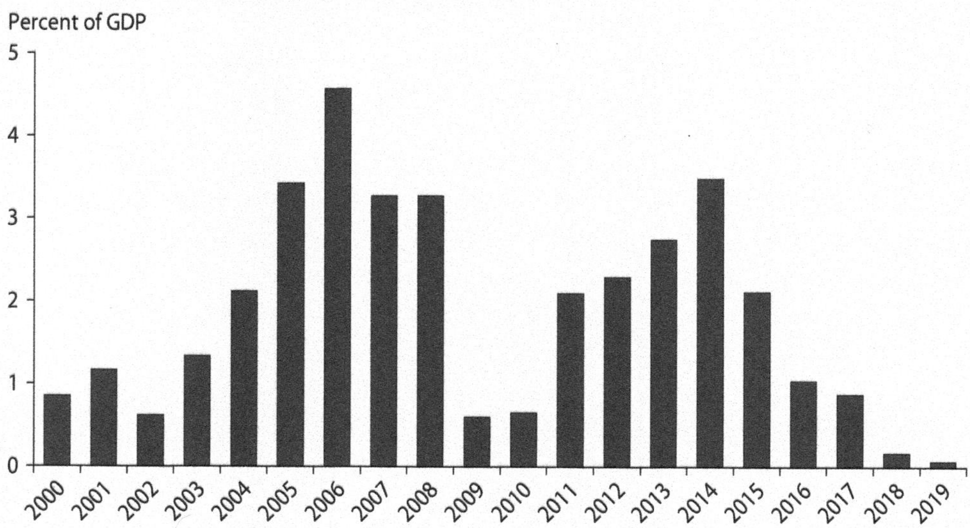

Source: Original figure for this publication based on World Economic Outlook Database, International Monetary Fund, https://www.imf.org/en/publications/sprolls/world-economic-outlook-databases.

(continued)

Box 2.8. Fiscal discipline without a formal rule: The case of the Philippines *(continued)*

Equally important is the role of credibility and consistency in policy implementation. The sustained alignment between fiscal plans and outcomes helped reinforce confidence in the fiscal framework, even in the absence of a formal rule. This experience suggests that, although rules can be valuable tools, credible medium-term planning can also support fiscal discipline.

TABLE 2.3 Association of fiscal rule adoption with countercyclical fiscal policy, East Asia
Dependent variable: cyclical component of real government expenditure

Variable	(1)	(2)	(3)
GDP cycle	0.398**	2.591	−2.010
	(0.170)	(1.839)	(2.054)
GDP cycle × Fiscal rule	−0.839***	−0.311	−0.826**
	(0.317)	(0.487)	(0.361)
GDP cycle × Low GE	—	—	1.893**
			(0.943)
GDP cycle × Fiscal rule × Low GE	—	—	0.455
			(0.491)
GDP cycle × Gov't effectiveness	—	−0.036	0.049
		(0.030)	(0.036)
GDP cycle × Financial openness	—	−1.330*	−2.047*
		(0.777)	(1.117)
Institutional controls	No	Yes	Yes
Financial openness	No	Yes	Yes
Low GE threshold	No	No	Yes
Country fixed effects	Yes	Yes	Yes

(continued)

TABLE 2.3 Association of fiscal rule adoption with countercyclical fiscal policy, East Asia *(continued)*

Variable	(1)	(2)	(3)
Observations	190	190	190
Countries	8	8	8
Within R^2	0.021	0.057	0.100

Source: Original table for this publication.
Note: Sample covers eight East Asian economies over 2000–23. Country fixed effects throughout. All fiscal rule variables lagged one period. Low GE is an indicator for government effectiveness (GE) below 47 (approximate mean of the East Asian sample). Institutional controls include government effectiveness. Financial openness is the Chinn-Ito KAOPEN index (Chinn and Ito 2006). — = not applicable.
$^*p < 0.10$ $^{**}p < 0.05$ $^{***}p < 0.01$

From fiscal discipline to fiscal space: The role of liquidity buffers

Liquidity buffers are essential to translate fiscal discipline into effective stabilization. Although fiscal rules can strengthen discipline, they do not ensure access to liquidity during downturns. Countries can build such access through accumulated savings, market financing, or contingent financing. Sovereign wealth funds, a key instrument for this purpose, provide readily available resources during shocks by saving in good times and drawing down during downturns, particularly in countries dependent on natural resources. Fiscal discipline can also improve access to borrowing, allowing governments to finance deficits during downturns. Many Pacific Island countries, however, have limited or no access to capital markets. In such cases, contingent financing can provide timely liquidity when shocks materialize.

The effectiveness of stabilization funds depends critically on credible withdrawal rules. Clear and transparent frameworks, typically linked to observable indicators and supported by limits on the pace of withdrawals, help ensure the predictable and sustainable use of resources. Chile provides a well-known example: a structural balance rule anchored in long-term copper prices and potential output guides both saving and dissaving decisions, supported by independent expert inputs and strong institutional oversight (Marcel Cullel et al. 2001; Medina and Soto 2007).

Experience in EAP economies illustrates that design alone is not sufficient. Credibility and consistent implementation are equally important. In Mongolia, weak compliance and repeated revisions to the fiscal framework have undermined stabilization funds linked to commodity price cycles, limiting the accumulation of savings over time

(World Bank 2025). In Timor-Leste, a clear withdrawal rule based on the Estimated Sustainable Income governs the Petroleum Fund, but frequent withdrawals above the benchmark have weakened its role as a buffer (IMF 2024). These cases illustrate that even well-designed frameworks require strong institutions and adherence to rules to function effectively.

Contingent financing provides an important source of liquidity, particularly for countries with limited or no access to capital markets. Unlike savings, which must be accumulated ex ante, contingent credit lines offer prearranged financing that can be drawn rapidly when shocks materialize, reducing the need for abrupt fiscal adjustment and helping preserve priority spending. In Pacific Island countries, where institutional capacity is also constrained, the effectiveness of these instruments depends on simplicity and external support. Facilities with clear triggers, standardized procedures, and technical assistance are more likely to be effective, allowing financing to be deployed quickly and reliably when shocks occur.

These findings highlight that fiscal discipline must be complemented by liquidity buffers that can be deployed when shocks materialize, particularly in countries with limited or no access to debt markets. Their effectiveness ultimately depends on credible rules and consistent implementation.

Conclusion

Macroeconomic stability in East Asia has been supported by fiscal discipline and broadly countercyclical or acyclical fiscal policy, even with relatively small governments. Effective stabilization, however, also depends on the scale of fiscal interventions, which in turn requires sufficient fiscal space. Rising debt, tighter financing conditions, and greater exposure to shocks are narrowing that space and constraining the scope for fiscal policy to respond. These constraints are most binding in Pacific Island countries, where limited market access and high vulnerability to shocks already severely restrict stabilization capacity. Preserving and strengthening the region's capacity to deliver macroeconomic stability will therefore require institutional frameworks that align revenues and spending over the medium term, strengthen fiscal discipline, and ensure access to liquidity during downturns. For Pacific Island countries, this strengthening of the region's capacity to deliver macroeconomic stability means prioritizing the accumulation of liquidity buffers, establishing clear and credible withdrawal rules to govern their use, and expanding access to prearranged contingent financing so that governments can deploy resources rapidly and predictably when shocks materialize.

Annex 2A. Supporting tables and figures

TABLE 2A.1 Relationship between mean growth and volatility, 1970–2023, 10-year period averages (conditional on Levine-Renelt variables)

Dependent variable: GDP per capita growth (10-year period)

Independent variable	145-country sample
Volatility (σ) (10-year period)	−0.273***
	(−4.06)
Average investment share of GDP (10-year period)	0.083***
	(3.52)
Average population growth rate (10-year period)	−0.291*
	(−1.73)
Initial human capital	0.854**
	(2.04)
Initial per capita GDP	−0.941***
	(−4.61)
Constant	8.885***
	(8.47)
Observations	788

Source: Original table for this publication based on Penn World Tables (Feenstra et al. 2015).

Note: Dependent variable is annual GDP per capita growth rate within each 10-year period over 1970–2023. Volatility is measured as the standard deviation of GDP growth per capita within each 10-year period over 1970–2023. All variables come from Penn World Table; *t*-statistics based on robust standard errors clustered by country are reported in parentheses.
$^{*}p < .1$ $^{**}p < .05$ $^{***}p < .01$

The countercyclicality or acyclicality of government spending in East Asia, as well as its procyclicality in Pacific Island countries, remains robust across alternative filtering techniques.

FIGURE 2A.1 Government size and cyclicality of primary expense, using different filtering techniques

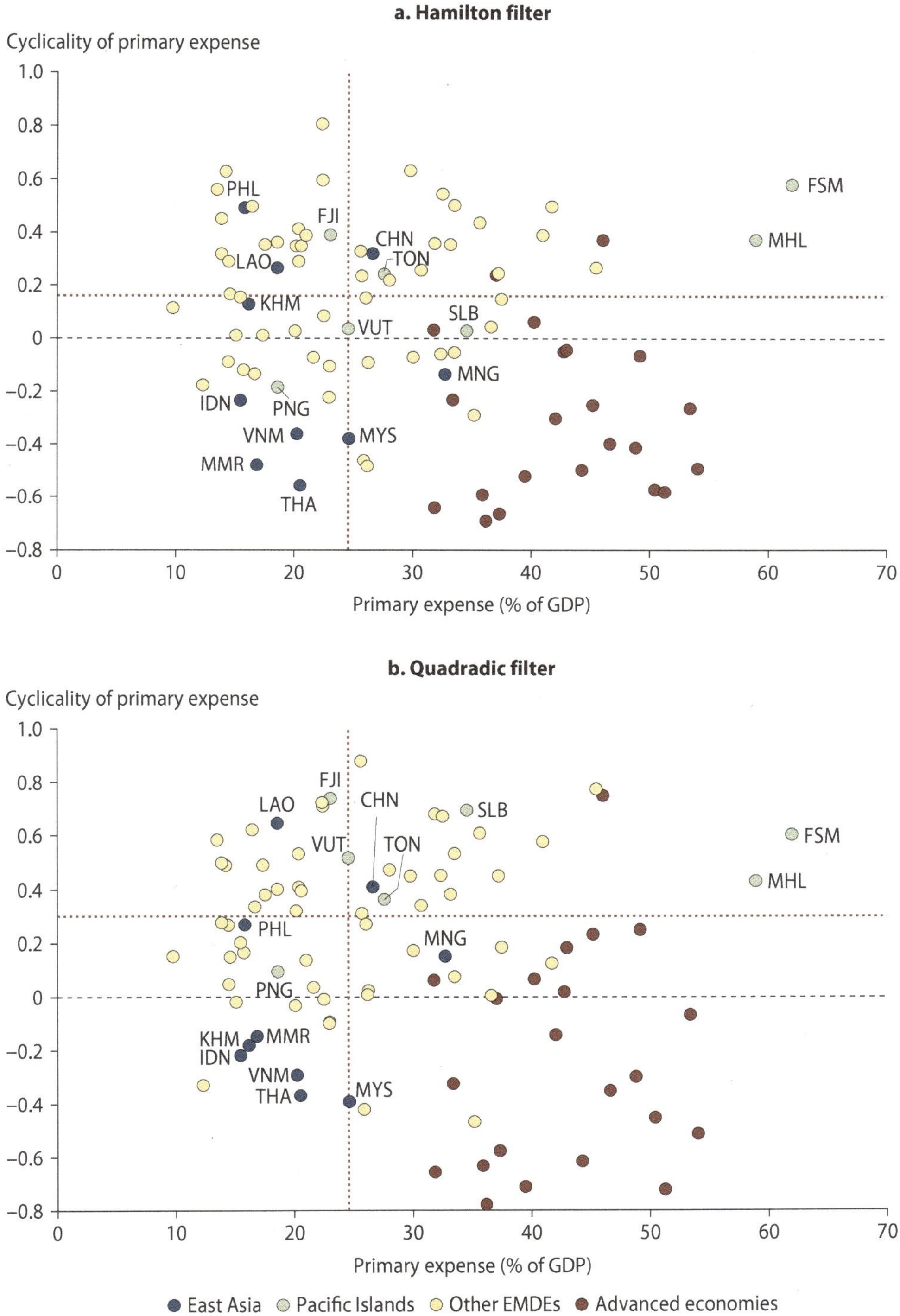

Source: Original figure for this publication based on World Economic Outlook Database, International Monetary Fund, https://www.imf.org/en/publications/sprolls/world-economic-outlook-databases. For a list of country codes, refer to https://www.iso.org/obp/ui/#search.

Forecast errors are uncorrelated with institutional quality, supporting their interpretation as a distinct measure of fiscal discipline.

FIGURE 2A.2 Correlation of primary balance forecast with government effectiveness and rule of law

a. Primary balance forecast error vs. government effectiveness

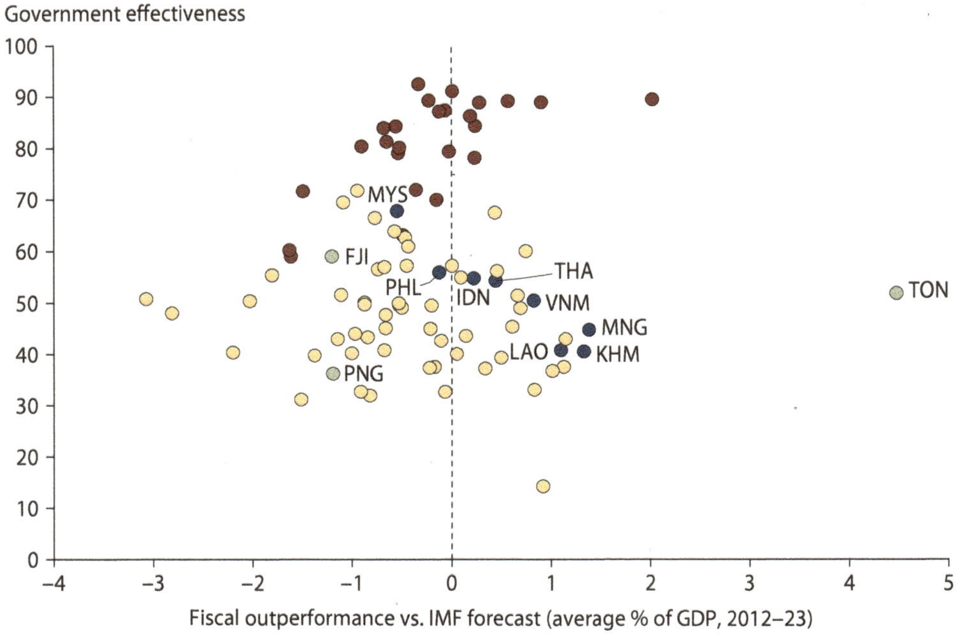

b. Primary balance forecast error vs. rule of law

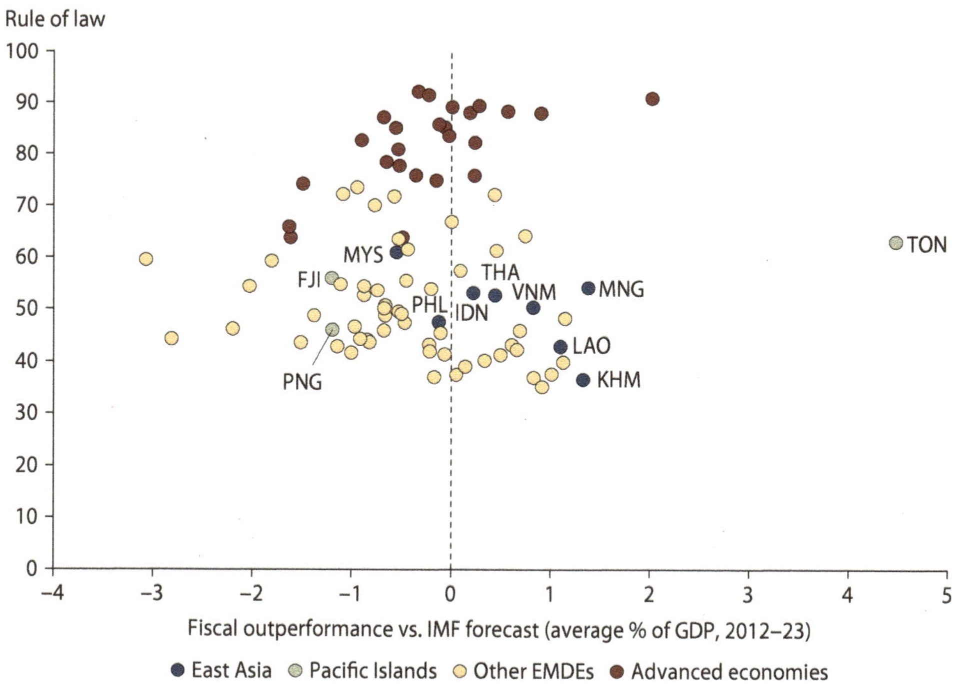

Source: Original figure for this publication based on World Economic Outlook Database, International Monetary Fund, https://www.imf.org/en/publications/sprolls/world-economic-outlook-databases.

Note: For a list of country codes, refer to https://www.iso.org/obp/ui/#search. IMF = International Monetary Fund.

Annex 2B. Debt accounting

The traditional accounting identity decomposes the changes in the ratio of government debt-to-GDP into the following equation:

$$d_t - d_{t-1} = \left(\frac{i_t}{1+g_t}\right)d_{t-1} - \left(\frac{g_t}{1+g_t}\right)d_{t-1} - \left(\frac{\pi_t}{1+g_t}\right)d_{t-1} + p_t \tag{2B.1}$$

where d is the ratio of debt-to-GDP, i is the nominal interest rate, g is the real growth rate, π is the inflation rate, and p is the primary deficit (the fiscal deficit excluding interest payments on the government's debt).[7] The first term on the right-hand side reflects the debt service, the second term reflects the erosion of the debt ratio that stems from the growth of output (the denominator in the debt ratio), the third term reflects the debt dilution associated with inflation rates, and the fourth term denotes the direct effect of primary deficits on debt accumulation.

To avoid debt explosion:

$$d_t = d_{t-1} \rightarrow \left(\frac{i_t - \pi_t - g_t}{1+g_t}\right)d_{t-1} = \left(\frac{r_t - g_t}{1+g_t}\right)d_{t-1} = p_t \tag{2B.2}$$

where $i_t - \pi_t = r_t$ denotes real interest rate at time t. Equation (2B.2) suggests that, when $r_t - g_t < 0$, governments can run moderate primary deficits without running the risk of a debt crisis. Although this has been the case for most East Asia and Pacific economies because of lower interest rates and high growth during the period after the global financial crisis of 2008–09, $r_t - g_t < 0$ is subject to reversals when either growth plummets or interest rates spike (World Bank 2021).

Notes

1. The analysis for this chapter follows Frankel et al. (2013) in measuring the cyclicality of government expenditure as the country-level correlation between the cyclical components of real government expenditure and real GDP, both estimated using the Hodrick-Prescott filter. Following Fuentes and Soto (2022), the analysis classifies fiscal policy as procyclical if the observed correlation is above 0.2, countercyclical if it is below –0.2, and acyclical otherwise.
2. These results are robust to other filtering techniques (refer to figure 2A.1 in annex 2A).
3. The Government Finance Statistics system defines Other Transfers as current transfers to nonprofit institutions serving households, capital transfers other than capital grants, and non-life insurance premiums and claims; refer to Government Finance Statistics, International Monetary Fund, https://data360.worldbank.org/en/int/dataset/IMF_GFSMAB.

4. World Economic Outlook Database, International Monetary Fund, https://www.imf.org/en/publications/sprolls/world-economic-outlook-databases.
5. World Economic Outlook Database, International Monetary Fund, https://www.imf.org/en/publications/sprolls/world-economic-outlook-databases.
6. The region offers a useful empirical setting, because East Asian economies adopted fiscal rules at different times: Indonesia in 2004, Mongolia in 2013, Viet Nam in 2016, Thailand in 2018, and Cambodia in 2019, creating a natural staggered adoption design. To account for the fact that treatment effects may vary across cohorts and evolve over time, the analysis uses an interaction-weighted difference-in-differences estimator (Wooldridge 2021), which avoids the biases that can affect standard two-way fixed effects regressions in staggered settings. The specification controls for the cyclical component of GDP, to ensure that results are not driven by business cycle dynamics, and for country-specific effects during 2020–21, to account for the heterogeneous fiscal impact of the COVID-19 pandemic across EAP economies.
7. The equation also can include the "stock-flow" residual that captures factors such as valuation effects due to changes in the exchange rate, privatizations and sales of other public assets, debt bailouts of entities that are not part of the general government (banks, state-owned enterprises), and central bank deficit financing, such as purchases of government debt (seigniorage). For debt denominated in foreign currency, we estimate the contribution of inflation to debt accumulation net of exchange rate depreciation.

References

Aaskoven, Lasse, and Wiese, Rasmus. 2022. "How Fiscal Rules Matter for Successful Fiscal Consolidations: New Evidence." *CESifo Economic Studies* 68 (4): 414–33. https://doi.org/10.1093/cesifo/ifac011.

Aghion, Philippe, and Abhijit Banerjee. 2005. *Volatility and Growth*. Oxford University Press.

Alesina, Alberto, Filipe R. Campante, and Guido Tabellini. 2008. "Why Is Fiscal Policy Often Procyclical?" *Journal of the European Economic Association* 6 (5): 1006–36.

Alonso, Virginia, Clara Arroyo, and Ozlem Aydin, et al. 2025a. "Fiscal Council Dataset: The 2024 Update." Fiscal Affairs Department, International Monetary Fund. https://www.imf.org/-/media/files/data/fiscal-council-docs/fiscal-council-database-technical-manual-2024.pdf.

Alonso, Virginia, Clara Arroyo, and Ozlem Aydin, et al. 2025b. "Fiscal Rules at a Glance: An Update 1985–2024." Fiscal Affairs Department, International Monetary Fund. https://www.imf.org/external/datamapper/fiscalrules/Release%20-%20Fiscal%20Rules%20at%20a%20Glance%201985-2024.pdf.

Alonso, Virginia, Clara Arroyo, and Ozlem Aydin, et al. 2025c. "Fiscal Rules Dataset: 1985–2024." International Monetary Fund. https://www.imf.org/en/topics/fiscal-policies/fiscal-rules-dataset.

Ardanaz, Martín, Eduardo Cavallo, Alejandro Izquierdo, and Jorge Puig. 2021. "Growth-Friendly Fiscal Rules? Safeguarding Public Investment from Budget Cuts Through Fiscal Rule Design." *Journal of International Money and Finance* 111: 102319. https://doi.org/10.1016/j.jimonfin.2020.102319.

Arslanalp, Serkan, Barry Eichengreen, and Peter Blair Henry. 2024. "Sustained Debt Reduction: The Jamaica Exception." *Brookings Papers on Economic Activity* (Spring): 133–81.

Badinger, Harald, and Wolf Heinrich Reuter. 2017. "The Case for Fiscal Rules." *Economic Modelling* 60: 334–43. https://doi.org/10.1016/j.econmod.2016.09.028.

Bergman, U. Michael, and Michael M. Hutchison. 2015. "Economic Stabilization in the Post-Crisis World: Are Fiscal Rules the Answer?" *Journal of International Money and Finance* 52: 82–101. https://doi.org/10.1016/j.jimonfin.2014.11.014.

Caselli, Francesca, and Julien Reynaud. 2020. "Do Fiscal Rules Cause Better Fiscal Balances? A New Instrumental Variable Strategy." *European Journal of Political Economy* 63: 101873. https://doi.org/10.1016/j.ejpoleco.2020.101873.

Chinn, Menzie D., and Hiro Ito. 2006. "What Matters for Financial Development? Capital Controls, Institutions, and Interactions." *Journal of Development Economics* 81 (1): 163–92 (October). https://web.pdx.edu/~ito/Chinn-Ito_website.htm.

Chowdhury, Ibrahim, Anders Hjorth Agerskov, Ekaterine T. Vashakmadze, and Christopher Wong. 2024. "Building Strong Fiscal Foundations: Essential Strategies for Pacific Island Countries to Withstand and Recover from Economic Shocks." *Let's Talk Development* (blog), June 2023. https://blogs.worldbank.org/en/developmenttalk/building-strong-fiscal-foundations--essential-strategies-for-pac0.

Cole, Harold L., and Timothy J. Kehoe. 2000. "Self-Fulfilling Debt Crises." *Review of Economic Studies* 67 (1): 91–116. https://doi.org/10.1111/1467-937X.00123.

Debrun, Xavier, and Manmohan Kumar. 2007. "Fiscal Rules, Fiscal Councils and All That: Commitment Devices, Signaling Tools or Smokescreens?" SSRN. https://papers.ssrn.com/sol3/papers.cfm?abstract_id=2004371.

Esquivel, Carlos, and Agustin Samano. 2026. "Expansionary Fiscal Rules Under Sovereign Risk." *Journal of International Economics* 159: 104198. https://doi.org/10.1016/j.jinteco.2025.104198.

Fardoust, Shahrokh, Justin Y. Lin, and Xubei Luo. 2012. "Demystifying China's Fiscal Stimulus." Policy Research Working Paper 6221, World Bank. http://hdl.handle.net/10986/12066.

Fardoust, Shahrokh, and V. J. Ravishankar. 2013. "Subnational Fiscal Policy in Large Developing Countries: Some Lessons from the 2008–09 Crisis for Brazil, China and India." Policy Research Working Paper 6409, World Bank. http://hdl.handle.net/10986/14447.

Feenstra, Robert C., Robert Inklaar, and Marcel P. Timmer. 2015. "The Next Generation of the Penn World Table." *American Economic Review* 105 (10): 3150–82. https://doi.org/10.1257/aer.20130954.

Frankel, Jeffrey A., Carlos A. Végh, and Guillermo Vuletin. 2013. "On Graduation from Fiscal Procyclicality." *Journal of Development Economics* 100 (1): 32–47.

Fuentes, J. Rodrigo, and Raimundo Soto. 2022. "Does Countercyclical Fiscal Policy Pay? The Relevance of Fiscal Acyclicality." World Bank. https://thedocs.worldbank.org/en/doc/351ffcd48af177a7b17fd29deb4009f5-0370012023/original/DC-conference-Oct-2022.pdf.

Gavin, Michael, and Roberto Perotti. 1997. "Fiscal Policy in Latin America." *NBER Macroeconomics Annual* 12: 11–61.

Government of Malaysia. 2023. *Fiscal Responsibility Act 2023 (Act 850)*. Government of Malaysia. https://www.mof.gov.my/portal/pdf/ekonomi/akta-850-en.pdf.

Government of the Philippines. 2022. *Medium-Term Fiscal Framework 2022–2030.* Department of Finance, Department of Budget and Management, National Economic and Development Authority, and Bangko Sentral ng Pilipinas. https://www.dbm.gov.ph/wp-content/uploads/DBCC/MTFF/MTFF-2022-2030-Midterm-Update_Final_Ad-Ref-Approved_Oct-2-2025.pdf.

Guerguil, Martine, Pierre Mandon, and René Tapsoba. 2017. "Flexible Fiscal Rules and Countercyclical Fiscal Policy." *Journal of Macroeconomics* 52: 189–220. https://www.sciencedirect.com/science/article/pii/S0164070417301519.

Hallerberg, Mark, Rolf Strauch, and Jürgen von Hagen. 2007. "The Design of Fiscal Rules and Forms of Governance in European Union Countries." *European Journal of Political Economy* 23 (2): 338–359. https://doi.org/10.1016/j.ejpoleco.2006.11.005.

Heinemann, Friedrich, Marc-Daniel Moessinger, and Mustafa Yeter. 2018. "Do Fiscal Rules Constrain Fiscal Policy? A Meta-Regression Analysis." *European Journal of Political Economy* 51: 69–92. https://doi.org/10.1016/j.ejpoleco.2017.03.008.

Hnatkovska, Viktoria, and Norman Loayza. 2005. "Volatility and Growth." In *Managing Economic Volatility and Crises: A Practitioner's Guide*, edited by Joshua Aizenman and Brian Pinto. Cambridge University Press.

Iara, Anna, and Guntram B. Wolff. 2014. "Rules and Risk in the Euro Area." *European Journal of Political Economy* 34: 222–36. https://doi.org/10.1016/j.ejpoleco.2014.02.002.

Ilzetzki, Ethan, and Carlos A. Végh. 2008. "Procyclical Fiscal Policy in Developing Countries: Truth or Fiction?" NBER Working Paper 14191, National Bureau of Economic Research.

IMF (International Monetary Fund). 2017. "Mongolia: 2017 Article IV Consultation and Request for an Extended Arrangement Under the Extended Fund Facility—Press Release; Staff Report." IMF. https://doi.org/10.5089/9781484302354.002.

IMF (International Monetary Fund). 2024. "Democratic Republic of Timor-Leste: 2024 Article IV Consultation—Press Release; Staff Report." *IMF Staff Country Reports* 2024/342. https://www.imf.org/en/publications/cr/issues/2024/12/17/democratic-republic-of-timor-leste-2024-article-iv-consultation-press-release-staff-report-559641.

Islamaj, Ergys, Agustin Samano Penaloza, and Scott Sommers. 2024. "The Sovereign Spread Compressing Effect of Fiscal Rules During Global Crises." Policy Research Working Paper 10741, World Bank. https://documents1.worldbank.org/curated/en/099249103282432838/pdf/IDU-5cfa7f6d-d6ab-4065-8cfe-57ccc6a3202a.pdf.

Islamaj, Ergys, and Jacek Rothert. 2024. "Cyclicality of Social Transfers in Emerging Markets: Did the COVID-19 Recession Signal Graduation to Counter-Cyclical Fiscal Policy?" SSRN. https://papers.ssrn.com/sol3/papers.cfm?abstract_id=5002672.

Kaminsky, Graciela L., Carmen M. Reinhart, and Carlos A. Végh. 2004. "When It Rains, It Pours: Procyclical Capital Flows and Macroeconomic Policies." *NBER Macroeconomics Annual* 19: 11–53.

Larch, Martin, Eva Orseau, and Wouter van der Wielen. 2021. "Do EU Fiscal Rules Support or Hinder Counter-Cyclical Fiscal Policy?" *Journal of International Money and Finance* 112: 102328. https://doi.org/10.1016/j.jimonfin.2020.102328.

Marcel Cullel, Mario, Marcelo Tokman Ramos, Rodrigo Valdés, and Paula Benavides Salazar. 2001. "Balance estructural: la base de la nueva regla de política fiscal Chilena." *Economía chilena* 4 (3): 5–27. https://repositoriodigital.bcentral.cl/xmlui/handle/20.500.12580/3440.

Medina, Juan Pablo, and Claudio Soto. 2007. *Copper Price, Fiscal Policy and Business Cycle in Chile* (Vol. 458). Banco Central de Chile. https://www.bcentral.cl/documents/33528/133326/DTBC_458.pdf.

Mendoza, Enrique G., and P. Marcelo Oviedo. 2006. "Fiscal Policy and Macroeconomic Uncertainty in Developing Countries: The Tale of the Tormented Insurer." NBER Working Paper 12586, National Bureau of Economic Research.

Michaud, Amanda, and Jacek Rothert. 2018. "Redistributive Fiscal Policies and Business Cycles in Emerging Economies." *Journal of International Economics* 112: 123–33.

Ministry of Finance Malaysia. 2024. "Budget 2025 Speech (Belanjawan 2025)." Government of Malaysia. https://belanjawan.mof.gov.my/pdf/belanjawan2025/ucapan/ub25-en.pdf.

Mueller, Johannes, Renaud Duplay, Luc Eyraud, Jason Harris, Murray Petrie, and Sagé de Clerck. 2015. *Philippines: Fiscal Transparency Evaluation.* IMF Country Report 2015/156, International Monetary Fund. https://doi.org/10.5089/9781513501161.002.

Ramey, Garey, and Valerie A. Ramey. 1995. "Cross-Country Evidence on the Link Between Volatility and Growth." *American Economic Review* 85 (5): 1138–51.

Rodden, Jonathan, and Erik Wibbels. 2010. "Fiscal Decentralization and the Business Cycle: An Empirical Study of Seven Federations." *Economics & Politics* 22 (1): 37–67.

Talvi, Ernesto, and Carlos A. Végh. 2005. "Tax Base Variability and Procyclical Fiscal Policy in Developing Countries." *Journal of Development Economics* 78 (1): 156–90.

Tornell, Aaron, and Philip R. Lane. 1999. "The Voracity Effect." *American Economic Review* 89 (1): 22–46.

Végh, Carlos A., and Guillermo Vuletin. 2015. "How Is Tax Policy Conducted over the Business Cycle?" *American Economic Journal: Economic Policy* 7 (3): 327–70.

Wooldridge, Jeffrey M. 2021. "Two-Way Fixed Effects, the Two-Way Mundlak Regression, and Difference-in-Differences Estimators." SSRN Electronic Journal. https://papers.ssrn.com/sol3/papers.cfm?abstract_id=3906345.

World Bank. 2017a. "Myanmar Public Expenditure Review 2017: Fiscal Space for Economic Growth." World Bank. http://hdl.handle.net/10986/28392.

World Bank. 2017b. "Taking Stock: An Update on Vietnam's Recent Economic Developments—Special Focus: Towards a High-Quality Fiscal Consolidation (Vietnamese)." World Bank. http://documents.worldbank.org/curated/en/530061500266807981.

World Bank. 2018. "Mongolia: Public Expenditure Review—Growing Without Undue Borrowing." World Bank. http://hdl.handle.net/10986/32033.

World Bank. 2020. "Indonesia Public Expenditure Review 2020: Spending for Better Results." World Bank. https://openknowledge.worldbank.org/entities/publication/118cb701-cc62-5d24-9d4d-df26496ae97b.

World Bank. 2021. *East Asia and Pacific Economic Update, April 2021: Uneven Recovery.* http://hdl.handle.net/10986/35272.

World Bank. 2023a. "Forging Ahead: Restoring Stability and Boosting Prosperity." Lao PDR Public Finance Review. World Bank. https://doi.org/10.1596/40861.

World Bank. 2023b. "Malaysia Economic Monitor, February 2023: Expanding Malaysia's Digital Frontier." World Bank. http://hdl.handle.net/10986/39438.

World Bank. 2023c. "Thailand Public Revenue and Spending Assessment: Promoting an Inclusive and Sustainable Future." World Bank. http://documents.worldbank.org/curated/en/099052523201510112.

World Bank. 2024a. "Cambodia Public Finance Review: From Spending More to Spending Better." World Bank. http://hdl.handle.net/10986/41034.

World Bank. 2024b. "Forging Ahead: Restoring Stability and Boosting Prosperity." Lao PDR Public Finance Review. World Bank. https://doi.org/10.1596/40861.

World Bank. 2025. "Mongolia Public Finance Review: Making This Time Different—Fiscal Reforms for Stable, Sustainable, and Inclusive Development." World Bank. http://hdl.handle.net/10986/43650.

World Bank. 2026. *Global Economic Prospects, January 2026*. World Bank. https://www.worldbank.org/en/publication/global-economic-prospects.

Fiscal Policy for Equity: Taxes, Spending, and Distributional Impacts

3

Introduction

The East Asia and Pacific (EAP) region has achieved the greatest reduction in poverty in history. In 1990, the region had a higher poverty rate than Sub-Saharan Africa. Rapid growth changed that. China alone lifted more than 800 million people out of extreme poverty over three decades. A further 210 million people in the rest of EAP exited poverty. Extreme poverty has now been nearly eradicated across the region (World Bank 2024a; refer to figure 3.1, panel a).

The gains, however, are incomplete. Over half of the population in EAP excluding China still lives in moderate poverty or is vulnerable to falling back into it. Poverty reduction has slowed, as has the growth of the middle class (Krah et al. 2026; refer to figure 3.1, panel b). As economies have moved into middle- and upper-middle-income status, the older model of unskilled, labor-intensive, export-driven growth is losing steam—even as households aspire to higher living standards and better public services. Inequality is rising in several economies. The middle and upper classes are increasingly opting out of public services in some economies, widening the quality gap between rich and poor and placing greater strain on the system.[1] EAP's traditional social contract is one built on low taxes and low spending, with broad-based gains distributed primarily through labor income. A new contract based on higher taxes with greater investments in public services becomes less viable if richer households who will shoulder much of the tax burden do not see the value in the public services that those taxes will finance.

Extreme poverty has nearly been eradicated in EAP; however, over half of the region excluding China lives in moderate poverty or is vulnerable, and growth of the middle class has slowed.

FIGURE 3.1 Poverty in EAP, 2001–24

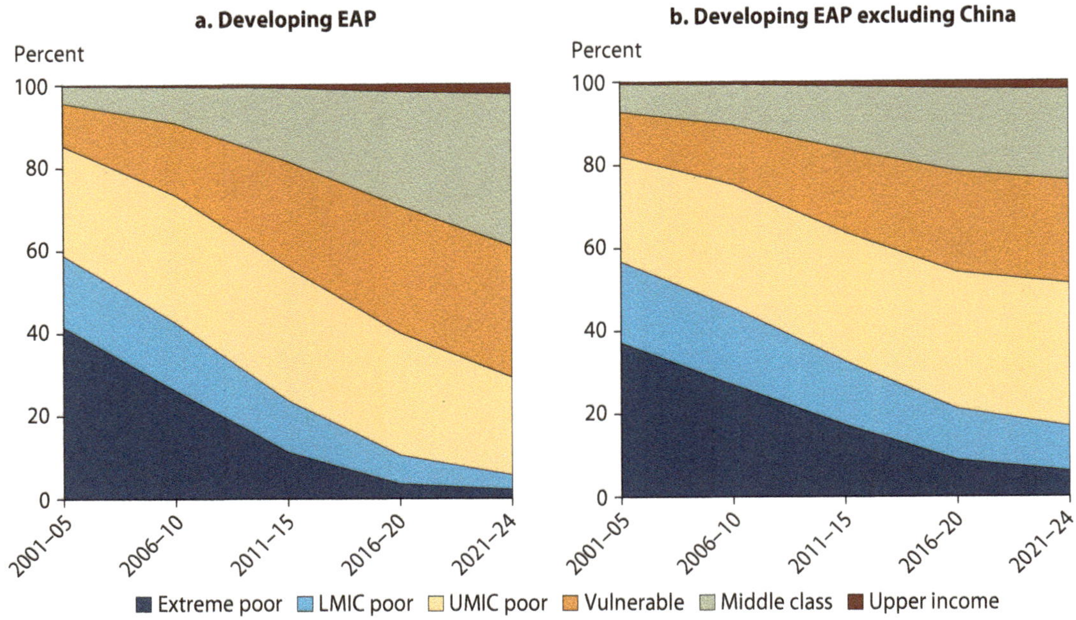

Source: Original figure for this publication based on Krah et al. 2026.
Note: LMIC poor individuals live on less than $4.20 per day; UMIC poor, on between $4.20 and $8.30 per day; vulnerable, on between $8.30 and $15.00 per day; middle class, on between $15.00 and $56.00 per day; and upper income, on above $56.00 per day. The $15.00 threshold follows Chaudhuri (2003) to identify the income or consumption level associated with a 10 percent probability of falling into poverty at the $8.30 (2021 purchasing power parity) line across 20 EAP economies. The median estimate ($15.20) was rounded to $15.00. The upper-income threshold, $56.00 per day, is twice the Prosperity Gap line of $28.00 per day, which reflects incomes typical of countries nearing high-income status; doubling that line better excludes the upper tail while maintaining focus on the middle of the distribution. EAP = East Asia and Pacific; LMIC = lower-middle-income country; UMIC = upper-middle-income country.

Expanding the middle class from below will require both growth and equity. The vulnerable and emerging middle classes together represent 56 percent of the region's population. Transforming EAP into a middle-class region means enabling these households to enter the secure middle class, safe from poverty and vulnerability, with rising disposable income and the skills needed for higher-value jobs. Better jobs and sustained growth are necessary, as are broader participation and greater equality of opportunity. Fiscal policy represents a central tool for driving both growth and equity.

Fiscal policy is unique in its size and temporal scope. Taxes and spending affect distributional outcomes immediately: taxes are paid today, transfers received today, and subsidies consumed today. At the same time, fiscal policy creates the space and the budget allocations that enable investments in infrastructure, health, education, and social protection. How governments create and use this fiscal space is a key function of fiscal policy that will also have strong distributional implications—now and tomorrow.

Many fiscal investments that promote equity also drive growth, and human capital investments do so most of all. Greater human capital accumulation among poorer individuals is the primary driver of longer-term economic mobility. At the aggregate level, human capital drives growth and is essential for middle-income countries to reach high-income status (World Bank 2024b). Adequate and well-targeted social assistance plays a complementary role: it protects productive assets from shocks, promotes human capital accumulation, and enables entrepreneurship (Wai-Poi et al. 2025; World Bank 2022c).[2] It also facilitates the politically difficult reforms that countries need. Any significant macroeconomic adjustment produces winners and losers. A well-functioning social assistance system can compensate those who lose, reducing adverse distributional impacts and softening political resistance, as illustrated by Indonesia's fuel subsidy reforms and the Philippines' TRAIN tax reform (Castillo et al. 2019; World Bank 2026).[3]

The evidence on well-designed social assistance is robust. A review of 165 studies across 56 cash transfer programs in 30 countries finds that well-designed transfers reduce monetary poverty, raise school attendance, improve dietary diversity, stimulate health service use, reduce child labor without reducing adult employment, and strengthen women's economic decision-making (Bastagli et al. 2018; refer to box 3.1).

Box 3.1. Social protection and growth

Social protection does more than protect the poor. It also promotes growth through three channels: resilience, human capital investment, and credit relief and local economic activity.

Resilience. Cash transfers reduce the likelihood that households cope with shocks by cutting food consumption, forgoing health care, withdrawing children from school, or selling productive assets (Alderman and Yemtsov 2012; Bowen et al. 2020; Hill et al. 2019). These negative coping strategies have lasting consequences. Avoiding them preserves a household's capacity to earn and invest over the medium and long term.

(continued)

Box 3.1. Social protection and growth *(continued)*

Human capital investment. Social protection encourages risk-taking and forward-looking decisions, particularly around children's health and education. Conditional cash transfers offer the best-known example: successful programs in Brazil and Mexico inspired similar designs worldwide and generated significant improvements in health and education outcomes (Bastagli et al. 2018; Fiszbein et al. 2009). A growing body of evidence also shows that unconditional cash transfers—particularly when accompanied by positive messaging about their purpose—can be equally effective (Baird et al. 2011). Beyond health and education, transfers generate positive effects on gender empowerment, food security, asset formation, savings, financial inclusion, and economic empowerment (Banerjee et al. 2015; Haushofer and Shapiro 2016; Hidrobo et al. 2018). A recent systematic review confirms strong positive effects on income, labor supply, school enrollment, and both financial and physical assets (Crosta et al. 2024).

Credit relief and local economic activity. Poor households often cannot borrow to invest, even when they would realize high returns. Transfers relieve that constraint. GiveDirectly's large-scale unconditional transfer experiment in Kenya found that cash injections increased local market activity, entrepreneurship, local production, and earnings—even among households that did not receive transfers directly. Inflation remained minimal. The estimated local fiscal multiplier was 2.5 (Egger et al. 2022). A systematic review confirms significant multiplier effects of cash transfers more broadly, though their magnitude depends on transfer size and predictability (Gassmann et al. 2023).

EAP's fiscal policy falls short on multiple dimensions. The region does not invest enough in human capital or social assistance. Moreover, what it spends it does not always spend effectively (Cho et al. 2025). Social assistance spending falls considerably below the upper-middle-income country (UMIC) average, and the region spends more, on average, on regressive and costly energy and agricultural subsidies. Health and education spending averages below that of low-income countries (LICs) and far below that of middle-income countries (MICs). Low spending compounds a problem of quality: In many of the region's economies, more than half of 10-year-olds cannot read or understand age-appropriate reading material, and 31 percent of enrolled 15-year-olds do not reach basic proficiency in mathematics and science. In most EAP economies, improving the quality of students currently enrolled would drive greater long-run growth than achieving universal enrollment at current quality levels, with quality improvements estimated to be 3.5 times more important than enrollment gains in Cambodia and Indonesia, 2.8 times in the Philippines, and 1.8 times in Thailand.

A core principle runs through this chapter: taxes should raise revenue efficiently, and spending should drive redistribution. The logic is one of cost-effectiveness. For each percentage point of gross domestic product (GDP), transfers reduce inequality by substantially more than either direct or indirect taxes. Direct taxes are more progressive than indirect taxes, but even they are far less cost-effective at redistribution than well-targeted transfers. Subsidies are the least cost-effective instrument of all. The clear implication is that the goal of taxation should be to raise revenue efficiently, not to redistribute directly. Redistribution can instead be achieved more cost-effectively through the spending that taxation finances.

A combination of value added tax (VAT) and transfers offers a key strategy for raising revenue while reducing poverty. With the scope for expanding personal income tax (PIT) limited by informality and administrative capacity, VAT will remain a core revenue source across the region for the medium term. This chapter examines the actual progressiveness or regressiveness of VAT and how governments can increase revenues while improving equity through targeted transfers. Social assistance plays a unique role. Its cash nature makes it the primary tool for offsetting the indirect tax burden on poorer households, and the most effective instrument for easing the distributional costs of broader reforms—new taxes, trade liberalization, and energy price adjustments. A well-functioning social assistance system is not just a welfare program. It is fiscal infrastructure.

The design and delivery of social protection programs matter as much as the level of spending. For any given social assistance budget, broader coverage means shallower benefits, and vice versa. The right balance depends on country context and policy objectives. Targeted transfers are the most cost-effective fiscal instrument for reducing poverty and inequality, but only if benefits reach poorer households. In some cases, targeting systems need to be strengthened before significantly increased spending is warranted. Targeting performance determines whether resources reach those who need them most. Indonesia illustrates both how targeting can be improved and how it must be maintained over time; Malaysia illustrates the fiscal cost of poorly targeted spending at scale; and the Philippines serves as a detailed case study in optimizing the coverage-adequacy trade-off.

Fiscal reforms are politically difficult, and design alone is not enough. A technically sound reform package can fail if it produces more losers than winners, or if the rationale is not communicated clearly. Expanding social assistance is politically sensitive in EAP. Across the region, policy makers and the public tend to prioritize work over welfare, worry about disincentive effects, and view income support as an individual rather than a government responsibility. Successful reform requires anticipating this resistance and addressing it directly through transparent communications and visible links between tax payments and tangible public benefits. The chapter reviews examples of successful and less successful reforms, with particular attention to fuel subsidy reform in Indonesia and the emerging option of a personalized VAT regime that links individual tax payments to direct cash rebates.

PIT, a progressive tax with most revenues coming from the richest and second-richest income deciles, can in principle be a key instrument for both raising revenue and achieving equity objectives. Nevertheless, most LICs and MICs have low effective tax rates for the richest households because of exemptions and evasion, reflecting weaknesses in both administrative capacity and the political will to tax the rich. Strengthening the PIT base through various policy changes can increase short-term revenues. Exemptions and deductions can be reduced or removed to increase the taxable income of rich households, and all sources of household income can be made subject to PIT, including capital income and capital gains. At the same time, top marginal PIT rates can be aligned with corporate income tax (CIT) rates to prevent avoidance. High employment informality and low incomes, however, can constrain PIT's scope in LICs and MICs.

Improving compliance and collection will require investments in tax administration capacity. Increased use of technology and data can make it easier to identify payers and verify their liability. In the longer term, bringing more households into the PIT base will require greater employment formality and higher incomes.

The chapter proceeds in five steps. First, it assesses EAP's distributional record—that is, how taxes and spending affect poverty and inequality across the region relative to global income level peers. Second, it examines the cost-effectiveness of different fiscal instruments, establishing the analytical foundation for the division of labor between revenue and redistribution. Third, it draws on that framework to outline the reform path for indirect taxes, direct taxes, and social protection spending. Fourth, it examines program design and delivery—that is, where poor targeting and inadequate benefit levels compound underspending. Finally, it addresses the political economy of reform: why technically sound packages fail, and how they can be made to succeed.

Impact of taxes and spending on poverty and inequality in EAP

Fiscal policy reduces income inequality in every country but to very different degrees. Global surveys using the Commitment to Equity (CEQ) methodology trace how taxes, transfers, and subsidies shift household incomes from market income to final consumption (Wai-Poi et al. 2025; World Bank 2022c).[4] Considering cash instruments only—taxes, transfers, and subsidies—the reduction in the Gini index ranges from near zero in Serbia to 11.9 points in Spain (refer to figure 3.2, diamonds).[5] Averages by country income level follow a clear gradient from 5.7 points for high-income countries (HICs) to 1.2 points for LICs (red lines). Adding the noncash benefits of public health and education substantially raises these figures, with inequality reduction rising in all income groups (gray lines). For most countries, in-kind health and education spending is the single largest driver of inequality reduction.

Within EAP, lower-middle-income countries (LMICs) perform at about the global average for their income level, whereas upper-UMICs mostly fall below it.[6] For example, Kiribati, the Philippines, and Viet Nam reduce inequality by roughly the average for LMICs, whether or not health and education benefits are included (refer to figure 3.3, panels a and b). Mongolia stands out as the exception: a universal and generous child money grant drives its inequality reduction well above the LMIC average. Cambodia and the Lao People's Democratic Republic fall below average, with Cambodia particularly underperforming.[7] Among EAP economies, only Thailand exceeds the UMIC global average when health and education are excluded, and only China reaches it when they are included. Indonesia and Malaysia consistently fall below the UMIC average, as does Fiji, though to a lesser extent.

Measured against spending, however, most EAP economies perform better than their budgets would predict. They generally spend less on health and education than the global average for their UMIC peers, yet most achieve above-average inequality reduction relative to that spending (refer to figure 3.3, panel c). China spends 0.7 percent of GDP below the UMIC average but reduces inequality by 1.6 Gini points more than predicted; Thailand spends 1.3 points below average but still achieves above-average inequality reduction. The exception, Indonesia, has both the largest spending gap (2.9 points below average) and the largest performance gap (5.7 Gini points below average) among EAP UMICs. Mongolia presents the inverse problem: it spends 3.1 points above the LMIC average but achieves only 0.6 points more inequality reduction than peers, well below what its spending would suggest. When the analysis is restricted to cash social spending and its direct inequality impact—excluding health and education—EAP economies look broadly in line with their global income-level peers (refer to figure 3.3, panel d).

In-kind benefits from health and education play the largest role in reducing inequality in most countries.

FIGURE 3.2 Change in Gini index, by type of fiscal instrument and income level, all countries

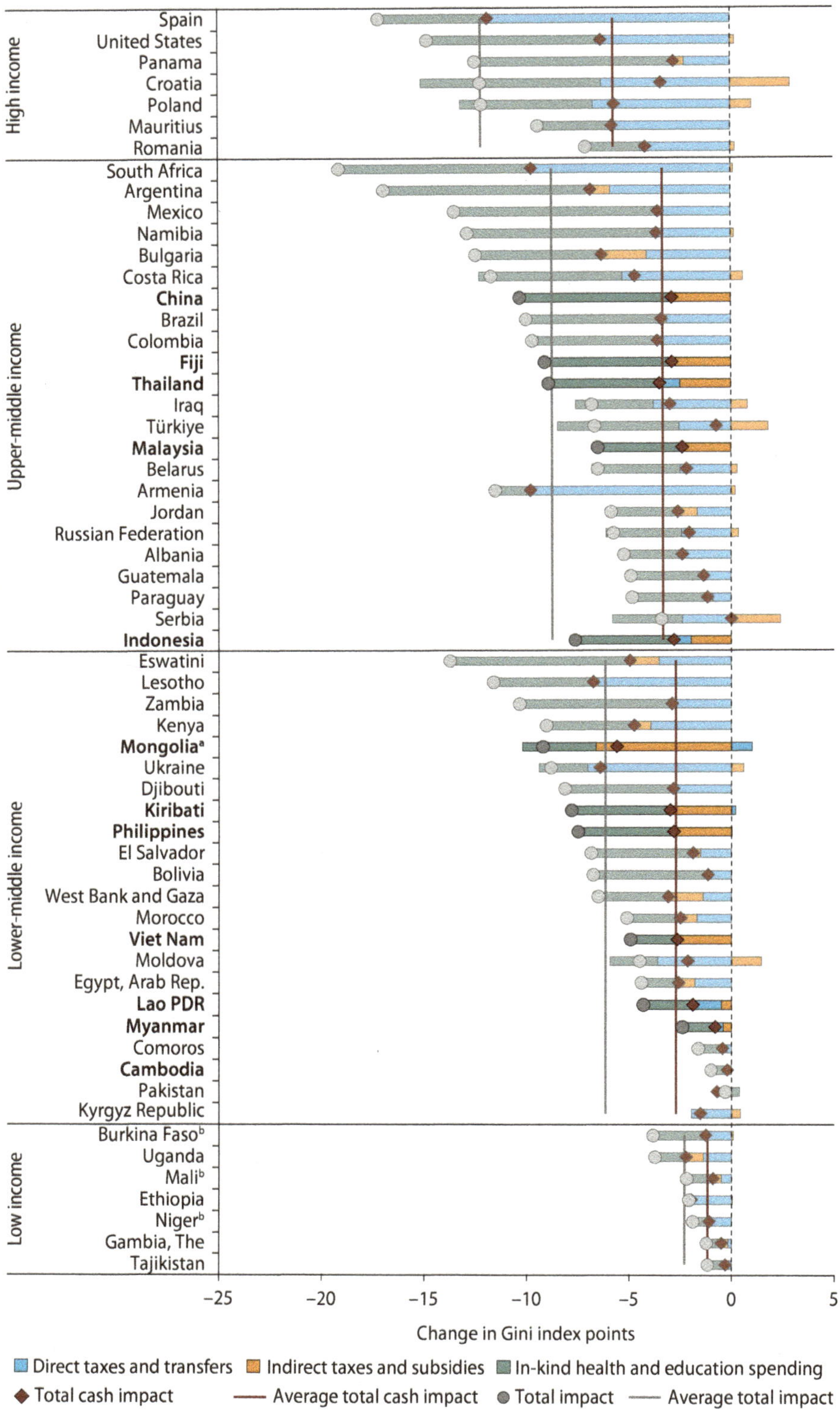

(continued)

FIGURE 3.2 Change in Gini index, by type of fiscal instrument and income level, all countries *(continued)*

Source: Original figure for this publication based on calculations from Wai-Poi et al. 2025.

Note: The latest available years range from 2010–19; refer to table 5 of Wai-Poi et al. (2025) for specific country years and sources. Bold countries and darker bars, dots, and diamonds indicate EAP economies. EAP = East Asia and Pacific.

a. Mongolia's Commitment to Equity result, from 2022, reflects significant social spending in response to the COVID-19 pandemic. Although similar spending occurred in many other countries, their results do not reflect that spending because analyses were conducted before the pandemic.

b. Pensions were treated as government taxes and transfers instead of the default pensions as deferred income. The former approach tends to overstate the impact on inequality relative to the latter approach; refer to Lustig (2022b) for discussion.

On inequality reduction, EAP LMICs achieve about the average for their global income level, but EAP UMICs generally fall below average.

FIGURE 3.3 Change in Gini index, by type of fiscal instrument and income level, EAP

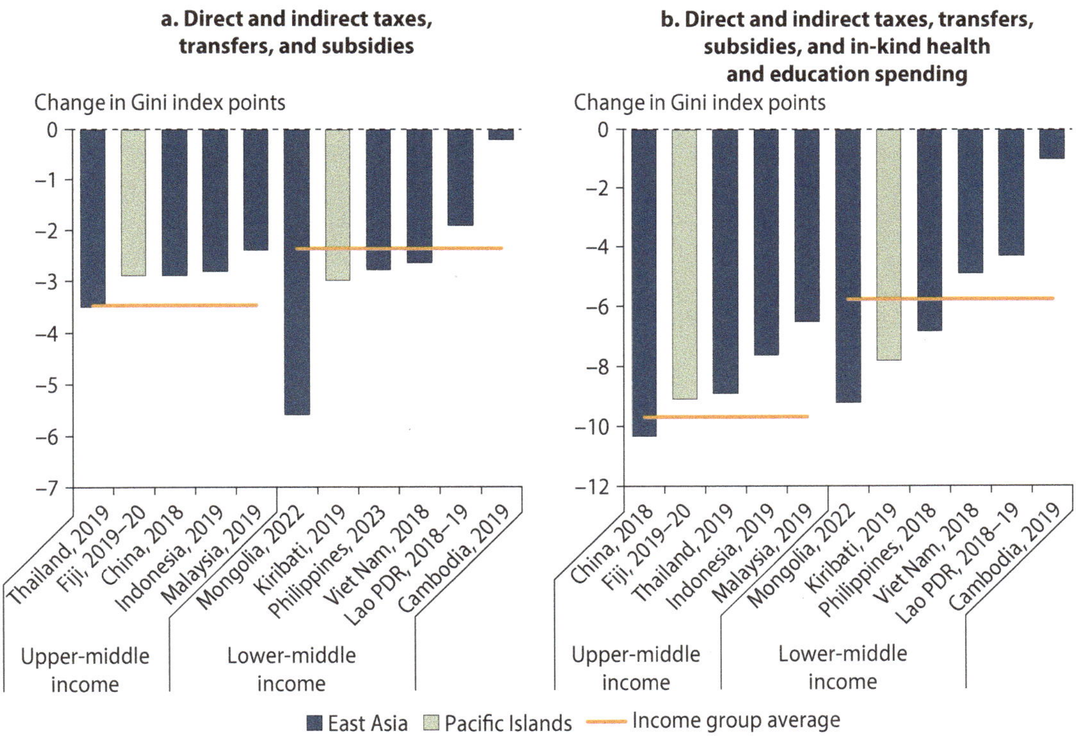

(continued)

FIGURE 3.3 Change in Gini index, by type of fiscal instrument and income level, EAP *(continued)*

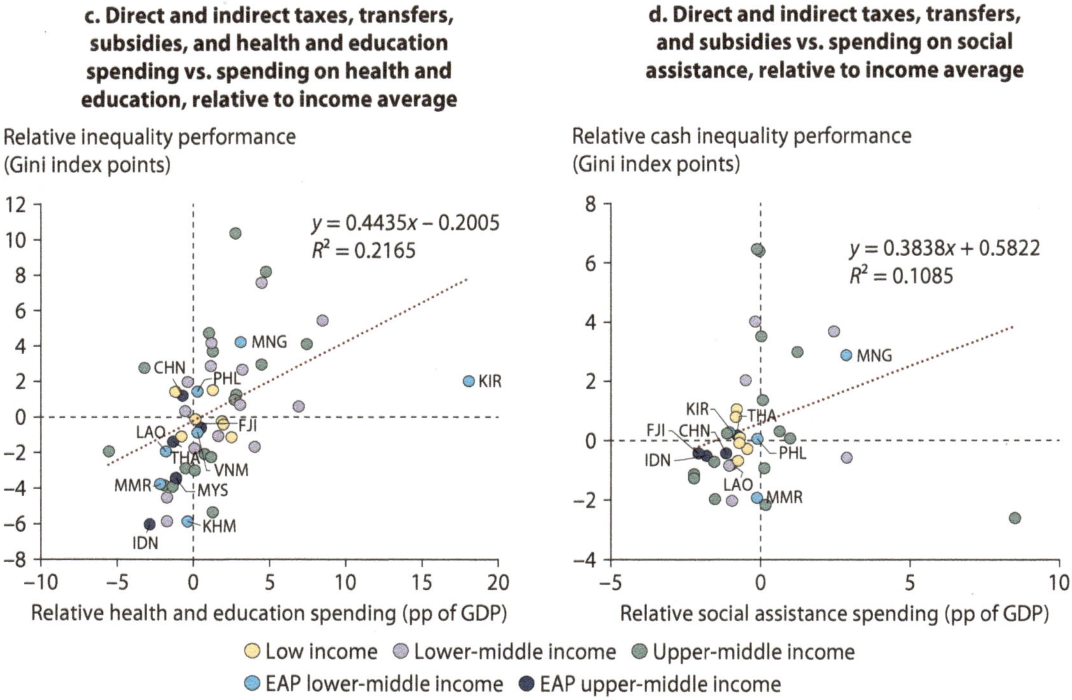

Sources: Original figure for this publication based on Atlas of Social Protection Indicators of Resilience and Equity (ASPIRE), World Bank, https://www.worldbank.org/en/data/datatopics/aspire (social assistance spending); individual EAP country studies (inequality impacts); Wai-Poi et al. 2025 (income average inequality impacts); World Development Indicators, World Bank, https://datatopics.worldbank.org/world-development-indicators/ (health and education spending).

Note: The figure excludes Kiribati, whose education and health spending exceed 25 percent of GDP because of its very small population and very large area, making it not comparable. For a list of country codes, refer to https://www.iso.org/obp/ui/#search. EAP = East Asia and Pacific; LMICs = lower-middle-income countries; pp = percentage point; UMICs = upper-middle-income countries.

Taxes and cash spending increase poverty in most MICs, and EAP LMICs are no exception. Setting aside noncash health and education benefits, the net cash impact of taxes, transfers, and subsidies increases poverty in virtually all LICs, most LMICs, and about half of UMICs (refer to figure 3.4). The mechanism is consistent: indirect taxes burden poor households more than direct transfers compensate them—few poor households pay much or any direct tax (included in the blue bars in figure 3.4).

For poverty, the pattern within EAP is the reverse of the inequality pattern. EAP UMICs mostly reduce poverty, whereas EAP LMICs mostly increase it (refer to figure 3.5, panel a). Malaysia and Thailand both reduce poverty, a better result than most UMICs globally. Indonesia's 4-point poverty reduction is among the strongest of any LIC or MIC. Fiji reduces poverty at the lower-middle-income

Taxes and cash spending increase poverty in most LMICs and half of UMICs.

FIGURE 3.4 Change in poverty rate, by type of fiscal instrument and income level

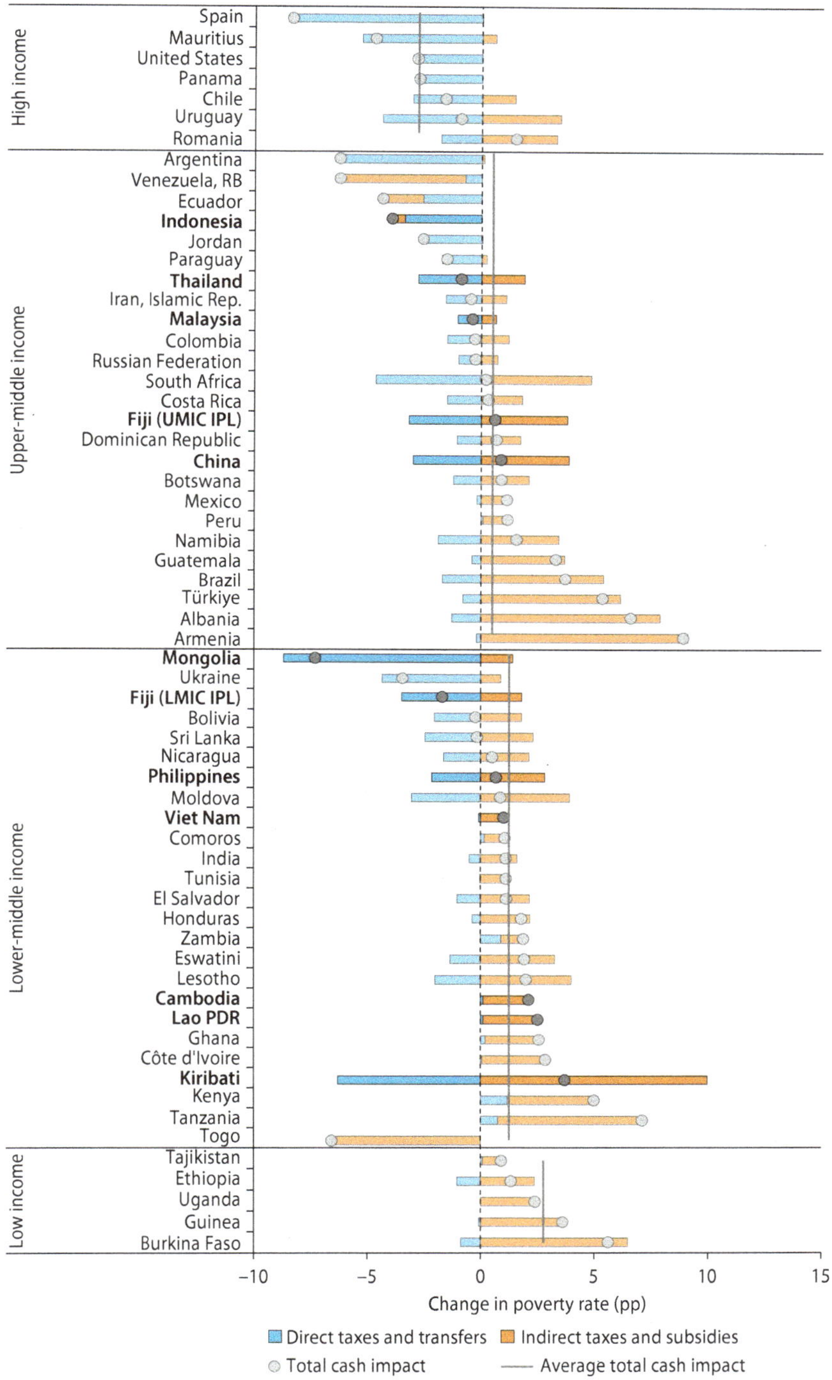

Source: Original figure for this publication based on calculations from Wai-Poi et al. 2025.

Note: Poverty rates at 2011 PPP lines for all countries except 2005 PPP lines used for Albania, Burkina Faso, Mauritius, and the Russian Federation, and 2017 PPP lines used for Lao PDR. Bold countries and darker bars and dots indicate EAP economies. Fiji appears as both an LMIC and a UMIC: it became a UMIC just before the Commitment to Equity study, and its national poverty line is closer to the LMIC line, so both are shown because they produce different results. IPL = international poverty line; LMICs = lower-middle-income countries; pp = percentage point; PPP = purchasing power parity; UMICs = upper-middle-income countries.

poverty line but increases it slightly at the upper-middle-income line.[8] Among LMICs, the Philippines achieves a small poverty reduction and Mongolia a large one—7.3 percentage points—driven by its universal child grant. All other EAP LMICs increase poverty through the combined effect of taxes and spending, with Cambodia, Kiribati, and Lao PDR performing below the LMIC average. As with inequality, these outcomes largely reflect the level of social assistance spending in each country (refer to figure 3.5, panel b).

Unlike inequality, most EAP LMICs increase poverty through taxes and spending, whereas EAP UMICs mostly reduce it.

FIGURE 3.5 Change in poverty rate, by type of fiscal instrument, selected EAP economies

a. Direct and indirect taxes, transfers, and subsidies, relative to income level

b. Direct and indirect taxes, transfers, and subsidies vs. spending on social assistance, relative to income average

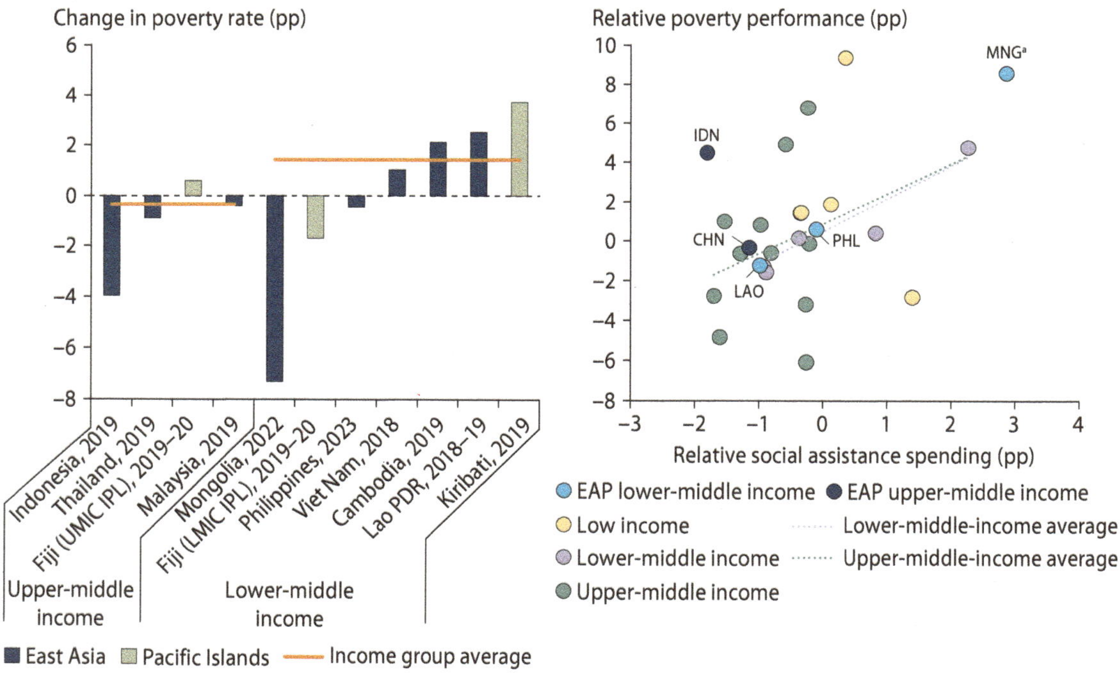

Sources: Original figure for this publication based on Atlas of Social Protection Indicators of Resilience and Equity (ASPIRE), World Bank, https://www.worldbank.org/en/data/datatopics/aspire (social assistance spending); individual EAP country studies (inequality impacts); Wai-Poi et al. 2025 (income average poverty impacts).

Note: Fiji became a UMIC just before the Commitment to Equity study, and its national poverty line is closer to the LMIC line, so both are shown because they produce different results. For a list of country codes, refer to https://www.iso.org/obp/ui/#search. EAP = East Asia and Pacific; IPL = international poverty line; LMICs = lower-middle-income countries; pp = percentage point; UMICs = upper-middle-income countries.

a. Mongolia's Commitment to Equity result, from 2022, reflects significant social spending in response to the COVID-19 pandemic. Although similar spending occurred in many other countries, their results do not reflect that spending because analyses were conducted before the pandemic.

The next section presents new evidence on inequality reduction and the use of four fiscal instruments: direct taxes, indirect taxes, subsidies, and transfers. It then focuses specifically on VAT and targeted transfers, examining their relative strengths, their interactions, and how combining them can increase revenues while reducing inequality.

Cost-effectiveness of fiscal redistribution: The roles of revenue and expenditures

Not all fiscal instruments are equally effective at reducing inequality. This section measures cost-effectiveness of a fiscal instrument as the reduction in the Gini index per percentage point of GDP spent (benefits) or raised (taxes)—that is, the marginal contribution of each instrument relative to its budget. This section compiles a new cost-effectiveness data set for this report.[9] The analysis covers four aggregate categories: direct taxes, indirect taxes, subsidies, and transfers.[10]

Transfers are by far the most cost-effective instrument for reducing inequality, and spending consistently outperforms taxes. Globally, transfers reduce the Gini index by 1.12 points per percentage point of GDP spent—more than six times the return from direct taxes (0.18 point) and over 50 times the return from indirect taxes (0.02 point) (refer to figure 3.6).[11] Subsidies deliver only 0.17 point of inequality reduction per point of GDP, with wide variation depending on design. No tax instrument comes close to transfers in cost-effectiveness at redistribution.

EAP economies tend to outperform other emerging market and developing economies on cost-effectiveness, but small budgets may limit total impact. Indonesia, Malaysia, the Philippines, and Thailand all achieve above-average cost-effectiveness from their transfer programs. Direct tax cost-effectiveness also appears favorable by international comparison, but this appearance is misleading: it reflects a very narrow tax base rather than efficient redistribution. When only the top of the income distribution is taxed, the instrument looks progressive but raises little revenue and leaves most of the population untouched. Subsidy cost-effectiveness in EAP slightly exceeds the global average, although it still falls well below that of transfers.

Transfers are much more cost-effective than subsidies or direct taxes at reducing inequality.

FIGURE 3.6 Cost-effectiveness of inequality reduction, by major fiscal instrument, global data

Points of Gini reduced per point of GDP spent

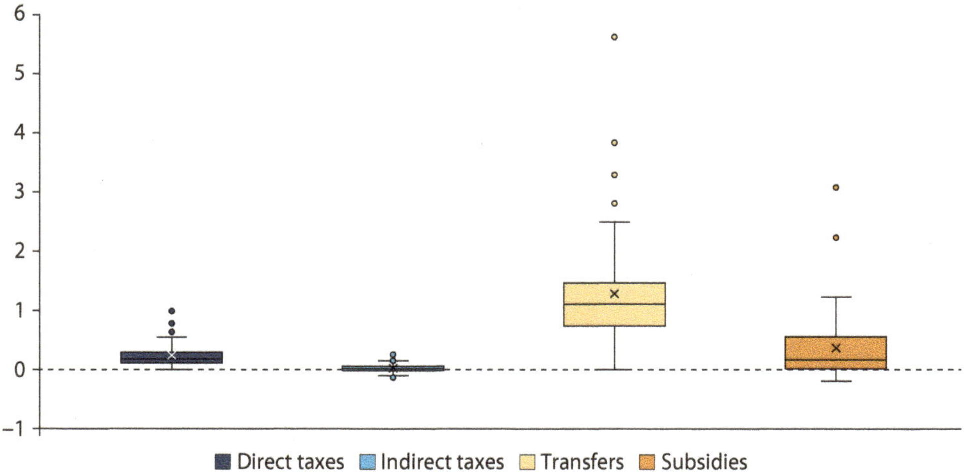

Source: Original figure for this publication based on analysis of global Commitment to Equity database from Wai-Poi et al. 2025.
Note: The upper line of each box represents the 75th percentile, the middle line the 50th percentile (median), and the bottom line the 25th percentile. × represents unweighted averages. The lines extending above and below the central box show the maximum and minimum values respectively, excluding outliers. Dots beyond the maximums and minimums represent outliers.

In every EAP economy examined, targeted transfers are substantially more cost-effective than subsidies at reducing poverty and inequality—by a factor of three to six (refer to figure 3.7).[12] Indonesia's experience during the 2005 fuel subsidy reform makes the point vividly: temporary unconditional cash transfers under the Bantuan Langsung Tunai (BLT) program, equivalent to about 15 percent of household consumption, more than compensated poor households for higher fuel prices, gave them time to adjust spending patterns, and were associated with broader gains in community-wide expenditure (World Bank 2012a).

These results point to a clear division of labor: taxes should focus on raising revenue efficiently, and spending should do the work of redistribution. Direct taxes are the most progressive tax instrument available, but high informality, low taxable incomes, and limited administrative capacity constrain how much revenue they can generate in MICs like those in EAP. A significant share of tax revenues across the region comes from less progressive indirect taxes. Even in Organisation for Economic Co-operation and Development (OECD) countries—where direct taxes account for three-quarters of revenue—three-quarters of redistribution still comes from the spending side. If progressive direct taxes cannot drive redistribution even in rich countries with deep tax systems, they cannot be the primary redistribution tool in EAP.

Social assistance spending is three to six times more cost-effective at reducing poverty and inequality in EAP than subsidy spending, with fuel subsidies the least cost-effective.

FIGURE 3.7 Cost-effectiveness in reducing poverty and inequality, by type of fiscal instrument, selected EAP economies

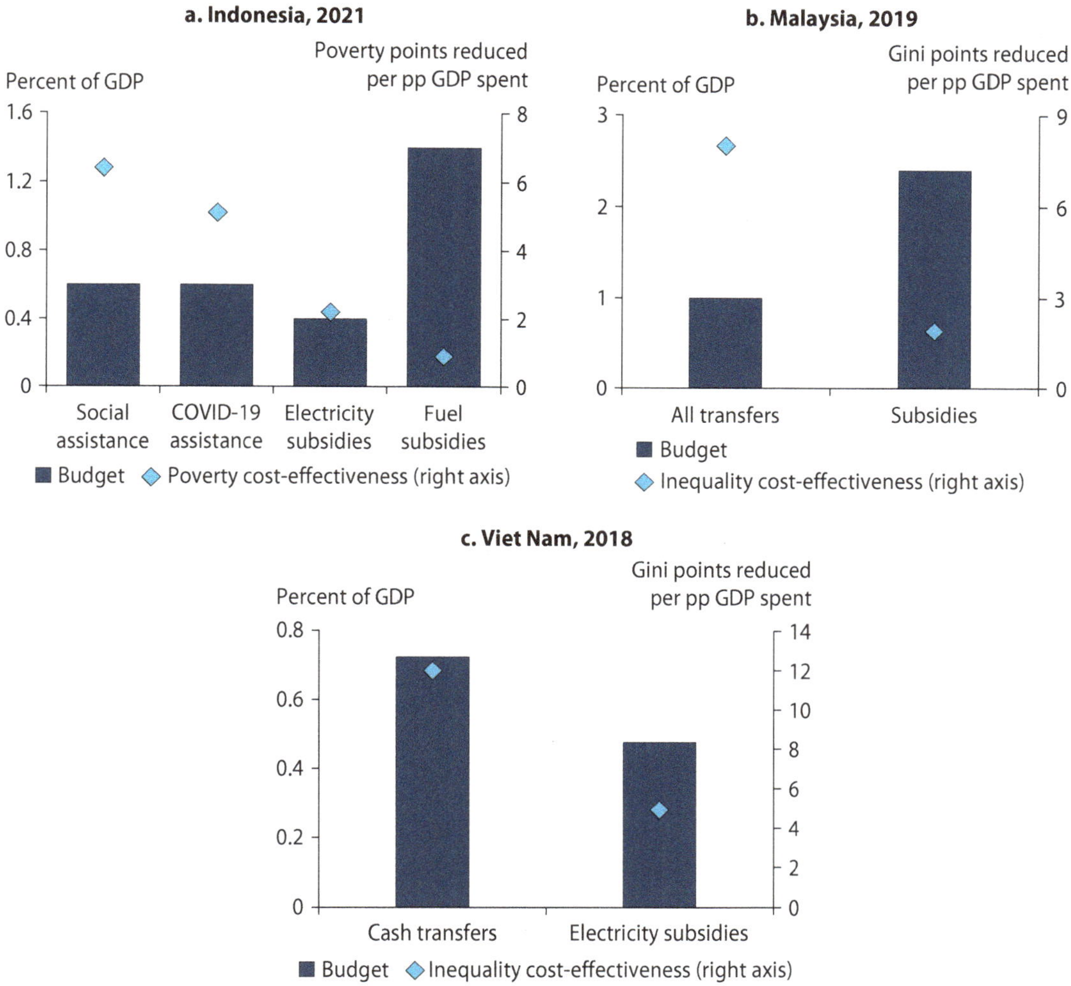

Sources: Original figure for this publication based on World Bank 2022a, 2022b, 2023a, 2023c.
Note: Inequality cost-effectiveness estimates in this figure are not comparable to those in figure 3.6 because this figure uses model-based budgets, whereas figure 3.6 uses administration-based budgets. EAP = East Asia and Pacific; pp = percentage point.

Direct taxes become less progressive as the base expands, whereas transfers maintain their progressivity as budgets grow. Figure 3.8 shows this asymmetry clearly: in every country, direct taxes are progressive—that is, the Kakwani Index is positive throughout (refer to panel a)—but progressivity declines on average as more revenue is raised.[13] The reason lies in the shape of the income distribution (Wai-Poi et al. 2025). PIT bases typically expand downward from the top of the distribution.

Direct taxes become less progressive as the tax base broadens, but direct transfers do not lose progressivity as they expand.

FIGURE 3.8 Progressivity of fiscal instruments, by income level

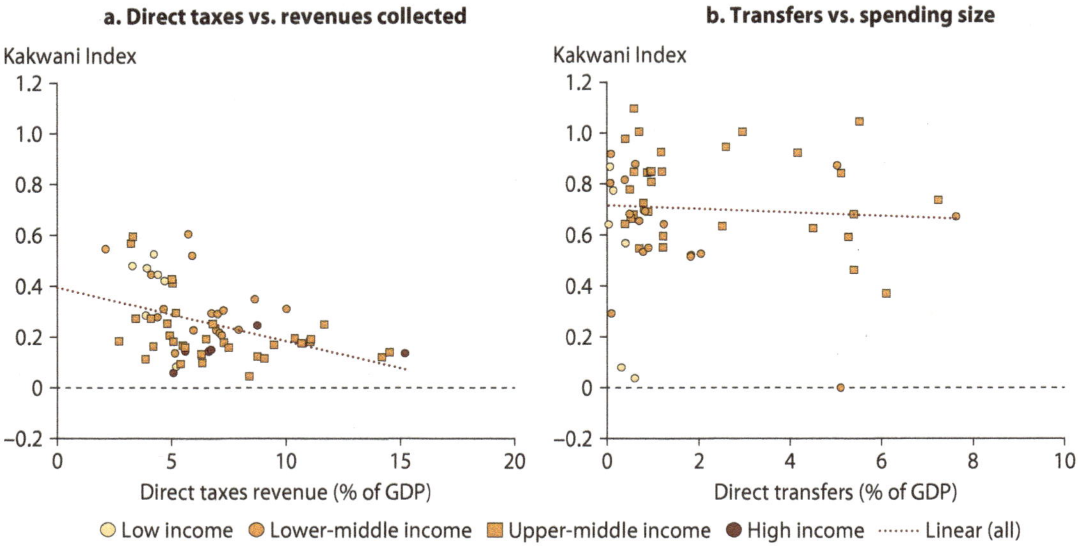

Source: Original figure for this publication based on Wai-Poi et al. 2025.

Note: The Kakwani Index reflects the difference between the concentration coefficient of a fiscal instrument and the Gini coefficient for market income. The concentration coefficient is an analog to the Gini coefficient, that is, the normalized area between the diagonal and the concentration curve of the fiscal instrument. For taxes, the Kakwani Index is the tax concentration coefficient minus the market income Gini coefficient. For transfers, it is the market income Gini minus the transfer concentration coefficient. This convention means that a positive Kakwani Index for a tax or transfer is progressive. Refer to Lustig (2022a) for greater discussion.

Because of the large income gap between the 9th and 10th deciles, which shrinks as one moves farther down the income distribution, each increment of base-broadening reduces the average tax rate paid as a share of income, eroding progressivity even as the tax remains positive.[14]

Transfers work in the opposite direction. Average transfer progressivity is higher than for direct taxes and does not fall as budgets expand (refer to figure 3.8, panel b). Coverage expansions move from the poorest to the second and third deciles; however, because of compression in the left-hand side of the income distribution, expanding coverage does not materially change the income profile of beneficiaries. Consequently, transfer progressivity is largely scale-invariant. A further implication follows from the skewed income distribution: taxing the top decile generates revenue that represents a far higher share of income for households at the bottom. Redistribution through the tax-transfer system exploits this asymmetry—and does so most efficiently when taxes are kept broad and transfers are kept well-targeted.

The greater redistributional efficiency of spending does not mean that tax design is irrelevant to equity. Governments should distribute the burden of taxation fairly and avoid regressive designs when possible. However, directing the revenue base toward exemptions to achieve equity comes at a high cost: it erodes the fiscal space needed to fund the transfers and public services that reduce inequality far more cost-effectively. The better approach is a broad, efficient tax base paired with well-targeted spending, a division of labor that the rest of this chapter develops in detail.

Designing fiscal policy for equity and growth

The picture so far is of a region that performs about or above average in reducing poverty but below average in reducing inequality. EAP's UMICs do relatively well on poverty because of low indirect tax burdens offset by targeted transfers; however, those same low indirect taxes constrain revenues, limiting spending on health and education and weakening inequality reduction over the long run. The central question becomes how to expand fiscal space for growth- and equity-enhancing investments without increasing the short-term burden on poorer households. This section draws on international experience and new country-level analysis to outline how governments can achieve that balance.

The right fiscal design depends on income level, but the direction of reform is consistent. At every income level, fiscal designs exist that can raise revenues while reducing poverty and inequality, but the instruments differ (refer to table 3.1). For LICs, indirect taxes are unavoidable: they are the primary revenue instrument, and investments in social assistance and tax administration capacity are the foundations on which everything else is built. Health taxes can raise revenue immediately while reducing long-term public health costs. Subsidies are a costly and inefficient substitute for social protection.

For EAP's LMICs and recently graduated UMICs, the priority is broad indirect taxation combined with targeted direct transfers and the elimination of subsidies. Greater administrative and economic capacity allows these economies to go further: rationalizing VAT exemptions and preferential rates, complementing VAT with health and property taxes, and building the targeting systems needed to direct transfers to the poor.[15] UMICs approaching high-income status should increasingly complement indirect taxes with progressive direct taxes.[16] As economies formalize and data availability and interoperability improve, supported by digital infrastructure and technological advances, more accurate targeting and benefit differentiation become feasible.[17]

TABLE 3.1 Progressive fiscal policies for all income levels

LICs: Increase revenues and build safety nets	LMICs and UMICs: Enact broad indirect taxation with targeted direct transfers	HICs: Enact direct taxation and targeted direct transfers
• Indirect taxes are inevitable. Taxes are not progressive and will burden households, but they are the main revenue-generation instruments. • Health taxes can raise short-term revenues directly and long-term revenues indirectly, and reduce long-term public health spending. • Investments in social assistance can help reduce inequality and offset the burden of indirect taxation for the poorest. • Subsidies are costly and inefficient ways to support the poor. • Administrative capacity for collecting direct taxes (such as the PIT and the property tax) will require investments.	• Indirect taxes can have a revenue-equity trade-off, yet exemptions are often inefficient to help the poor; personalized VAT schemes are difficult. • Indirect taxes combined with targeted transfers can be progressive; each instrument should be used for its best purpose (raising revenue and supporting the poor). • Indirect taxes have limitations: – Indirect taxes create a greater burden to offset, and targeting has more errors because of data constraints, making transfers less effective. – High prices of basic goods could make VAT a greater burden on the poor. • Political economy issues include closing exemptions, targeting errors, and coverage rates. • Indirect tax revenue should be augmented with progressive health tax revenue. • Investing in the capacity to conduct direct taxation and expand the PIT and property tax base.	• Direct taxes are progressive, raising revenues from those who can afford to pay, which can then be used for progressive spending. • The use of progressive health tax revenue should continue. • Targeted direct transfers are progressive: – They are the most cost-effective way of reducing poverty and inequality. – Richer countries with more formal economies and more data can target more precisely (eligibility and benefit levels).

Source: Original table for this publication based on Wai-Poi et al. 2025.
Note: HICs = high-income countries; LICs = low-income countries; LMICs = lower-middle-income countries; PIT = personal income tax; UMICs = upper-middle-income countries; VAT = value added tax.

Indirect taxes and targeted transfers: Raising revenues while reducing poverty

For MICs, the combination of indirect taxes and targeted transfers is the primary driver of distributional outcomes.[18] Progressive direct tax and transfer systems used by HICs are not yet feasible across most of EAP, but revenues can be built around a strong VAT while transfers offset the burden on poorer households. In practice, many countries undermine both prongs of this strategy. They forgo revenue through preferential VAT rates and exemptions, and they keep social assistance budgets too small and too poorly targeted to compensate poorer households adequately.

Consequently, even the VAT-transfer combination leaves poor households less well off in many MICs. On average, HICs collect indirect taxes equivalent to 18 percent of market income from the poorest decile but provide transfers worth 70 percent of prefiscal income, leaving the poorest households 53 percent more well off in net cash terms (refer to figure 3.9). That net gain drops to just 21 percent in UMICs. In LMICs, the poorest decile barely breaks even, and the second-poorest decile is less well off.

In EAP, despite low indirect taxes, transfers are often insufficient to offset even that modest burden. The poverty increases seen in most EAP LMICs—Cambodia, Kiribati, Lao PDR, and Viet Nam—reflect very modest social protection spending that fails to offset relatively low indirect tax burdens (refer to figure 3.9). Only Kiribati and Mongolia impose an indirect tax burden on poorer households above the LMIC average. In both cases, generous transfers leave the poorest decile more well off; however, in Kiribati's case this result does not extend far enough up the distribution to prevent an overall rise in poverty. In EAP UMICs, larger social assistance budgets mean that transfers for the poorest one or two deciles offset low indirect tax burdens, but usually just barely. Combined with relatively low poverty rates, this result is enough to prevent poverty from rising in most EAP UMICs. The existence of reasonably well-targeted transfer systems in these economies offers an important signal: they have scope for significantly higher VAT revenues, provided they maintain and improve transfers.

Thailand shows the feasibility of simultaneously raising VAT revenues and cutting poverty. Thailand's base VAT rate stands at 7 percent—low even by regional standards—and a range of goods and services benefit from preferential rates, mostly accruing to richer households. Removing all exemptions and raising the rate to 10 percent could generate an estimated 1.5 percent of GDP in new revenues (refer to table 3.2). At the same time, a significant share of Thailand's social assistance currently reaches nonpoor households (World Bank 2023d). Redirecting those transfers to the poorest would reduce poverty by an additional 0.4 percentage point without any increase in spending. Expanding budgets for the Social Welfare Card and Old Age Allowance, combined with improved targeting, would reduce inequality by 2.6 Gini points and poverty by 3.6 percentage points while still generating 0.6 percent of GDP in net new revenues. A less aggressive expansion would leave even greater fiscal gains. For comparison, a reduction in the diesel excise tax would cost half the new VAT revenues while offsetting only a third of the poverty impact, a far less efficient use of fiscal space.

EAP economies collect less in indirect taxes and spend less in transfers than income level peers, leading to both lower revenues and less redistribution.

FIGURE 3.9 Indirect taxes, transfers, and net impact relative to market income, by decile, selected EAP economies and comparators

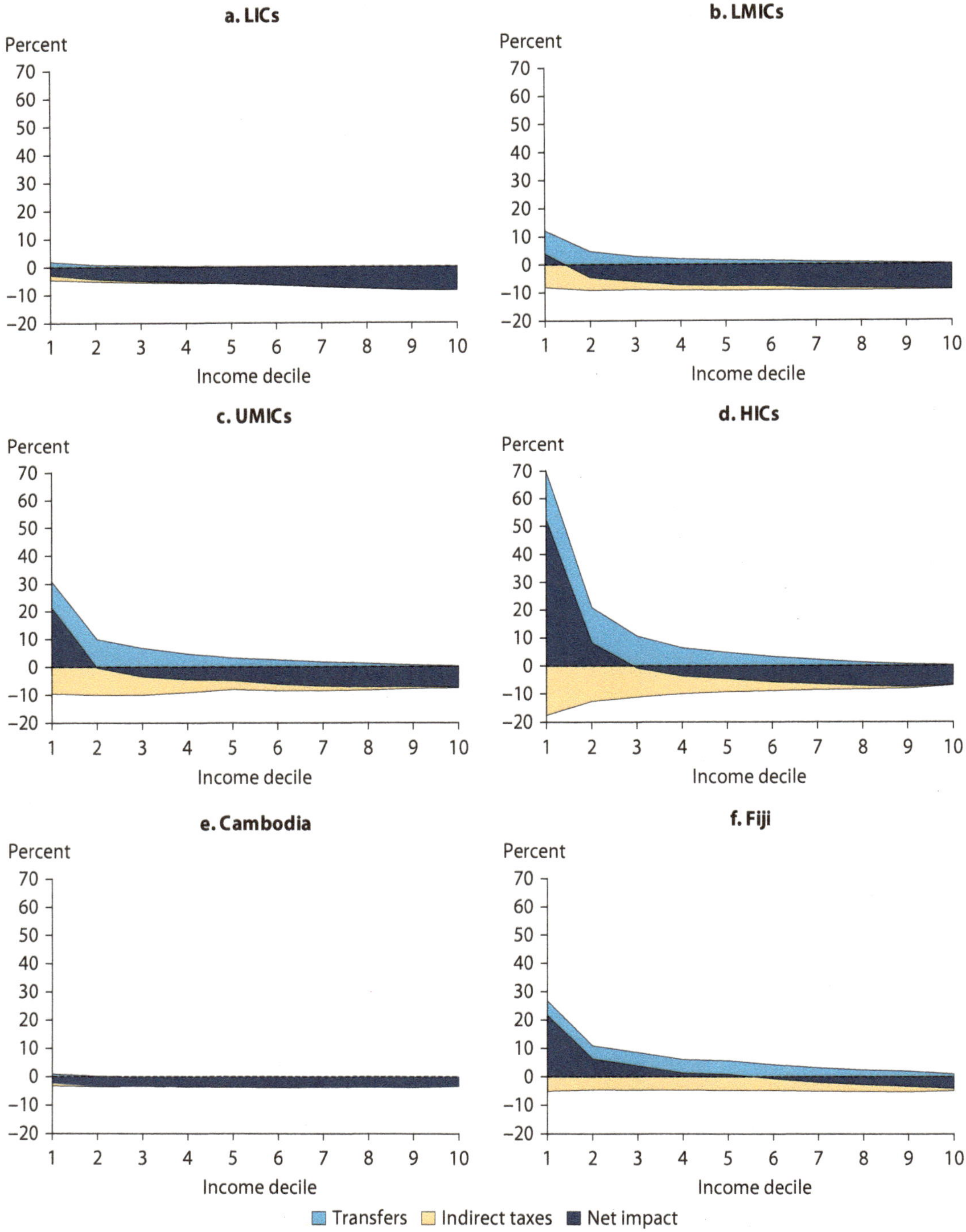

(continued)

FIGURE 3.9 Indirect taxes, transfers, and net impact relative to market income, by decile, selected EAP economies and comparators *(continued)*

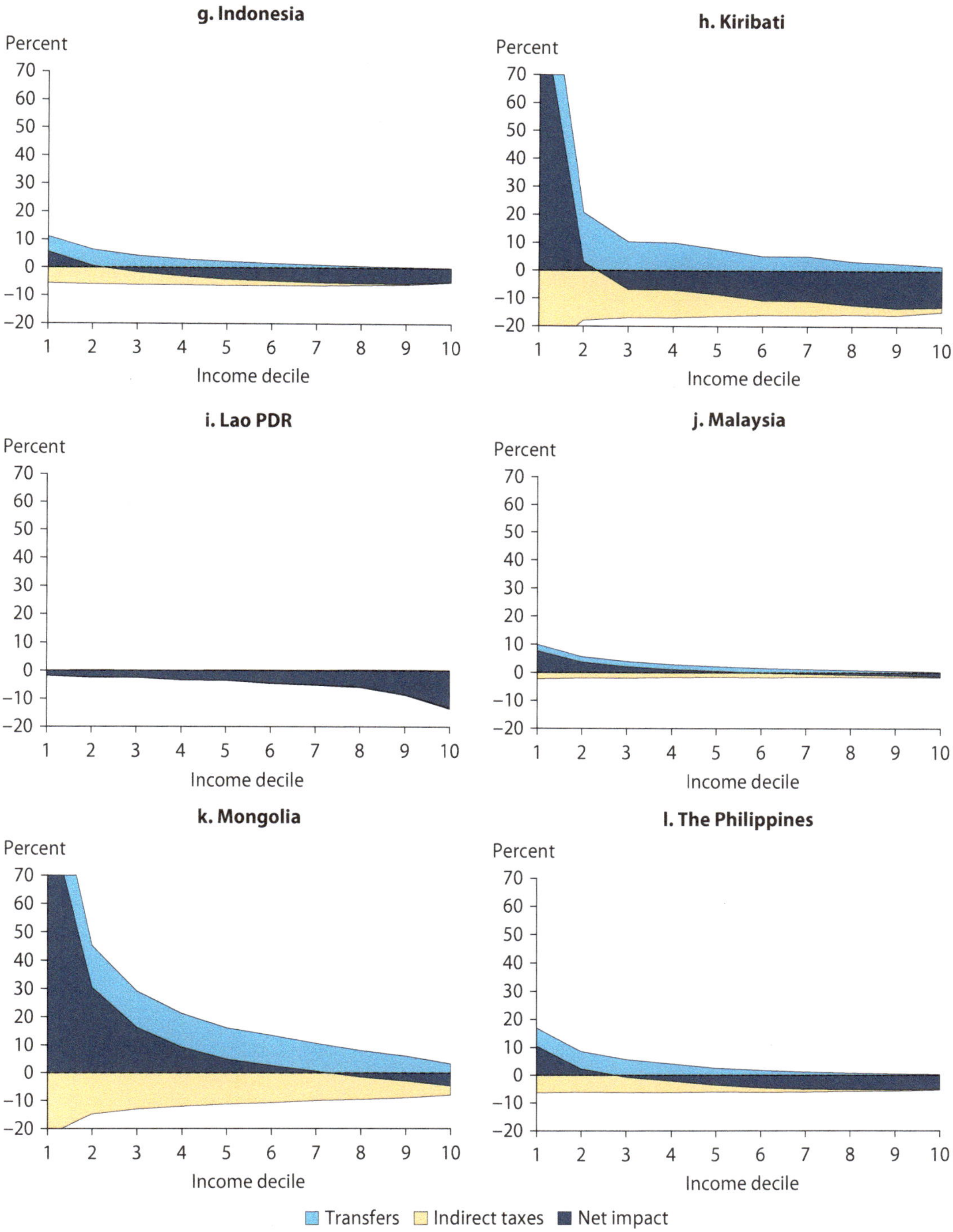

(continued)

FIGURE 3.9 Indirect taxes, transfers, and net impact relative to market income, by decile, selected EAP economies and comparators *(continued)*

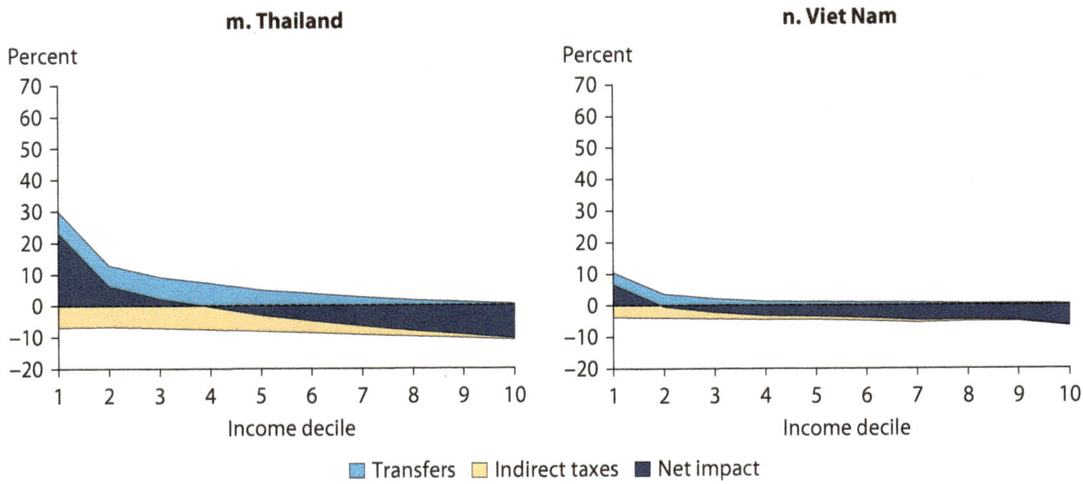

Sources: Original figure for this publication based on individual EAP economy studies; Wai-Poi et al. 2025 (income averages).
Note: EAP = East Asia and Pacific; HICs = high-income countries; LICs = low-income countries; LMICs = lower-middle-income countries; UMICs = upper-middle-income countries.

TABLE 3.2 Effects of combined VAT and social assistance reform on net revenues, poverty, and inequality, Thailand

	Fiscal (B, billions)	Inequality (Gini change)	Poverty (percentage points)	Cost per point (B, millions)	Fiscal (% of GDP)
a. Revenue reform					
7% VAT, no exemptions	111	−0.1	0.8		0.7
10% VAT, with current exemptions	87	−0.2	0.4		0.5
10% VAT, no exemptions	245	−0.3	1.5		1.5
b. Household compensation					
Improved targeting of SWC	−2	−0.1	−0.4	4.0	0
Increase OAA and SWC (improved targeting)	−145	−2.3	−4.4	32.9	−0.9
B 10.00 price reduction of diesel	−133	0.2	−0.5	276.2	−0.8
c. Preferred combination					
10% VAT, no exemptions, increase OAA and SWC	100	−2.6	−3.6	−27.8	0.6

Source: Original table for this publication adapted from World Bank 2023d.
Note: B = Thai baht; OAA = Old Age Allowance; SWC = Social Welfare Card; VAT = value added tax.

Lao PDR points to the same conclusion from a different starting point. In 2022, Lao PDR cut its VAT rate from 10 percent to 7 percent as part of a post-COVID-19 recovery package. Combined with changes to excise taxes, this cut is estimated to have reduced revenue and increased inequality (World Bank 2023b). Restoring the rate to 10 percent and raising excise taxes on beer and cigarettes would increase revenues by 40 percent. Pairing this change with a cash transfer equivalent to 10 percent of the poverty line, targeted at the poorest 20 percent of the population (Lao PDR currently has no significant social assistance program), would still leave a net revenue gain of 16 percent while reducing poverty by 1.9 percentage points and inequality by 1 Gini point.

Transfers in EAP also improve human capital outcomes and help households absorb shocks without reducing work incentives. Evaluation of Indonesia's temporary BLT transfer finds modest improvements in education, labor, and health outcomes among BLT recipient households, with stronger effects on child labor (World Bank 2012a); increased use of health services; and no effect on nutrition or consumption of harmful goods. BLT households found new work at higher rates and did not reduce hours or leave employment more frequently than nonrecipients.[19] Program Keluarga Harapan (PKH), Indonesia's targeted conditional cash transfer program for the extreme poor, showed still stronger results (World Bank 2012b). PKH increased incomes, drove large increases in health service expenditure, improved protein-rich food consumption, and kept children in school for longer. Spillover effects—improved health behaviors among poor but nonrecipient households in PKH areas—suggest that PKH benefits extend beyond direct recipients.

VAT: A significant revenue opportunity

Low base rates and broad exemptions across the region constrain VAT. As chapter 1 documents, EAP has VAT revenues well below what income levels would predict, a gap driven by both below-average base rates and an expanding array of preferential rates and exemptions. Globally, preferential rates on goods and services have grown from under 20 percent of all tax forgone in 1990 to just over 60 percent by 2021, with two-thirds of this amount from VAT (von Haldenwang et al. 2023).

Contrary to common assumption, VAT is not strongly regressive; instead, once informality is accounted for, it is broadly progressive. All households consume taxed goods and services, but poorer households are significantly more likely to purchase from vendors that do not charge VAT—such as street markets, informal traders, and own production—even for nonexempt items (Bachas et al. 2024).[20] In both Indonesia and the Philippines, the poorest decile purchases roughly twice as much at informal locations compared with the richest decile (refer to figure 3.10). This difference has two implications: poorer households have a lower effective VAT burden, and the value of VAT exemptions to them is also lower because they would not have paid VAT on those items even without the exemption. Across 32 LMICs, VAT is found to be broadly progressive after accounting for consumption informality (Bachas et al. 2024).

Accounting for transfers further improves the distributional picture. Measuring VAT incidence against disposable income, rather than market income,[21] results in a materially lower effective burden on poor households, because transfers have already raised their purchasing power and allowed them to consume more. With their increased disposable income and greater consumption, poorer households pay more VAT. The combined effect shifts VAT from appearing regressive in HICs and UMICs and slightly regressive in LMICs to broadly neutral or slightly progressive at all three income levels.

Poorer households are more likely to make purchases from locations that do not charge VAT, reducing both the existing VAT burden and the value of exemptions.

FIGURE 3.10 Consumption patterns, by income decile, Indonesia and the Philippines

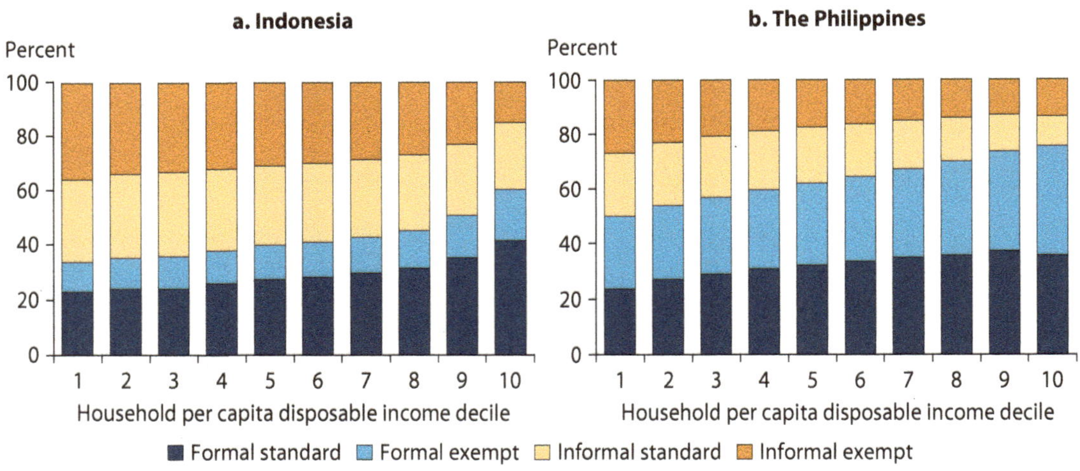

Sources: Original figure for this publication based on National Socioeconomic Household Survey, Rand, https://www.rand.org/health/surveys/bps/susenas.html (Indonesia); Family Income and Expenditure Survey, Philippine Statistics Authority, https://psa.gov.ph/statistics/income-expenditure/fies (Philippines).

Note: Informal purchases can be from a vendor below the threshold for VAT registration who does not need to charge and remit final VAT or from a vendor above the threshold who is noncompliant. Informality estimates for Indonesia and the Philippines are imputed using countries with similar VAT efficiency gaps in Bachas et al. (2024). VAT = value added tax.

VAT exemptions and preferential rates are poorly targeted and costly instruments for achieving distributional goals. Almost every country applies some preferential VAT rates, primarily to protect poorer households from the burden of indirect taxation; however, the evidence consistently shows these instruments do not achieve their intended purpose.[22] In Viet Nam, two-thirds of forgone VAT revenues benefit the richest half of the income distribution, with 31 percent going to the richest two deciles alone (refer to figure 3.11, panel a). In Thailand—where household survey data allow for direct measurement of consumption informality—76 percent of VAT exemption benefits go to the richest five deciles and 45 percent to the richest two (refer to figure 3.11, panel b). Despite their fiscal cost—estimated at 0.7 percent of GDP in Thailand—preferential rates provide little income support to any decile: in Thailand, they are worth about 2 percent of income across the entire distribution and, in Viet Nam, less than 1 percent (refer to panels c and d).

The case against exemptions extends beyond poor targeting. Multirate VAT systems increase administrative complexity, raise compliance costs, lower compliance rates, generate legal disputes, and invite lobbying.[23] The efficiency arguments sometimes advanced in their favor—supporting labor-intensive services or home production substitutes—find no significant employment effect in the empirical literature, and more direct instruments are consistently found to be more effective and less costly (Copenhagen Economics 2007; European Commission 2003).

EAP countries could raise significant revenues simply by removing VAT exemptions (refer to Aguirre and Shome 1988; Hutton 2017). In the Philippines, nearly 3 percent of GDP in VAT revenues goes uncollected because of exemptions and reduced rates; preferential rates alone in 2018 represented ₱503 billion, almost two-thirds of the ₱768 billion actually collected (refer to figure 3.12). This policy gap grew to an estimated 3 percent of GDP by 2022. In Indonesia, forgone revenues from VAT exemptions are estimated at about 1 percent of GDP (refer to figure 3.13)—larger than the current social assistance budget.

In Thailand and Viet Nam, most VAT preferential rate expenditures benefit richer households while providing little income support to poorer households.

FIGURE 3.11 Share and value of VAT preferential rates, by household income decile, Thailand and Viet Nam

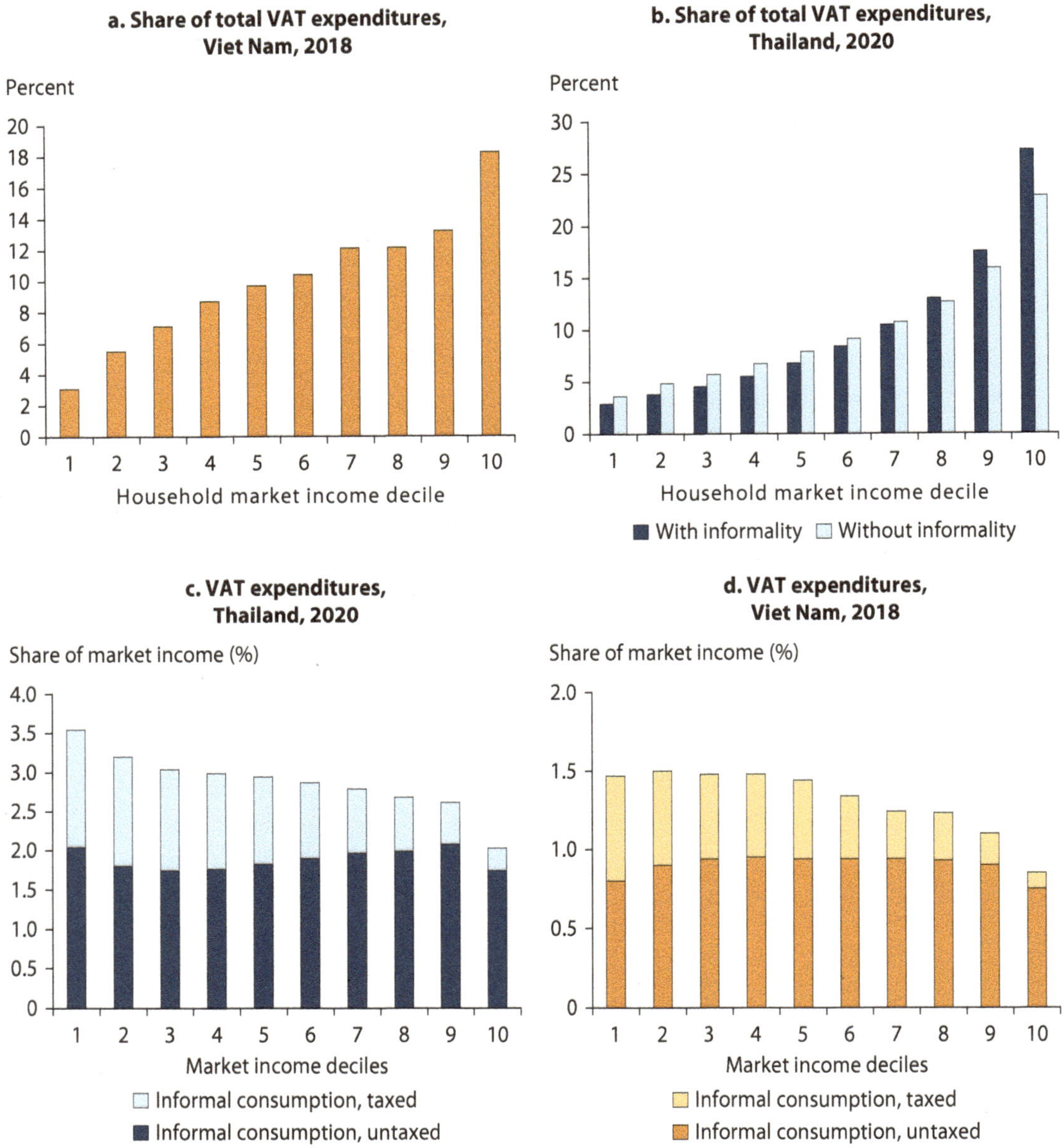

Sources: Original figure for this publication based on Thailand Socioeconomic Survey, 2020 (panels a and c); Viet Nam Household Living Standards Survey (panels b and d); Wai-Poi et al. 2025 (panels a and c).

Note: VAT = value added tax.

The Philippines forgoes about 3 percent of GDP in VAT preferential rates.

FIGURE 3.12 Actual VAT revenue, administrative gap, and compliance gap, the Philippines, 2018

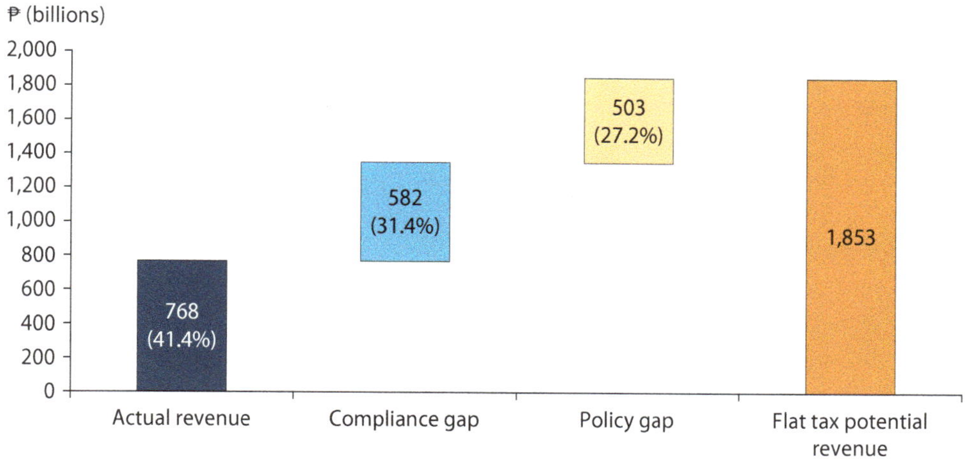

Source: Original figure for this publication based on World Bank 2025d.
Note: Numbers in parentheses show the share of potential flat tax revenue. ₱ = Philippine peso; VAT = value added tax

Indonesia forgoes about 1 percent of GDP in VAT preferential rates.

FIGURE 3.13 VAT policy gap in Indonesia, 2016–21

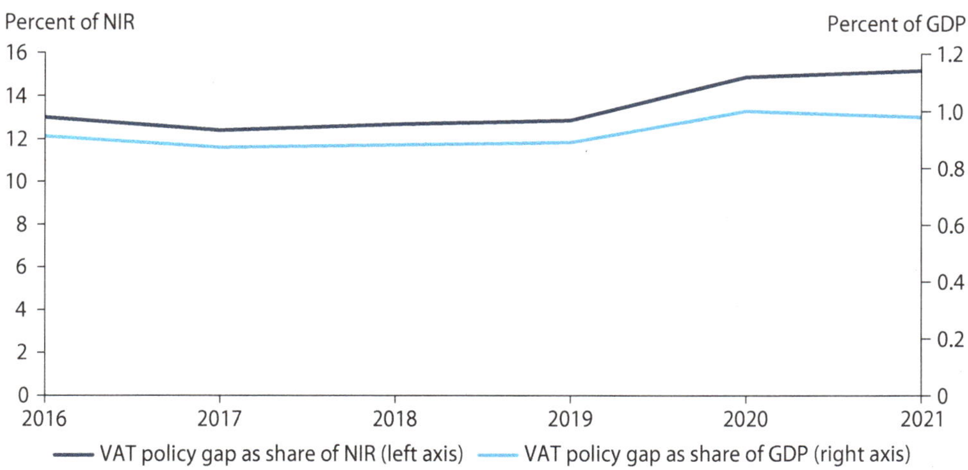

Source: Original figure for this publication based on World Bank 2025a.
Note: NIR = notional ideal revenue; VAT = value added tax.

Broadening the PIT base: Raising revenues while maintaining progressivity

Indirect taxes will remain the central revenue instrument across EAP in the medium term, but direct taxes, particularly PIT, can provide important complementary revenues without requiring mitigating transfers. The case for expanding PIT rests on a structural pattern visible in global data: as countries grow richer and labor markets formalize, the direct tax base broadens downward from the top of the distribution, generating more revenue while retaining strong progressivity.

In LICs, the richest decile pays 71 percent of all direct taxes. As incomes rise, more households cross taxable thresholds and employment formalizes: the share paid by the richest decile falls to about 55 percent in UMICs, 47 percent in non-OECD HICs, and 40 percent in OECD countries (refer to figure 3.14). Crucially, this broadening is accompanied by rising effective rates across all deciles: each decile pays more, but the rate curve steepens, maintaining strong progressivity throughout (refer to figure 3.15). In OECD countries, where direct taxes account for three-quarters of revenues, even the poorest decile pays an average effective rate of 6 percent of market income—higher than the rate for the richest decile in LICs—yet the system remains highly progressive because all other deciles pay substantially more.

A sequenced approach to PIT reform follows from this pattern. In the short term, many EAP economies can increase PIT collection from rich households by reviewing taxable thresholds, marginal rates, deductions, and excluded income

The direct tax base broadens as countries get richer.

FIGURE 3.14 Share of total direct taxes, by decile and country income level

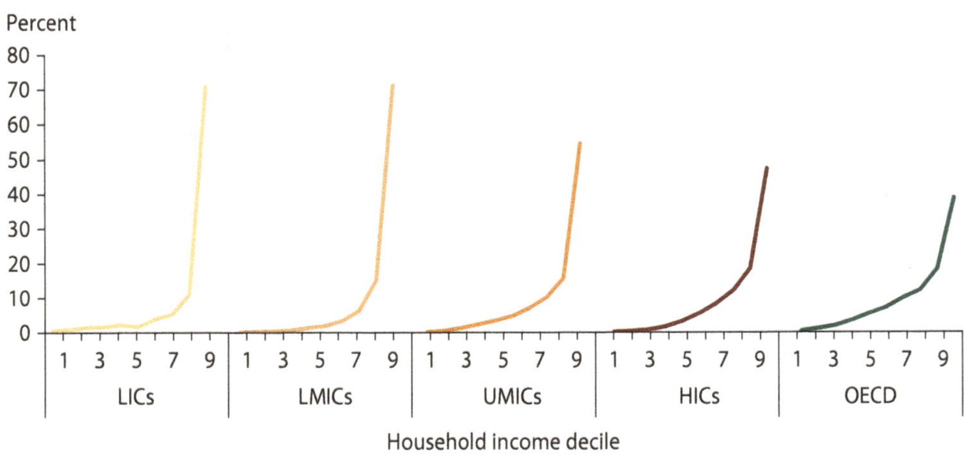

Source: Original figure for this publication based on Wai-Poi et al. 2025.
Note: The figure shows direct tax concentration shares, aggregated by income group, which is taxes paid by each decile as a percentage of total taxes paid by the population. HICs = high-income countries; LICs = low-income countries; LMICs = lower-middle-income countries; OECD = Organisation for Economic Cooperation and Development; UMICs = upper-middle-income countries.

As the base broadens with higher incomes, the direct tax incidence increases for all deciles.

FIGURE 3.15 Direct taxes as a share of market income, by decile and country income level

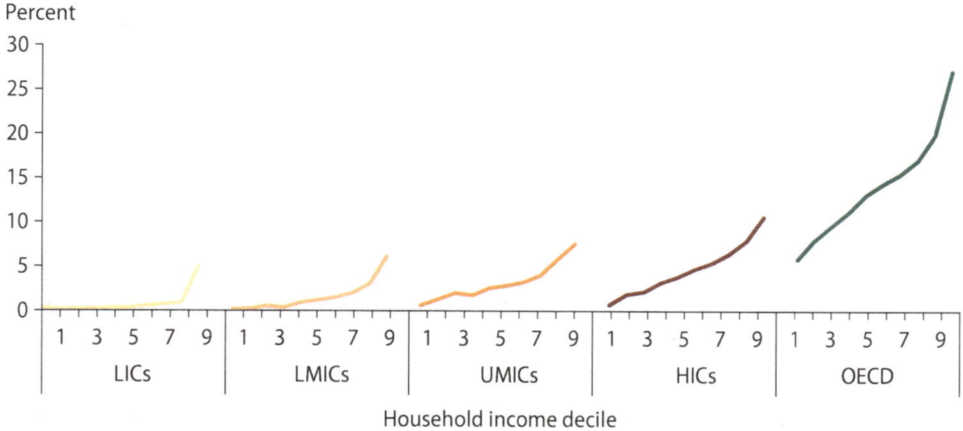

Source: Original figure for this publication based on Wai-Poi et al. 2025.
Note: The figure shows direct tax incidence, aggregated by income group, which is taxes paid by each decile as a percentage of that decile's market income. HICs = high-income countries; LICs = low-income countries; LMICs = lower-middle-income countries; OECD = Organisation for Economic Cooperation and Development; UMICs = upper-middle-income countries.

sources—particularly capital income and capital gains. In the medium term, investments in tax administration capacity and technology offer significant potential to improve compliance, identify taxable entities, and verify liabilities (Okunogbe and Tourek 2024). Over the longer term, bringing more households into the PIT base will require greater employment formality and rising incomes.

Thailand illustrates both the potential and the pitfalls of direct tax reform. On aggregate, the richest decile pays 47 percent of direct taxes, in line with the HIC average but concealing a highly uneven structure. PIT is narrow, with 68 percent paid by the richest decile and fewer than 5 percent of households in deciles 1–7 paying anything; social security contributions are broad, covering significant shares of every decile including the poorest (refer to figure 3.16). The result is a direct tax system that looks progressive in aggregate but places a disproportionate burden on low-income formal workers through payroll taxes; effective social security rates are both high and regressive for those who pay them but create strong incentives to remain informal (refer to figure 3.17). Over a third of Thai workers in the richest decile are informal; the share exceeds half for all other deciles.

Expanding Thailand's direct tax base in a way that advances both fiscal and equity objectives means broadening PIT—that is, reducing the concentration at the top and bringing deciles 7–9 into the base—while reconsidering the design of social security contributions to expand coverage without placing high regressive burdens on lower-income formal workers.

Only in decile 10 do more than 20 percent of Thais pay PIT, and almost no one in deciles 1–5 does. However, significant numbers of all deciles make social security contributions.

FIGURE 3.16 Share of individuals paying direct taxes, by income decile, Thailand, 2019

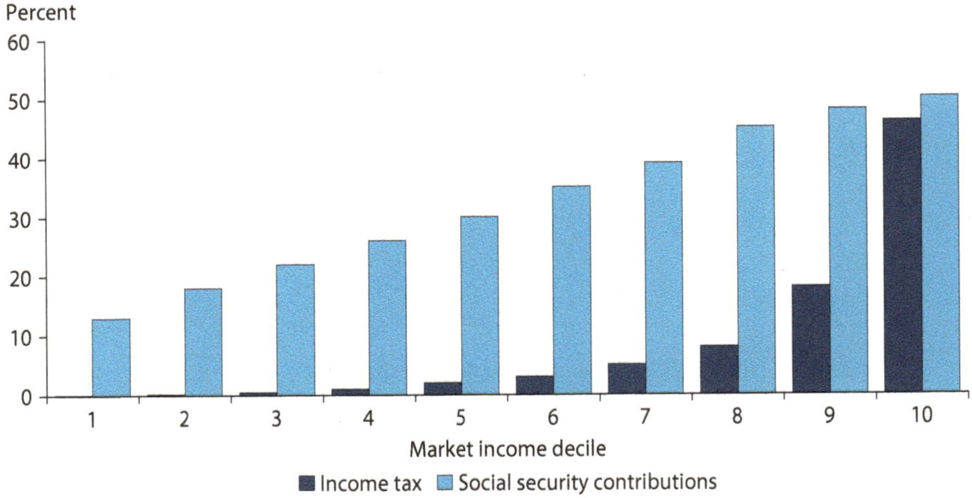

Source: Original figure for this publication based on World Bank 2023d.

Social security contributions are a high share of income for regularized workers in poorer Thai households.

FIGURE 3.17 Total tax incidence (decile average) and social security incidence (decile average for payers) by decile (percentage of market income), Thailand, 2019

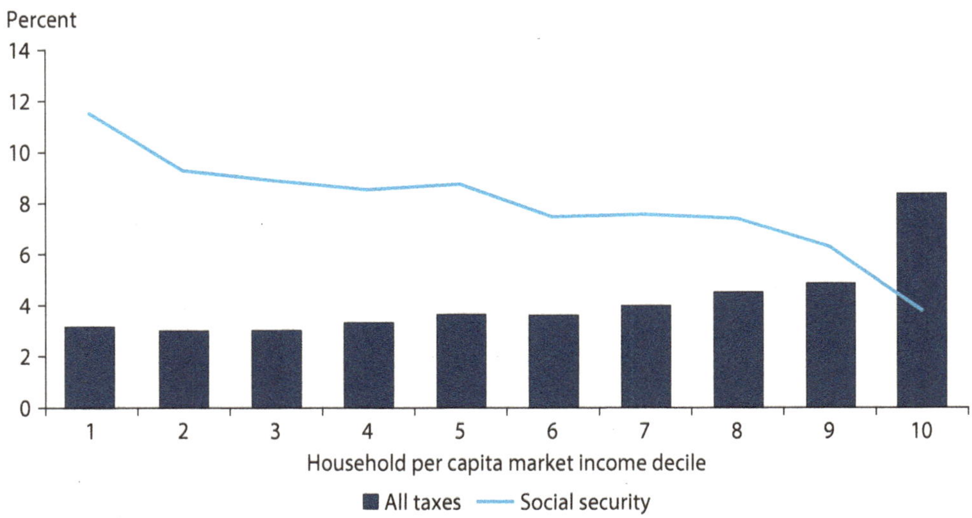

Source: Original figure for this publication based on data from World Bank 2023d.
Note: Tax incidence for social security contributions shows the average for households in the decile with formal workers who make contributions; all taxes show the average for all households in the decile whether they pay social security taxes or not.

The state of EAP: Not raising enough, not spending enough, not spending effectively

EAP does not raise enough revenue, spends too little on social protection, and allocates too much to subsidies. As chapter 1 documents, EAP has lower revenues than every other region except South Asia, and those lower revenues constrain spending on health, education, and social protection. Average EAP health and education spending falls below the LIC average and far below the LMIC and UMIC averages. Social assistance spending, although slightly above the LMIC average, falls considerably below the UMIC average—and lower, on average, than what EAP spends on energy and agricultural subsidies (refer to figure 3.18).

EAP spends comparatively little on social protection compared to other regions and income averages, and less than it spends on energy and agricultural subsidies.

FIGURE 3.18 Social assistance, energy, and agriculture subsidy spending, by region and income level

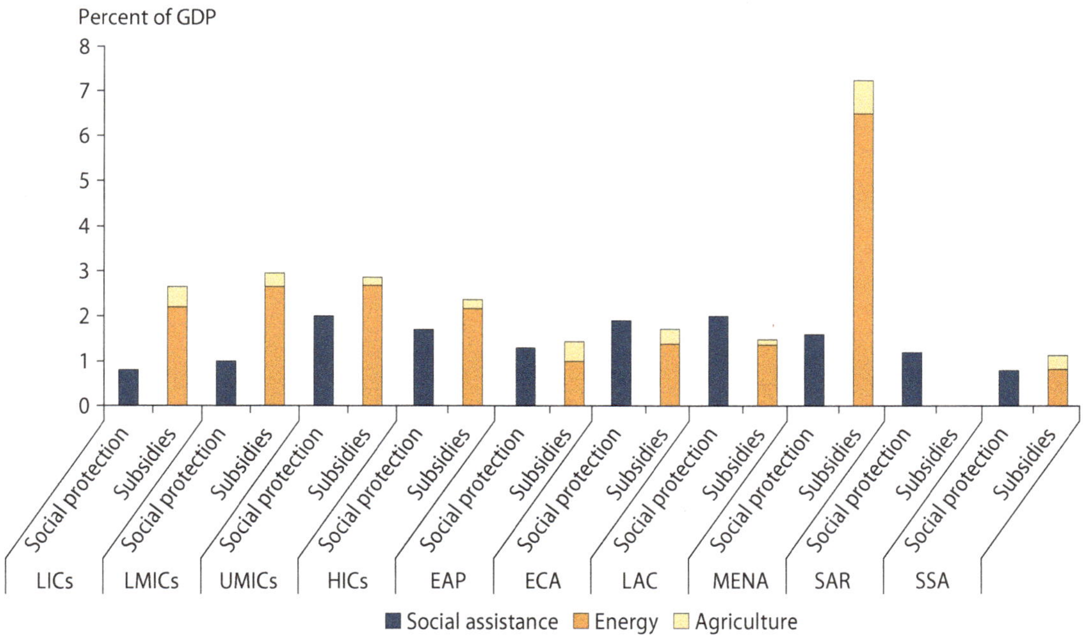

Sources: Original figure for this publication based on Wai-Poi et al. 2025 (agricultural and energy subsidies); World Bank 2025c (social assistance spending; for more details, refer to Tesliuc and Fonteñez 2025). Original agricultural data from AgInventives Consortium, http://www.ag-incentives.org/; original energy data from International Institute for Sustainable Development, https://www.iisd.org/.
Note: Agricultural subsidies are calculated as averages for the period 2016–18. Energy subsidies are calculated as average subsidies for the period 2017–19. Data are aggregated by income group. The figure uses data for the World Bank–defined MENA region rather than the later expanded region. EAP = East Asia and Pacific; ECA = Europe and Central Asia; HICs = high-income countries; LAC = Latin America and the Caribbean; LICs = low-income countries; LMICs = lower-middle-income countries; MENA = Middle East and North Africa; SAR = South Asia; SSA = Sub-Saharan Africa; UMICs = upper-middle-income countries.

As noted earlier, low spending compounds a quality problem. On health, EAP economies underperform their income levels on stunting and noncommunicable diseases—both of which carry significant long-term costs for cognitive development, educational attainment, and adult earnings. On education, in many of the region's economies, more than half of 10-year-olds cannot read or understand age-appropriate reading material, and 31 percent of enrolled 15-year-olds do not reach basic proficiency in mathematics and science (refer to figure 3.19). In most EAP economies, improving the quality of education for currently enrolled students would generate greater long-run growth than would achieving universal enrollment at current quality levels; for instance, compared to increasing enrollment, improving the quality of education would contribute an estimated 3.5 times more GDP growth in Indonesia and Cambodia, 2.8 times more in the Philippines, and 1.8 times more in Thailand (refer to figure 3.20).

Poor quality public services also risk fracturing the social contract by pushing the middle class to private alternatives. The economically secure middle class,[24] safe from poverty and vulnerability, represents the richest one to three deciles in most EAP economies, except Malaysia where it accounts for the majority (World Bank 2018). These households pay the bulk of indirect taxes and virtually all direct taxes. Their continued engagement with public services, and their willingness to finance improvements through taxation, is essential for sustaining and improving those

About one-third of EAP children cannot read a basic sentence and lack basic skills in math and science.

FIGURE 3.19 Learning poverty and lack of basic skills, by region

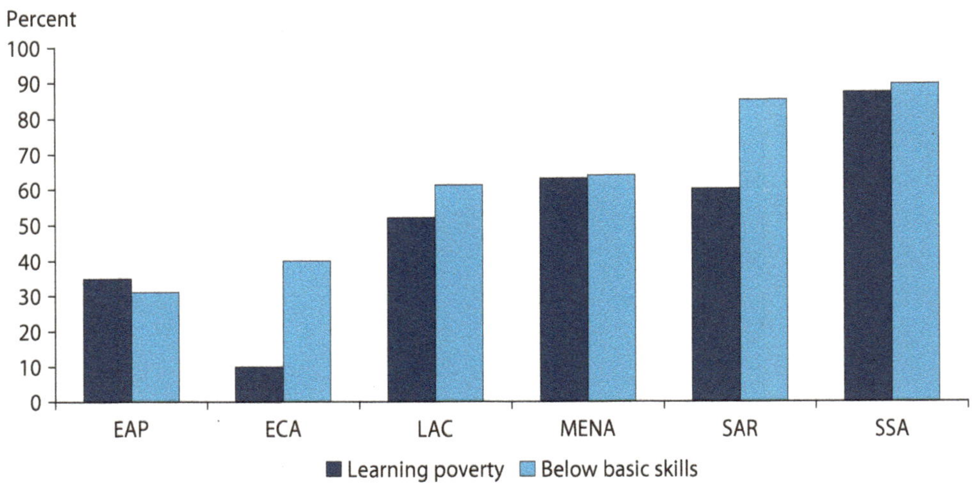

Sources: Original figure for this publication based on Gust et al. 2024 (basic skills data); World Bank et al. 2022 (learning poverty data).

Note: Learning poverty means that a 10-year-old child cannot read and understand a simple passage. Below basic skills means that a 15-year-old child is not at Level 1 on the Programme for International Student Assessment or equivalent test. The figure uses data for the World Bank–defined MENA region rather than the later expanded region. EAP = East Asia and Pacific; ECA = Europe and Central Asia; LAC = Latin America and the Caribbean; MENA = Middle East and North Africa; SAR = South Asia; SSA = Sub-Saharan Africa.

Most EAP economies would gain more growth through improving the quality of education for existing students than through universal enrollment at existing quality levels.

FIGURE 3.20 Contribution to GDP of quality vs. quantity, and GDP increase by 2100 of doing both

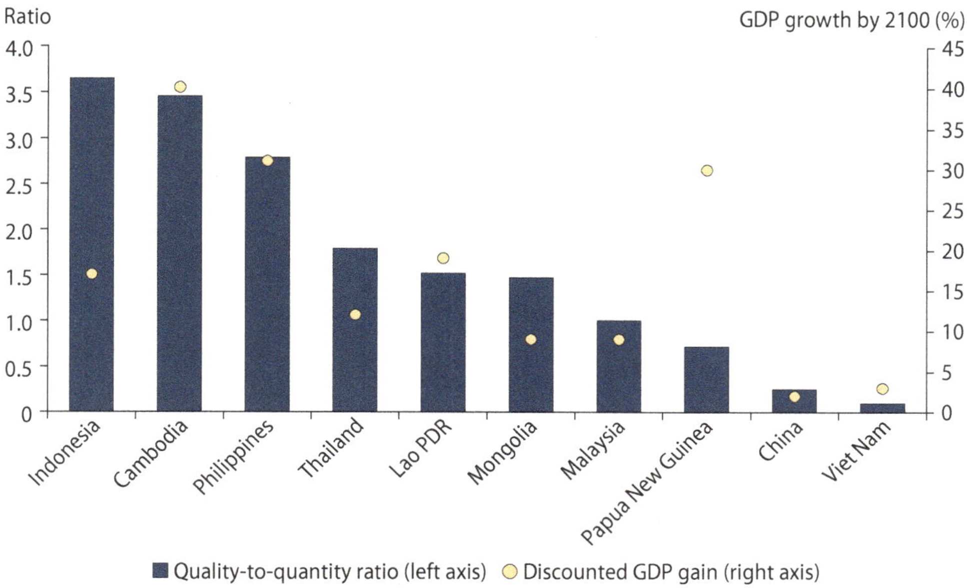

Source: Original figure for this publication based on Gust et al. 2024.
Note: The figure shows three modeled growth scenarios: Scenario 1 assumes currently enrolled children can reach at least basic skill levels; Scenario 2 assumes universal enrollment at current skill levels; and Scenario 3 assumes both. The quality-to-quantity ratio is the ratio of growth improvements from Scenario 1 over Scenario 2. The (discounted) GDP gain by 2100 is for Scenario 3. EAP = East Asia and Pacific.

services. Nonetheless, significant and growing shares of EAP's middle class already rely on private health care and, to a lesser extent, private education.[25] At the extreme, planned private urban developments in cities like Jakarta offer complete amenities—security, utilities, schools, and recreational facilities—that substitute for public services entirely. Where the middle class opts out, it tends to disengage from public discourse on service quality and become less willing to support the taxation needed to finance improvements, a dynamic that would compound EAP's existing fiscal gaps.

Moving to a fiscal architecture for equity and growth requires comprehensive reforms on both the revenue and expenditure sides. An example proposed for Malaysia would achieve net fiscal gains, reduce poverty and inequality, and expand social spending. A recent report on inequality in Malaysia examines how fiscal policy could be reformed to create net fiscal and distributional gains (World Bank 2025b). The different scenarios include a "big bang" reform involving increased revenues from both direct and indirect taxes, coupled with increased spending on social assistance and health. Modeling of this scenario indicates that, even with social assistance spending increased by 0.5 percent of GDP and health spending by an additional 1.0 percent, the aggregate reform would still raise 2.1 points in net revenues. Moreover, the reform would reduce poverty by 1.3 points and inequality by nearly 8.0 points (refer to box 3.2).

Box 3.2. Examining a comprehensive revenue and spending reform for Malaysia

A phased fiscal reform was analyzed for Malaysia to simultaneously generate new revenues, increase development spending, and reduce poverty and inequality.

Phase 1 removes fuel subsidies and compensates poorer households through expanded social assistance. Doing so saves over 2.5 percent of gross domestic product (GDP) in subsidy spending while increasing social assistance from 1.0 to 1.5 percent of GDP, with a slight net decline in poverty. Fiscal savings from subsidy removal do not, however, represent a sustainable long-term revenue source because their size fluctuates with international fuel prices, as does much of Malaysia's existing revenue base.

Phase 2 builds sustainable revenue through indirect and direct tax reform. Malaysia's indirect tax collection, at 3 percent of GDP, sits below even the average for low-income countries. Replacing the current sales and services tax with a broad-based goods and services tax at 10 percent with few exemptions would generate an estimated 1 percent of GDP in additional revenue. Lowering taxable income thresholds, applying higher rates in upper-income brackets, and capping the total value of relief claimed could raise a further 1 percent of GDP from personal income tax. Both measures are highly progressive.

Better targeting of transfers, combined with a goods and services tax rebate for poorer households, offsets the distributional burden on low-income households and still leaves a net fiscal gain of 2 percent of GDP. Part of these revenues finances a 1 percent of GDP increase in health spending, which, distributed broadly, reduces inequality by a further 1.3 Gini points.

The combined effect moves Malaysia from the bottom half to the top half of countries globally in terms of the inequality-reducing impact of its fiscal system (refer to figure B3.2.1).

(continued)

Box 3.2. Examining a comprehensive revenue and spending reform for Malaysia *(continued)*

Comprehensive tax and spending reform in Malaysia would increase net revenues while reducing inequality enough to move from the bottom half to the top half of the global rankings.

FIGURE B3.2.1 Impact on inequality of taxes, transfers, subsidies, and in-kind services, by scenario and income level

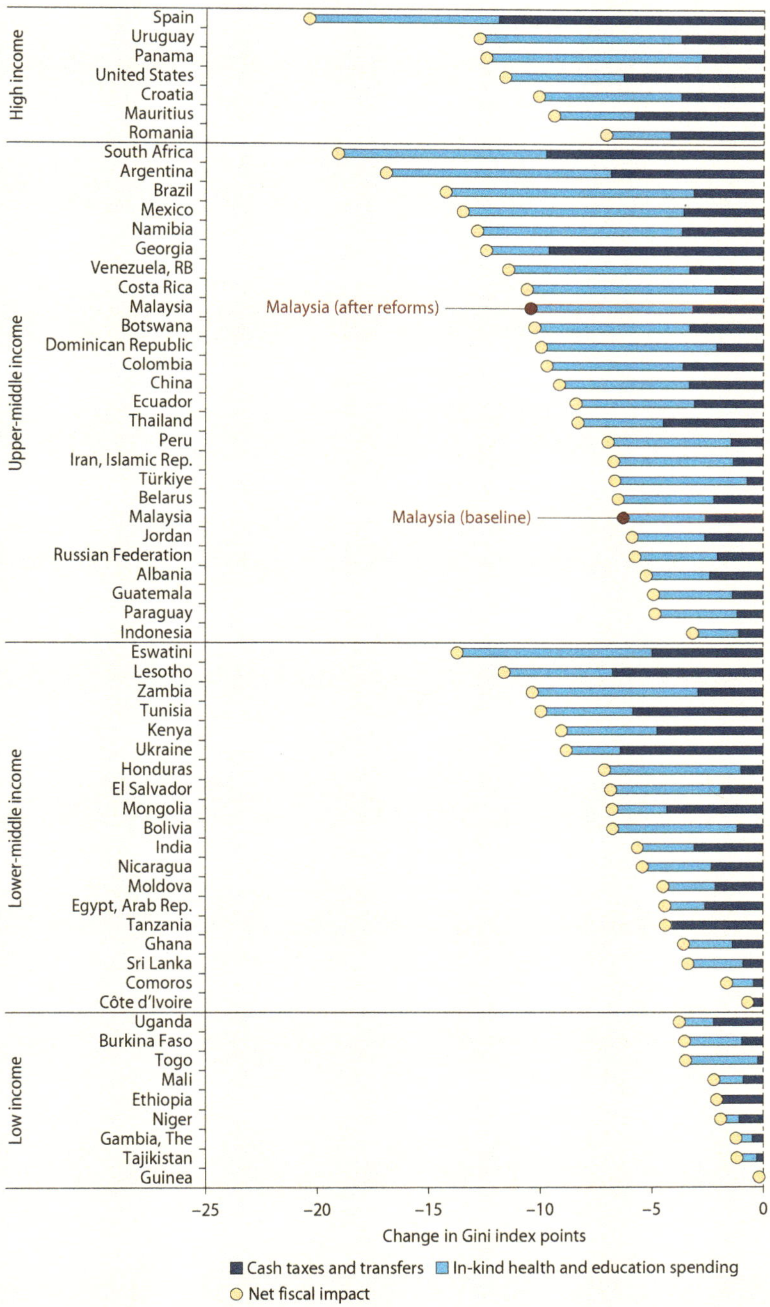

Source: Original figure for this publication based on World Bank 2025b.

Spending more effectively: Program design and implementation

Adequate budgets are necessary but not sufficient. Many social protection programs, although sufficiently funded, fail to deliver their intended impact because their benefits are too shallow, their coverage too narrow or too wide, their targeting too imprecise, or their delivery systems too fragmented. Economies will realize the fiscal gains from the revenue and spending reforms outlined in the previous section only if the programs that receive those resources are well designed and well run. This section examines two design issues in depth: the trade-off between coverage and benefit adequacy, and the targeting and delivery systems that determine whether resources reach the right households.

Balancing coverage and adequacy in the design of social assistance

For any given social assistance budget, policy makers face a fundamental trade-off: broader coverage at lower benefit levels or narrower coverage at higher benefit levels. Neither extreme is efficient. Spreading limited resources too wide produces benefits too shallow to meaningfully reduce poverty or enable households to invest in health and education. Concentrating benefits too narrowly, even at generous levels, limits the number of households reached and mutes aggregate poverty impacts.

The right balance depends on the budget available, the shape of the poverty distribution, and what the policy maker wants to achieve. Two considerations favor somewhat broader coverage than the poverty headcount alone would suggest. First, poverty dynamics are fluid: most households do not remain poor year after year but cycle in and out from a larger group of near-poor and vulnerable households.[26] A program designed to support the poor should thus cover not only the poor but also the vulnerable. Second, adequacy matters: benefits must be large enough to lift households meaningfully closer to the poverty line. Evidence from developing countries consistently shows that transfer levels are rarely high enough to discourage work; if anything, they often enable it by financing transportation, childcare, or small business capital.

Simulations for the Philippines illustrate how these trade-offs play out in practice. Before social assistance, the pre-COVID-19 poverty rate is 20 percent; after social assistance (0.82 percent of GDP, covering 35 percent of the population at an average benefit of 0.15 times the lower-middle-income poverty line), it falls to 16 percent—a reduction of 3.8 percentage points. Fifteen simulated designs—with varying budget levels (0.5, 1.0, and 1.5 percent of GDP) and coverage-benefit combinations (from wide-low to narrow-high)—reveal a consistent finding: virtually all simulated designs outperform the current one on poverty reduction and cost-effectiveness (refer to figure 3.21).

All simulated scenarios would reduce the poverty rate more cost-effectively than current social assistance in the Philippines. In particular, the wide coverage of current programs relative to budget means low benefits that constrain poverty reduction.

FIGURE 3.21 Impact on poverty rate of simulated designs, by budget level and coverage, the Philippines

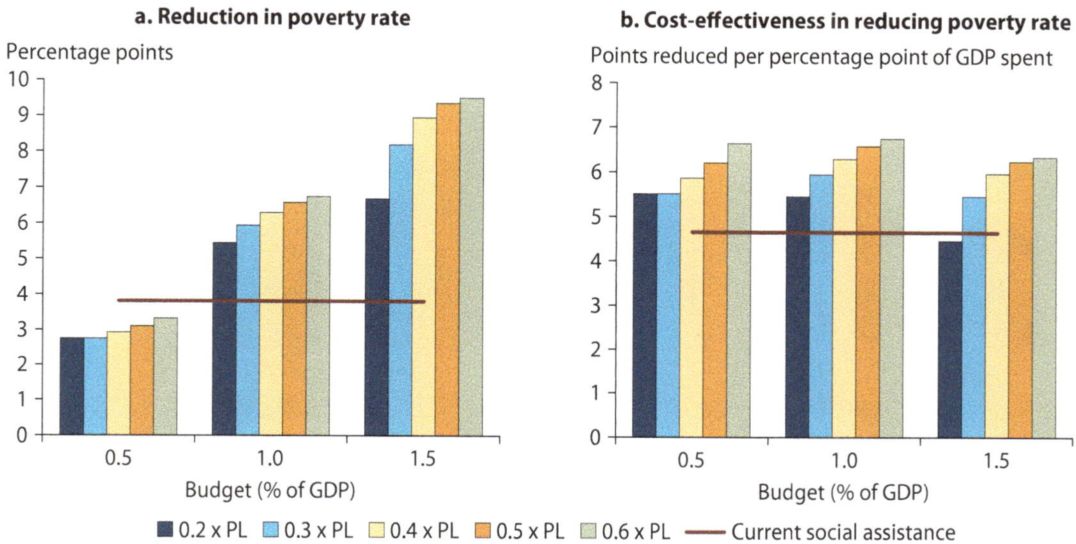

Source: Original figure for this publication based on 2018 Family Income and Expenditure Survey, Philippine Statistics Authority, https://psa.gov.ph/statistics/income-expenditure/fies.

Note: The lower-middle-income country poverty line is used for benefit level ratios. Each simulation shows a different budget: 0.5, 1.0, and 1.5 percent of GDP. Within each fixed budget size, five coverage-benefit designs are presented with benefit levels set at 0.2 times, 0.3 times, 0.4 times, 0.5 times, and 0.6 times the poverty line with coverage then determined as budget / benefit. PL = poverty line.

The optimal design, however, depends on the welfare objective. For reducing the poverty rate, concentrating higher benefits on a narrower set of beneficiaries is most effective—particularly at larger budget levels, where broad coverage is already achieved even under the narrowest designs. For reducing the poverty gap, a more balanced coverage-benefit approach performs best: a poor household that does not cross the poverty line still moves closer to it, reflected in a lower poverty gap even when the poverty rate does not change. On both measures, however, the current design—wide coverage with low benefits—consistently performs worst (refer to figure 3.21, panels a and b; refer to figure 3.22, panels a and b).

The simulations have clear implications for the Philippines: concentrating higher benefits, about 0.4–0.5 times the poverty line, on a narrower set of beneficiaries (13–16 percent of the population), with improved targeting, could nearly double the poverty reduction impact of current spending at a budget of about 1 percent of GDP.

Designs that better balance the coverage and benefit trade-off have the greatest impact on reducing the poverty gap, whereas narrow-coverage and high-benefit designs reduce poverty rates the most. Thus, policy maker objectives matter for design.

FIGURE 3.22 Impact on poverty gap of simulated designs, by budget level and coverage, the Philippines

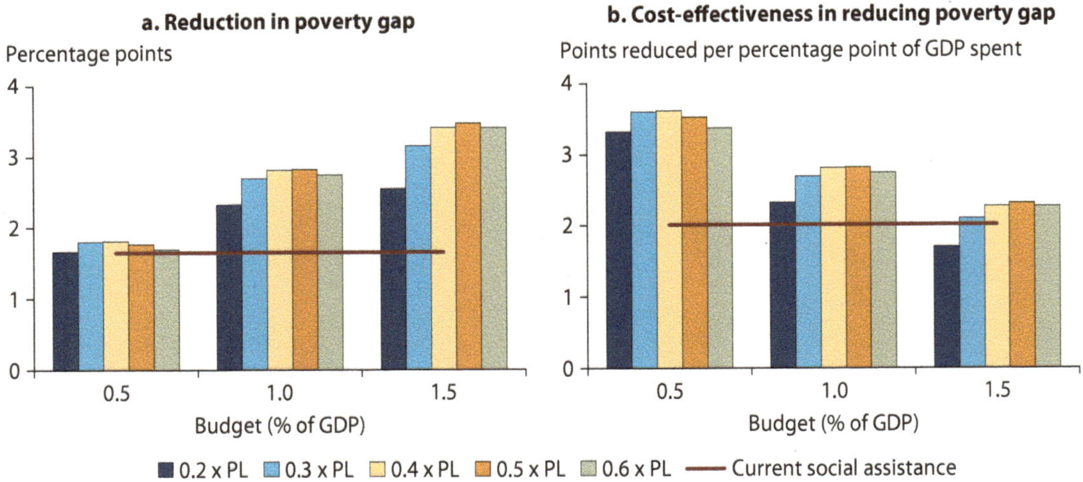

Source: Original figure for this publication based on 2018 Family Income and Expenditure Survey, Philippine Statistics Authority, https://psa.gov.ph/statistics/income-expenditure/fies.
Note: The lower-middle-income country poverty line is used for benefit level ratios. Each simulation shows a different budget: 0.5, 1.0, and 1.5 percent of GDP. Within each fixed budget size, five coverage-benefit designs are presented with benefit levels set at 0.2 times, 0.3 times, 0.4 times, 0.5 times, and 0.6 times the poverty line with coverage then determined as budget / benefit. PL = poverty line.

Strengthening delivery systems

Program design cannot deliver results without the infrastructure to identify beneficiaries, make payments, and share data across government systems. EAP's pandemic response exposed significant preexisting weaknesses in its infrastructure. The economies that fared best were those with robust, digitalized delivery systems already in place.

The region has had uneven progress since the COVID-19 pandemic (refer to table 3.3). For instance, Indonesia and Viet Nam now have nearly universal identification coverage, following major overhauls, and the Philippines accelerated its national identification rollout after pandemic delivery failures exposed the cost of the gap. By contrast, Myanmar has no digitalized system. Digital government payments are most advanced in Malaysia and Thailand; Indonesia, the Philippines, and Viet Nam, although moving in this direction, have significant remaining gaps. On data sharing—the infrastructure that allows targeting systems, payment platforms, and service registries to work together—progress is weakest: countries with shared data platforms, including Cambodia and Thailand, do not yet use them systematically; others rely on bilateral data exchanges on an ad hoc basis (World Bank 2020).

TABLE 3.3 Digital delivery infrastructure, selected EAP economies

Economy	National ID coverage	Digital payments	Data sharing capacity
Cambodia	Lagging	Pilots under way	Platform exists, underutilized
Indonesia	Nearly universal, recently overhauled	In progress	Comprehensive ecosystem in development
Lao PDR	Lagging	Small CCT pilots	Ad hoc bilateral exchanges
Malaysia	Universal, leveraged during COVID-19	Advanced	Platform exists, underutilized
Myanmar	No digitalized system	Limited	Limited
Philippines	Fast-tracked rollout after COVID-19	In progress	Ad hoc bilateral exchanges
Thailand	Universal, leveraged during COVID-19	Advanced	Platform exists, underutilized
Viet Nam	Nearly universal, recently overhauled	In progress	Ad hoc bilateral exchanges

Source: Original table for this publication based on World Bank 2021a.
Note: CCT = conditional cash transfer; EAP = East Asia and Pacific; ID = identification.

Where delivery systems are weak, improving targeting can deliver larger poverty reduction gains than increasing budgets can, as Malaysia illustrates (World Bank 2023c). About three-quarters of Malaysian households receive some form of social assistance although programs nominally target the poorest 40 percent. Half of all social assistance goes to households in the top 60 percent of the income distribution, spread across a highly fragmented system of overlapping programs. A simulation applying a Proxy Means Test to the existing 1.0 percent of GDP budget—redirecting it to the poorest 40 percent—would more than double total poverty reduction from 0.9 percentage point to 2.0 percentage points at no additional cost (refer to figure 3.23). This result matches the impact of increasing the budget by 50 percent without improving targeting. Combining both, better targeting and a 50 percent budget increase, would reduce poverty by 3.1 percentage points.

Governments must also actively maintain targeting systems. Indonesia's Unified Targeting Database, introduced in 2012, significantly improved targeting outcomes and contributed to poverty and inequality reduction (World Bank 2026); however, the underlying data and models were last updated in 2015. Analysis shows that the 2015 models correlated strongly with actual household welfare in 2015 (correlation of 0.80) but that the correlation has steadily declined—to 0.67 in 2017, 0.64 in 2019, and 0.61 in 2021 (refer to figure 3.24). With updated models, the correlation returns to 0.80–0.81 across all four years. This example shows that targeting systems do not maintain themselves. Without regular reestimation, the quality of targeting and the equity impact of spending erode quietly over time and do not trigger the kind of visible failure that prompts corrective action.

Improved targeting of existing social assistance budgets in Malaysia would double poverty reduction, the same impact as increasing the budget by 50 percent with current targeting; doing both triples the impact.

FIGURE 3.23 Fiscal policy impact on poverty under different social assistance budgets and targeting scenarios, Malaysia

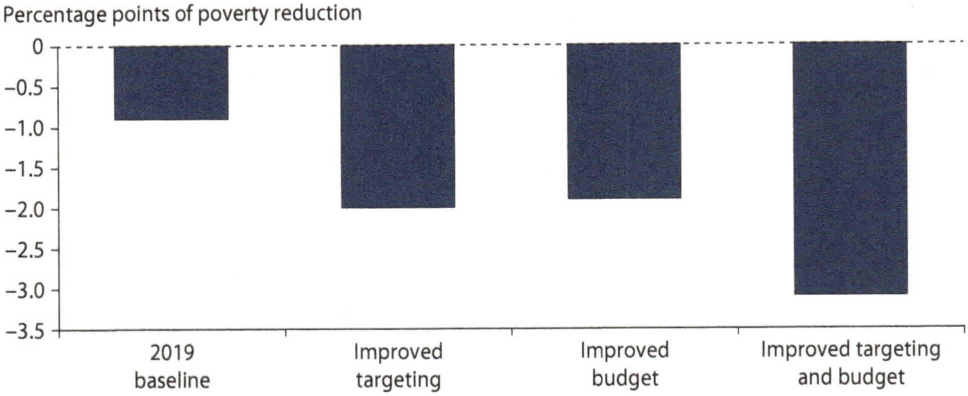

Source: Original figure for this publication based on World Bank 2023c.
Note: The 2019 baseline is the reduction in national poverty from the main Commitment to Equity analysis. Improved targeting simulates a PMT across the whole population; the 2019 social assistance budget is then allocated to the poorest 40 percent of people according to their PMT scores. The improved budget increases all 2019 social assistance beneficiary benefits by 50 percent. "Improved targeting and budget" is the same as the improved targeting scenario with 50 percent higher benefits. PMT = Proxy Means Test.

In Indonesia, existing 2015 targeting models have a strong correlation with true household welfare in 2015 but have become less accurate over time.

FIGURE 3.24 Predicted log household per capita consumption using 2015 PMT models vs. true log household per capita consumption, Indonesia

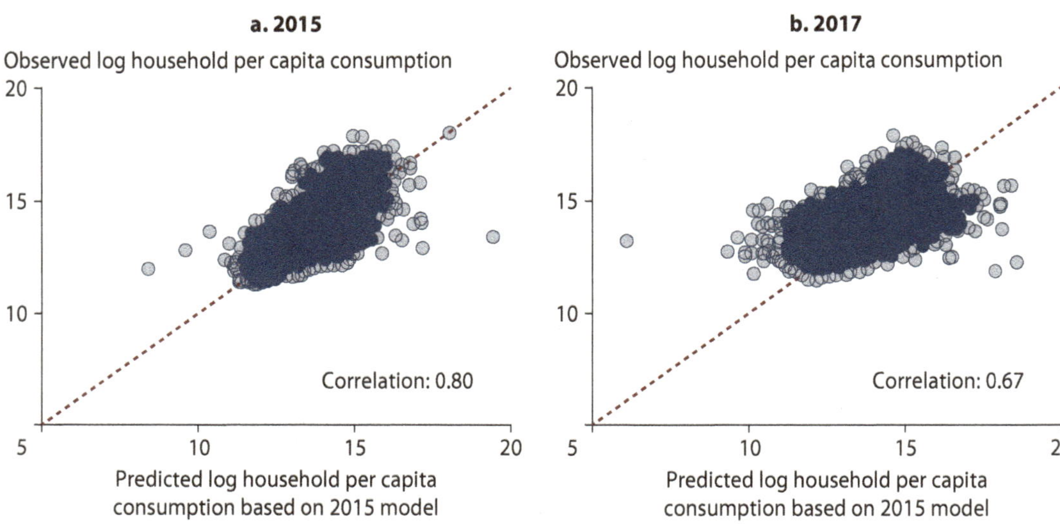

(continued)

FIGURE 3.24 Predicted log household per capita consumption using 2015 PMT models vs. true log household per capita consumption, Indonesia *(continued)*

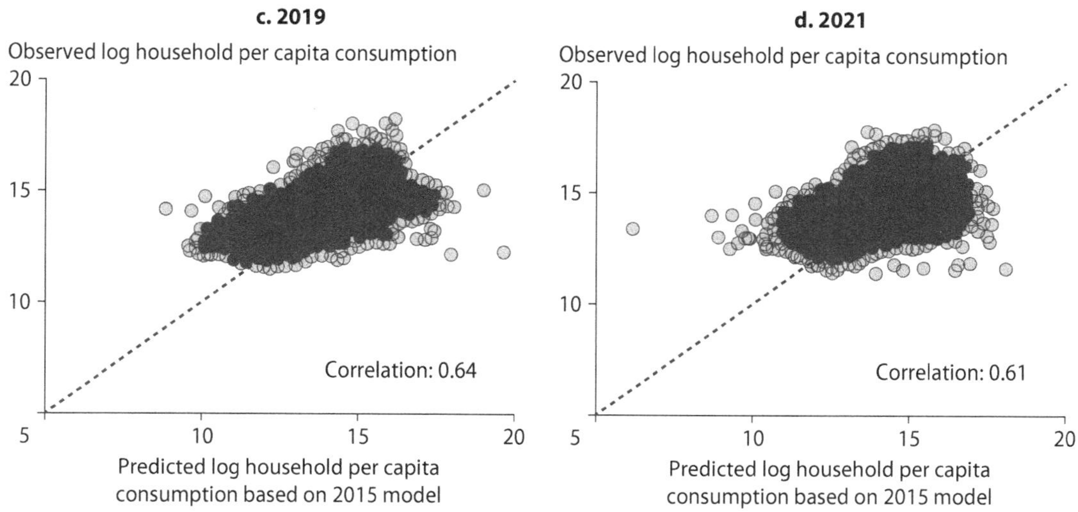

Source: Reproduced from World Bank 2026.
Note: Predicted household welfare is based on a 2015 PMT regression model of log household per capita consumption on a range of demographic, housing, and asset characteristics. The model coefficients applied to a household's characteristics in the 2015, 2017, 2019, and 2021 National Socio-Economic Household Survey. The PMT model uses LASSO for variable selection and fivefold cross-validation to evaluate the model's out-of-sample fit. LASSO = Least Absolute Shrinking and Selection Operator; PMT = Proxy Means Test.

The political economy of fiscal reform

Technical soundness is necessary but not sufficient for fiscal reform. A well-designed package can fail if it generates more visible losers than winners, if policy makers fear the political consequences of implementation, or if public perceptions are negative enough to make the reform politically toxic—before or after enactment. This section examines the political economy constraints that shape what is feasible, how public communications can improve the odds of success, and how an emerging instrument, the personalized VAT, addresses some of these constraints directly.

Public perceptions and the case for proactive communications

Implementing fiscal reforms can be politically very difficult, despite a strong technical case. Key challenges arise in designing a reform package that has more winners than losers (or, for a package that has more losers, it also has a relatively small and unobjectionable degree of loss). Challenges also arise in communicating the rationale and advantages of the package clearly to the public (and often a broad range of policy makers and politicians, as well as special interest groups).

In many cases, it is critical to provide evidence to the broader public, either because fiscal incidence outcomes are not well-known or because of a need to correct misperceptions. For example, although the large fiscal costs of fuel subsidies are often well-known and discussed, tax expenditures (for example, CIT holidays, PIT deductions, and VAT exemptions) can be invisible, representing forgone tax revenues rather than an expenditure explicitly made in the budget. Meanwhile, a common concern over the use of targeted cash transfers is that they will create a disincentive to work or be spent on "bad" consumption items, such as alcohol and tobacco. In fact, very little evidence of this problem exists (refer to box 3.3), although spending levels reflect the concern (refer to later discussion). Similarly, the public often has mistaken perceptions about who benefits from particular spending or who pays a particular tax.

Box 3.3. Little evidence that cash transfers lead to labor market disincentives or "bad" consumption in developing countries

Evidence shows that, with appropriately set benefit levels, well-designed social assistance programs that involve cash transfers do not create dependency or reduce labor market incentives. They also do not lead to undesirable consumption. With developing countries increasingly using targeted cash transfer programs as a mainstay of social assistance, policy makers and the wider public often express concerns about potential negative consequences, including that the transfers will discourage work or increase consumption of "bad" things, such as alcohol and tobacco. The more widely a country believes that poverty occurs because of laziness, the less it spends on cash transfers (Evans and Popova 2017). Systematic reviews of the evidence, however, find little grounds for these concerns in developing countries. For example, a systematic review of 21 studies finds that, even after pooling and reanalyzing data from seven rigorous randomized controlled trial studies, including in Indonesia and the Philippines, the studies find no systematic evidence of an impact of transfers on work behavior, either for men or women (Banerjee et al. 2017).

One reason is that the transfers often do not provide enough that beneficiaries can afford to stop working. In Indonesia, the temporary cash transfers used to offset the impact of fuel subsidy reforms in 2005 and 2008 did not create work disincentives because their value "was not enough to fulfill all living needs" (World Bank 2012a, 20). In fact, whereas working heads of households of recipient families did not change employment status any more than nonrecipients, nonworking recipient heads

(continued)

Box 3.3. Little evidence that cash transfers lead to labor market disincentives or "bad" consumption in developing countries *(continued)*

were 10 percentage points more likely to move into employment than nonworking nonrecipient heads. In the short run, one explanation is that cash transfers relieve credit constraints, allowing for participation in economic activity. In the long run, such transfers have been shown to facilitate the accumulation of human capital, again with positive employment impacts (World Bank 2012c). Among studies with significant effects on employment, reductions in work are more likely among people with good reasons to work less, such as the elderly, persons with disabilities, and women with care responsibilities. Studies also show reallocation of labor from casual work to investing in one's own business activities (Handa et al. 2018). Furthermore, a global review of transfer programs finds no evidence of increased spending on alcohol and tobacco (Evans and Popova 2017).

Source: Based on World Bank 2023c.

In rich and developing countries alike, the public has a poor understanding of fiscal incidence. In the United States, survey respondents believe that 20 percent of households pay the top PIT rate, but the actual share is 1 percent; they believe 25 percent of households pay no PIT, but the real share is 44 percent; and they believe 364 in every 1,000 households pays the estate tax, but fewer than 1 in 1,000 do (Stantcheva 2021). Misperceptions about spending are equally widespread in developing countries. In Malaysia, fuel subsidies are popular in part because most people do not know that richer households capture the largest share of their benefits: in 2019, the richest 20 percent of households received the same share of total fuel subsidy benefits (29 percent) as the poorest 40 percent; however, only 38 percent of survey respondents correctly believed the rich benefited more, and the poorest households were the most likely to overestimate their own share (World Bank 2023c).

These misperceptions have direct fiscal consequences. Countries where most respondents believe that laziness or lack of will power causes poverty spend significantly less on cash transfers than those where most people attribute poverty to an unfair society (refer to figure 3.25; Banerjee et al. 2017). EAP faces a particular version of this challenge. Across the region, public attitudes reflect what Cho et al. (2025) describe as a "productivist mindset" emphasizing economic growth, labor market participation, and the belief that social policy should reinforce self-reliance

Countries where people believe that the poor are lazy spend much less on cash transfers than those where people believe that an unfair society causes poverty.

FIGURE 3.25 Cash transfer spending compared to beliefs in why people are poor, selected countries

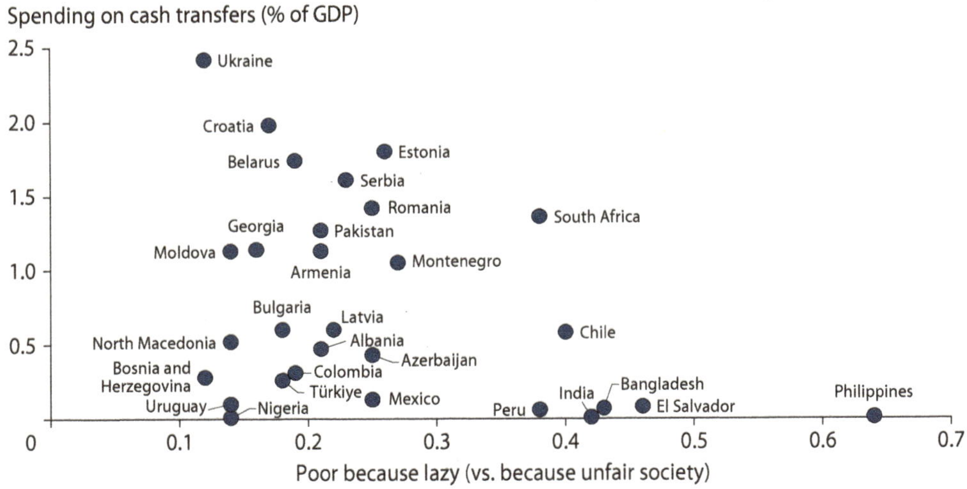

Source: Original figure for this publication based on Banerjee et al. 2017. Constructed using data concerning beliefs from the World Values Survey. Data on national spending on social assistance come from the Atlas of Social Protection Indicators of Resilience and Equity, (ASPIRE) World Bank, https://www.worldbank.org/en/data/datatopics/aspire, for the latest available year.
Note: The horizontal axis plots the national average answer to the World Values Survey (1995 wave) question: "Why, in your opinion, are there people in this country who live in need? Poor because of laziness and lack of will power (= 1), or, Poor because of an unfair society (= 0)."

rather than provide welfare. EAP economies are more likely than income peers to believe individuals are responsible for their own welfare: globally, about 40 percent of survey respondents hold this view regardless of income level,[27] but most EAP economies exceed this average, particularly Mongolia, the Philippines, and Viet Nam (refer to figure 3.26, panel a). The public in EAP economies also places higher value on work relative to leisure than income peers,[28] particularly in China, Indonesia, and Viet Nam (refer to figure 3.26, panel b).

Reform packages that anticipate these attitudes, and that visibly link new revenues to popular spending, consistently outperform those that do not. Perceptions data from Indonesia show that the public cares more about inequality reduction than growth, and that job creation is the most popular framing for new public investment. This finding suggests that redirecting fuel subsidy savings to

The public in EAP countries is much more likely to believe that individuals are responsible for their own welfare and that work is more important than leisure.

FIGURE 3.26 Beliefs about self-sufficiency and the importance of work

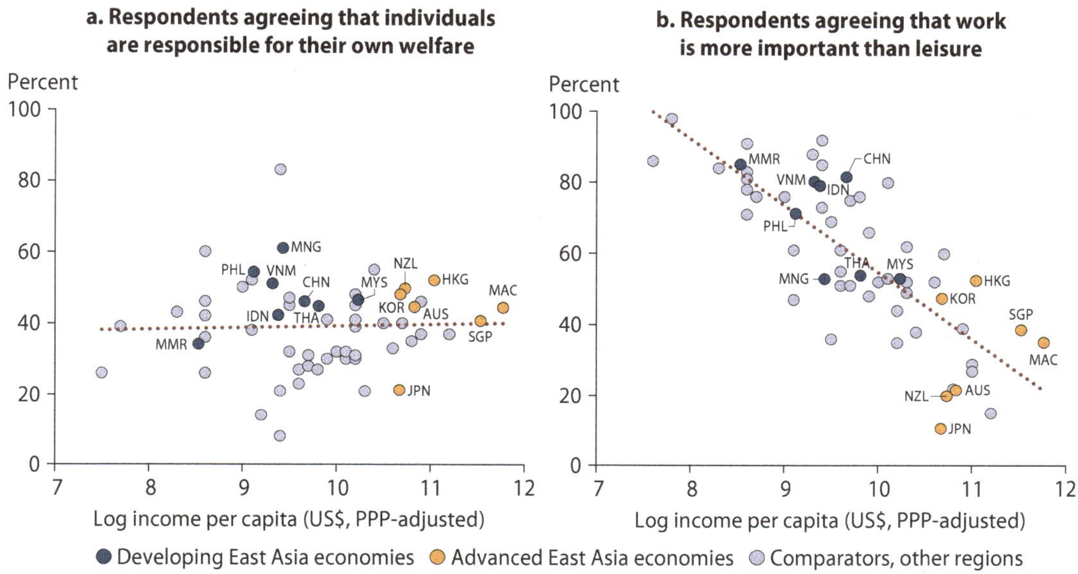

Source: Original figure for this publication based on Cho et al. 2025. Constructed using World Values Survey (7th wave, 2017–22) data concerning beliefs.

Note: The vertical axis in panel a plots the national average response to the statements: "People should take more responsibility to provide for themselves" (= 1) or "Governments should take more responsibility to ensure that everyone is provided for" (= 0). The vertical axis in panel b plots the national average response to the statements: "Work comes first before leisure" (= 1) or "Leisure comes first before work" (= 0). For a list of country codes, refer to https://www.iso.org/obp/ui/#search. EAP = East Asia and Pacific; PPP = purchasing power parity.

infrastructure should be communicated through job creation benefits rather than aggregate growth, a shift that subsequent messaging incorporated. The same analysis finds that, whereas raising taxes on the rich ranks low in public support, linking new revenues to health, education, and social protection spending substantially increases public support (World Bank 2015). A study of 12 middle-income countries confirms that baseline support for fuel subsidy removal, already low, doubles or triples when the reform is packaged with credible compensatory policies (Hoy et al. 2023).

Box 3.4 draws on the international experience of fuel subsidy reform to illustrate how these dynamics play out in practice—that is, where strong communications and credible compensation made the difference between success and failure.

Box 3.4. International experience of fuel subsidy reforms

Energy subsidies have well-documented costs: they are regressive, distortionary, fiscally expensive, and environmentally damaging; and they encourage overconsumption of subsidized products, driving wasteful energy use and exacerbating climate change.[a] Removing them, however, is among the most politically difficult fiscal reforms a government can attempt. A review of over 30 distinct reform episodes (Inchauste and Victor 2017) and a systematic review of 24 reform episodes across 18 countries (Mukherjee et al. 2023) yield consistent lessons.

The core political economy challenge is to make a credible offer—that is, to convince the public that the removal of visible benefits will deliver new, currently invisible gains. Doing so is hardest when subsidies benefit large numbers of households: even when richer households receive more, poorer households may still value their share significantly as a share of income. When concentrated interest groups also benefit, the central task is inoculating the reform against their political power or offering them an acceptable alternative.[b] In both cases, the costs of reform are diffuse and abstract (fiscal savings), whereas the losses are immediate and personal (higher fuel prices).

Social protection systems must be in place before reform begins. In every successful reform episode reviewed, policy makers built or expanded cash transfer systems before or simultaneously with subsidy removal, not after. In five months, Indonesia collected new targeting data covering 30 percent of the population to enable temporary cash compensation for the 2005 reform. It progressively improved the database, which became the foundation for subsequent reforms in 2008, 2013, and 2014–15, as well as the COVID-19 response. In the Dominican Republic, getting targeting, payment channels, and grievance mechanisms right was identified as central to the 2008 reform's success.

Communications play a decisive role. In Indonesia, the successful 2005 and 2014–15 reform episodes were accompanied by coordinated, professionally managed communications campaigns, including governmentwide messaging, prominent public endorsements, and factoids such as the number of schools that could be built with annual subsidy savings. The 2012 failure had no communications strategy, no link between savings and popular spending, and no

(continued)

Box 3.4. International experience of fuel subsidy reforms *(continued)*

response to media inaccuracies or political opposition. In Jordan, a major public campaign preceding reform was coordinated across parliament, nongovernmental organizations, the business community, and labor representatives. Both Jordan's successful fuel reform and the Islamic Republic of Iran's large-scale 2011 reform—one of the largest energy subsidy removals in history—deployed strong, proactive communications.

Reform windows open unpredictably. Most reform episodes occur when prices are either low (making the fiscal cost of reform low) or high (making the cost of inaction high). Ukraine implemented a sixfold fuel price increase in a difficult geopolitical environment by rapidly scaling up cash transfers. What matters is not the price environment per se, but whether the government can credibly deliver visible alternative benefits before opposition consolidates.

Compensation through cash transfers is the most effective approach, but with transfers often tapering over time. Countries either expanded existing programs (40 percent of cases) or created new ones (60 percent); in countries with multiple reform episodes, programs built for earlier reforms were expanded in later ones. Jordan offers a key lesson illustrating that political capital from one reform does not automatically transfer to the next: a well-communicated fuel subsidy reform succeeded, but failure to socialize a subsequent personal income tax reform half a decade later led to the prime minister's resignation.[c]

a. As Inchauste and Victor (2017) observe, below-market costs encourage overconsumption of subsidized products as well as distortionary efforts by consumers to switch toward subsidized products. In Indonesia, for example, large differences in fuel costs affected motorists' choice of vehicles.

b. In the Dominican Republic, for example, the replacement of liquefied petroleum gas subsidies was accompanied by a sister program benefiting taxi drivers who use that fuel, and monthly diesel quantities were awarded to powerful transportation unions (refer to Gallina et al. 2017).

c. Jordan introduced personal income tax reform against a backdrop of austerity, subsidy reduction, and excise tax increases, without prior stakeholder consultation. This introduction triggered demonstrations across multiple cities. King Abdullah accepted the prime minister's resignation four days later. Later analysis finds that, because of its high income threshold, the draft law would not have affected most Jordanians, but the measure was never adequately explained (Rodriguez and Wai-Poi 2020). Refer also to al-Omari and Fishman (2018).

An emerging alternative to VAT exemptions: Personalized VAT

As noted earlier in the chapter, the standard approach to addressing VAT's distributional impact—granting preferential rates and exemptions on goods consumed disproportionately by the poor—is poorly targeted and fiscally costly. An emerging alternative routes the distributional correction through the household rather than the product: instead of reducing the rate on specific goods, governments provide rebates to eligible households based on their VAT payments or estimated VAT burden.

The most sophisticated version, a fully personalized VAT, tracks individual household purchases in real time through e-invoicing systems, identifies eligible households through biometric or digital identification, and refunds VAT at the point of sale or periodically. Brazil's state of Rio Grande do Sul implemented a version of this approach in 2021 through the Devolve-ICMS program (refer to box 3.5), a model now part of Brazil's national tax reform debate. OECD examples also exist, though they tend to be closer to transfers in design.[29] An International Monetary Fund paper released in 2024 examines in detail the case for a progressive VAT through personalized rates (de la Feria and Swistak 2024), and other examples from Latin America include Argentina, Bolivia, and Ecuador.[30]

Box 3.5. Personalized value added tax in Brazil

The Brazilian state of Rio Grande do Sul offers a notable example of a developing country that has implemented a personalized value added tax rebate, increasing progressivity and formalization of consumption. The Devolve-ICMS (for Imposto de Circulação de Mercadorias e Serviços) program, introduced in 2021, returns a portion of value added tax paid by low-income households based on their tracked invoiced consumption. It targets Bolsa Família beneficiaries, leveraging existing transfer infrastructure, and applies to households with per capita income below half the national minimum wage or total family income below three times the minimum wage. Refunds are delivered via a state bank card usable at supermarkets, bakeries, and pharmacies, combining a fixed rebate with a variable component based on invoiced purchases.

Administrative data show an average refund equal to 16 percent of income for households below one minimum wage. Before the reform, the effective value added tax burden was regressive: 9.9 percent for the lowest income group versus 7.5 percent for those above four times the minimum wage. After the reform, the lowest income group received a net transfer equivalent to 1.4 percent of income. The number of monthly invoices submitted by recipients increased by 21–46 percent and total invoiced values by 20–50 percent, indicating a meaningful formalization effect on consumption.

Source: Based on Tonetto et al. 2023.

The personalized VAT has genuine advantages but also important limitations that determine when it makes sense relative to simpler alternatives (refer to table 3.4). On the advantages side, rebates can be more finely calibrated to actual household tax burdens than uniform transfer levels can. In addition, tracking household purchases may increase formalization of consumption, as the Rio Grande evidence suggests. Finally, and critically for EAP, framing the benefit as a tax reduction rather than a welfare payment may make it more politically palatable in environments where public attitudes are skeptical of transfers. A point-of-sale rebate is also psychologically more salient than a delayed transfer.

TABLE 3.4 Advantages and disadvantages of VAT-mitigating options

<table>
<tr><th rowspan="2"></th><th rowspan="2">Preferential rates</th><th rowspan="2">Targeted transfers</th><th colspan="2">Personalized rebates</th></tr>
<tr><th>POS rebate</th><th>Periodic transfer</th></tr>
<tr><td rowspan="2">Advantages</td><td rowspan="2">• No exclusion errors
• Exempt items (such as food) often have emotional salience</td><td rowspan="2">• Very high cost-effectiveness
• Benefit levels can provide much greater support
• Can be tiered to achieve broad coverage
• Can leverage existing programs
• Can be called a VAT rebate</td><td colspan="2">• May be more politically palatable than transfers
• Can be tiered to achieve broad coverage
• E-invoicing may increase formalization of consumption over the longer term</td></tr>
<tr><td>• Can be applied at POS
• Retains more net revenue than other options</td><td>• High benefits (can receive more than VAT owed)</td></tr>
<tr><td rowspan="2">Disadvantages</td><td rowspan="2">• Significantly lowers revenues
• Very low cost-effectiveness
• Benefits capped at very low levels
• Preferential rates not always passed on to consumers</td><td rowspan="2">• Will always have targeting (exclusion) errors
• Consumes much of the new revenue if coverage is too broad, but may not build political consensus if coverage is too narrow
• Transfers are not embraced by all policy makers and the public</td><td colspan="2">• High technology consumption tracking requirements
• Will always have targeting (exclusion) errors</td></tr>
<tr><td>• Low benefit levels
• High POS technology requirements</td><td>• Lower net revenue than POS rebate
• Does not reduce price at POS</td></tr>
</table>

Source: Original table for this publication based on Wai-Poi et al. 2024.
Note: POS = point of sale; VAT = value added tax.

On the limitations side, the approach addresses VAT in isolation, when what matters to households is the net effect of all taxes and spending together. Capping refunds at the VAT paid constrains the maximum benefit, potentially far below what a targeted transfer could deliver. In Rio Grande, the average benefit was 16 percent of income for the poorest group; the average social assistance benefit for the poorest quintile in UMICs is 23 percent, and 38 percent including social protection overall (World Bank 2025c). Moreover, the fully personalized version requires substantial investment in e-invoicing infrastructure and raises genuine privacy concerns, an issue that warrants careful consideration given the sensitivity of household-level consumption data (World Bank 2021b). Finally, program eligibility still requires targeting systems, which means the exclusion errors that affect cash transfers also affect personalized rebates.

The case for a personalized VAT is therefore strongest where political resistance to direct transfers is high, e-invoicing infrastructure already exists, and increased formalization of consumption is a policy priority. In the absence of these conditions, a simpler approach—a transfer labeled as a VAT rebate, calibrated to the estimated VAT paid by a particular income group—can achieve most of the political economy advantages at a fraction of the administrative cost.

Singapore takes exactly this approach with its enhanced VAT voucher.[31] This voucher differentiates benefit levels by household income and demographics, not by tracked VAT payments, yet the government communicates the net effective VAT rate across the income distribution after the voucher is accounted for, making the distributional impact of the combined system visible and credible (refer to figure 3.27; Lustig 2022b; Wai-Poi et al. 2025; World Bank 2022c). The instrument is, in substance, a targeted transfer. As communicated, however, it is a VAT correction. Both things are true, and both matter.

This chapter outlines a technically sound reform agenda: broader VAT, reduced subsidies, and expanded and better-targeted transfers. Making this agenda politically viable requires three things that successful reform episodes consistently demonstrate: sequencing that builds delivery capacity before asking for public sacrifice; communications that make the distributional consequences of both the current system and the proposed reform visible; and packaging that links less popular elements (new taxes or subsidy removal) to more popular ones (health, education, and job creation). In EAP's political environment, where people value work over welfare and individual responsibility over state provision, this need for sequencing and framing is not a communications afterthought. It is a core design requirement.

Singapore's enhanced VAT voucher does a good job of communicating the net VAT burden across the income distribution after netting out the voucher's benefit.

FIGURE 3.27 Effective VAT rate, by income decile, after accounting for the enhanced VAT voucher, Singapore

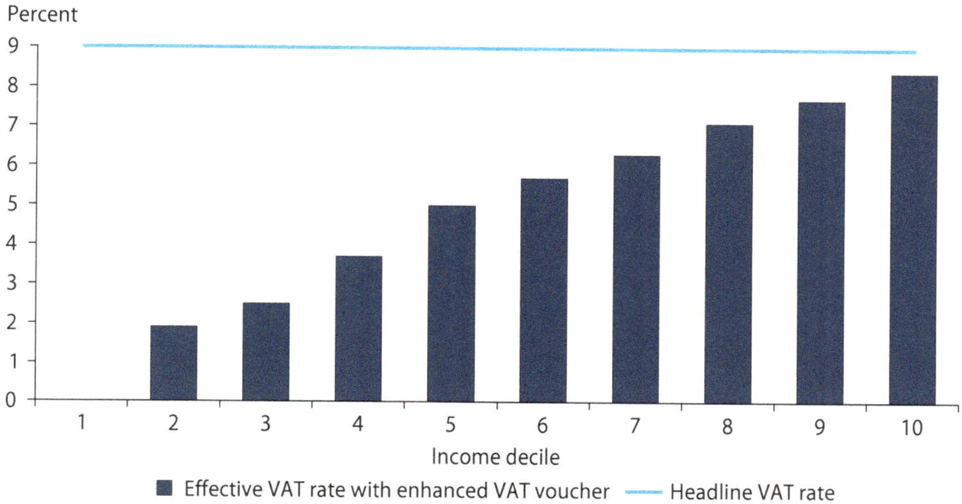

Source: Original figure for this publication based on Government of Singapore, "GST Voucher: Overview," https://www.govbenefits.gov.sg/about-us/gst-voucher/overview/.
Note: Although Singapore calls it a goods and services tax, the tax is equivalent to a VAT. VAT = value added tax.

Notes

1. For Indonesia, refer to World Bank (2019); for Malaysia, World Bank (2014); for Thailand, World Bank (2023c); for the EAP region, Wai-Poi et al. (2016) and World Bank (2018).
2. For a discussion of the role of social assistance in EAP, refer to Cho et al. (2025).
3. Nonfiscal reforms include agricultural liberalization in Mexico during the North American Free Trade Agreement, where farmer compensation in the face of anticipated declines in crop prices enabled trade liberalization (Sadoulet et al. 2001), and the expansion of mandatory coverage of the national pension system in the Republic of Korea to farmers and fishermen in 1995 in response to the Uruguay Round trade negotiations (Cho et al. 2025).
4. These analyses represent a comprehensive survey of fiscal incidence data from over 90 different countries. The results are based on the CEQ framework. This approach was developed by the CEQ Institute at Tulane University. For information concerning the methodology, implementation guidelines, applications, and software of the CEQ approach, refer to Lustig (2022a).
5. Taxes generally include PIT, payroll taxes, VAT, and excise taxes but exclude CIT. Transfers include cash and near-cash benefits, and subsidies include those for energy, food, and sometimes agriculture. All data come from 2010–19, before the COVID-19 pandemic; refer to Wai-Poi et al. (2025) annex for detailed country years and sources.

6. This chapter uses the following income designations for EAP economies: LMICs include Cambodia, Kiribati, Lao PDR, Mongolia, Myanmar, the Philippines, and Viet Nam; UMICs include China, Fiji, Indonesia, Malaysia, and Thailand. Note that Indonesia became a UMIC in 2019, the year of the CEQ study included here, but was an LMIC before then.
7. Cambodia data come from 2019. Social assistance expanded significantly in response to the COVID-19 pandemic, and impacts on inequality and poverty are likely larger now.
8. Fiji became a UMIC in 2012, the Fiji CEQ was conducted using 2019–20 data.
9. The section draws underlying data on marginal contributions and size of fiscal instruments from the Wai-Poi et al. (2025) data set.
10. Because of data limitations, the analysis does not include health and education spending, and the analysis is restricted to inequality impacts rather than poverty.
11. Although health and education indicators are not available in the current data set, in most individual CEQ studies, transfers have a much higher redistribution cost-effectiveness. Governments generally make health and education services available to the entire population, making this spending less targeted than transfers tend to be. Health and education spending still reduces inequality because, even though the cost of providing these public services is the same for each household, the same benefit represents a far larger percentage of poor household incomes than of rich ones.
12. These estimates cannot be compared to the global data set because they use modeled budgets rather than administrative data.
13. The Kakwani Index reflects the difference between the concentration coefficient of a fiscal instrument and the Gini coefficient for market income. The concentration coefficient is an analog to the Gini coefficient, that is, the normalized area between the diagonal and the concentration curve of the fiscal instrument. For taxes, the Kakwani Index is the tax concentration coefficient minus the market income Gini coefficient. For transfers, it is the market income Gini minus the transfer concentration coefficient. This convention means that a positive Kakwani Index for a tax or transfer is progressive. Refer to Lustig (2022a) for greater discussion.
14. It is well-established that a small fraction of the richest PIT payers accounts for most of the PIT paid.
15. As well as spending on quality public services and the expansion of social insurance, which benefits households in the middle of income distribution (discussed further in this chapter's final section on political economy).
16. Health taxes, traditionally on cigarettes and alcohol but recently increasingly on sugar-sweetened beverages and foods high in sodium, raise modest revenues but can significantly reduce future health spending. Such taxes are often held to be regressive when considered relative to current household spending on such items across income deciles as a share of total consumption; however, accounting for enhanced future earnings through greater life and quality of life expectations and lower health spending, along with the greater elasticity of consumption in the face of price increases for poorer households, shows that such taxes tend to be quite progressive (refer to BMJ 2018; Fuchs et al. 2019).
17. On technology and targeting, refer to Grosh et al. (2022). On the role that technology plays in boosting tax revenues through helping identify who is liable for tax, the extent of that liability, and how to ensure payment, refer to Okunogbe and Tourek (2024).
18. This section draws from Wai-Poi et al. (2025).
19. The transfers potentially facilitated a wide job search.

20. Locations may not charge VAT because they fall below the threshold at which they have to register for VAT or because they exceed this level but nonetheless do not register; both of these locations are called "informal" for the following discussion, although the former are not evading charging VAT. If an informal establishment purchases inputs from a formal source, VAT will be charged, with the cost usually passed on to the consumer's final price. The final value added of the informal seller plus informal inputs will not include VAT.
21. In addition to the issue of transfers and direct taxes discussed here, there is also the issue of savings. Income saved this year is usually consumed (and taxed) in a later year, but the tax paid is not captured in the current year analysis. Conversely, some of the consumption tax paid this year and included in the analysis is out of saved income from previous periods. Savings rates generally increase with income, with Thomas (2022, 6) noting that "this biases income-based VAT burden results downwards at higher income levels." Wai-Poi et al. (2025) add that poorer households are more likely to dissave, thus biasing income-based VAT incidence upward at lower income levels. Thomas (2022) shows that the VAT burden in OECD countries is regressive relative to income deciles but broadly neutral to slightly progressive relative to expenditure deciles. However, in most EAP CEQ studies, the savings issue is not applicable because they use a consumption-based household survey, equate consumption to disposable income, add back direct taxes, and subtract direct transfers to recover market income. In this case, all income concepts are after savings, being derived from consumption.
22. In addition, preferential rates are sometimes argued for on the basis that they can promote the consumption of "merit goods" that generate positive externalities. For example, many OECD countries apply preferential rates to books and newspapers or cinema, theater, museums, zoos, amusement parks, and sporting facilities. Preferential rates are not well-targeted if underconsumption is specific to a subset of the population, such as young people or the elderly (Thomas 2022).
23. Particularly for substitutes for goods already subject to preferential rates (IFS 2011), with lobby group pressure influencing decisions to extend concessions (IFS and Mirrlees 2011). It is much easier to deny special treatment in all cases than to allow it in some cases and not in others (Benge et al. 2013).
24. The World Bank defines the middle class in EAP as economically secure, meaning that households have high enough incomes this year (or period) that they have a low probability of being poor or vulnerable next year (or period). Refer to Wai-Poi et al. (2016) for the initial class definitions used in World Bank (2018) and updated in Krah et al. (2026).
25. For regional data, refer to Wai-Poi et al. (2016) and World Bank (2018); for private health care use in China and private education in Indonesia, refer to Wai-Poi et al. (2016); for patterns of the Indonesian and Malaysian middle classes as a whole, refer to World Bank (2019) and World Bank (2014), respectively.
26. For discussion and examples, refer to Grosh et al. (2022).
27. The World Values Survey question asks respondents to choose between two statements: "People should take more responsibility to provide for themselves" and "Governments should take more responsibility to ensure that everyone is provided for."
28. The World Values Survey question asks whether respondents agree that "work comes first before leisure."

29. Tonetto et al. (2023) discuss Canada and Japan as OECD examples, but those approaches appear closer to a transfer in nature.
30. For a regional overview of Latin American personalized VAT experiments, refer to Pineda et al. (2022).
31. Although formally called a goods and services tax voucher, Singapore's instrument is functionally equivalent to a VAT voucher. This chapter uses VAT terminology throughout for consistency.

References

Aguirre, Carlos A., and Parthasarathi Shome. 1988. "The Mexican Value Added Tax (VAT): Methodology for Calculating the Base." *National Tax Association* 41 (4): 543–54.

Alderman, Harold H., and Ruslan G. Yemtsov. 2012. *Productive Role of Safety Nets: Background Paper for the World Bank 2012–2022 Social Protection and Labor Strategy.* Social Protection and Labor Discussion Paper 1203. World Bank. http://documents.worldbank.org/curated/en/338111468336856525.

al-Omari, Gaith, and Ben Fishman. 2018. "Jordan's Economic Protests: Repackaging Reform." Policy Analysis. Washington Institute for Policy Analysis. https://www.washingtoninstitute.org/policy-analysis/jordans-economic-protests-repackaging-reform.

Bachas, Pierre, Lucie Gadenne, and Anders Jensen. 2024. "Informality, Consumption Taxes, and Redistribution." *Review of Economic Studies* 91 (5): 2604–34. https://doi.org/10.1093/restud/rdad095.

Baird, Sarah, Craig McIntosh, and Berk Özler. 2011. "Cash or Condition? Evidence from a Cash Transfer Experiment." *Quarterly Journal of Economics* 126 (4): 1709–53.

Banerjee, Abhijit, Rema Hanna, Gabriel E. Kreindler, and Benjamin Olken. 2017. "Debunking the Stereotype of the Lazy Welfare Recipient: Evidence from Cash Transfer Programs." *World Bank Research Observer* 32 (2). http://hdl.handle.net/10986/31221.

Banerjee, Abhijit, Dean Karlan, and Jonathan Zinman. 2015. "Six Randomized Evaluations of Microcredit: Introduction and Further Steps." *American Economic Journal: Applied Economics* 7 (1): 1–21.

Bastagli, Francesca, Jessica Hagen-Zanker, and Georgina Sturge. 2018. "The Impact of Cash Transfers: A Review of the Evidence from Low- and Middle-income Countries." *Journal of Social Policy* 48 (3): 569–94. https://doi.org/10.1017/S0047279418000715.

Benge, Matt, Marie Pallot, and Hamish Slack. 2013. "Possible Lessons for the United States from New Zealand's GST." *National Tax Journal* 66 (2): 479–98.

BMJ. 2018. "The Health, Poverty, and Financial Consequences of a Cigarette Price Increase Among 500 Million Male Smokers in 13 Middle Income Countries: Compartmental Model Study." April 11, 361: k1162. https://doi.org/10.1136/bmj.k1162.

Bowen, Thomas, Carlo del Ninno, Colin Andrews, et al. 2020. *Adaptive Social Protection: Building Resilience to Shocks*. International Development in Focus. World Bank. http://hdl.handle.net/10986/33785.

Castillo, Czar Joseph, Ramon Clarete, Marjorie Muyrong, and Philip Tuaño. 2019. "Impacts of TRAIN Fuel Excise Taxes on Employment and Poverty." PIDS Policy Notes No. 2019-10, Philippine Institute for Development Studies. https://pidswebs.pids.gov.ph/CDN/PUBLICATIONS/pidspn1910.pdf.

Chaudhuri, Shubham. 2003. "Assessing Vulnerability to Poverty: Concepts, Empirical Methods and Illustrative Examples." Department of Economics, Columbia University. http://www.econdse.org/wp-content/uploads/2012/02/vulnerability-assessment.pdf.

Cho, Yoonyoung, Robert Palacios, and Matthew Wai-Poi. 2025. "Why Social Protection Matters for Inclusive Growth in East Asia and the Pacific." Unpublished working paper, World Bank.

Copenhagen Economics, 2007. "Study on Reduced VAT Applied to Goods and Services in the Member States of the EU." *Taxation Studies* 0018, Directorate General Taxation and Customs Union, European Commission. https://ideas.repec.org/p/tax/taxstu/0018.html.

Crosta, Tommaso, Dean Karlan, Finley Ong, Julius Rüschenpöhler, and Christopher R. Udry, 2024. "Unconditional Cash Transfers: A Bayesian Meta-Analysis of Randomized Evaluations in Low and Middle Income Countries." NBER Working Paper 32779, National Bureau of Economic Research.

de la Feria, Rita, and Artur Swistak. 2024. *Designing a Progressive VAT*. IMF Working Paper 2024/078. International Monetary Fund. https://doi.org/10.5089/9798400271830.001.

Egger, Dennis, Johannes Haushofer, Edward Miguel, Paul Niehaus, and Michael Walker. 2022. "General Equilibrium Effects of Cash Transfers: Experimental Evidence from Kenya." *Econometrica* 90 (6): 2603–43.

European Commission. 2003. "Experimental Application of a Reduced Rate of VAT to Certain Labour-Intensive Services." Report from the Commission to the Council and the European Parliament, COM(2003)309 final. European Commission. https://eur-lex.europa.eu/LexUriServ/LexUriServ.do?uri=COM:2003:0309:FIN:EN:PDF.

Evans, David K., and Anna Popova. 2017. "Cash Transfers and Temptation Goods." *Economic Development and Cultural Change* 65 (2).

Fiszbein, Ariel, Norbert Schady, Francisco H. G. Ferreira, et al. 2009. *Conditional Cash Transfers: Reducing Present and Future Poverty.* World Bank Policy Research Report. World Bank. http://hdl.handle.net/10986/2597.

Fuchs, Alan, Fernanda Gonzalez Icaza, and Daniel Paz. 2019. "Distributional Effects of Tobacco Taxation: A Comparative Analysis." Policy Research Working Paper 8805, World Bank. http://hdl.handle.net/10986/31534.

Gallina, Andrea, Gabriela Inchauste, Pavel Isa, Catherine Lee, and Miguel Sánchez. 2017. "The Political Economy of Energy Subsidy Reform in the Dominican Republic." In *The Political Economy of Energy Subsidy Reform*, edited by Gabriela Inchauste and David G. Victor. World Bank.

Gassmann, Franziska, Ugo Gentilini, Julieta Morais, et al. 2023. "Is the Magic Happening? A Systematic Literature Review of the Economic Multiplier of Cash Transfers." Policy Research Working Paper 10529, World Bank. http://hdl.handle.net/10986/40113.

Grosh, Margaret, Phillippe Leite, Matthew Wai-Poi, and Emil Tesliuc, eds. 2022. *Revisiting Targeting in Social Assistance: A New Look at Old Dilemmas*. World Bank. http://hdl.handle.net/10986/37228.

Gust, Sarah, Eric Hanushek, and Ludger Woessmann. 2024. "Global Universal Basic Skills: Current Deficits and Implications for World Development." *Journal of Development Economics* 166: 103205.

Handa, Sudhanshu, Silvio Daidone, Amber Peterman, et al. 2018. "Myth-Busting? Confronting Six Common Perceptions about Unconditional Cash Transfers as a Poverty Reduction Strategy in Africa." *World Bank Research Observer* 33 (2): 259–98. https://doi.org/10.1093/wbro/lky005.

Haushofer, Johannes, and Jeremy Shapiro. 2016. "The Short-Term Impact of Unconditional Cash Transfers to the Poor: Experimental Evidence from Kenya." *Quarterly Journal of Economics* 131 (4): 1973–2042.

Hidrobo, Melissa, John Hoddinott, Neha Kumar, and Bastien Olivier. 2018. "Social Protection, Food Security, and Asset Formation." *World Development* 101: 88–103. https://doi.org/10.1016/j.worlddev.2017.08.014.

Hill, Ruth Vargas, Emmanuel Skoufias, and Barry Maher. 2019. "The Chronology of a Disaster: A Review and Assessment of the Value of Acting Early on Household Welfare." World Bank. https://documents1.worldbank.org/curated/en/796341557483493173/pdf/The-Chronology-of-a-Disaster-A-Review-and-Assessment-of-the-Value-of-Acting-Early-on-Household-Welfare.pdf.

Hoy, Christopher, Yeon Soo Kim, Minh Nguyen, Mariano Sosa, and Sailesh Tiwari. 2023. "Building Public Support for Reducing Fossil Fuel Subsidies: Evidence Across 12 Middle-Income Countries." Policy Research Working Paper 10615, World Bank. https://doi.org/10.1596/1813-9450-10615.

Hutton, Eric. 2017. *The Revenue Administration–Gap Analysis Program: Model and Methodology for Value Added Tax Gap Estimation*. Technical Notes and Manuals 2017/004. International Monetary Fund. https://doi.org/10.5089/9781475583618.005.

IFS (Institute for Fiscal Studies). 2011. "Quantitative Analysis of VAT Rate Structures." In *A Retrospective Evaluation of Elements of the EU VAT System*, report prepared for the European Commission, TAXUD/2010/DE/328. https://taxation-customs.ec.europa.eu/system/files/2016-09/report_evaluation_vat.pdf.

IFS (Institute for Fiscal Studies), and James Mirrlees, eds. 2011. *Tax by Design: The Mirrlees Review*. Oxford University Press.

Inchauste, Gabriela, and David G. Victor, eds. 2017. *The Political Economy of Energy Subsidy Reform*. Directions in Development. World Bank.

Krah, Kwabena, Veronica Sonia Montalva Talledo, and Sailesh Tiwari. 2026. "Striving for Economic Security: Emerging Middle Class in the East Asia and Pacific Region." Policy Research Working Paper 11301, World Bank. https://doi.org/10.60572/sy4m-nz07.

Lustig, Nora, ed. 2022a. *Commitment to Equity Handbook: Estimating the Impact of Fiscal Policy on Inequality and Poverty*, Second Edition. Brookings Institution Press.

Lustig, Nora. 2022b. "Fiscal Policy, Income Redistribution, and Poverty Reduction in Low- and Middle-Income Countries." Chapter 10 in *Commitment to Equity Handbook: Estimating the Impact of Fiscal Policy on Inequality and Poverty*, Second Edition (Volume 1). Brookings Institution Press.

Mukherjee, Anit, Yuko Okamura, Ugo Gentilini, et al. 2023. "Cash Transfers in the Context of Energy Subsidy Reforms: Insights from Recent Experience." Energy Subsidy Reform in Action Series. World Bank. http://hdl.handle.net/10986/39948.

Okunogbe, Oyebola, and Gabriel Tourek. 2024. "How Can Lower-Income Countries Collect More Taxes? The Role of Technology, Tax Agents, and Politics." *Journal of Economic Perspectives* 38 (1): 81–106.

Pineda, Emilio, Martin Bes, and Alberto Barreix. 2022. "Revisando el IVA Personalizado: Una herramienta para la consolidación fiscal con equidad." *CIAT* (blog), April 25. https://www.ciat.org/ciatblog-revisando-el-iva-personalizado-una-herramienta-para-la-consolidacion-fiscal-con-equidad/.

Rodriguez, Laura, and Matthew Wai-Poi. 2020. "Fiscal Policy, Poverty and Inequality in Jordan: The Role of Taxes and Public Spending." Working paper, World Bank. http://documents.worldbank.org/curated/en/113451615905549990.

Sadoulet, Elisabeth, Alain de Janvry, and Benjamin Davis. 2001. "Cash Transfer Programs with Income Multipliers: PROCAMPO in Mexico." *World Development* 29 (6): 1043–56.

Stantcheva, Stefanie. 2021. "Understanding Tax Policy: How Do People Reason?" *Quarterly Journal of Economics* 136 (4): 2309–69.

Tesliuc, Emil Daniel, and Maria Belen Fonteñez. 2025. "Adaptive Social Protection Agenda Lessons from Responses to COVID-19 Shock: The State of Social Protection Report 2025 Background Paper #2." Social Protection Discussion Paper 2509, World Bank. http://hdl.handle.net/10986/43038.

Thomas, Alastair. 2022. "Reassessing the Regressivity of VAT." *Journal of Applied Public Economics* 43 (1): 23–38. https://doi.org/10.1111/1475-5890.12290.

Tonetto, Jorge Luis, Adelar Fochezatto, and Giovanni Padilha da Silva. 2023. "Refund of Consumption Tax to Low-Income People: Impact Assessment Using Difference-in-Differences." *Economies* 11 (6): 153. https://doi.org/10.3390/economies11060153.

von Haldenwang, Christian, Augustin Redonda, and Flurim Aliu. 2023. *Tax Expenditures in An Era of Transformative Change*. GTED Flagship Report. German Institute of Development and Sustainability. https://doi.org/10.23661/r2.2023.

Wai-Poi, Matthew, Ririn Purnamasari, and Matthew Goldman. 2024. "Implementing a Progressive GST in Malaysia: Evidence and Options." Unpublished working paper, World Bank.

Wai-Poi, Matthew, Ririn Purnamasari, Taufik Indrakesuma, Ikuko Uochi, and Laura Wijaya. 2016. "East Asia's Rising Middle Classes." Background paper for *Riding the Wave: An East Asian Miracle for the 21st Century*. World Bank.

Wai-Poi, Matthew, Mariano Sosa, and Pierre Bachas. 2025. *Taxes, Spending, and Equity: International Patterns and Lessons for Developing Countries*. Prosperity Insight Series. World Bank. https://doi.org/10.1596/44281.

World Bank. 2012a. "BLT Temporary Unconditional Cash Transfer." Social Assistance Program and Public Expenditure Review 2, World Bank. http://hdl.handle.net/10986/26698.

World Bank. 2012b. "PKH Conditional Cash Transfer." Social Assistance Program and Public Expenditure Review 6, World Bank. http://hdl.handle.net/10986/26697.

World Bank. 2012c. "Protecting Poor and Vulnerable Households in Indonesia." World Bank. http://hdl.handle.net/10986/13810.

World Bank. 2014. "Malaysian Economic Monitor December 2014: Towards a Middle-Class Society." World Bank. http://hdl.handle.net/10986/21057.

World Bank. 2015. "Indonesia's Rising Divide." World Bank. http://documents.worldbank.org/curated/en/267671467991932516.

World Bank. 2018. *Riding the Wave: An East Asian Miracle for the 21st Century*. World Bank. https://openknowledge.worldbank.org/entities/publication/50703ffb-9d87-5cfd-b6eb-38dc29ed0253.

World Bank. 2019. "Aspiring Indonesia: Expanding the Middle Class." World Bank. http://hdl.handle.net/10986/33237.

World Bank. 2020. "Scaling Up Social Assistance Payments as Part of the COVID-19 Pandemic Response." G2Px research, World Bank. https://thedocs.worldbank.org/en/doc/655201595885830480-0090022020/original/WBG2PxScalingupSocialAssistancePaymentsasPartoftheCovid19PandemicResponse.pdf.

World Bank. 2021a, *East Asia and Pacific Economic Update, October 2021: Long COVID*. World Bank.

World Bank. 2021b. *World Development Report 2021: Data for Better Lives*. World Bank. http://hdl.handle.net/10986/35218.

World Bank. 2022a. "From the Last Mile to the Next Mile—2022 Vietnam Poverty and Equity Assessment." World Bank. http://hdl.handle.net/10986/37952.

World Bank. 2022b. *Philippines Country Climate and Development Report*. CCDR Series. World Bank. https://doi.org/10.1596/38280.

World Bank. 2022c. *Poverty and Shared Prosperity Report 2022: Correcting Course*. World Bank.

World Bank. 2023a. *East Asia and Pacific Economic Update, April 2023: Reviving Growth*. World Bank. http://hdl.handle.net/10986/39598.

World Bank. 2023b. "Lao PDR Fiscal Incidence Analysis, Raising the Bar: Toward an Equitable and Inclusive Fiscal Policy." World Bank. http://hdl.handle.net/10986/40815.

World Bank. 2023c. "Raising the Tide, Lifting All Boats." Malaysia Economic Monitor (October), World Bank. http://documents.worldbank.org/curated/en/099100623063032359.

World Bank. 2023d. "Thailand Public Revenue and Spending Assessment: Promoting an Inclusive and Sustainable Future." World Bank. http://documents.worldbank.org/curated/en/099052523201510112.

World Bank. 2024a. *Poverty, Prosperity, and Planet Report 2024: Pathways Out of the Polycrisis*. World Bank. https://doi.org/10.1596/978-1-4648-2123-3.

World Bank. 2024b. *World Development Report 2024: The Middle-Income Trap*. World Bank. http://hdl.handle.net/10986/41919.

World Bank. 2025a. "Estimating Value Added Tax (VAT) and Corporate Income Tax (CIT) Gaps in Indonesia." Prosperity Insight Series, World Bank. http://hdl.handle.net/10986/42959.

World Bank. 2025b. "A Fresh Take on Reducing Inequality and Enhancing Mobility in Malaysia." World Bank. http://documents.worldbank.org/curated/en/099011125013533848.

World Bank. 2025c. *State of Social Protection Report 2025: The 2-Billion-Person Challenge*. World Bank. http://documents.worldbank.org/curated/en/099042725111568158.

World Bank. 2025d. "Value Added Tax Gap in the Philippines." Unpublished note.

World Bank. 2026. *An Eventful Decade: Taxes, Spending and Equity in Indonesia, 2012–21*. Unpublished, World Bank.

World Bank, United Nations Educational, Scientific and Cultural Organization (UNESCO), United Nations Children's Fund (UNICEF), Foreign Commonwealth and Development Office (FCDO), United States Agency for International Development (USAID), and Bill & Melinda Gates Foundation. 2022. "The State of Global Learning Poverty: 2022 Update." World Bank, UNESCO, UNICEF, FCDO, USAID, and Bill & Melinda Gates Foundation. https://www.worldbank.org/en/topic/education/publication/state-of-global-learning-poverty.

Policy Implications: A Growth-Enhancing Fiscal Compact in EAP

4

Introduction

A growth-enabling fiscal approach—low tax rates, spending within means, and comparatively high public investment in infrastructure—supported decades of rapid growth, macroeconomic stability, and poverty reduction in East Asia and Pacific (EAP). It also produced persistent underinvestment in health, education, social protection, and climate adaptation, leaving the region ill-equipped for the pressures it now faces: climate shocks, rapidly aging populations, and slowing productivity.

The path forward requires a growth-enhancing fiscal compact built on the following three mutually reinforcing pillars (refer to box 4.1).

Spending prioritization: scaling up investment in human capital, infrastructure, social protection, and climate adaptation. In each area, state spending is warranted because social returns exceed private returns: markets underprovide public goods, under-internalize externalities, and leave persistent gaps in access that compound over generations. Spending expansion alone is insufficient; each pillar requires institutional and sectoral reforms that raise the efficiency of public expenditure, crowd in private investment, and improve service delivery.

Revenue mobilization: broadening and deepening the domestic tax base to finance the transition. In a world where capital and skills are mobile and employment is often informal, the largest untapped revenue opportunities lie in levying uniform indirect taxes, property taxes, and taxes on negative externalities—carbon and health-damaging products. Well-designed reforms in these areas can simultaneously increase revenues, reduce distortions, and improve health and climate outcomes.

Box 4.1. Policy actions for a growth-enhancing fiscal compact in East Asia and Pacific

A growth-enhancing fiscal compact for the East Asia and Pacific region could rest on three mutually reinforcing pillars and their supporting policy actions.

1. Prioritize spending on health, education, infrastructure upgrades, climate adaptation, and social protection:

- Scale up investment in health, education, and physical infrastructure, with a shift in composition to high-externality activities: primary health care, early childhood development, foundational learning, and connectivity in lagging areas.
- Strengthen climate adaptation planning and investment, integrating climate risk into public investment management and developing shock-responsive social protection systems.
- Reform pension systems to close the gap between actual and actuarially fair contribution rates, extend coverage to informal workers, and anchor long-run fiscal sustainability.
- Rationalize subsidies, replacing untargeted price subsidies with direct transfers, and implement sectoral reforms that raise spending efficiency and crowd in private provision where markets function.

2. Improve the efficiency and effectiveness of domestic revenue mobilization:

- Broaden the value added tax base by rationalizing exemptions and zero-rated items; pair that base-broadening with direct transfer mechanisms to protect the poor, rather than relying on exemptions.
- Strengthen the personal income tax base by raising compliance among high earners, reducing excessive thresholds and deductions, and leveraging digitalization to identify taxable income in informal labor markets.
- Increase property tax revenues—the most underused yet efficient and progressive revenue instrument available to most East Asia and Pacific governments—through updated valuations, simplified administration, and removal of outdated exemptions.
- Price negative externalities through carbon taxes or emissions trading systems and excise taxes on health-damaging products, capturing a revenue-environmental double dividend.

(continued)

Box 4.1. Policy actions for a growth-enhancing fiscal compact in East Asia and Pacific *(continued)*

3. Strengthen fiscal capacity and public support for reform:

- Implement institutional and technological improvements—including digital public infrastructure, e-filing, and integrated spending and benefit systems—to reduce compliance costs, compress leakages, and improve targeting.
- Link revenue mobilization to spending priorities through credible medium-term fiscal frameworks with binding budget constraints, fiscal rules, and adequate liquidity buffers.
- Build public support through transparent communication of reform benefits and distributional safeguards, making visible the connection between what citizens pay and what they receive.

Fiscal capacity and public support: linking revenue and spending reforms within credible institutional frameworks. Spending and taxation are jointly determined—that is, the optimal fiscal scale is reached when the marginal benefit of the last dollar spent equals the marginal cost of raising it. Explicitly connecting new or higher taxes to clear, well-targeted spending priorities strengthens political feasibility. Anchoring reforms in a medium-term fiscal framework—supported by fiscal rules, liquidity buffers, and transparent communication—builds the public trust on which sustained reforms depend.

Spending prioritization

Prioritizing spending on health, education, infrastructure upgrades, climate adaptation, and social protection can simultaneously support growth, resilience, and inclusion. Importantly, spending priorities reinforce each other, and public investment can crowd in private investment. Investments in basic human capital create the conditions for further investments in higher education, supporting long-term growth. Such investments also reduce inequality by equipping a larger share of the population with skills that act as springboards for upward mobility. Infrastructure investment raises productivity and strengthens resilience to shocks, both of which spur private investment. Climate adaptation similarly protects existing assets and livelihoods, leading to more stable economic activity over time, and encourages investment by reducing risk.

Human capital and infrastructure investments

Higher spending on human capital, combined with reforms of education and health, supports growth and reduces inequality. Narrowing the region's human capital spending gaps could yield substantial economic and social returns (refer to figure 4.1). For example, raising education spending in EAP economies to the average levels of Japan and the Republic of Korea could boost annual gross domestic product (GDP) per capita growth by an estimated 0.97 percentage point on average. The economies with the largest gaps stand to gain the most.

Modernizing infrastructure is essential to build resilience and sustain growth. Infrastructure gaps in transportation and digital networks raise logistics costs and inhibit productivity growth. In Indonesia, for instance, infrastructure deficiencies contribute to logistics costs of about 15 percent of firms' total expenditure (Kasyanenko et al. 2023). Mobile connectivity has expanded rapidly across the region, but disparities in broadband quality and connection speeds remain pronounced both within and across economies. The returns to closing these gaps are high. Benefit-cost ratios for investments in energy and transportation

Narrowing the education spending gap in EAP economies could increase annual growth, on average, by 0.97 percentage point.

FIGURE 4.1 Additional growth from aligning education spending with average of aspirational countries, selected EAP economies

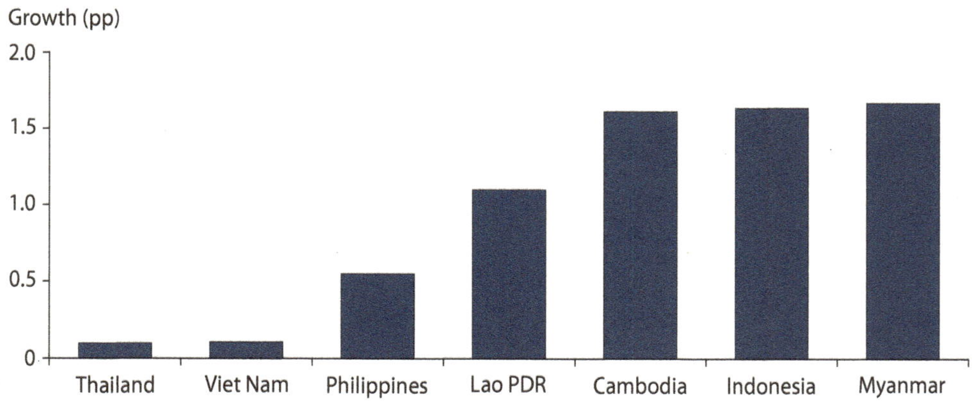

Source: Original figure for this publication based on Acosta-Ormaechea and Morozumi 2013.
Note: The bars represent additional annual growth (pp) if the average government spending on education between 2010 and 2019 equaled the average spending on education by Japan and the Republic of Korea in the same period. The figure does not include Malaysia and Mongolia because they both have higher average education spending within the period than the aspirational average. EAP = East Asia and Pacific; pp = percentage point.

exceed 1 in almost all of EAP—meaning that additional investment passes a basic social rate of return threshold in virtually every economy in the region (as discussed in chapter 1). Public investment is warranted where the social returns to investment are higher than the private returns, even after the relevant regulatory reforms have been implemented.

Climate adaptation planning and investment

Climate adaptation investments can deliver a triple dividend. First, adaptation measures reduce the physical and economic losses associated with climate shocks. For example, upgraded and climate-informed infrastructure reduces direct exposure to floods, storms, heat waves, droughts, and sea level rise. Second, such measures also generate induced economic benefits by lowering uncertainty and enabling investment and productivity. At the same time, many adaptation interventions yield social and environmental co-benefits, such as improved access to services, stronger livelihoods, and better ecosystem management. The public good and positive externality character of many adaptation measures provides a strong case for public investment—provided that public financing strengthens rather than crowds out private action.

Despite these benefits, adaptation remains underfunded. Financing, however, is not the only, and perhaps not even the main, constraint to scaling up climate adaptation. Few governments have costed out adaptation strategies in their Nationally Determined Contributions or National Adaptation Plans. Moreover, few governments are ready with good economic and financial analysis of adaptation finance policies and projects.[1]

Governments need to think about how to allocate adaptation funding across sectors and between ex ante risk reduction (spanning such options as short-term flood management and long-term agricultural research) and ex post risk management (such as contingency finance, insurance schemes, and safety nets). Donor lending and concessional finance instruments can support these efforts across sectors and levels, from macrolevel contingency finance to climate-informed community-driven development. Nonetheless, available international climate finance remains far below estimated needs for mitigation, adaptation, and loss and damage (refer to box 4.2).

Adaptation investments are routinely undervalued because project appraisal focuses on avoided losses alone. The triple dividends framework corrects this undervaluation by accounting for all three return categories: avoided losses,

Box 4.2. The cost and benefits of building climate resilience

Adaptation policy spans two broad categories. Ex ante risk reduction covers investments in infrastructure and agriculture and policies that reduce exposure, restricting development in flood-prone areas, protecting natural ecosystems, and building climate-resilient transportation and energy networks. Ex post risk management covers early warning systems, sovereign risk insurance, and social safety nets that absorb losses after shocks occur. Cost-benefit analysis consistently shows that ex ante risk reduction delivers higher returns than ex post risk management, except for low-cost early warning systems (World Bank 2023a).

Analysis of the Nationally Determined Contributions (NDCs) submitted by East Asia and Pacific economies provides insight into the sectors that governments prioritize for adaptation interventions (refer to figure B4.2.1). Agriculture tops the list, followed by efforts to strengthen the institutional capacity and data needed to better plan and implement adaptation strategies.

NDCs of EAP economies reveal sectoral priorities for adaptation actions.

FIGURE B4.2.1 Adaptation actions cited, by sector

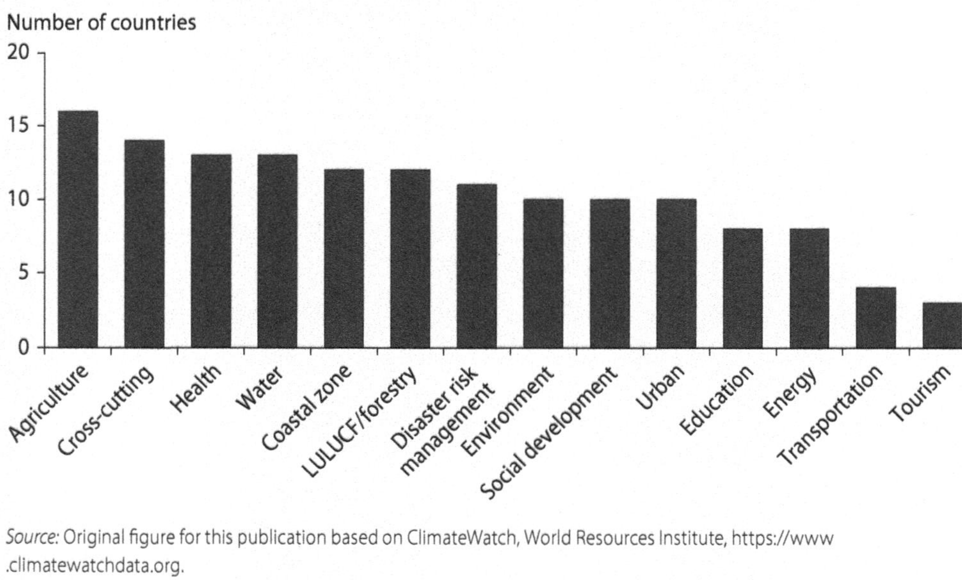

Source: Original figure for this publication based on ClimateWatch, World Resources Institute, https://www.climatewatchdata.org.

Note: Data extracted from 21 developing countries in EAP that identify priority sectors. Examples of "Cross-cutting" include capacity-building, contingency risk management, and climate information services. EAP = East Asia and Pacific; LULUCF = land use, land use change, and forestry; NDCs = Nationally Determined Contributions.

(continued)

Box 4.2. The cost and benefits of building climate resilience *(continued)*

Prioritization has not translated into cost strategies, however. Among 21 East Asia and Pacific economies submitting NDCs for the 2021 United Nations Climate Change Conference, only five provided even rough cost estimates, ranging from a few hundred to several thousand dollars per capita over the NDC period (refer to table B4.2.1). The complexity of adaptation also explains why recent Country Climate and Development Reports often provide only tentative estimates of adaptation costs and frequently rely on rules of thumb across infrastructure, buildings, food systems, health, education, and environmental sectors.

Adaptation investment needs are substantial and vary widely across countries, but they also offer significant economic returns. Global estimates place adaptation costs at about 0.25 percent of world gross domestic product (GDP) annually, with requirements exceeding 1 percent of GDP in many developing economies and surpassing 10 percent in some small island states (Aligishiev et al. 2022). In East Asia and Pacific, estimated adaptation needs range from about 0.7 percent of GDP in the Philippines to 1.5–2.0 percent in China and 3.0–5.4 percent in Viet Nam; in Samoa prioritized adaptation projects for 2022–26 total about 11 percent of 2021 GDP (Chai et al. 2019; IMF 2022; World Bank 2022a, 2022b). These investments can yield substantial benefits: in Samoa, an additional 2 percent of GDP invested in adaptation over five years could avoid output losses estimated at about 4.5 percent of GDP; in the Philippines, adaptation investments of less than 1 percent of GDP could avert losses of 1–2 percent of GDP across multiple sectors (IMF 2022; World Bank 2022a). Refer to figure B4.2.2 for more on the sectoral benefits in the Philippines.

TABLE B4.2.1 Adaptation costs in NDCs submitted to COP26, selected EAP economies, 2021

Economy	Adaptation finance needs according to NDC (US$, millions)	Population (millions)	Finance needs per capita (US$)
Cambodia	2,041	16.6	123
Kiribati	75	0.13	577
Mongolia	5,200	3.3	1,576
Solomon Islands	1,267	0.71	1,784
Viet Nam	35,000	97.5	359

Source: Original figure for this publication based on ClimateWatch, World Resources Institute, https://www.climatewatchdata.org.
Note: COP26 = 2021 United Nations Climate Change Conference; EAP = East Asia and Pacific; NDCs = Nationally Determined Contributions.

(continued)

Box 4.2. The cost and benefits of building climate resilience *(continued)*

Adaptation investments in the Philippines will have a broad range of employment benefits.

FIGURE B4.2.2 Sectoral benefits from climate adaptation investments, the Philippines

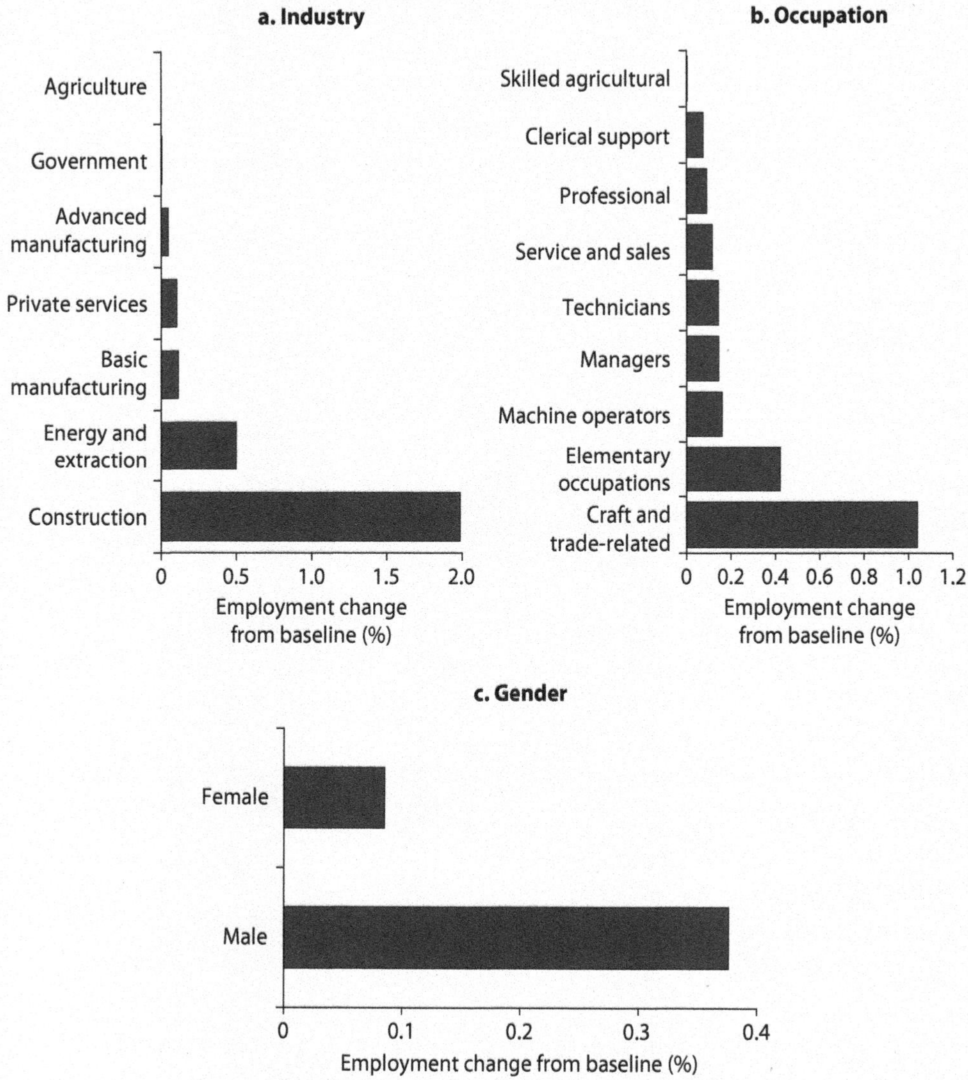

Source: Original figure for this publication based on World Bank 2022a.

Note: Estimates using the Multi-Regional Input-Output model from World Bank 2022a.

induced economic and development benefits, and social and environmental co-benefits. Across six project types covering wildfires, urban flooding, stormwater management, coastal flooding, urban heat islands, and drought, valuing all three dividend streams consistently transforms marginally viable projects into clearly high-return ones. This systematic undervaluation has also led to systematic underfinancing: many adaptation projects generate high economic returns even without concessional climate finance, but the structure of private benefit capture and public good spillovers means that private investment does not materialize without public co-investment or blended finance mechanisms. Governments can address this problem through property and betterment taxes that capture private beneficiaries' share of adaptation gains, public-private partnerships structured around de-risked project pipelines, and fiscal frameworks that integrate climate risk into public investment planning.

Reforming pension systems

Pension systems play an increasingly important role as populations age, providing old-age income security while shaping labor markets, national savings, and fiscal sustainability. In systems with large unfunded liabilities and generous civil service schemes, demographic pressure translates directly into rising pension deficits.

The core parametric levers for reform include raising the retirement age, better aligning benefits and contributions, expanding coverage, and shifting from defined benefits to defined contribution designs (refer to box 4.3). For instance, China announced a retirement age increase in 2024; Viet Nam is raising its retirement age incrementally through 2028; and Indonesia's pension legislation already includes provisions to reach age 65 by 2043. These steps head in the right direction, but more comprehensive reform remains necessary (OECD 2025)—particularly to avoid large deficits as defined benefit schemes mature.

The transition from defined benefit to defined contribution creates temporary fiscal pressure—that is, the need to continue financing existing liabilities while contributions accumulate in funded accounts—but the long-term result is stronger sustainability, prefunded liabilities, and higher national savings.

Box 4.3. Population aging and pension reform in East Asia and Pacific

The most pressing fiscal challenge associated with aging in East Asia and Pacific relates to the sustainability and coverage of old-age income security. Most countries face two simultaneous pressures: extending coverage to informal workers who will reach retirement without contributory pension entitlements, and reforming existing contributory schemes—especially those for civil servants—to address unsustainable unfunded liabilities.

Financing structures. In pay-as-you-go defined benefit schemes, the dominant model across East and Southeast Asia, rising old-age dependency ratios make exclusive reliance on payroll contributions increasingly untenable. Consequently, governments play a larger financing role, blurring the distinction between social insurance and social assistance, as seen in Japan and Mongolia. Defined contribution provident funds—found in Malaysia, Singapore, and Pacific Island countries—face a different challenge: adequacy at retirement, not structural deficit.

Contribution-benefit misalignment. As shown in chapter 1 (refer to figure 1.38, panel b), contribution rates in most East Asia and Pacific defined benefit pension schemes, except in Viet Nam, fall well below actuarially fair levels—the rate at which the present value of contributions equals the present value of promised benefits. This shortfall is the quantitative expression of unfunded pension liabilities.

Parametric reforms. Common priorities include raising retirement ages in line with life expectancy, adjusting overly generous benefits, adopting automatic price indexation, and increasing contribution rates that fall well below actuarially fair levels (refer to table B4.3.1). Reducing disparities between civil service and private sector schemes—such as in Thailand, where civil servant replacement rates are roughly three times higher—could improve both equity and fiscal sustainability.

Integrating formal and informal sectors. Many workers cycle between formal and informal employment, a pattern intensifying with gig work and labor mobility. Contributory pensions, social pensions, and voluntary savings schemes must be designed as an integrated system: social pensions should not crowd out voluntary contributions, and incentives for informal workers should not inadvertently encourage informality. Australia and Chile have addressed this need through a pension test that progressively reduces the social pension as contributory benefits rise. Applying such a mechanism in East Asia and Pacific could reduce the long-run cost of an adequate social pension while improving aggregate welfare.

(continued)

Box 4.3. Population aging and pension reform in East Asia and Pacific *(continued)*

TABLE B4.3.1 Parametric reforms to defined benefit schemes in East Asia and Pacific

Economy (scheme)	Retirement age increase	Reduction in target replacement rate	Move to automatic price indexation	Increased contribution rate
Cambodia (civil service)	x	x	x	x
Cambodia (private sector)	x	—	—	x
China	x[a]	—	x	—
Indonesia (civil service)	x	x	—	—
Indonesia (private sector)	—	—	—	x
Lao PDR	x	x	x	x
Malaysia (civil service)	—	—	—	—
Myanmar (civil service)	x	—	x	x
Philippines (civil service)	—	—	—	—
Philippines (private sector)	x	x	x	x
Thailand (civil service)	x	x	x	x
Thailand (private sector)	x	—	x	x
Viet Nam	x	x	x	—

Source: Original table for this publication.
Note: — = not available.
a. China announced that it would raise its retirement age in 2024.

Integrating civil service and private sector schemes. International practice increasingly favors integrating civil service and national pension schemes, which can reduce unfunded liabilities, improve labor mobility, and narrow disparities in retirement benefits. Among Organisation for Economic Co-operation and Development countries, only four of 27 still maintain parallel systems, down from 16 a few decades ago. In East Asia and Pacific, China, the Lao People's Democratic Republic, and Viet Nam have integrated pension systems, although with long transition periods. Cambodia and Indonesia have announced integration reforms but have not finalized the transition design. The Philippines and Thailand have not currently announced any integration plans.

Systemic reform. A shift from unfunded defined benefit to funded defined contribution design fully prefunds the pension liability and can raise national

(continued)

Box 4.3. Population aging and pension reform in East Asia and Pacific *(continued)*

savings, but it creates a transition deficit as legacy liabilities are financed simultaneously with the accumulation of individual accounts. Indonesia has announced its intention to implement systemic reform for its civil service scheme, although the legislative framework has yet to be finalized. Whether in defined benefit reserves or defined contribution accounts, investment policy matters significantly: Indonesia and Viet Nam currently invest more than 90 percent of reserves in government bonds, which erases the savings effect and gives governments access to a captive credit source they might otherwise not have.

A growing social pension is effectively inevitable given the scale of informal sector coverage gaps. The design imperative is to integrate social pensions with contributory schemes in ways that minimize costs and preserve incentives to formalize—separating the instruments aimed at poverty prevention from those aimed at consumption smoothing, and designing tapers carefully to avoid discouraging contributory participation.

Improving spending efficiency

The growth-enhancing role of fiscal policy will require more effective use of existing spending. Most EAP economies could achieve significant gains through sectoral reforms that improve the quality and targeting of public services, as well as through the rationalization of poorly targeted subsidies that often absorb substantial fiscal resources while delivering limited social or economic benefits. Improving spending efficiency can help create fiscal space for priority investments in human capital, infrastructure upgrades, climate adaptation, and social protection.

Sectoral reforms

Improving spending efficiency can expand effective fiscal space without requiring additional revenue, and experience in EAP demonstrates large gains from doing so. Some economies achieve strong outcomes relative to their level of public spending, whereas others spend more but achieve comparatively weak results. Policy choices and the regulatory environment largely explain this difference, confirming the importance of sectoral reforms in increasing the returns to public investment.

Experiences across the region demonstrate that higher spending alone does not guarantee better outcomes. Viet Nam's consistently strong performance on the

Programme for International Student Assessment (PISA), despite spending levels below many advanced economies, reflects a strong emphasis on teacher quality, accountability, and parent involvement (Afkar et al. 2023). Korea built world-class human capital by sequentially concentrating education spending at the primary level before expanding investment at higher levels of education, ensuring that each stage functioned effectively before scaling up further (World Bank 2018b). Thailand's expansion of universal health coverage paired increased funding with provider payment reforms and centralized pharmaceutical procurement, generating gains in both coverage and efficiency (Tangcharoensathien et al. 2011). As populations age and noncommunicable diseases become more prevalent, economies such as China and Thailand increasingly emphasize prevention, screening, early diagnosis, and care management to contain long-term health costs while preserving productivity (Debebe et al. 2026).

At the same time, several economies illustrate the costs of inefficient spending allocation. Despite substantial increases in education spending, Thailand's PISA scores have stagnated, partly reflecting an oversized network of small schools and insufficient spending at preprimary and secondary levels, which would have higher returns (Afkar et al. 2023; World Bank 2023c). Timor-Leste spends per student at levels broadly comparable to Indonesia, the Philippines, and Viet Nam, yet literacy and child survival outcomes remain significantly weaker, pointing to inefficiencies in teacher deployment and budget allocation rather than insufficient resources (World Bank 2023c). These experiences highlight that institutional quality, spending composition, and sectoral reforms are often as important as overall spending levels in determining development outcomes.

Subsidy rationalization

Redirecting spending from inefficient and regressive subsidies creates fiscal space for more productive and inclusive priorities—without expanding the overall fiscal envelope. Consumption and energy subsidies, in particular, tend to disproportionately benefit higher-income households while absorbing substantial fiscal resources that could instead support human capital development, infrastructure, and social protection. Redirecting even a portion of these expenditures to productive development spending would promote more inclusive growth without requiring a major expansion of overall government spending.

Well-targeted transfers are significantly more effective than generalized subsidies at reducing poverty and inequality (refer to figure 3.7 in chapter 3). In Indonesia, Malaysia, and Viet Nam, direct social transfers reduce poverty and inequality by far more per unit of currency spent than subsidies do—by a factor of three to six. As illustrated by Indonesia's 2005 fuel subsidy reform, temporary unconditional cash transfers under the Bantuan Langsung Tunai program, equivalent to about 15 percent of household consumption, more than compensated poor households for higher fuel prices, allowed households time to adjust spending patterns, and generated broader gains in community-wide expenditure (World Bank 2012).

Consolidating fragmented social programs and improving targeting through integrated beneficiary registries and digital delivery systems can reduce leakages and ensure that support reaches those most in need. Combined with broad-based indirect taxes (discussed in the next section), well-targeted transfers can achieve equity objectives more efficiently while preserving fiscal sustainability.

Domestic revenue mobilization

As EAP economies seek to finance growing spending needs, they face the challenge not only of raising more revenue but also of doing so in ways that are efficient, equitable, and growth-friendly. Broadening tax bases through the rationalization of value added tax (VAT) exemptions and zero-rated items, strengthening personal income taxation, increasing property tax revenues, and pricing environmental and health externalities can mobilize substantial fiscal resources while limiting economic distortions. Together, these reforms can help create the fiscal space needed to finance investments in human capital, infrastructure, social protection, and climate resilience.

Rationalizing value added tax exemptions and zero-rated items

Economies in the region could raise an additional 2 percent of GDP through more effective collection of goods and services taxes—the largest single revenue opportunity available to most EAP governments. The key lever involves broadening the tax base by rationalizing exemptions and reducing preferential treatment, not by raising statutory rates. The largest opportunities are concentrated in Malaysia, the Philippines, and Viet Nam, where goods and services tax revenues currently fall substantially below potential levels (refer to box 1.2 in chapter 1).

VAT is often viewed as regressive; however, in economies with high informality, VAT is more progressive than commonly assumed (as discussed in chapter 3). In Indonesia and the Philippines, informal consumption—largely outside the VAT net—accounts for a much larger share of total consumption among lower-income households than among higher-income groups. The high informal consumption of standard-rated items among poorer households implies that broadening the VAT base can raise revenue while maintaining progressivity (Bachas et al. 2024). As coverage expands and more consumers are brought into the tax net, this implicit progressivity may diminish. Nonetheless, deliberate VAT exemptions offer an ineffective and inefficient way to mitigate indirect tax impacts on the poor. The high informal consumption of exempt items means the poor do not benefit from the exemption; at the same time, exemptions mean forgoing considerable revenues from richer households (Wai-Poi et al. 2025).[2]

An alternative to VAT exemptions is to maintain a broad tax base while compensating vulnerable households through targeted transfers, as noted earlier, or through rebates. In practice, such instruments can achieve similar or better distributional outcomes than exemptions, which tend to be poorly targeted and distort the tax base (Wai-Poi et al. 2025). Although countries such as Brazil have introduced personalized VAT rates with point-of-sale or periodic rebates (refer to box 3.5 in chapter 3), simple mechanisms—such as VAT rebate vouchers calibrated to household income—can replicate the intended benefits of exemptions without requiring complex tracking of individual consumption (Bachas et al. 2024; Cebreiro-Gómez et al. 2022). This approach preserves revenue efficiency while strengthening equity, and has been implemented in practice, for example through Singapore's VAT voucher system (as discussed in chapter 3).[3]

Strengthening the personal income tax base

EAP economies have low personal income tax (PIT) revenues relative to income-level peers. High informality makes it difficult to identify taxable earners and verify their liabilities, but digitalization is reducing this constraint. Beyond informality, effective PIT rates are depressed by high filing thresholds, generous exemptions and deductions, and bracket structures that rarely reach top earners.

The top of the distribution offers the most tractable near-term opportunity. Because households in the richest income decile account for most PIT revenue, raising effective rates for higher earners does not require mitigating cash transfers. Governments can increase effective rates by reducing income exemptions and permitted deductions, adjusting bracket thresholds and rates, including all income sources (capital income and capital gains alongside labor income), and aligning the corporate income tax rate with the top PIT marginal rate to close avoidance channels.

Payroll taxes require separate treatment. Their design must avoid placing undue burdens on lower-income workers or discouraging labor formalization—a real risk where minimum contribution floors create high effective tax rates for marginal earners. Replacing minimum contribution floors with minimum income thresholds for contributing would reduce this distortion; modest increases in contribution rates or maximum contribution ceilings for higher earners could preserve revenue neutrality. Social security design is inherently complex, with coverage, adequacy, sustainability, and equity objectives frequently in tension. Any reform of contribution structures should be embedded in a broader review of social security effectiveness and sustainability.

Increasing property tax revenues

The property tax—although efficient, progressive, and administratively tractable—is the most underused revenue instrument in EAP. Property is visible, immobile, and concentrated in the ownership of higher-income households—attributes that make recurrent property taxes simultaneously less distortionary to labor and investment decisions, more progressive than most alternatives, and harder to evade.

The revenue gap is striking. Recurrent taxes on immovable property generate well below 0.5 percent of GDP in most EAP economies, against an average in Organisation for Economic Co-operation and Development countries of about 1.9 percent (Wai-Poi et al. 2025). Indonesia collects 0.10 percent of GDP, Thailand 0.20 percent, Viet Nam 0.05 percent, and Malaysia effectively nothing from recurrent property taxes. In the Philippines, the regional outlier, property taxes account for nearly 9 percent of local tax revenues; however, even there, collection rates reach only about 50 percent of assessed liabilities, and the tax base rests on outdated valuations, leading to property tax collections accounting for only 0.47 percent of GDP in 2020.

Beyond political resistance from property owners, economies face consistent obstacles: incomplete land registers, assessed values disconnected from market prices and updated infrequently if at all, and limited administrative capacity at the local government level where property taxes are typically assigned. Closing even a fraction of the gap with structural peers would meaningfully expand fiscal space, particularly for subnational governments responsible for service delivery.

Pricing externalities through carbon and health taxes

Carbon pricing, through carbon taxes or emissions trading systems, can mobilize substantial and stable revenues while addressing environmental externalities. Establishing a predictable and gradually increasing carbon price trajectory, however, is critical to guide private investment and avoid policy uncertainty. In EAP, economies such as Singapore have implemented a carbon tax with a preannounced path of increases, increasing credibility and enabling firms to adjust investment decisions over time. China has developed the world's largest emissions trading system, demonstrating the feasibility of scaling up carbon pricing instruments in large emerging economies. Evidence shows that well-designed carbon pricing can generate significant fiscal revenues while supporting decarbonization objectives (World Bank 2024).

Health taxes—particularly on tobacco, alcohol, and sugar-sweetened beverages—can raise revenue while addressing negative health externalities. These taxes are relatively easy to administer, have low efficiency costs, and are good for health. Several EAP economies provide examples: the Philippines significantly increased excise taxes on tobacco and alcohol, generating revenues exceeding 1 percent of GDP while helping finance universal health coverage, and Thailand has long used earmarked excise taxes to fund health promotion initiatives (Kaiser et al. 2016; World Bank 2023c). Together, carbon and health taxes illustrate how fiscal policy can expand revenue mobilization while remedying negative externalities, particularly when supported by transparent communication, predictable policy frameworks, and effective administration.

Fiscal capacity and public support

The growth-enhancing role of fiscal policy also requires stronger institutions and greater public trust. Improvements in tax administration, public financial management, and the use of digital technologies can enhance both revenue mobilization and spending efficiency. At the same time, credible fiscal frameworks that clearly link additional revenues to visible spending priorities can help strengthen public support for reform. Ultimately, the success of fiscal reforms depends not only on their technical design but also on their political feasibility and the ability of governments to build broad-based coalitions in support of change.

Improving spending efficiency and revenue mobilization through reforms and technology

Government spending and taxation are jointly determined. The economically optimal fiscal scale is reached when the marginal benefit of the last dollar spent equals the marginal cost of raising it through taxation (Barro 1990). That optimal scale is not fixed but rather expands as the effectiveness of public spending improves and the cost of revenue collection falls. Both are shaped by institutional reform and technological investment (refer to box 4.4).

Box 4.4. From low-revenue traps to high-capacity states: A simple framework of taxation and spending

East Asia and Pacific economies risk remaining in low-revenue, low-spending equilibriums despite large unmet needs for public goods. This box presents a simple framework for determining fiscal outcomes by the interaction between the marginal cost of raising revenue and the marginal benefit of public spending, both shaped by institutions and technology.

Following Barro (1990), consider a government choosing spending G financed by distortionary taxation T, where output depends on private inputs and productive public services: $Y = F(K, L, G; \theta)$.[a] The variable represents institutional improvements or new technologies that facilitate revenue collection or increase the effectiveness of public spending. The planner's problem yields a simple marginal condition:

$$MB_G\,(G; \theta) = MC_T\,(T; \theta),$$

where MB_G is the marginal benefit of public spending, and MC_T is the marginal excess burden of taxation, including distortions to labor supply, investment, and the costs of evasion and enforcement.

Two canonical properties shape these schedules. MB_G is downward sloping: returns to public inputs diminish as higher-return projects are exhausted (Barro 1990). MC_T is upward sloping: distortions rise as tax rates increase, consistent with the classical optimal taxation literature (Diamond and Mirrlees 1971a, 1971b; Ramsey 1927). The equilibrium is determined by the intersection of the two curves, which endogenously defines the optimal scale of government.

At low levels of spending, the marginal benefit of additional public expenditure is high; at low levels of taxation, the marginal cost of raising additional revenue is relatively low. Consequently, the equilibrium occurs at a positive level of taxation and public spending. Institutional reform and technological adoption can shift both marginal schedules through distinct but complementary channels. Improvements in tax administration, enforcement capacity, and digitalization reduce the marginal cost of raising revenue—even though some new technologies can make it easier to avoid taxes; and better public investment management, targeting mechanisms, and monitoring systems increase the marginal benefit of public spending. Together, these channels can shift the economy to a higher-revenue, higher-spending equilibrium that strengthens fiscal capacity (refer to figure B4.4.1).

(continued)

Box 4.4. From low-revenue traps to high-capacity states: A simple framework of taxation and spending *(continued)*

Government spending and taxation are jointly determined, but the optimal fiscal scale is not fixed; as public spending becomes more effective and revenue collection more efficient, economies can sustain higher levels of taxation and expenditure.

FIGURE B4.4.1 Marginal benefit of spending and marginal cost of taxation

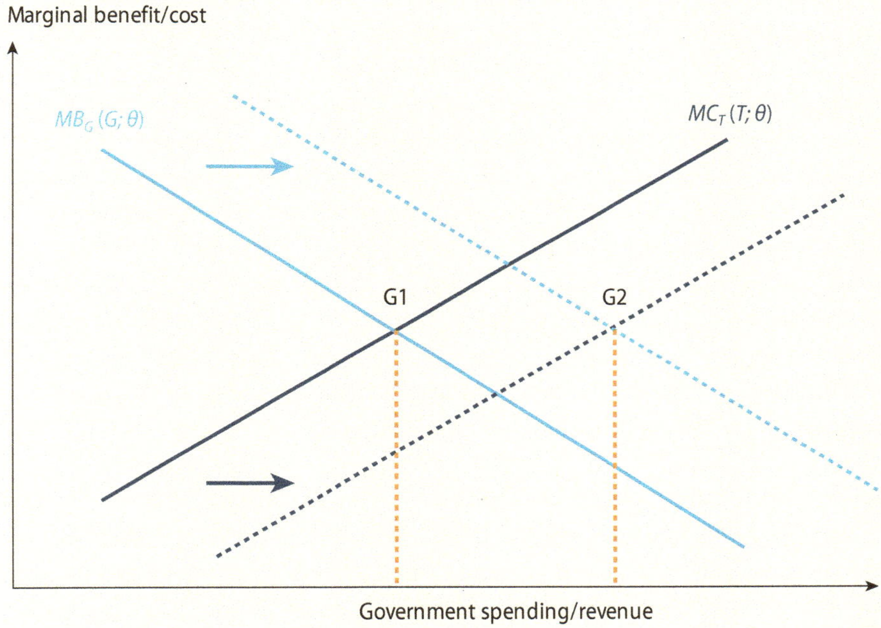

Source: Original figure for this publication.

a. Abstracting from deficits and debt, $G = T$.

Institutional reforms

Strengthening public investment management can substantially raise the effectiveness of spending. Transparent procurement systems, standardized project appraisal, and independent evaluation help reduce leakages and improve project selection. In developing EAP, leakages in public investment have been estimated at 50–60 percent of funds invested in some economies, implying that institutional failure cuts the effective return to a dollar of spending roughly in half before it reaches its intended purpose (Riera-Crichton et al. 2014; World Bank 2018a).

Taxation reforms such as simplified payment procedures and risk-based audits can lower compliance costs and strengthen enforcement. Bribery demands, arbitrary audits, and opaque enforcement increase compliance costs and discourage participation in the formal economy (Junquera-Varela et al. 2017). Firms in the Lao People's Democratic Republic and Viet Nam spend 540 and 362 hours per year, respectively, meeting tax obligations, compared to 67 hours in Singapore (World Bank Group and PwC 2017).

Institutional reforms following the Asian financial crisis strengthened fiscal institutions across much of EAP, but the reform momentum has slowed. In the decade after the crisis, Country Policy and Institutional Assessment scores on budget management and revenue mobilization improved for most EAP economies eligible for assistance from the International Development Association.[4] These gains reflected a wave of first-generation reforms, including fiscal responsibility laws (Indonesia, 2003), medium-term expenditure frameworks (Viet Nam, 2016; Philippines, 2022), and the broad expansion of Public Expenditure and Financial Accountability–assessed Public Financial Management systems (IMF 2016, 2023; PEFA Secretariat 2022; World Bank 2008). Repeated Public Expenditure and Financial Accountability assessments for economies such as Cambodia, Indonesia, the Philippines, and Viet Nam confirm measurable improvements in budget credibility, revenue administration, and fiscal transparency over this period.

However, progress has broadly plateaued since the mid-2010s. Country Policy and Institutional Assessment scores have remained flat or drifted marginally lower across most countries, and Public Expenditure and Financial Accountability assessments continue to reveal persistent weaknesses in external audit effectiveness, legislative scrutiny, and multiyear fiscal planning.[5] Myanmar stands out as a case of outright institutional reversal following the 2021 political crisis. The pattern points to a region that successfully captured first-generation institutional gains but faces growing difficulty advancing toward higher-order reforms—precisely the reforms needed to shift the revenue-expenditure frontier most significantly.

Technological improvements

Technological change can strengthen fiscal capacity by improving both revenue mobilization and the effectiveness of public spending. Technological improvements such as e-filing, e-payments, e-invoicing, automated audits, and integrated taxpayer databases allow governments to identify taxpayers more effectively, verify liabilities, and improve compliance. Evidence suggests that the largest fiscal gains come from technologies that generate verifiable third-party transaction trails and use them for automated cross-checking and enforcement actions. Electronic invoicing systems in

Ethiopia, for example, increased VAT revenues significantly, and computerized VAT risk analysis in Pakistan reduced fraudulent refund claims by half (Bachas et al., forthcoming; Mascagni et al. 2021; Okunogbe and Tourek 2024). Digital systems can also reduce discretionary interactions between taxpayers and tax officials, improving transparency and limiting opportunities for collusion and evasion.

Digitalization can also increase the effectiveness and efficiency of public spending. Linking tax systems with digital identification systems, payment platforms, and cross-government databases allows governments to identify beneficiaries more accurately, automate transfers, and monitor program implementation in real time. Estonia's X-Road platform, for example, reduced administrative costs by an estimated 2 percent of GDP through automated data exchange and highly efficient online public services.[6] Digital project monitoring tools can also improve transparency and reduce cost overruns in public infrastructure projects, as observed in Honduras and Thailand (CoST Infrastructure Transparency Initiative 2023; Straub et al. 2026).

Linking revenue mobilization to spending priorities through credible fiscal frameworks

Even well-designed reforms can fail without credibility and public support. Their immediate and certain costs but diffuse and delayed benefits make tax increases particularly difficult to implement. When citizens do not trust the government to translate revenue into better services, they resist contributing, and that resistance is individually rational (Besley and Persson 2013). The collective outcome, however, presents a low-level equilibrium trap: low revenues constrain service delivery, poor services erode trust and compliance, and depressed compliance further limits fiscal capacity. Breaking out of this trap requires mechanisms that make the tax-spending link observable and credible.

Three instruments are particularly effective. First, earmarking revenue to visible spending priorities—such as a VAT surcharge for health insurance or a fuel levy for road maintenance—converts abstract fiscal promises into verifiable commitments that citizens can monitor. Second, front-loading improvements in spending efficiency—demonstrating better service delivery before asking for more revenue—builds the compliance culture on which deeper fiscal capacity rests. Third, anchoring reforms in a medium-term fiscal framework (MTFF) moves policy beyond annual budgeting cycles, establishes multiyear revenue and expenditure targets, and allows the tax-spending link to become observable over time (Junquera-Varela et al. 2017).

MTFFs can strengthen the credibility of reform by making the link between revenue mobilization and spending commitments observable over time. As discussed in chapter 2, MTFFs are most effective when they function as binding operational anchors that integrate medium-term fiscal objectives into annual budget decisions. By establishing credible multiyear fiscal paths, they help align fiscal sustainability with development objectives while enhancing accountability and transparency.

In practice, many MTFFs in EAP remain weakly integrated into the budget process. Medium-term targets are frequently revised, implemented with discretion, or based on overly optimistic projections, which limits their credibility as fiscal anchors. Weak enforcement mechanisms and limited external oversight further reduce their effectiveness. Strengthening MTFFs requires better integration into budget decisions; simple, flexible fiscal rules equipped with well-designed escape clauses; and independent fiscal councils to provide external scrutiny (refer to boxes 4.5 and 4.6).

Box 4.5. Improving fiscal rules in East Asia and Pacific: The role of escape clauses

Fiscal rules are most effective when they are simple enough to monitor, flexible enough to accommodate shocks, and credible enough to function as binding policy anchors. Without adequate design, rules risk being ignored or repeatedly revised, which weakens rather than strengthens fiscal discipline.

Economies in East Asia and Pacific generally have simple and transparent, but weakly enforceable, fiscal rules. Most economies rely on observable deficit or debt ceilings; however, Cambodia, Indonesia, Malaysia, Thailand, and Viet Nam do not incorporate cyclical adjustments or automatic correction mechanisms. Responses to shocks remain largely discretionary, rules are frequently suspended, and paths to returning to compliance are rarely defined. In practice, adherence depends more on political commitment than on binding institutional constraints.

(continued)

Box 4.5. Improving fiscal rules in East Asia and Pacific: The role of escape clauses *(continued)*

Well-designed escape clauses address this weakness. Over the past two decades, escape clauses have become an increasingly common feature of fiscal frameworks globally (refer to figure B4.5.1). When well-designed, they provide institutionalized flexibility—reducing discretion without rigidity, and specifying clear, verifiable conditions for activation alongside credible return paths. By reducing uncertainty about how rules operate during crises, they support more countercyclical fiscal policy, limit the amplification of downturns, and preserve market confidence (Davoodi et al. 2022; Eyraud et al. 2018).

The adoption of fiscal rules with escape clauses has become increasingly common over the past two decades.

FIGURE B4.5.1 Number of fiscal rules with and without escape clauses

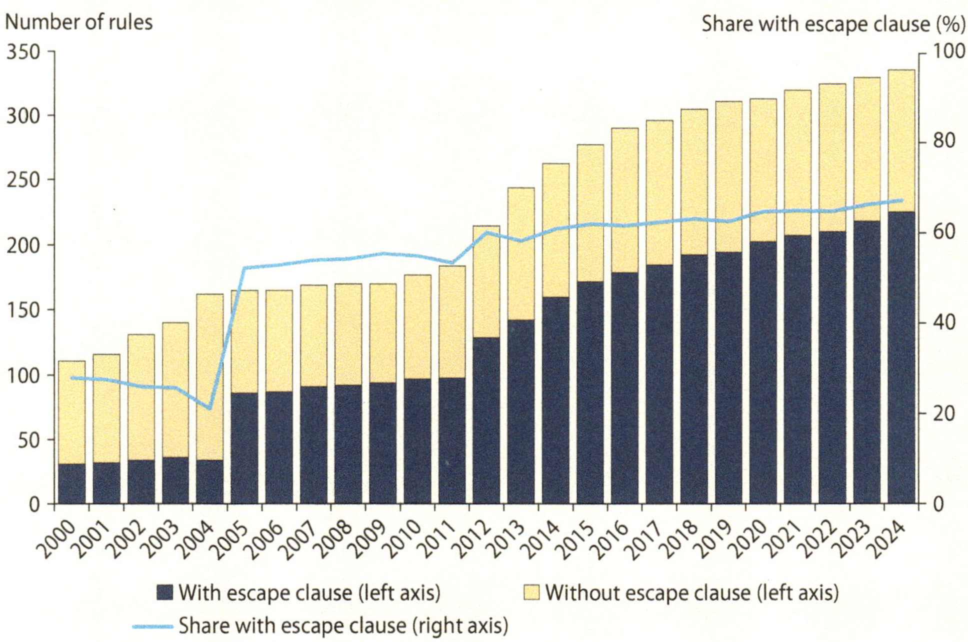

Source: Original figure for this publication based on Alonso et al. 2025b.

Box 4.6. Fiscal councils and fiscal credibility

Fiscal councils strengthen the credibility of fiscal frameworks by providing independent assessment of fiscal projections and compliance with fiscal rules. They reduce optimism bias in forecasts, increase transparency, and anchor market expectations. Their adoption has increased significantly over the past decade, particularly among emerging market and developing economies (refer to figure B4.6.1).

Evidence from Europe and Latin America shows that fiscal councils improve compliance with fiscal rules and reduce optimism bias in fiscal forecasts (Beetsma et al. 2019). Fiscal council adoption is also associated with lower sovereign spreads in low- and middle-income countries, particularly those with operationally independent councils (refer to figure B4.6.2 and table B4.6.1). Chile's Consejo Fiscal Autónomo monitors compliance with the structural balance rule and publicly evaluates deviations from targets. Peru's Fiscal Council assesses macrofiscal projections and debt sustainability risks.

The adoption of independent fiscal councils has increased in EMDEs.

FIGURE B4.6.1 Number of independent fiscal councils, by type of economy, 1985–2024

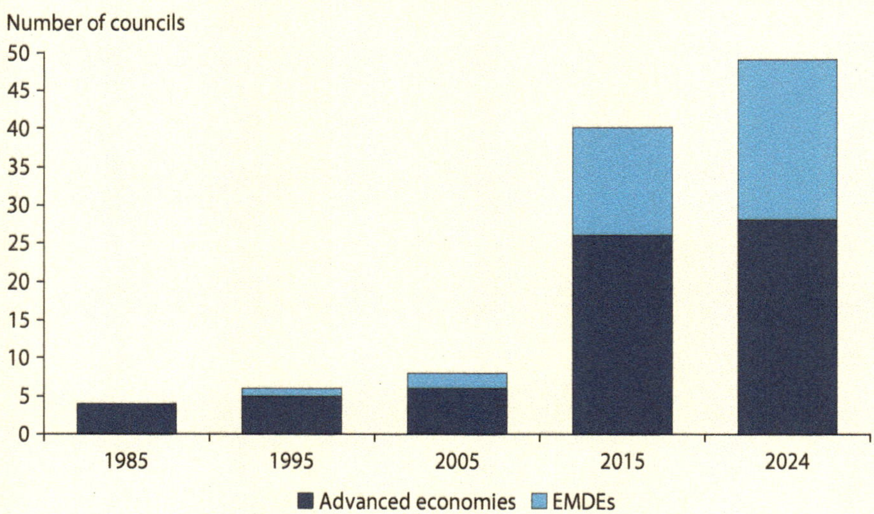

Source: Original figure for this publication based on Alonso et al. 2025a.

Note: Independent fiscal councils are defined as institutions that satisfy at least one of two criteria: legal independence or operational independence. The figure excludes Mexico, North Macedonia, and Uganda—the only countries with fiscal councils that do not meet either criterion. EMDEs = emerging market and developing economies.

(continued)

Box 4.6. Fiscal councils and fiscal credibility *(continued)*

Most East Asia and Pacific economies either lack fiscal councils entirely or rely on advisory bodies housed within ministries of finance with limited independence and narrow mandates. The Republic of Korea is the only economy in East Asia and Pacific with an independent fiscal council. For the rest of the region, implementing credible fiscal councils—with operational independence, clear mandates, adequate technical capacity, and transparent public communication—could transform fiscal rules from commitments on paper into enforceable policy anchors.

Fiscal council adoption is associated with a significant and sustained reduction in sovereign spreads for EMDEs.

FIGURE B4.6.2 Association between fiscal council adoption and sovereign spread

ATT on spread, by horizon

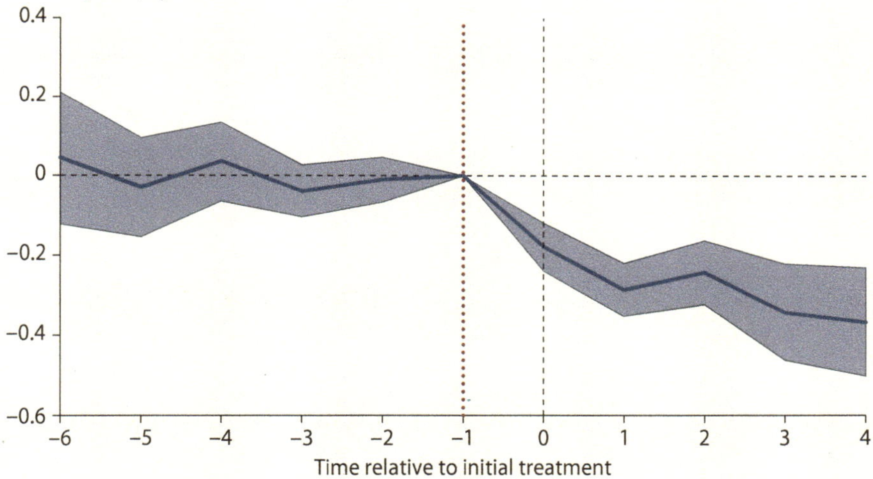

Sources: Original figure for this publication based on Alonso et al. 2025a; proprietary data from J.P. Morgan EMBI Global; World Economic Outlook (WEO) Database, International Monetary Fund, https://www.imf.org/en/publications/sprolls/world-economic-outlook-databases; Worldwide Governance Indicators (WGI), World Bank, https://www.worldbank.org/en/publication/worldwide-governance-indicators.

Note: The figure shows interaction-weighted difference-in-differences estimates of the effect of fiscal council adoption on sovereign spreads for 41 EMDEs (2000–19), following Wooldridge (2021). The plotted blue line shows ATT estimates; the shaded band shows 90 percent confidence intervals. The dotted vertical line marks treatment onset ($t = 0$); estimates are normalized to zero in the year before adoption ($t = -1$). The dependent variable is the log of year-end sovereign spread. The figure includes the following East Asian economies: Indonesia, Malaysia, Mongolia, Philippines, Thailand, and Viet Nam. Countries that adopt fiscal councils during the sample period constitute the treated group; never-adopters serve as the control group. Always-treated countries (those with a fiscal council throughout the entire sample) are excluded. Standard errors are clustered by country. Controls include lagged gross debt (percent of GDP), lagged government effectiveness index (WGI), and the EMBI global spread. ATT = average treatment effect on the treated; EMDEs = emerging market and developing economies.

(continued)

Box 4.6. Fiscal councils and fiscal credibility *(continued)*

TABLE B4.6.1 Association between fiscal council adoption and reduction in sovereign spread

	Dependent variable: log sovereign spread			
	(1)	(2)	(3)	(4)
Fiscal council	−0.036	0.087*	−0.092*	0.029
	(0.057)	(0.047)	(0.052)	(0.036)
Fiscal council × Operational independence		−0.179**		−0.175***
		(0.067)		(0.049)
Debt-to-GDP (lagged)			0.005**	0.005**
			(0.002)	(0.002)
Cyclical component of GDP			1.336	1.254
			(0.798)	(0.799)
Government effectiveness (lagged)			−0.008***	−0.008***
			(0.002)	(0.002)
Lagged spread	Yes	Yes	Yes	Yes
Year FEs	Yes	Yes	Yes	Yes
Country FEs	Yes	Yes	Yes	Yes
Observations	547	547	510	510
Countries	44	44	44	44
R^2	0.763	0.764	0.782	0.783

Source: Original table for this publication.
Note: The dependent variable is the logarithm of sovereign spreads. The sample covers annual observations from 2000 to 2019. All specifications include country and year fixed effects. Standard errors are clustered at the country level and shown in parentheses. FE = fixed effects.
$^*p < .10$ $^{**}p < .05$ $^{***}p < .01$

The political economy of fiscal reforms

Even with a strong technical case, making fiscal reforms is politically difficult. The core challenge is designing a package in which winners outnumber losers—or in which losses are small enough to be acceptable—and communicating that design credibly to a skeptical public.

A critical first step is making implicit fiscal costs and benefits visible. Tax expenditures—corporate income tax holidays, personal income tax deductions, and VAT exemptions—appear as forgone revenues rather than explicit spending and receive far less scrutiny than equivalent outlays. Populations similarly misunderstand subsidy incidence: in Malaysia in 2019, the richest 20 percent of households received the same share of total fuel subsidy benefits (29 percent) as the poorest 40 percent, yet a national survey found that only 38 percent of respondents correctly believed the rich benefited more; moreover, those least likely to benefit in reality (the poorest quintile) were the most likely to believe they benefited disproportionately (World Bank 2023b). In the United States, survey respondents believe that 20 percent of households pay the top PIT rate, against a true figure of 1 percent, and that 25 percent pay no PIT, against a true figure of 44 percent (Stantcheva 2021). Misperceptions of this scale represent the norm rather than the exception, and they directly shape reform feasibility.

Public concerns about cash transfers are a second source of misperception that reform communications must address. Policy makers and the public frequently worry that transfers discourage work or increase spending on alcohol and tobacco. The empirical evidence does not support either concern (refer to box 3.3 in chapter 3). Systematic reviews find little to no effect of well-designed cash transfers on labor supply in developing countries; for example, studies from Indonesia and the Philippines find no impact on work behavior for either men or women (Banerjee et al. 2017). A global review finds no evidence of increased spending on alcohol and tobacco (Evans and Popova 2017).

Perceptions data can be invaluable in calibrating reform communications. In Indonesia, surveys show that the public cares more about reducing inequality than accelerating growth, and that job creation is the most popular mechanism for achieving that reduction—suggesting that the government's plan to redirect fuel subsidies to infrastructure should emphasize employment benefits rather than aggregate growth (World Bank 2015). The same analysis finds that linking increased revenues to health, education, and social protection spending significantly increases public support for progressive tax reforms. A study of 12 middle-income countries confirms the pattern: baseline support for fuel subsidy removal is low, but support doubles or triples when reform is packaged with credible compensatory policies (Hoy et al. 2023).

EAP presents a specific communications challenge. Across the region, attitudes reflect what Cho et al. (2025) describe as a "productivist mindset," one emphasizing economic growth, labor force participation, and individual self-reliance over collective welfare provision. Most EAP economies sit above the global average (approximately 40 percent, consistent across income levels) in the share of respondents who believe individuals rather than governments are responsible for their own welfare, with shares particularly high in Mongolia, the Philippines, and Viet Nam (refer to figure 3.26 in chapter 3). EAP economies—particularly China, Indonesia, and Viet Nam—also prioritize work over leisure more than comparator countries at the same income level. Reform communications that frame expanded social spending as an investment in individual productivity and resilience, rather than as welfare dependency, are more likely to build durable public support in this context. Box 4.7 draws out lessons from international fuel subsidy reform experience discussed in chapter 3 in more detail.

Box 4.7. International experience of fuel subsidy reforms

Fuel subsidy reform is among the most politically difficult fiscal reforms, but a substantial body of international experience points to consistent design and communications lessons.

The political economy challenge. The negative consequences of energy subsidies are well-documented: they are regressive, distortionary, fiscally costly, and environmentally harmful. The political problem is that their benefits are visible and immediate whereas their costs—borne by the public through the state budget—are diffuse and opaque. Inchauste and Victor (2017), reviewing over 30 reform episodes, identify two dominant political economy problems: mitigating opposition from organized interest groups when subsidies are concentrated, and credibly compensating the broader public when benefits are widely diffused. The latter is more difficult but also more common across East Asia and Pacific.

The binding condition: credible commitment. As noted in the main text, support for subsidy removal doubles or triples when reform comes with credible compensatory policies (Hoy et al. 2023). The key mechanism is credibility: subsidies are embedded in the social contract, and reform requires demonstrating, before removal of subsidies, that the government can deliver alternative benefits. Those benefits can be cash or in-kind; what matters is citizens' confidence that the commitment will be honored.

(continued)

Box 4.7. International experience of fuel subsidy reforms *(continued)*

Social protection as a precondition. In every successful reform episode reviewed by Inchauste and Victor (2017) and Mukherjee et al. (2023), reformers laid the groundwork for better-targeted social assistance before removing subsidies. Over five months, Indonesia collected new targeting data covering 30 percent of the population to support the temporary cash compensation program in 2005; during the following decade, this database evolved into the backbone of a social protection system that enabled reform episodes in 2008, 2013, and 2014–15, and supported the COVID-19 response. A review of 24 reform episodes in 18 countries finds that 60 percent created new cash transfer programs where none existed and that those programs created in earlier episodes were expanded in later ones (Mukherjee et al. 2023).

Communications. Effective communication is consistently identified as a decisive factor. Indonesia's successful 2005 and 2014–15 reforms were accompanied by coordinated, professional communications campaigns—including participation by prominent economists and public figures, fact-driven messaging (for example, the number of schools fundable with annual subsidy savings), and cross-government alignment. The failed 2012 episode had none of those features: no communications strategy, no link to popular spending priorities, and no response to sustained media criticism. Jordan's 2011 reform involved broad stakeholder consultations and a large public information campaign; half a decade later, failure to socialize a personal income tax reform led to the prime minister's resignation. The contrast in both cases illustrates that political capital built through good reform communication can also rapidly erode with its absence.

Windows of opportunity. Reforms cluster around periods of falling energy prices (when the fiscal cost of reform is low) or energy price spikes (when the fiscal cost of inaction is high). Of 24 recent reform episodes reviewed, 20 occurred between 2008 and 2012. Ukraine demonstrates the feasibility of a very large (sixfold) price adjustment even in a difficult geopolitical environment, when the rapid scaling of cash transfers provides credible compensation.

Conclusion

EAP's growth-enabling fiscal approach—low tax rates, spending within means, and comparatively high public investment in infrastructure—supported decades of rapid growth, macroeconomic stability, and poverty reduction. By taxing little and spending within their means, most economies in EAP successfully transitioned to middle-income status through private investment and export-led growth. This approach also led, however, to underinvestment in health, education, social protection, and climate adaptation. Consequently, growth has slowed, becoming less resilient and less inclusive, and putting the region's high-income aspirations increasingly at risk. To achieve its development ambitions, EAP will need to transition to a new growth-enhancing fiscal compact in which the state plays a stronger role in supporting productivity, resilience, and inclusion.

That transition involves three mutually reinforcing pillars, outlined in this chapter. The first is to prioritize spending on human capital, infrastructure, climate adaptation, and social protection—areas that generate strong positive externalities, crowd in private investment, and reduce persistent inequalities in access to opportunity. The second is to improve the efficiency and effectiveness of domestic revenue mobilization through broader indirect taxes, stronger property taxation, and taxes on negative externalities, while minimizing distortions to investment and formal employment. The third is to strengthen the institutional and political foundations needed to sustain reform over time. Institutional reforms and digital technologies can improve spending efficiency, strengthen revenue mobilization, and increase the credibility and political feasibility of reform. The current fiscal approach served EAP well. Delivering on the region's higher ambitions will require a more efficient and proactive fiscal state.

Notes

1. Governments have a growing realization of the need to do so, not only because of rising physical climate change risks but also because the International Monetary Fund, World Bank, and other donors are demanding better understanding of those risks. Donors are also helping to highlight the links between reducing climate risk and the development benefits of doing so—from community-level benefits (income and welfare) to national-level benefits (reduced fiscal, trade, financial sector, and debt sustainability risks).
2. Over time, a sustainable and equitable revenue system can combine indirect taxes with stronger direct taxation, including personal income and property taxes.
3. Government of Singapore Ministry of Finance, "GST Voucher: Overview," https://www.govbenefits.gov.sg/about-us/gst-voucher/overview/.

4. World Bank DataBank, "CPIA Efficiency of Revenue Mobilization Rating," https://data.worldbank.org/indicator/IQ.CPA.REVN.XQ; "CPIA Quality of Budgetary and Financial Management Rating," https://data.worldbank.org/indicator/IQ.CPA.FINQ.XQ.
5. Based on Public Expenditure and Financial Accountability, "Assessments," https://www.pefa.org/assessments, for the following assessment rounds: Cambodia, 2010, 2015, 2021; Indonesia, 2008, 2012, 2017; Myanmar, 2013, 2020; the Philippines, 2010, 2016; Thailand, 2009; and Viet Nam, 2011, 2024.
6. e-Estonia, "X-Road—Interoperability Services," https://e-estonia.com/solutions/interoperability-services/x-road/.

References

Acosta-Ormaechea, Santiago, and Atsuyoshi Morozumi. 2013. "Can a Government Enhance Long-Run Growth by Changing the Composition of Public Expenditure?" IMF Working Paper No. 13/162, International Monetary Fund. https://www.imf.org/external/pubs/ft/wp/2013/wp13162.pdf.

Afkar, Rythia, Tara Béteille, Mary E. Breeding, et al. 2023. *Fixing the Foundation: Teachers and Basic Education in East Asia and Pacific*. World Bank East Asia and Pacific Regional Report. World Bank. http://hdl.handle.net/10986/40332.

Aligishiev, Zamid, Emanuele Massetti, and Matthieu Bellon. 2022. *Macro-Fiscal Implications of Adaptation to Climate Change*. IMF Staff Climate Note 2022/002. International Monetary Fund. https://doi.org/10.5089/9798400201608.066.

Alonso, Virginia, Clara Arroyo, Ozlem Aydin, et al. 2025a. "Fiscal Council Dataset: The 2024 Update." Fiscal Affairs Department, International Monetary Fund. https://www.imf.org/-/media/files/data/fiscal-council-docs/fiscal-council-database-technical-manual-2024.pdf.

Alonso, Virginia, Clara Arroyo, Ozlem Aydin, et al. 2025b. "Fiscal Rules Dataset: 1985–2024." International Monetary Fund. https://www.imf.org/en/topics/fiscal-policies/fiscal-rules-dataset.

Bachas, Pierre, Lucie Gadenne, and Anders Jensen. 2024. "Informality, Consumption Taxes, and Redistribution." *Review of Economic Studies* 91 (5): 2604–34. https://doi.org/10.1093/restud/rdad095.

Bachas, Pierre, Oyebola Okunogbe, Mahvish Shaukat, and Dario Tortarolo. Forthcoming. *Raising Revenue Right: A Roadmap to Domestic Resource Mobilization*. Policy Research Report. World Bank.

Banerjee, Abhijit, Rema Hanna, Gabriel E. Kreindler, and Benjamin Olken. 2017. "Debunking the Stereotype of the Lazy Welfare Recipient: Evidence from Cash Transfer Programs." *World Bank Research Observer* 32 (2). http://hdl.handle.net/10986/31221.

Barro, Robert J. 1990. "Government Spending in a Simple Model of Endogenous Growth." *Journal of Political Economy* 98 (S5): 103–25. https://doi.org/10.1086/261726.

Beetsma, Roel M. W. J., Xavier Debrun, Xiangming Fang, et al. 2019. "Independent Fiscal Councils: Recent Trends and Performance." *European Journal of Political Economy* 57 (March): 53–69.

Besley, Timothy, and Torsten Persson. 2013. "Taxation and Development." Chapter 2 in *Handbook of Public Economics*, Vol. 5, edited by Alan J. Auerbach, Raj Chetty, Martin Feldstein, and Emmanuel Saez. North Holland.

Cebreiro-Gómez, Ana, Colin Clavey, Marcello Estevao, Jonathan Leigh-Pemberton, and Benjamin Stewart. 2022. "Digital Services Tax: Country Practice and Technical Challenges." Equitable Growth, Finance and Institutions Insight. World Bank. http://hdl.handle.net/10986/36840.

Chai, Qimin, Fu Sha, Wen Xinyuan, et al. 2019. "Financial Needs in Implementing China's Nationally Determined Contribution to Address Climate Change by 2030." *China Population, Resources and Environment* 29 (4): 1–9. https://caod.oriprobe.com/articles/56479871/Financial_needs_in_implementing_China_s_nationally.htm.

Cho, Yoonyoung, Robert Palacios, and Matthew Wai-Poi. 2025. "Why Social Protection Matters for Inclusive Growth in East Asia and the Pacific." Unpublished working paper.

CoST Infrastructure Transparency Initiative. 2023. "Business Plan 2017–2020." CoST Thailand. https://infrastructuretransparency.org/resource/cost-2017-2020-business-plan/.

Davoodi, Hamid R., Paul Elger, Alexandra Fotiou, et al. 2022. "Fiscal Rules and Fiscal Councils: Recent Trends and Performance During the COVID-19 Pandemic." IMF Working Paper No. 22/11, International Monetary Fund.

Debebe, Zelalem, Damien de Walque, Young Eun Kim, et al. 2026. *A Healthy Future: Primary Health Care and the Chronic Disease Epidemic in East Asia and Pacific.* East Asia and Pacific Development Studies. World Bank. https://doi.org/10.1596/978-1-4648-2284-1.

Diamond, Peter A., and James A. Mirrlees. 1971a. "Optimal Taxation and Public Production I: Production Efficiency." *American Economic Review* 61 (1): 8–27.

Diamond, Peter A., and James A. Mirrlees. 1971b. "Optimal Taxation and Public Production II: Tax Rules." *American Economic Review* 61 (3): 261–78.

Evans, David K., and Anna Popova. 2017. "Cash Transfers and Temptation Goods." *Economic Development and Cultural Change* 65 (2).

Eyraud, Luc, Xavier Debrun, Andrew Hodge, Victor Duarte Lledó, and Catherine A. Pattillo. 2018. "Second-Generation Fiscal Rules: Balancing Simplicity, Flexibility, and Enforceability." IMF Staff Discussion Note 2018/004, International Monetary Fund. https://doi.org/10.5089/9781484350683.006.

Hoy, Christopher, Yeon Soo Kim, Minh Nguyen, Mariano Sosa, and Sailesh Tiwari. 2023. "Building Public Support for Reducing Fossil Fuel Subsidies: Evidence Across 12 Middle-Income Countries." Policy Research Working Paper 10615, World Bank. https://doi.org/10.1596/1813-9450-10615.

IMF (International Monetary Fund). 2016. *Vietnam: 2016 Article IV Consultation.* IMF Country Report No. 16/240. International Monetary Fund. https://www.elibrary.imf.org/view/journals/002/2016/240/002.2016.issue-240-en.xml.

IMF (International Monetary Fund, Fiscal Affairs Department). 2022. "Samoa: Technical Assistance Report—Climate Macroeconomic Assessment Program." IMF Staff Country Report 2022/083. IMF. https://doi.org/10.5089/9798400205569.002.

IMF (International Monetary Fund). 2023. "The Medium-Term Fiscal Framework for the Philippines." *Philippines: Selected Issues* 2023 (415). IMF Asia and Pacific Department. https://www.elibrary.imf.org/view/journals/002/2023/415/article-A002-en.xml.

Inchauste, Gabriela, and David G. Victor, eds. 2017. *The Political Economy of Energy Subsidy Reform*. Directions in Development. World Bank.

Junquera-Varela, Raúl Félix, Marijn Verhoeven, Gangadhar P. Shukla, Bernard Haven, Rajul Awasthi, and Blanca Moreno-Dodson. 2017. *Strengthening Domestic Resource Mobilization: Moving from Theory to Practice in Low- and Middle-Income Countries*. Directions in Development. World Bank. http://hdl.handle.net/10986/27265.

Kaiser, Kai, Caryn Bredenkamp, and Robert Iglesias. 2016. *Sin Tax Reform in the Philippines: Transforming Public Finance, Health, and Governance for More Inclusive Development*. Directions in Development. World Bank. http://hdl.handle.net/10986/24617.

Kasyanenko, Sergiy, Philip George Kenworthy, Franz Ulrich Ruch, Ekaterine T. Vashakmadze, Dana Lauren Vorisek, and Collette Mari Wheeler. 2023. "Investment in Emerging Market and Developing Economy Regions: Trends, Prospects, and Policy Options." Policy Research Working Paper 10369, World Bank. http://documents.worldbank.org/curated/en/099542403162311587.

Mascagni, Giulia, Andualem T. Mengistu, and Firew B. Woldeyes. 2021. "Can ICTs Increase Tax Compliance? Evidence on Taxpayer Responses to Technological Innovation in Ethiopia." *Journal of Economic Behavior & Organization* 189 (September): 172–93.

Mukherjee, Anit, Yuko Okamura, Ugo Gentilini, et al. 2023. "Cash Transfers in the Context of Energy Subsidy Reforms: Insights from Recent Experience." Energy Subsidy Reform in Action Series. World Bank. http://hdl.handle.net/10986/39948.

OECD (Organisation for Economic Co-operation and Development). 2025. *Pensions at a Glance 2025: OECD and G20 Indicators*. OECD Publishing. https://doi.org/10.1787/e40274c1-en.

Okunogbe, Oyebola, and Gabriel Tourek. 2024. "How Can Lower-Income Countries Collect More Taxes? The Role of Technology, Tax Agents, and Politics." *Journal of Economic Perspectives* 38 (1): 81–106. https://doi.org/10.1257/jep.38.1.81.

PEFA (Public Expenditure and Financial Accountability) Secretariat. 2022. *Global Report on Public Financial Management 2022*. PEFA Secretariat. https://www.pefa.org/global-report-2022.

Ramsey, F. P. 1927. "A Contribution to the Theory of Taxation." *Economic Journal* 37 (145): 47–61.

Riera-Crichton, Daniel, Carlos A. Végh, and Guillermo Vuletin. 2014. "Fiscal Multipliers in Recessions and Expansions: Does It Matter Whether Government Spending Is 'Bricks or Mortar'?" Policy Research Working Paper 6993, World Bank. http://hdl.handle.net/10986/19389.

Stantcheva, Stefanie. 2021. "Understanding Tax Policy: How Do People Reason?" *Quarterly Journal of Economics* 136 (4): 2309–69.

Straub, Stéphane, He He, Yue Li, et al. 2026. *Infrastructure Foundations: From Current Assets to Future Growth*. Sustainable Infrastructure Series. World Bank. https://openknowledge.worldbank.org/entities/publication/c35564b6-20e5-4606-a9df-d5735f8481d3.

Tangcharoensathien, Viroj, Walaiporn Patcharanarumol, Phusit Prakongsai, et al. 2011. "Health-Financing Reforms in Southeast Asia: Challenges in Achieving Universal Coverage." *The Lancet* 377 (9768): 863–73.

Wai-Poi, Matthew, Mariano Sosa, and Pierre Bachas. 2025. *Taxes, Spending, and Equity: International Patterns and Lessons for Developing Countries*. Prosperity Insight Series. World Bank. https://doi.org/10.1596/44281.

Wooldridge, Jeffrey M. 2021. *Econometric Analysis of Cross Section and Panel Data,* 3rd ed. MIT Press.

World Bank. 2008. "Indonesia Public Expenditure Review: Spending for Development." World Bank. http://documents.worldbank.org/curated/en/370501468041427374.

World Bank. 2012. "Protecting Poor and Vulnerable Households in Indonesia." Social Assistance Program and Public Expenditure Review 1. World Bank. http://hdl.handle.net/10986/13810.

World Bank. 2015. "A Perceived Divide: How Indonesians Perceive Inequality and What They Want Done About It." World Bank. http://hdl.handle.net/10986/23602.

World Bank. 2018a. *East Asia and Pacific Economic Update, April 2018: Enhancing Potential.* World Bank. https://doi.org/10.1596/978-1-4648-1283-5.

World Bank. 2018b. *Growing Smarter: Learning and Equitable Development in East Asia and Pacific*. World Bank East Asia and Pacific Regional Report. World Bank. https://doi.org/10.1596/978-1-4648-1261-3.

World Bank. 2022a. *Philippines Country Climate and Development Report*. CCDR Series. World Bank. https://doi.org/10.1596/38280.

World Bank. 2022b. *Vietnam Country Climate and Development Report*. CCDR Series. World Bank. http://hdl.handle.net/10986/37618.

World Bank. 2023a. *East Asia and Pacific Economic Update, April 2023: Reviving Growth*. World Bank. http://hdl.handle.net/10986/39598.

World Bank. 2023b. "Raising the Tide, Lifting All Boats." Malaysia Economic Monitor (October), World Bank. http://documents.worldbank.org/curated/en/099100623063032359.

World Bank. 2023c. "Thailand Public Revenue and Spending Assessment: Promoting an Inclusive and Sustainable Future." World Bank. http://documents.worldbank.org/curated/en/099052523201510112.

World Bank. 2024. *State and Trends of Carbon Pricing 2024*. World Bank. https://hdl.handle.net/10986/41544.

World Bank Group and PwC. 2017. *Paying Taxes 2017*. PwC, World Bank, and International Finance Corporation. https://www.pwc.at/de/publikationen/steuern-und-recht/pwc-paying-taxes-2017-at.pdf.